THE ALLYN & BACON SOURCEBOOK
FOR
WRITING PROGRAM ADMINISTRATORS

Lindemann
Tate

Comp Studies

THE ALLYN & BACON SOURCEBOOK
FOR
WRITING PROGRAM ADMINISTRATORS

Irene Ward
Kansas State University

William J. Carpenter
Lafayette College

New York San Francisco Boston
London Toronto Sydney Tokyo Singapore Madrid
Mexico City Munich Paris Cape Town Hong Kong Montreal

Vice President/Publisher: Eben W. Ludlow
Marketing Manager: Christopher Bennem
Senior Production Manager: Eric Jorgensen
Project Coordination, Text Design, and Electronic Page Makeup: Electronic
Publishing Services Inc., NYC
Cover Design Manager: John Callahan
Cover Design: Keithley & Associates
Senior Manufacturing Buyer: Dennis J. Para
Printer and Binder: Courier Stroughton
Cover Printer: Phoenix Color Corp.

Library of Congress Cataloging-in-Publication Data

The Allyn & Bacon sourcebook for writing program administrators / [compiled by]
Irene Ward, William J. Carpenter. — 1st ed.
          p. cm.
     Includes bibliographical references and index.
     ISBN 0-205-31687-5
     1. English language —Rhetoric—Study and teaching. 2. Report writing—Study
and teaching (Higher) 3. Writing centers—Administration. I. Title: Allyn and Bacon
sourcebook for writing program administrators. II. Ward, Irene, 1950- III. Carpenter,
William J. (William James) IV. Allyn and Bacon.

     PE1404 .A46 2002
     808'.042'0711—dc21
                              2001029129

Please visit our website at http://www.ablongman.com

ISBN 0-205- 31687-5

1 2 3 4 5 6 7 8 9 10—CRS—04 03 02 01

CONTENTS

Foreword
Gary A. Olson   ix

Preface   xi

Introduction
William J. Carpenter   1

PART I   WHO ARE YOU AS ADMINISTRATOR?   7

David Schwalm
**The Writing Program (Administrator) in Context: Where Am I, and
Can I Still Behave Like a Faculty Member?   9**

Katherine K. Gottschalk
The Writing Program in the University   23

Richard Gebhardt
**Administration as Focus for Understanding the
Teaching of Writing   34**

Barry M. Maid
Working Outside of English   38

PART II   ADMINISTERING, MANAGING, LEADING   47

Irene Ward
**Developing Healthy Management and Leadership Styles:
Surviving the WPA's "Inside Game"   49**

Joyce Kinkead and Jeanne Simpson
The Administrative Audience: A Rhetorical Problem   68

Hildy Miller
Postmasculinist Directions in Writing Program Administration   78

Thomas Amorose
WPA Work at the Small College or University:
Re-Imagining Power and Making the Small School Visible   91

Edward White
Use It or Lose It: Power and the WPA   106

PART III   TEACHING ASSISTANT TRAINING
AND STAFF DEVELOPMENT   115

Irene Ward and Merry Perry
A Selection of Strategies for Training Teaching Assistants   117

Catherine G. Latterell
Training the Workforce: Overview of
GTA Education Curricula   139

William J. Carpenter
Professional Development for Writing Program Staff   156

*Timothy Catalano, Will Clemens, Julia Goodwin,
Gary McMillin, Jeff White, and Stephen Wilhoit*
TA Training in English: An Annotated Bibliography   166

PART IV   CURRICULUM DESIGN AND ASSESSMENT   183

David Smit
Curriculum Design for First-Year Writing Programs   185

Brian A. Huot and Ellen E. Schendel
A Working Methodology of Assessment for Writing Program
Administrators   207

Todd Taylor
Ten Commandments for Computers and Composition   228

Geoffrey Chase
Redefining Composition, Managing Change, and the
Role of the WPA   243

Daniel Mahala and Michael Vivion
The Role of AP and the Composition Program   252

Martha Townsend
Writing Across the Curriculum   264

Barbara E. Walvoord
The Future of WAC   275

PART V   PROMOTION AND PROFESSIONAL ISSUES FOR WPAs   297

Douglas D. Hesse
Understanding Larger Discourses in Higher Education: Practical
Advice for WPAs   299

Jeanne Gunner
Professional Advancement of the WPA: Rhetoric and Politics in
Tenure and Promotion   315

Charles I. Schuster
The Politics of Writing Promotion   331

PART VI   APPENDICES   343

Appendix A: Statement of Principles and Standards for the
              Postsecondary Teaching of Writing   345
Appendix B: "The Portland Resolution"   352
Appendix C: WPA Outcomes Statement
              for First-Year Composition   357
Appendix D: Guidelines for the Workload
              of the College English Teacher   360
Appendix E: Position Statement on the Preparation and
              Professional Development of
              Teachers of Writing   362
Appendix F: Evaluating the Intellectual Work of Writing
              Administration   366

Appendix G: ADE Guidelines for Class Size and Workload for
               College and University Teachers of English:
               A Statement of Policy   379
Appendix H: The Buckley Amendment: "Protection of the Rights
               and Privacy of Parents and Students"   383
Appendix I: Guidelines for Self-Study to Precede WPA Visit   388

Index   395

FOREWORD

At last, compositionists have a bible of writing program administration. *The Allyn and Bacon Sourcebook for Writing Program Administrators* is a comprehensive, informative, and eminently useful compendium of articles, essays, position statements, historical documents, and general good advice for anyone involved in directing a writing program. This book is a truly impressive contribution to program administration and is likely to remain the authoritative statement on the subject for years to come.

Writing program administration is one of the most difficult, most demanding, yet least rewarded positions in today's English departments. In some institutions—such as my own—the writing program administrator (WPA) is responsible for hundreds of sections of classes staffed by a few hundred instructors (adjuncts, faculty, and teaching assistants) servicing thousands of undergraduate students. This is a daunting job, yet there has been very little support for those heroes who daily must confront the inevitable difficulties and pitfalls that such an important job involving so many individuals entails. Finally, help has arrived. Irene Ward and William Carpenter have compiled the first major sourcebook providing substantive advice and guidance to those of us committed to directing pedagogically sound, administratively effective programs.

Whether it be teacher training or curriculum design, program assessment or administrative authority, professional advancement or nuts-and-bolts administrative techniques, The Allyn & Bacon Sourcebook for Writing Program Administrators contains concise, authoritative, well-written essays on all the key issues of concern to WPAs written by the foremost scholars in the discipline. What's more, this valuable text contains nine historical documents related to program administration, including WPA's "The Portland Resolution," NCTE's "Guidelines for the Workload of the College English Teacher," ADE's "Guidelines for Class Size and Workload for College and University Teachers of English," and even "The Buckley Amendment." *The Allyn &*

Bacon Sourcebook is a "must own" for any compositionist concerned with how to translate contemporary composition theory and pedagogy into dependably effective writing programs.

The publication of this important book is a good sign. First, it indicates that the field of rhetoric and composition has reached a new level of disciplinary maturity in that finally, specialists in the field are setting the standards for our writing programs; we have finally gained a degree of control over how writing will be taught in institutions across the nation. Second, the fact that a major publisher like Allyn & Bacon has agreed to publish this book indicates that as a field, we have indeed grown in importance, not to mention numbers. I applaud the editors, the authors, and the publisher for producing this ambitious and historically important project.

Gary A. Olson
University of South Florida

PREFACE

Some of us arrive at our first jobs as writing program directors having taken some graduate courses in writing program administration. However, in most English departments those who take on the job of writing program administrator (WPA) have little or no graduate coursework to aid them in running a writing program. Even if you acquired such training, you may discover that in one or more areas you are not as knowledgeable as you might wish to be, or it may simply have been a long time since you had to deal with certain kinds of issues. Whether you are at a community college, a small liberal arts college, or a large research university, this book will be of use to you if you are taking graduate courses in composition and rhetoric; are a veteran or new WPA; have extensive, some, or little background in composition and run a writing program; or are a department head supervising running a writing program.

We hope this book will help any person who administers a writing program face the day-to-day challenges of the job by offering sound theory and practical wisdom. We hope that this book sits on or near the WPA's desk and that when problems arise this book will provide a source for finding the right solution for a particular program and institution. We don't claim to have all the answers, but hope that this book will help you form an accurate picture of your problem and a workable plan for moving forward.

We think of this book as a new family member in the long line of professional books that have been published in the field of rhetoric and composition. The forebears on this family tree are those books that tried to help solve some of the immediate, day-to-day problems we face as we learn the best ways to teach students of all kinds learn to write. In the area of program administration the book that first comes to mind is Gary A. Olson's collection, *Writing Centers: Theory and Administration* (NCTE 1984), published as the writing center movement took shape and developed a body of both theoretical and practical knowledge about how writing centers work and what makes them successful. Erika Lindeman's third edition of *A Rhetoric for Writing Teachers* (Oxford 1995) and Gary Tate, Edward P. J. Corbett, and now Nancy Meyers's fourth edition of *The Writing Teachers Sourcebook* (Oxford 2000) have introduced many of us to program administration and composition as a body of theoretical and practical knowledge.

The first two parts of *The Allyn & Bacon Sourcebook for Writing Program Administrators* will be especially helpful for the newer WPA who has not held an administrative position before or may be unfamiliar with higher education administration. Parts III and IV highlight the relevant research in instructor and TA training, curriculum design, and assessment. We hope these essays help WPAs understand the parameters of these issues by providing a discussion of the scholarship and by providing extensive bibliographies. Part V contains articles concerning the WPA's professional development and career future. Part VI is a collection of professional position statements and other documents that we have found essential to have close at hand.

Eleven articles were written specifically for this book. The contributors are experienced writing program directors with years of experience and deep knowledge of the scholarship in their fields. In alphabetical order they are:

Jeanne Gunner, editor of *College English*, University of Santa Clara. Member of both the executive and editorial boards of *WPA: Writing Program Administrator*.

Doug Hesse, director of graduate studies and former WPA, Illinois State University; Hesse is also the former editor of *WPA: Writing Program Administration* and the current president of the Council of Writing Program Administrators.

Brian A. Huot, director of composition, University of Louisville; cofounder and coeditor of *Assessing Writing*, the only scholarly journal devoted to assessing writing.

Barry M. Maid, head of faculty of technical communication at Arizona State University-Mesa, former WPA and department head

David Schwalm, vice provost and former WPA, Arizona State University-Mesa, member of the editorial board of *WPA: Writing Program Administrator* and executive board of the Council of Writing Program Administrators and list owner of WPA-L

David Smit, director of expository writing, Kansas State University

Todd Taylor, assistant director of the writing program, University of North Carolina-Chapel Hill and former coordinator, Computers and Writing Program, department of English, University of South Florida

Martha Townsend, director of campus writing program at University of Missouri-Columbia

Irene Ward, former director of expository writing, Kansas State University, and member of the editorial board of *WPA: Writing Program Administration*

Two bright newcomers, Merry Perry, University of South Florida, and
  Ellen E. Schendel, Grand Valley State University, appear as coauthors
  of substantial articles. William J. Carpenter, assistant director of the college writing program, Lafayette College, and former assistant WPA at
  University of Kansas, writes about providing professional development
  opportunities for adjunct faculty.

Most of the reprinted articles are from *WPA: Writing Program Administration*, a journal devoted to writing program research and scholarship. These
articles also are among the best to be published in the journal, and the authors
have credentials similar to the contributors of original material. Two additional articles come from *ADE*, the journal of the Associated Departments of
English, which focuses on administration in English departments, and from
College English, a journal that deals with many aspects of teaching writing and
literature. So whether you are just beginning your career as a graduate student, a new WPA in your first job, returning to WPA work after a break, or a
department head who supervises the writing program, we think you will find
this book helpful.

ACKNOWLEDGEMENTS

Both of us wish to express our gratitude to the Council of Writing Program
Administrators, especially President Doug Hesse, the executive board, and
Dennis Lynch for assistance reprinting from *WPA: Writing Program Administration* and for sustaining one of the most helpful and nurturing professional
academic organizations there is. We also want to thank each of the contributors for their professionalism and willingness to work with us on this project.
Each of these people played major roles in supporting writing programs and
their administrators. We feel honored to be in such illustrious company. We
want to thank Sandy Kirshner, president of Allyn & Bacon, and Doug Day,
Longman's English sales specialist, for their initial enthusiasm and support
of this project. We also thank our editorial team—Eben Ludlow, vice president of Longman, and his editorial assistant, Grace Trudo. Thank you, Grace,
for answering our endless questions with tact and patience. Thank you, Eben,
for your confidence in us, for your wise counsel, and for everything else
you've done to make this book a reality.

—*IPW and WJC*

I would like to acknowledge Professor Amy J. Devitt and the students in her
1997 WPA seminar at the University of Kansas. The course taught me to view
program administration as intellectual work, a perspective that has greatly
informed my editorial duties here. Lafayette College has been generous with
its secretarial and financial support. Thanks go to Jill A. Riefenstahl for her
help with the manuscript preparation, and to Professors Carolynn Van Dyke
and Patricia Donahue for their support and encouragement during the final

busy days. Additional funding was made available through a manuscript preparation grant awarded by the Lafayette College academic research committee. Finally, I thank Stephanie Pelkowski Carpenter for her fine editorial comments and her constant support in this and all endeavors.

—WJC

I thank Mindy McAlexander for her work in preparing the final manuscript. I also thank the graduate advisory committee of the English department and the graduate school at Kansas State University for supporting her work. I want to thank Gary A. Olson, as always, for his time and generosity in editorial advice and for writing the Foreword. I thank Professor Ronald G. Downey of the industrial/organizational psychology program at Kansas State for help in understanding the literature on workplace burnout and for his helpful comments on my essay on management and leadership (see Part II). Also, I want to take this opportunity to most sincerely thank Robin Mosher and Deborah Murray not only for patient reading of my contributions to the book but also for the years of collaborative administration of Kansas State's writing program. I have learned a great deal about being a WPA and human being from them both.

—IPW

INTRODUCTION

William J. Carpenter

As with so many projects taken on by writing program administrators (WPAs), this book responds to a specific need: namely, to have a handy resource that provides valuable advice and information on running a college or university writing program. I was struck by the absence of a book such as this while in the midst of preparing for my Ph.D. exams at the University of Kansas. In amassing the articles and resolutions and position statements found on my reading list, I weaved through library stacks, made copies of journal articles, and surfed web pages, keeping my copies and notes in a three-ring binder. The result was a sourcebook of texts I could draw on not only in my exam but in my career as a writing teacher and WPA. In a phone call to Irene I mentioned my three-ring binder, and by the end of that conversation we had a plan for what would become *The Allyn and Bacon Sourcebook for Writing Program Administrators*.

WPAs are the people who take on such challenges as planning a program's curriculum, handling its budget, training its teachers, and scheduling its courses, all while juggling their own teaching and research. The work of WPAs proves vital to the daily existence of our colleges and universities, even though it is often underappreciated or misunderstood by the controlling departments, administrations, and legislatures. Because of this precarious situation, WPAs have formed their own support network in the shape of journals, discussion lists, and conferences. At these sites, WPAs across the country engage in an active conversation regarding the practical and theoretical aspects of their positions—positions that directly affect the educational experiences of every student on campus. And this conversation does not stop there: it is carried into graduate courses in writing program administration, faculty and TA seminars, workshops at the annual conferences, staff meetings at two- and four-year institutions, and writing centers. Never has this conversation engaged as many people in as many different situations as it does today: from graduate students in composition and rhetoric programs at our nation's research institutions, to the department chairs of local community colleges, to the groups of faculty members who rotate in and out of the positions at their institutions.

The purpose of this book is to provide you with some starting points and perhaps some guiding principles, and to point you in the direction of sources that will help you on a day-to-day basis to run a writing program. This book can be another resource for all WPAs, regardless of their experience, training, or position. We hope it will help you solve problems, gain background knowledge, devise workable policies, and deal with the upper administration in productive ways that benefit the students and teachers in your program. It can also inform graduate seminars on program administration and be used in development workshops and conferences. We've assembled essays that are practical and informative and that discuss issues pertinent to a wide range of programs. The authors, many of whom are or have been WPAs, present strategies and advice for dealing with some of the common challenges and demands faced by program directors. They are neither prescriptive nor authoritarian; they assume a general audience composed of individuals in unique situations. The strength of this book, we think, comes from the authors' abilities to communicate their ideas in helpful, thought-provoking manners.

Of the 23 essays found here, 11 have been written just for this collection. We asked the authors to write on the issues they feel are most important for WPAs to consider. As a result, this book contributes new essays on curriculum design, technology and writing, professional development and advancement, teacher training, writing across the curriculum (WAC), and administrative strategy. The remaining 12 essays have been reprinted from journals such as *WPA: Writing Program Administration*, *ADE Bulletin*, *Composition Chronicle*, and *College English*. We chose these pieces for their broad coverage of topics ranging from small-college administration and proactive leadership to TA training and administrative rhetoric. Many of the essays here cite resources beyond those traditionally associated with composition and rhetoric, and some offer extensive bibliographies. The appendices unite important position statements and guidelines with which WPAs should be familiar.

We've divided the book into six sections, each focused on an important aspect of writing program administration. Depending on your situation and need, you may want to read the book straight through or skip around to find the essays and documents most helpful to you.

PART I: WHO ARE YOU AS ADMINISTRATOR?

We begin this collection with a group of essays that examine the position of WPA in terms of the administrative, political, and social structures of institutions and departments. Knowing how these structures affect you and your position proves vital to performing your WPA duties as efficiently and productively as possible. David Schwalm points out in his essay that many WPAs often bring to their positions "a faculty-centered view of the academic world," one that doesn't always recognize the administrative workings of an institution. By exploring a series of deceptively simple questions, Schwalm explains how you can "cross the line" into administrative work without forsaking your faculty-member values. In "The Writing Program in the University," Katherine K. Gottschalk describes Cornell University's collaboratively administered writing program. In so doing, she examines some strategies for "securing and enhancing the role of the writing program" in an institution. Richard Gebhardt presents administration as "macrolevel teaching," arguing that WPAs should see themselves as teachers who affect students through their administrative duties and decisions, rather than through direct interacting in the classroom. Lastly, Barry M. Maid surveys issues related to writing programs that are separate from English departments.

PART II: ADMINISTERING, MANAGING, LEADING

The authors in this part examine the concepts of management and leadership as they pertain to the WPA position. Irene Ward discusses research in occupational health and offers strategies for avoiding job stress and burnout. Joyce Kinkcad and Jeanne Simpson advise WPAs on how to "talk the (administrative) talk." Their glossary of administrative terms accompanies an insightful discussion of how and when to use those terms in proposals and reports. In "Postmasculinist Directions in Writing Program Administration," Hildy Miller explores the concept of "feminist directing," analyzing the tensions between feminist ideology and traditionally masculine administrative structures. Thomas Amorose discusses WPA work at small colleges and universities. He argues that the experiences of WPAs at these institutions can "enlarge the repertoire of instruments available to all WPAs for addressing their political scene." We conclude this section with Edward White's important essay "Use It or Lose It: Power and the Writing Program Administrator," in which he encourages WPAs to recognize the power associated with their positions and to use it to improve the conditions surrounding their programs.

PART III: TEACHER ASSISTANT TRAINING AND STAFF DEVELOPMENT

An important component of may WPAs' jobs is the recruiting and training of teachers, many of whom are graduate students and adjuncts. In Part III, the authors discuss methods and strategies for preparing writing program staffs for their professional duties. Irene Ward and Merry Perry provide an overview of the current theories and practices informing the training of teaching assistants, including a bibliography of literature from 1996. Catherine Latterell presents findings from a survey of WPAs on "the kinds and range of writing pedagogy courses required for teaching assistants." In my essay, I argue the importance of professional development initiatives for writing program staff and offer some suggestions for activities. The last essay, "TA training in English: An Annotated Bibliography" by Timothy Catalano, Will Clemens, Julia Goodwin, Gary McMillin, Jeff White, and Stephen Wilhoit, offers an excellent overview of the literature before 1996 on this important topic.

PART IV: CURRICULUM DESIGN
AND ASSESSMENT

This part unites seven authors who are interested in curriculum and assessment issues. Many WPAs have the responsibility of designing first-year writing programs, and others must develop or implement ways of assessing student learning and program effectiveness. David Smit provides a detailed discussion of the theories and practices that have informed first-year writing programs. In "A Working Methodology of Assessment," Brian A. Huot and Ellen E. Schendel argue that assessment initiatives "can instigate valuable program-wide discussions about curricular and programmatic issues." They contend that assessment decisions can and should be connected to decisions regarding curriculum, teaching, and faculty development. Todd Taylor's essay lists ten principles to observe when considering instructional technology for the writing program. Geoffrey Chase examines how the relationship among a writing program's local conditions, internal coherence, and external relevance can inform a WPA's decisions about curriculum and program structure. In their essay on Advanced Placement exams and composition programs, Daniel Mahala and Michael Vivion encourage program staffs to review their policies concerning AP credit for writing courses. Martha Townsend discusses some trends in the WAC movement and analyzes their implications for WPAs. She includes a useful annotated bibliography. The part concludes with Barbara Walvoord's look into "The Future of WAC."

PART V: PROMOTION AND PROFESSIONAL
ISSUES FOR WPAs

The three authors in this part, Douglas D. Hesse, Jeanne Gunner, and Charles Schuster, offer some practical advice about the professional aspects of writing program administration. Hesse argues the importance of WPAs' understanding the discourses that define higher education. He provides a helpful list of the associations, organizations, and publications from which WPAs can draw support and information. Gunner examines some of the issues surrounding tenure and the WPA. By discussing her own tenure case, she outlines necessary strategies for successful professional advancement. Last, Schuster's "The Politics of Promotion" discusses some of the potential pitfalls facing compositionists and WPAs seeking tenure and professional advancement.

PART VI: APPENDICES

The appendices unite documents we think serve as valuable resources for all WPAs. These documents can often inform and shape program proposals, hiring practices, budget requests, training programs, etc. As a WPA, you should become familiar with the positions, guidelines, and laws detailed in these documents.

Of course, no one book can serve as the only resource for WPAs. There exists an ever-growing body of research and scholarship on program administration, and directors should make themselves aware of its sources. If you're interested in starting a WPA library, here are a few suggestions for collections and books:

- *Kitchen Cooks, Plate Twirlers & Troubadours: WPAs Tell Their Stories*. Diane George, editor. Boynton/Cook 1999.
- *Administrative Problem-Solving for Writing Programs and Writing Centers: Scenarios in Effective Program Management*. Linda Myers-Breslin, editor. NCTE 1999.
- *Border Talk: Writing and Knowing in the Two-Year College*. Howard B. Tinberg. NCTE 1997.
- *Resituating Writing: Constructing and Administering Writing Programs*. Joseph Janangelo and Kristine Hansen, editors. Boynton/Cook 1995.
- *Evaluating Teachers of Writing*. Hult, Christine A., ed. Urbana, IL: NCTE, 1994.
- *Developing Successful College Writing Programs*. Edward White. Jossey-Bass 1989.
- *Evaluating College Writing Programs*. Stephen P. Witte and Lester Faigley. Southern Illinois UP 1983.
- Your institution's *Student Handbook* and *Faculty Handbook*.

If you don't already, consider subscribing to journals such as *College English, College Composition and Communication*, and *ADE Bulletin*. These publication often present articles focused on or related to program administration. You might also consider attending the annual Conference on College Composition and Communication (CCCC), as well as the National Council of Teachers of English conference. These events are excellent opportunities to meet others in similar positions and to hear from your colleagues and peers.

Most important—and we cannot stress this enough—join the Council of Writing Program Administrators. The council, started in 1976, is a professional organization composed of individuals interested in any aspect of program administration. Its journal, *WPA: Writing Program Administration*, publishes scholarship of interest to WPAs at all institutions, and its annual summer conference includes an extensive workshop for new WPAs. In addition, the council offers research grants and a valuable consultant-evaluator service. To join the Council of Writing Program Administrators, contact Jenne Dautermann, Department of English, Miami University, Oxford, OH 45056. The 2001 annual membership fee is $30. The journal and newsletter subscription are included in this price. You should also consider signing on to the WPA listserv, a nationwide electronic discussion list with over 700 members. The listserv is an excellent source for immediate, practical information and advice, and it frequently hosts some lively and spirited debates. To subscribe to the WPA-L, send the following message to listserve@asu.edu: subscribe WPA-L [your name].

This discussion about the council and the listserv should make one thing clear: WPAs do not have to work in isolation. Across the country there are people in similar situations experiencing similar successes and trials. While we should recognize that each situation is unique in its context and participants, we must also recognize the commonalities that unite us and the principles that guide us. Irene and I hope this book makes such recognition easier. And we hope it provides you with the resources you need to make your WPA experiences as productive and enriching as they can be.

PART I

WHO ARE YOU AS ADMINISTRATOR?

The Writing Program (Administrator) in Context: Where Am I, and Can I Still Behave Like a Faculty Member?

David E. Schwalm

Arizona State University—East

The position of writing program administrator is often a first administrative position for the WPA, who may be a veteran faculty member or—as is frequently the case—a new untenured junior faculty member. In either case, new WPAs tend to have a career orientation toward traditional faculty concerns—their discipline, their students, and their scholarship. The perfect environment for most faculty members is the one that interferes least with their main concerns. They often have little interest in the institution that contains them, except when elements of that institution intrude on their academic space. They tend not to be especially knowledgeable about organizational charts, personnel policies, or budgets. Faculty usually know *who* they are but prefer to be in a position in which it does not matter *where* they are—that is, located in a particular place in a particular academic institution operating under particular constraints and policies. This is probably as it should be, for such focus is critical to faculty members' single-minded and uncompromising dedication to knowledge, to academic integrity, and to student learning.

But a faculty-centered view of the academic world is not adequate once the faculty member crosses the line into administration at any level, including administration of a writing program. This chapter is intended to serve as a kind of primer to help new WPAs achieve the point of view they must have in order to be successful as WPAs.

WHERE AM I?

When I was a junior faculty member, I could tell you who my department chair was (it was a small department), but I'm not sure I knew what college my department was in or who was dean. I neither knew nor cared who or what a provost was. This information wasn't a secret; all of it was in the college catalog. But I had no apparent reason to know it, and there was nothing in my graduate education that suggested that it was any of my business. My business was teaching and research in my discipline. Many faculty who suddenly find themselves in WPA positions come to the job—regardless of age or experience—with nearly as little knowledge or awareness. Basically they do not know where they are institutionally. Some of the following questions may seem a little rudimentary, but all will help new WPAs progressively to discover where they are in their institutions and the general universe of higher education. The answers to the following set of questions will provide the basis for a very useful job description.

IS MY JOB REAL?

Your chair says, "We're making you director of the writing program." You need to know right up front whether this is just a *task* or also a *position*. A position—i.e., director of composition—usually has a place in the departmental organizational chart, along with the chair, associate chair, director of graduate studies, etc. It often has positional authority, a term of appointment, and a set of responsibilities stipulated in departmental bylaws, and these stipulations may include performance standards, expectations about allocation of time and effort, criteria for reappointment, and resources for support.

A task—i.e., directing the composition program—is something that needs to be done around the campus, but it includes no positional standing in the administrative hierarchy and often is quite open-ended or ill-defined in terms of responsibilities, expectations, and rewards. It is a "quasi administrative" appointment, characterized by lots of responsibility but no positional authority and no budget. You may be called "director of composition," but the position exists only as a line on your nameplate and business card.

WPA *as position* tends to be more common in larger institutions, *as task* in smaller institutions or in community colleges where managing the composition program is a major part of the job of the department or division chair. One type of responsibility is not necessarily better than the other, but, before you accept the position or task, you ought to know what sort of job you have, what its scope is, and under what conditions you are doing it. If you have already accepted the position or task, it becomes even more important for you to determine which it is. (I once thought I had a position until I got involved in revising the departmental bylaws and discovered that there was no such position.) Two documents prepared by the Council of Writing Program Administrators can be of great help. "The Portland Resolution" (Appendix B) can help you define your position, or task as the case may be. "Evaluating the

Intellectual Work of Writing Administration" (Appendix F) can help you identify appropriate criteria by which your work can be evaluated.

WHAT AM I DIRECTING?

By "writing program," different institutions mean different things, and the range is enormous. On the one end may be a collection of writing courses taught by various faculty according to their own lights and probably not desiring much direction. This is not really a writing program. A writing *program* minimally consists of one or more courses (usually first-year courses) with multiple sections of each, governed by a common set of objectives. They might also have a common course syllabus, some consistency in teaching methods, and common assessment and placement procedures. There are lots of add-ons and variations. As WPA, your portfolio might include additional courses, such as advanced composition, technical communication, or business writing. The responsibilities sometimes include basic writing, a writing center, and placement and assessment processes. You may be responsible for writing across the curriculum programs (WACs) as well. Composition classes may be taught by regular faculty or, as is common at larger institutions, by some combination of regular faculty, part-time faculty, and graduate assistants who are novice teachers in training. Thus, in addition to determining course objectives and designing curriculum, you may have responsibility for managing instructional staff and training TAs and tutors. There is no agreed-upon concept of "writing program." There is no reason why there must be agreement, and, again, no particular model is necessarily better than another, but you ought to know the scope of your program and responsibilities and be aware of opportunities to do more, or less, or differently.

WHERE IS MY PROGRAM?

Most writing programs, wherever they fall in the range of "programness" described above, are located in English departments. In other instances they may actually be located in rhetoric or writing or communication departments. It is worth noting whether the program is an official structural subset of a department and faculty or a responsibility generally shared across the department—as is usually the case in most community colleges and small colleges. If it is a departmental subunit, you may have colleagues who share your academic interest in rhetoric and composition and bring knowledge and experience to the program and classroom, but you may also have to deal with cultural differences between the "literature faculty" and the "composition faculty," along with possible conflicts over resources. In the second case you may well be "the writing person" and you may be working with faculty who resent having to teach writing classes.

Writing programs occasionally wind up in other locations. Some may be located—along with introductory math or language courses—in a lower-division college or university college. Others may be freestanding units, outside of a department, separately budgeted, yet not having departmental status or offering degrees. In such cases you may report to a department chair as a faculty member but to someone else as a program administrator. You may, in some circumstances, be the "coordinator" of a "distributed" program, where courses that meet the university writing requirement are distributed across a range of departments in the university. The location of the program will suggest rather different administrative challenges, opportunities, and responsibilities. Under any circumstances, you should identify the location of your program and its various pieces and the person or persons to whom you are responsible.

WHERE IS MY PROGRAM, RELATIVELY?

Once you understand the immediate environs of your program, it becomes useful to see where that location is in the larger institution. It is at this point that you need to look at the organization of your college or university to see where you and your program fall.

There are lots of different institutional structures, determined by historical accident and local conditions. Most universities, small colleges, and community colleges are composed of three major administrative units: academic affairs, student affairs, and administrative affairs. The president or chancellor of the institution is the chief executive officer (CEO), and each of these three major units is led by a vice president (or vice chancellor), although the head of academic affairs is often called a provost. Frequently, one of the vice presidents (usually—but not always—the vice president for academic affairs) is identified as the *senior* vice president, and this is worth noting. All of the vice presidents report directly to the president, but the senior vice president may have authority to resolve disagreements among the vice presidents. Academic affairs is made up primarily of colleges or college-shaped objects such as "schools" or "divisions." Each of these college-type units is usually made up of departments (like a typical college of liberal arts), although smaller professional colleges often function more or less like big departments. Each college-type unit is led by a dean, and there seems to be considerable consistency in the use of that term. There are often an array of assistant or associate deans (a.k.a. "deanlets") in the larger colleges. The academic deans often include the dean of the library—but not the dean of students, who usually reports to the vice president for student affairs. All of the academic deans report to the provost, who is also identified as the chief academic officer (CAO). In institutions where the colleges are very independent, deans wield a great deal of institutional power, sometimes reflecting the size of the college (e.g., liberal arts and sciences) and sometimes its ability to generate outside funding (engineering). There are some institutions (often those with strong faculty unions) where the deans don't have much power. In most institutions, the provost is the dominant figure on the academic side, especially if he or she controls the flow of money to the colleges.

Because writing requirements tend to cut across academic boundaries, you need to understand the relationships among academic units and be ready to work across boundaries. Because your WPA responsibilities inevitably extend beyond the limits of academic affairs you should attend to the staff and organization of other major units on campus. The vice president for student affairs tends to vie with the provost for power on most campuses, especially those with residential opportunities and national recruiting programs. Typically, the vice president for student affairs is responsible for the whole range of activities relating to the cocurricular and nonacademic aspects of a student's college experience—student life and student business processes. Thus, student affairs manages admissions, registration, records, residence life, financial aid, student conduct, athletics, student health, clubs and organizations, student government, student union, alumni affairs, and so on. (*Note:* Big-time athletics may be an independent unit, with the athletic director reporting directly to the president.) There seems to be less consistency in the manner in which student affairs is organized. But academic affairs and student affairs frequently operate independently of each other, often without much communication between them, often with some hostility where their domains touch, and often with duplication of effort—in areas that are relevant to WPAs such as tutoring, orientation, or leadership education. It is a good idea to explore what student affairs people know, especially about "student development," something most people on the academic side of the house do not know much about but should. The best place to start is with *How College Affects Students* (Jossey-Bass), a major synthesis of research by Ernest Pascarella and Patrick Terenzini (1991).

Administrative affairs is probably the most poorly understood and least respected unit at most campuses. It includes personnel functions (hiring, affirmative action, benefits, payroll, etc.), comptroller, training and development, room scheduling, facilities management, and buildings and grounds—essentially all of the components that colleges and universities have in common with business and industry. Administrative affairs manages the stuff we either take for granted or complain about. Administrative affairs is sometimes the largest employer on campus, although most of the employees are in the lower classifications—custodians, groundskeepers, painters, mail delivery, maintenance. The employees of administrative affairs are often ill-treated by employees of the other two units, but they are well-positioned to make our lives miserable—or pleasant. You are likely to have lots of dealings with administrative affairs, especially with regard to personnel matters and room scheduling, and you should make some friends among the operational staff.

Information Technology (IT)—the computer and technology unit— is sometimes combined with the library and sometimes not. It is sometimes located in academic affairs and sometimes in administrative affairs. As a comparatively new part of higher education institutions, IT has not yet reached a conventional place in the system. Just look for it. You will need to be able to work with IT if you want to offer computer-based sections of your program courses or do anything with your program that may put a new tax on the technological infrastructure.

Small-college administration is often a little less complicated (structurally if not politically), and the organizational divisions may be a bit less rigid. Generally speaking, however, the three basic administrative components—academic affairs, student affairs, administrative affairs—will be present and readily identifiable. The president is the CEO. The CAO may be a provost, a vice president, or a dean of faculty. Most small colleges do not have subcolleges with deans, although professional programs—usually business or nursing—may achieve college status if they offer masters' degrees. While power and authority in small campuses tend to be centrally held, department chairs assume something like the power position of deans. The dean of students may be the head of student affairs, and a vice president for business may be in charge of the traditional functions of administrative affairs.

Faculty are sometimes inclined to see themselves at the top of this large supporting structure. That may be the way it should be, but this hierarchy is usually conceived not in terms of the function of the institutions (which would actually put students at the top) but in terms of decision-making authority and responsibility/accountability. The president is at the top, the vice presidents at the next level, the deans and the deanlets at the next, then department chairs and department-level administrators, then individual faculty, followed by an assortment of staff. Thus, the typical WPA, directing a writing program that is a subprogram of an English department, is buried pretty deeply in the administrative hierarchy, with direct access only to the department chair. And that's the way it is, notwithstanding the fact that composition programs in many universities offer more sections, serve more students, produce more credit hours, and involve more faculty than most departments and some colleges. If your WPA job is more of a task than a formal position, you may have responsibilities equal to those of a dean but little more positional authority than a typical faculty member.

If you are buried deeply in the hierarchy with little authority, you lack direct access to resources and you may have difficulty attracting institutional focus to the accomplishments or objectives of your program. It is hard to get around a chair, for example, who does not want to emphasize composition or support appropriate class size or staffing. On the other hand, the same levels of bureaucracy can protect you from wrath flowing down from above. Authority and accountability usually go together. Clear understanding of this hierarchy and your place in it is essential for understanding how you will do your work. There is a simple rule to follow regardless of where you fall: make friends among the master sergeants. One friendly associate registrar is worth more than a roomful of deans when it comes to getting things done.

WHERE IS MY UNIVERSITY?

Once you have located yourself and your writing program in the institutional hierarchy, you need to consider how your institution relates to other institutions. If you are in any kind of public institution, you must recognize that your institution is not totally independent. Students constantly move back and forth among institutions; at my university, 2500 students every semester are concurrently enrolled for one or more courses at the community colleges. Students from elite liberal arts colleges take summer courses at their hometown universities. Your campus will be involved with other universities, colleges, and community colleges in statewide (if not national) "articulation agreements" that govern the transfer of courses from one campus to another. Models for articulation agreements vary widely across the country. Florida has a common lower-division curriculum among all public universities and community colleges, with common course numbers and course prefixes. Arizona has a more flexible system: a statewide electronic course equivalency guide updated continually, a "plug in anywhere" general education package that includes first-year composition, and a set of "transfer pathways" that lead from the community colleges into various university majors. Other states have "transfer contracts" between and among different institutions. Almost all but the most selective small colleges participate in articulation agreements with one another and public institutions in their service areas. Because first-year composition is the course most frequently transferred from one institution to another you will need to become very familiar with the transfer processes and the procedures whereby course equivalencies are established. You must be willing to work collegially with faculty from other institutions (and other kinds of institutions) to conduct the business of articulation. You will also be among the first who will have to address the transfer of a whole range of courses delivered via technology by a range of mysterious providers. Similarly, you will be involved in determining how your institution handles credit earned through advanced placement, international baccalaureate, CLEP, or other test-based sources of credit—in the face of intense lobbying by the test marketers and promoters. As educational institutions become increasingly interdependent, articulation is going to become an increasingly important part of the WPA's responsibilities.

WHERE IS HIGHER EDUCATION?

You should ask all of the questions above and assemble the answers in a paragraph that will add up to a comprehensive yet specific position (or task) description. This will serve as a good starting point for the task (or position) ahead. But there is one more matter that a WPA must address. You need to be current on trends in higher education and to locate your programs in the general landscape. In addition to reading professional literature written especially for WPAs, you must read the general professional literature in higher education that is read by trustees, presidents, provosts, and deans. They all have their own professional organizations and publications. They, too, go to conferences and bring ideas back to their campuses. It is extremely important to read what they read so that you can anticipate what is going to follow them home from their conferences and possibly get out in front of whatever that is. Because faculty tend to read about what is happening in their discipline but not about what is happening in higher education, they are almost always in the position of *reacting* to the latest administrative initiative—maybe a good one, maybe a bad one. Thus, they are often in a posture of resistance to innovation rather than in finding out ways to incorporate innovation into their own agendas.

Doug Hesse's excellent essay "Understanding Larger Discourses in Higher Education: Practical Advice for WPAs" [see Part V] provides a survey and analysis of the professional literature of higher education. From Hesse's comprehensive list, I would select four publications that are must reading for all WPAs and often serve as ways into the rest of the literature Hesse cites. The first is the *Chronicle of Higher Education*, a weekly report of news and trends in education. The second is *Change: The Magazine of Higher Learning*, a bimonthly publication of the American Association for Higher Education (AAHE). The third is the *AAHE Bulletin*, a monthly publication of the AAHE that addresses current trends in higher education, reports on the status of AAHE projects and publications, and includes news about the activities of AAHE members. The fourth publication (of special interest to smaller colleges) is *Liberal Education*, a quarterly publication of the American Association of Colleges & Universities (AAC&U), dedicated to carrying forward the values of liberal education in a climate of change and innovation.

By regularly reading these publications, you can assume more aggressive postures with regard to higher education trends, and you will not be caught off-guard, unable to talk the talk of higher education. Kinkead and Simpson, in "The Administrative Audience: A Rhetorical Problem" [see Part II], point out that "by communicating well with the administrative culture in the terminology of administration, we stand to gain resources and respect" (72). The remainder of their essay contains a critical lexicon of "dean-speak" and an excellent lesson in administrative rhetoric.

If you have worked your way through the series of questions above, you will have made great progress in moving toward the administrative point of view. Yet there is one other matter about which you must be concerned and about which faculty who are not administrators tend to know very little. Once you know where you are, then you have to find out where the money is.

WHO'S GOT THE MONEY?

Faculty who are not administrators have a knack for developing wonderful academic programs that will never be implemented because they do not take into account the budget realities of the institution. You ignore budget issues at your peril. Any plan that has a chance of being put into place must include an estimate of its costs as well as some indication of where the money will come from. Because WPAs tend to come out of an "English" background, there is a high likelihood that budgets have not been their strong suit, a weakness that has often been used to their disadvantage by those who do understand budgets. But it's not all that tough. It's just addition and subtraction.

First, we all have to get past some popular-culture myths about budget management. We are very much taken by stereotypical stories coming from critics of business and industry: about products that are made poorly because the company is cutting corners in order to line the pockets of the owners or investors and about employees who are exploited in this or that way to increase profits for the rich. Some of this thinking carries over into our thinking about university budgets—especially because our programs have historically been underfunded. For that reason you should understand the difference between *cost accounting*, which is what for-profit businesses do, and *fund accounting*, which is what most colleges and universities do.

For-profit businesses have identified a product or service for which more or fewer customers are willing to pay a lower or higher price. The quality of the product will be determined by finding the place where the product is good enough that enough people will buy it at a price that allows a margin in excess of production costs to reward investors and owners with a profit. There is an ongoing effort to remain in the range of acceptable quality while minimizing cost (supplies, materials, processing, labor, equipment, etc.) and maximizing profit. This is the realm of cost accounting.

Fund accounting is a rather different activity. The key point is that there is no profit; there are no greedy owners or investors who stand to gain from cutting costs. In the university the goal is to spend all of the money we have in order to produce the best program we can with the resources available. The resources available generally bear no relationship to the actual costs of producing an education of a specified quality. Resources available—especially at tax-supported institutions—are a reflection of public-policy decisions, political bargains, and other historical accidents. As a "product" or "service," education is almost totally open-ended, unlimited in scope. There is no limit on the quality. It should be as good as possible and can *always* be better. Generally, the goal of fund accounting is to allow the institution to do as much as possible of an open-ended mission as well as possible with resources that bear no relationship to the mission or to expectations of quality. What this means, of course, is that there are no greedy capitalists to blame here. The funding that doesn't go to the writing program probably goes to the math program or maybe to the creation of a new women's studies department. People who share your general goals and values get the money that you don't. You are competing with your friends. There's no one to demonize, although the deans and provosts are usually identified as the enemy because they have the responsibility of rationing the money. The provost and the deans don't get to keep it. Fund accounting is a process of allocating too little money to do too big a job.

There are generally four sources of money in most public educational institutions: tuition, government (state, local, federal) appropriations, outside money in the form of gifts and grants, and revenue from auxiliary enterprises. Private institutions have all of these sources as well, but a larger portion tends to come from tuition and gifts and a smaller portion from the taxpayers. The distribution of funds across these sources varies considerably from institution to institution, and what you are allowed to do with different kinds of money varies as well. At the main campus of my university, for example, 40 percent of the total (all funds) budget comes from a state allocation; about 15 percent from tuition; about 15 percent from gifts, grants, and contracts; and 30 percent from what we call "unrestricted local funds" (income from auxiliary enterprises such as the bookstore or student union, investments, financial aid funds, and indirect cost recovery from grants, summer-school revenues, etc.). At our new small campus the state appropriation equals 53 percent of our all-funds budget; tuition provides 21 percent; about 16 percent comes from gifts, grants, and contracts; and another 10 percent is "unrestricted local funds" from the sources described above. Usually, money from the government appropriation and from tuition has severe restrictions on what can be done with it. Similarly, use of money generated by gifts, grants, and contracts may be even more narrowly restricted and more carefully audited. The really cool funds in any institution are those "unrestricted" local funds that the institution can use for about any purpose that is otherwise legal.

If you are in a public institution, your campus budget is probably a matter of public record. You can look at it, although most institutions do not go out of their way to make this information easily accessible. (I never saw a university budget until I became a central administrator. Once you're done looking up everyone's salaries, it's actually pretty interesting reading.)

The budgets of private schools, large or small, are usually not matters of public record and are often difficult or impossible to access. It never hurts to ask to see the budget. However, the sources of money for these schools are about the same, although the dependence on tuition and endowment earnings tends to be higher. With notable exceptions, most public institutions do not have huge endowments.

The current budget of your institution, whatever it is, has resulted from a history of purposeful and political decisions, and it is what it is. The usual problem for most campuses is figuring out how to get *more* money. To figure out how tuition and state appropriations are determined is often difficult. In my state tuition setting is a political process that bears no relationship to educational costs. The state constitution says that higher education should be "as close to free as possible." The state appropriation is supposedly driven, to some extent, by formulas. We have, for example, an "enrollment growth" (or alas, shrinkage) formula of 22:1. That is, for every 22 new full-time-equivalent student (FTE student—also FTSE—full-time student equivalent), we get funding for one new full-time faculty line, one quarter of a staff line, and some additional operating funds for both. To determine the number of FTEs, the total number of student credit hours (SCH) for which students are enrolled on the twenty-first day of the fall semester is divided by 12, the equivalent of four 3-credit-hour courses, the official definition of a full-time load. If enrollment shrinks, the formula works the other way. There is also a formula based on square footage for generating maintenance dollars for existing space. The legislature is not obliged, however, to fund either of these formulas fully, and it usually doesn't. Funds for new or enhanced programs that cannot be managed with the continuing budget must be specially requested in "decision packages," which the legislature may or may not choose to fund. Increasingly, funds for "capital projects" (e.g., new buildings, major renovations, campus infrastructure) are being raised through bond issues, the institutional equivalent of a mortgage.

Our local community college district—one of the largest in the nation—is funded mainly through tuition and a county property tax that is earmarked for support of the community college. Increased funding for the district can be generated either by an increase in the tax rate or by riding up local property values. However, the district delivers funding to its constituent campuses according to enrollment formulas and square footage. Private colleges are heavily dependent on a booming stock market or tuition/fee increases to generate new money. You should make an effort to discover how your campus is funded, where the money comes from, and how important *incremental* funding can be generated. Nationally, public funding for higher education has been declining as a percentage of all funds budgets. Legislatures think that we can free up bags of money by becoming more efficient. In fact, most of the burden is shifting to tuition, while all institutions are making an effort to generate more funds through gifts, grants, and contracts. There is usually a sponsored projects office or a research and creative activity office reporting to the provost that will help with the writing and submission of grant applications. More and more campuses have a development office and an independent foundation to help generate gifts. Get to know these folks.

Once you get a global sense of where the money comes from, you should also try to understand where money in your institution goes and how it gets there, which costs are fixed and which are flexible, and which monies are fungible (i.e., interchangeable) and which are not.

The point about fundibility is often poorly understood. As WPAs, we often work in departments and programs that are seriously underfunded and involve poorly paid graduate assistants and adjunct faculty. Thus, we (and they) sometimes feel resentful when we see new buildings going up or other kinds of construction on campus. We recognize that the money spent on repairing a sidewalk on the campus mall would be enough to give all of our adjunct faculty a significant raise. If we raise questions about this funding, we get the annoying response, "different pocket." Annoying or not, it is fundamentally correct—at least in public institutions. Funding available for building projects is "capital" funding and cannot be used to fund "operations," such as instruction. This is especially true if the funds were raised by the sale of bonds. Capital funds are usually not included in the operating budget.

There are eight standard categories of expenditure for university operating budgets. I will describe each and indicate what my university spends in each category in order to provide one fairly typical example of how the money is distributed. This represents the allocation of funds to certain categories of activities, not to functional areas (i.e., academic affairs, student life, administrative affairs).

1. *Instruction:* The big item in this category is faculty salaries, including regular faculty, adjunct faculty, and graduate assistants. (Technically, the research that most faculty do is hidden in the instruction budget.) At my institution the expenditures for instruction account for 50 percent of the total operating budget.

2. *Organized research:* This refers to the costs of conducting basic and applied research, and it is almost totally funded by outside agencies. At my institution about 8 percent of the total budget is spent on organized research, but only a third of that amount comes from the state appropriation.

3. *Public service:* Public services are services that the university provides for the benefit of the general public, such as operating a public television or radio station. My university devotes 1.5 percent of its operating budget to this purpose.

4. *Academic support:* The big-ticket items include the library, information technology, audiovisual services, and academic administration (provost, deans, etc.). My institution devotes about 8 percent of its operating budget to academic support.

5. *Student services:* This category includes admissions, registrar, student activities, student health, career counseling, and financial aid administration. These functions receive a little over 4 percent of my institution's operating budget.

6. *Institutional support:* This category includes executive management (nonacademic administration), financial operations, utilities, human resources, security, alumni relations, and community outreach. A large portion of this money goes to nearly fixed costs such as utilities and campus security. The total amount spent on institutional support at my university is 13 percent of the operating budget.

7. *Scholarships/fellowships:* This category includes student awards not requiring repayment or direct service. About 7 percent of my university's operating budget is committed to this kind of aid. This figure may be higher at other institutions, since our tuition is among the lowest among public universities nationwide.

8. *Auxiliary enterprises:* These are fee-driven services such as bookstore, housing, and meal plans. They are essentially self-supporting. A little over 11 percent of our budget is spent on auxiliary enterprises.

As an administrator, you should take a comprehensive view of the institutional budget. As I have suggested above, fund accounting at the university is a zero-sum game. Your gain is almost always someone else's loss, even when new resources become available. If your project is funded, some other project is cut or not funded. But the game gets a little looser when played on a bigger court. You don't want to think only in terms of the departmental budget. For example, if the boundary of your thinking is the departmental budget only, then more funding for composition will almost inevitably be seen as less funding for literature and your project may get lost in intradepartmental squabbles while the dean looks on smiling as the chair manages an allocation problem. If the college budget is the boundary of your thinking, then the pain of freeing up more funding for a high-impact project in composition can be diffused across a wider area with little impact in any one place, although the dean now has the allocation problem while the provost smiles. If the whole academic affairs budget is the boundary of your thinking, the sources to draw from become greater, while the allocation problem falls on the once-smiling provost. It is especially audacious to take the whole university budget as the boundary of your thinking, since it is generally unthinkable that funds could cross the boundary from one of the big three administrative areas into another. But they can, if the scowling president decides that they can.

There is very little flexibility and waste in most university budgets (notwithstanding the opinions of trustees or state legislators). Most of the operating budget is tied up in salaries or more-or-less fixed costs such as the gas and electric bills or student financial aid. Yet there is always some play in the system. The main source of slack is "salary savings." At any given time there will always be a certain number of funded faculty, staff, or administrative positions that are not occupied; and, while they remain unoccupied, those salaries can be used for other purposes. Most often, this money is used to pay for temporary instructional staff such as adjunct faculty, yearly appointed nontenure faculty, or graduate assistants. If the money is used in this way, it can be recouped when someone is hired to fill the empty line. If salary savings are used to increase the rate of pay for adjuncts or to increase other faculty salaries permanently, then the money cannot be recovered and the lines must remain empty. There is also a hidden dimension to salary savings. For every salary saved, there is also a saving (equaling about 25 percent of the salary) in employee-related expenses (ERE). ERE is the employer's contribution to retirement, health benefits, and so on. The ERE pool is often held centrally, while salaries are distributed to college budgets. Thus the ERE savings are held centrally as well. This is often the provost's or president's deep pocket for emergencies. At many financially stressed institutions, however, salary savings and the ERE pool are no longer slack in the system; they are an integral part of the budget planning. Too many of the basic functions of the institution depend on the existence of a fairly constant level of salary/ERE savings from year to year. In such cases the zero-sum game becomes a serious game indeed.

CROSSING THE LINE: CAN I STILL BEHAVE LIKE A FACULTY MEMBER?

As I noted at the beginning, faculty are almost *countertrained* for administrative roles. Yet once you cross the line from a pure faculty role to an administrative role, your effectiveness as an administrator depends on your willingness to think institutionally and to look beyond the institution to the larger universe of higher education. This is not necessarily something that comes naturally or easily, and the ambiguous nature of WPA roles is such that you may have to maintain a faculty perspective and an administrative perspective simultaneously. This is not a bad thing. There have to be people in colleges and universities who sustain an uncompromising commitment to knowledge, academic quality, and student learning. Without them, it would be all too easy for institutions to settle for doing what they can with the resources they have. It is the faculty's relentless pressure to do more and better that keeps administrators from caving in to "reality." And that truly is crossing the line—when our open-ended mission stops pushing on our finite resources, when we are tempted to move from fund account to cost accounting. One of the most valuable features of the typical WPA role is that this creative tension is constantly at work in your daily life and work. And this is a valuable experience if you return to being a faculty member, and maybe even more valuable if you choose to pursue an administrative career.

WORK CITED

Pascarella, Ernest, and Patrick Terenzini. *How College Affects Students.* San Francisco: Jossey-Bass, 1991.

The Writing Program
in the University

Katherine K. Gottschalk
Cornell University

For a number of years now, Cornell faculty and administrators have been meeting to discuss trends that will affect teaching and learning at universities. As a tuition-paying parent, I could have told members of the committees I have been on that in the future economic considerations will be a driving force. But they already knew, as we all know that colleges and universities are struggling with economic issues and that these issues affect how, and what, we teach our students. We all know that an unwelcome urgency can develop to make teaching cost-effective at the expense of educational goals. My particular concern is that too often the candidates singled out for financial pressure are writing programs: How about forty students rather than thirty in a class? A good deal of lip service is paid to writing— "[F]or most faculty and administrators, the importance of writing is axiomatic, rather like the need for higher salaries or more parking space" (White 1)—but the difficulty is to turn plaintive talk into practice. It's worth considering what can make a writing program an integral part of the mission of a university, so that it doesn't become a target when unpleasant cuts have to be made.

Too often writing programs, like parking lots, are situated on the fringes of the university. A writing program that is set up in a marginalized position, that sees itself as marginalized, and that carries out its activities in a marginalized way will have trouble with long-term survival; it will in fact have trouble doing its job well at any point. Yet that is often the situation in which writing programs find themselves. Some programs survive only about as long as the special grant on which they are founded survives; they are not given permanent funding or control of funding. Administrators and teachers in writing programs may occupy precarious lines, or they may be expected to develop a program and educate the rest of the (resistant) faculty while

carrying heavy teaching loads. Probably the heaviest burden a writing program can bear is having been established by top-down fiat and then being virtually abandoned: "We've hired a writing-across-the-curriculum director,
we've hired a writing program administrator, and now our work is done—
you do the rest or get someone else to do it." The program then operates in a
state of anxiety or in opposition to the rest of the institution.

Observing the difficulties under which some writing programs labor, I
have come to appreciate deeply the collaborative principle that is central to
Cornell's writing program. An examination of it yields useful observations
about the role of collaboration in the establishment and operation of a writing program, about the ways in which such a program may assist in the integration of writing into a university's life.

Our writing program's history has taught me that successful collaboration does not necessarily require unity—that difference and even separation
may be positive forces. Oddly enough, at the heart of Cornell's highly collaborative writing program is a tradition of department territorialism, a force
that a writing program can put to good use. Back in the 1960s, when it was
questioned whether the English department should have sole responsibility
for freshman composition, eight other departments offered to take up a share
of the job and make the teaching of writing an aspect of educational responsibility in their own fields. They recognized that departments other than English could and should provide excellent teachers as well as stimulating topics
about which to write. In 1966, therefore, humanities seminars at Cornell were
born, with offerings in such departments as art history, government, philosophy, and history, as well as in English; the English department became the
coordinator of these efforts. Perhaps this is how many successful collaborative programs begin: departments and individual faculty members initiate a
program and claim it as their own.

Maintaining this initiative is an ongoing challenge; good intentions and
goodwill alone are not enough. Administrative arrangements are important
when many departments in a large university are involved in a joint endeavor,
when a program is trying to do its work. The most decentralized program
needs a steady center. For a long time Cornell's new humanities seminars
were run exclusively by the English departments, with various faculty members appointed to act as director and manage attention to TA training—a situation much like that found today at many colleges and universities. Excellent
work was done, but the program ran into difficulties during the late 1970s,
when familiar complaints arose: the seminars weren't teaching writing,
weren't requiring enough papers, and so on. Recognizing that solutions
imposed by one administrator or by a few members of a department are seldom popular, a university-wide task force of faculty members investigated
the place of writing in the curriculum and proposed ways in which to develop
a more affective and rigorous program.

The enemies of a program's success are, as Toby Fulwiler and Art Young
have observed, "uncertain leadership" and the lack of a secure place in the aca-

demic structure (288–89). The Cornell task force produced recommendations that merit examination here, as they suggest ways in which a writing program may function optimally within and for its institution. One noteworthy recommendation was that the writing seminars be administered by an independent program with its own director. Another significant recommendation was that the directorship be rotated regularly, with a tenured faculty member—not necessarily from the English department—appointed to the position.

The question of whether or not English departments should house writing-across-the-curriculum and writing programs has been a locus for continuing discussion (e.g., Smith; Blair; White). Sound arguments can be made both pro and con, especially because so much depends on an institution's particular situation and traditions. Creating a separate niche for the writing program at Cornell, however, improved the program's strength and opportunities for interdisciplinary work, and observation of Cornell's experience suggests possible benefits of independent status, given an institution's commitment to writing. A separate program, we learned immediately, can be effective because it *is* separate: it can keep its mind, energy, and resources on its sole charge, the teaching of writing. In Cornell's writing program, newly reorganized and reestablished in 1982, we could attend to the charges the university's task force had agreed on: we established guidelines for the teaching of writing in all seminars and monitored their observance; we set up training programs and faculty incentives; we wrote and published a handbook, *Teaching Prose* (Bogel and Gottschalk). We added Writing to the title Freshman Seminars. With every step we concentrated on eliminating merely "additive" writing so that the seminars would truly offer writing in the universities, or writing across the curriculum in both senses: "cognitively based (on the idea of writing as a mode of learning) or rhetorically based (on the idea of introducing students to the discourse communities of various disciplines)" (McLeod 342).

Regardless of where a writing program is housed, our experience suggests that some independent control of funding can help it work from a position of strength. A writing program should not have to fear for its survival, as may happen when a home department, rather than provide security and support, only reluctantly cooperates. If a university believes in the importance of writing, then surely it should established funding that will enable the writing program to do its work without begging each year for photocopying money, let alone funds for courses. "[J]ust as in our private lives we determine our real priorities by what we spend our money on (whatever we may pretend), so does a university" (White 149).

And writing programs need money to spend; adequate funding and control of that funding can make it possible to encourage not just participation but excellence of participation. To that end it was decided at Cornell that the writing program should help distribute funds to departments that offered freshman writing seminars, namely, support for graduate students who taught in the program. Considerations entering into the distribution are faculty members' mentorship of TAs during the year, the quality of TAs being proposed by departments, and the student evaluations submitted each semester. Other kinds of tangible support encourage faculty members and graduate students to have a stake in the writing program—for instance, giving graduate students summer support for internships with experienced teachers or financially rewarding faculty members who participate in our Faculty Seminar for Writing Instruction. Financial incentives may not be needed once a program is under way, as many faculty members are interested in the teaching of writing whether or not they are rewarded financially, but it can help with initiating projects and encouraging active participation. Just as important, the tangible support demonstrates university commitment, and that in itself may encourage the commitment of individuals.

The directorship and staffing of a writing program can also be crucial to its success, to its recognition within the university, and to the quality of its work. Will a writing program disappear when someone retires or tires of the job and returns to teaching literature or other courses in a specialized field? Are the program's permanent teachers too overworked to put energy into outreach and administrative tasks? Cornell's writing program has found appropriate a rotating directorship held by a tenured faculty member from one of the participating departments; the faculty member receives released time from teaching to take on this position. As part of the writing program's administration for over twelve years, I have seen what it can mean to appoint faculty members new to the field of composition as such who are enthusiastic about investing themselves in the role of director. It is well understood that writing programs need the support of key administrators, and at Cornell we have found that the director of the writing program, who works closely with the dean and sometimes the provost, acts as just such a key administrator. A tenured faculty member in the role of director represents a discipline and a faculty committed to the teaching of writing; he or she works from within instead of being imposed from above to promote attention to language. Such directors, we have found, labor steadily and successfully for the program's financial security, for development and funding of new projects, and for the well-being and effectiveness of the writing program's staff—for instance, in the matter of released time and satisfactory course loads. (For a writing program's staff, the presence of an administrator who understands and acts as an advocate is essential).

It may help to look at a few of our directors in action as examples. The first director of the newly reorganized writing program made sure we established a TA training program suitable for participants from the many disciplines and that standards were high for all seminars. He also attended to grant writing, which resulted in a major endowment and a new name: the John S. Knight Writing Program. Our second director collaborated with administration and faculty for further improvements, such as a guarantee that seminars would be fixed at a maximum of seventeen students no matter what increases occurred in the size of the freshman class. Turning his attention to the faculty, he began the six-week summer Faculty Seminar in Writing Instruction. He also kept in constant contact with the administration, collaborating with the dean of the College of Arts and Sciences to invent an important new program, Writing in the Majors, and to win an internal grant for it. Through consultation with faculty and administration he thoroughly established the prestige of Writing in the Majors. The university now uses its own funds to keep it going, perhaps the most important sign of success a program can have. Jonathan Monroe, the third and present writing program director, like his predecessors, arrived with the vigor of new ideas and a new perspective and has already initiated a peer collaboration program for instructors of freshman writing seminars and negotiated agreements with the division of biological sciences for a "bio-writing lecturer," who has a joint appointment in the writing program, and for a new cost-sharing arrangement to increase the number and diversity of courses in Writing in the Majors.

In addition to realizing how important it is that a writing program director have sufficient time to work with faculty members and administrators, we have discovered the vital role members of a small committed full-time professional staff can play when they are given released time from teaching basic writing courses to work with other faculty members and graduate students and to develop programs. Long-term staff members become expert voices as well as valuable resources for teachers new to thinking about writing. Many of our projects depend on efforts and initiatives that come from the writing program's cadre of permanent senior lecturers. My job, for instance, is to direct the freshman writing seminars, a position that includes TA training and faculty development. Another senior lecturer directs Writing in the Majors, which again largely involves working with faculty and TAs; another gives special assistance to ESL students and their seminar teachers; and still another directs a writing center.

Such outreach across the university is invaluable. A writing program, we have learned, cannot depend only on its own efforts to provide true service to the university. Money and top-down program building alone do not suffice. As David Russell notes of writing-across-the-curriculum programs, "Finding ways to harness the efforts of the disciplines—where the faculty's primary loyalty and interest lie—will perhaps achieve more in the long run than structurally separate programs, no matter how well intentioned and well financed" (304). The successful integration of a writing program into the university indeed depends on the efforts of the disciplines. In fact, the role of a writing program—structurally separate or otherwise—may be less to "harness" those efforts for its own ends than to find ways of encouraging the disciplines themselves to discover and use their understanding of language. The writing program increases its value, and hence its security, as it works with and for the rest of the university.

As indicated above, the disciplines at Cornell early claimed freshman writing seminars as their own to teach. The seminars are successful with students and faculty members alike because, while coordinated by the writing program, the classes are actually designed and taught by many departments.

In any one semester students may choose from over a hundred different courses, ranging from American Literature and Culture (English) and The History and Politics of Scientific Methods (science and technology studies) to You Are What You Eat: Anthropological Perspectives on Culture, Society and Cuisine (anthropology). One-third of the freshman writing seminars are taught by faculty members; the rest are taught by graduate students. The writing program therefore puts much of its energy into encouraging and enabling the efforts of faculty members and graduate students from the thirty-some departments and programs actively involved in teaching the freshman writing seminars. It must help faculty members from music and graduate students from biology discover how to teach writing and how to use writing as a part of learning in their disciplines. Needless to say, the task is not always easy, as many begin with the idea that teaching writing means getting students to follow prescriptive rules.

How does the program help these teachers? What makes widespread participation possible? Possible stumbling blocks abound, given that when writing is incorporated into subjects other than English, it can be "perceived as an additional burden rather than an intrinsic part of learning" (Russell 297). It helps that Cornell did not impose the "burden" of teaching writing from above, which can indeed fatally weigh down an interdisciplinary writing program. Even now, new departments join the program voluntarily, because they see how freshman writing seminars can serve their purposes—when, for instance, they are interested in improving contact with undergraduates or when graduate students want a chance to teach a small course that is all their own. We have learned that the freshman writing seminars should offer these opportunities in a supportive, collaborative environment, that we do not want to dictate exactly what is going to be taught and how it's going to be taught. We try to work with and for the teacher in the discipline.

When, for instance, in a recent semester a professor from a science department taught a freshman writing seminar for the first time, he did so by choice. Talking with me beforehand, however, he was concerned about his qualifications for teaching writing; one of his first questions, as often happens, was how much grammar he needed to know. Thinking of writing as an addition to rather than part of his course, he was apprehensive. Before he began his teaching, the professor was encouraged to take part in the Faculty Seminar in Writing Instruction, a summer program established by the writing program for faculty members who wish to improve their teaching in freshman writing seminars or in other writing-intensive courses. From the seminar he learned about an emphasis that is also fundamental in Teaching Writing, the writing program's six-week training course required of all graduate students who teach a writing seminar.

Teaching Writing and the faculty seminar emphasize designing writing assignments that grow out of the nature and interests of the discipline and that help students discover the discipline through writing. The writing program encourages teachers of freshman writing seminars to consider what students will learn about writing. Instructors are encouraged to ask for rough drafts and revisions, to design assignments that are connected to each other, to assist students with preliminary writing that prepares them for the successful completion of essay assignments—the various methods familiar to those who wish to emphasize the process of writing, writing as a method of inquiry, writing even as a way of becoming part of a discipline's conversation. Just as important, we try to help faculty members and TAs discover that, as writing and reading scholars, they are more prepared to teach writing than they realize and that approaches they develop for a seminar may also improve their other teaching.

Rather than tell the science professor what to do, then, we helped him think about and act on what he knew already about language in his discipline in order to decide on the methods and concerns he considered central to communication in his field. He wasn't actually interested in grammar; matters of particular importance to him were having students investigate the use of persuasive devices in public writing about controversial subjects and having them do collaborative research and writing, a crucial mode of work in the sciences. Through the faculty seminar discussions and his own experience, the professor realized he did not have to run a grammar course (although he did teach grammar along the way, as needed. He taught a course in which students wrote to learn and learned to write, a course in which the students and he engaged in a productive dialogue. Having now taught the freshman writing seminar, he says he has never had a better teaching experience and spreads the word about the program.

While already familiar with the idea that students in writing courses are constantly inventing the university (Bartholomae), we've come to realize that the writing program needs to be constantly reshaped, revitalized—reinvented—by faculty members and graduate students as they discover ways to teach their students and as they explore the rhetoric of their own discourses. Clearly, this revitalizing and reshaping also occurs through our promoting of the collaboration of instructors. Our faculty members return as experienced teachers to Teaching Writing, the training course for graduate students, in order to work with TAs from their departments, and thy participate as alumni and alumnae in the Faculty Seminar in Writing Instruction. Faculty members and graduate students are thus encouraged to claim the freshman writing seminars and the training programs as their own. This approach worked in the science department mentioned above, where another faculty member and a graduate student decided to participate because of the enthusiasm of the first teacher.

When collaboration and the sense of ownership break down, faculty members and graduate students participate less successfully in a program. If faculty members neglect to mentor thoughtfully the graduate students who are teaching the freshman writing seminars, some graduate students may have a negative attitude toward teaching. To avoid such tensions, the writing program needs to work steadily to help faculty members remain aware of and be supportive of their graduate students as teachers. Occasionally faculty members who try teaching seminars for the first time find to their surprise that the seminars take a lot of time and effort. Some do not return, or return reluctantly. Without support and encouragement from the writing program, still more teachers might be unwilling to take on the challenge of this important work. We do find that those who have participated in the faculty seminar or worked with TAs, perhaps in Teaching Writing, often become committed participants despite the time investment and effort required. They see that the work matters and that it is theirs.

To promote further faculty involvement, the John S. Knight Writing Program also concentrates on an important initiative that it began in 1987: Writing in the Majors. This upper-level program has taught us further important lessons about how a writing program functions best through genuine collaboration. In Writing in the Majors we work with upper-level, required courses in disciplines that traditionally focus less on writing, courses such as biology, astronomy, and economics. We do not encourage faculty members of these courses to teach writing; in fact, we have learned that we should not work with faculty members who want the writing program to supply the "writing segment," that is, to supply an unwanted addition to the "real" subject. Instead, the writing program's goal for faculty members is one they already have: to improve their teaching of their subject matter, through improved attention to language. The Knight Writing Program provides financial support for one TA or more who will help with the increased burdens of the course. These TAs take our six-week training seminar, during which time they work closely with the Writing in the Majors director. The director also consults with the faculty.

Writing in the Majors continues to grow steadily. Since 1988, it has supported initiatives in forty courses in fifteen departments, courses that have enrolled, over the years, about 4,200 upper-division students. The program has worked directly with about sixty faculty members and a hundred TAs. Faculty members and TAs alike love the program. So do the students— although usually they don't know they are in a Writing in the Majors course. They just know they are in a good one. What is special about Writing in the Majors? And what are its attractions for faculty members?

Its director, Keith Hjortshoj, makes an important point. He believes that many interdisciplinary writing programs encounter resistance because "they attempt to distribute responsibility for writing instruction throughout the curriculum while retaining centralized authority over language" (Hjortshoj, Letter). Writing in the Majors courses have no mandates and fulfill no special requirements in writing. The program encounters little resistance because, as its director says, it offers little to resist. Faculty members respond to the program because most good teachers are perpetually looking for a better way to teach, and they see in our help an "opportunity to enrich education through active uses of language" (Hjortshoj, "Developments" [16]). Accordingly,

> We [encourage] people to pay attention to the uses of language in their courses and disciplines, both in writing and in reading, and sometimes in speaking and listening too. This, at least, is the central goal of Writing in the Majors, which emphasizes the vital connections between language and learning at upper levels of the curriculum. It doesn't…attach any kind of exclusive significance to writing, or even to writing instruction. Initiatives evolve, instead, from faculty members' concerns about learning issues that involve uses of language in many forms…. That's why we quickly engaged so many people in the sciences, who sensed a need for kinds of instruction and practice that were not included in the traditional science curriculum, but were essential to scientific learning and professions. (Hjortshoj, Letter)

Success in Writing in the Majors, then, is a result of working from the concerns and knowledge of faculty members. What we know about writing and pedagogy acts as a springboard for teachers to explore and perhaps even transform the use of language in their own disciplines. As Robert Jones and Joseph Comprone have urged, "This dialogue [between faculty and writing teachers] must work toward balancing humanistic methods of encouraging more active and collaborative learning in Writing Across the Curriculum courses with reinforcing the ways of knowing and the writing conventions of different discourse communities" (61). We do not provide experts in rhetoric to plan courses or correct papers. Rather, faculty members and graduate students within the fields provide the insights. A physics professor, for instance, recently completed a fascinating study on the rhetorical uses of citations in publications. This kind of process has led faculty members sometimes to abandon exams but always to explore richer, fuller uses of writing for students. In a laboratory course, students may produce carefully constructed experiment abstracts; in a senior-level course on particle physics, they may write research papers that draw on the professional literature and that are written in a professional manner.

TAs trained in the writing program's Teaching Writing course contribute new ideas and energy crucial to the program's success. "TAs tend to have energy and enthusiasm," Ellen Strenski has observed, "and most research universities have at least a minimal TA training program where TAs, unlike professors, can be given explicit instruction" (37). At Cornell, the energy and enthusiasm of faculty members also abound, and when TAs and faculty members combine these qualities, splendid things happen. Accordingly, as attention to the connection between language and leaning has increased, attention to the general training and contributions of TAs has increased—drawing TAs into closer collaboration with faculty members as well as with the students in their courses.

The collaborative approach and emphasis on language employed by Writing in the Majors recently received a vote of institutional confidence. When the university applied for a Lilly Endowment grant to develop teaching skills among junior faculty members, it chose to emphasize language and learning in the sciences and engineering through Writing in the Majors and the Engineering Communications Program. Cornell received the grant.

A final comment. At Cornell, as at any institution, we know that the writing programs's success would be impossible without the backing of an administration that believes in the importance of writing as part of the undergraduate experience. The deans of the College of Arts and Sciences have wholeheartedly supported the writing program, even in budget-cutting times. It is significantly that our deans participate in the writing program as teachers. One taught seminars regularly before becoming a dean and also took the Faculty Seminar in Writing Instruction, to which he returns most years as a participating alumnus. Even without these experiences, he would have supported the writing program, but his having been a successful participant surely contributed to his continuing interest and involvement. An outspoken and constant supporter of our work, he knows firsthand what it is. A previous dean, to whom we constantly turned for support as we developed new programs, is now teaching a course for Writing in the Majors, the program he helped get under way.

Every university must find its own strategies for securing and enhancing the role of the writing program. A writing program that occupies an adversarial or "janitorial" position is unlikely to succeed. Writing programs must work collaboratively with faculty and administration, helping them explore and benefit from their beliefs, their enthusiasm. The writing program becomes a means through which the university can develop and accomplish its ends. As I explain to seminar teachers, When you step into the classroom, *you* are the writing program. Be a good one.

WORKS CITED

Bartholomae, David. "Inventing the University." *When a Writer Can't Write: Studies in Writer's Block and Other Composing-Process Problems.* New York: Guilford, 1985. 134–65.

Blair, Catherine Pastore. "Only One of the Voices: Dialogic Writing Across the Curriculum." *College English* 50 (1988): 383–89.

Bogel, Fredric V., and Katherine K. Gottschalk, eds. *Teaching Prose: A Guide for Writing Instructors.* New York: Norton, 1988.

Fulwiler, Toby, and Art Young. "Afterword: The Enemies of Writing Across the Curriculum." *Programs That Work: Models and Methods for Writing Across the Curriculum.* Ed. Fulwiler and Young. Portsmouth, NH: Boynton, 1990, 287–94.

Jones, Robert, and Joseph J. Comprone. "Where Do We Go Next in Writing Across the Curriculum?" *College Composition and Communication* 44 (1993): 59–68.

Hjortshoj, Keith. "Developments in Writing in the Majors: 1991–1993." In-house report. Cornell Univ. 19 Sept. 1992.

———. Letter to the author. 28 Feb. 1994.

McLeod, Susan H. "Writing Across the Curriculum: The Second Stage, and Beyond." *College Composition and Communication* 40 (1989): 337–43.

Russell, David. *Writing in the Academic Disciplines, 1870–1990: A Curricular History.* Carbondale: Southern Illinois UP, 1992.

Smith, Louise Z. "Why English Departments Should 'House' Writing Across the Curriculum.' *College English* 50 (1988): 390–95.

Strenski, Ellen. "Writing Across the Curriculum at Research Universities." *Strengthening Programs for Writing Across the Curriculum.* Ed. Susan H. McLeod. San Francisco: Jossey, 1988. 31–41.

White, Edward M. *Developing Successful College Writing Programs.* San Francisco: Jossey, 1989.

Administration as Focus for Understanding the Teaching of Writing

Richard Gebhardt

Bowling Green State University

In "Writing Administration as Scholarship and Teaching," Duane Roen recounts how frequently phone calls from former graduate students begin like this: "I know you always told us not to do administration until after tenure, but they really need me to direct composition." "I try—and fail—to dissuade the caller," Roen writes. "Then we discuss strategies for negotiating assurances that their work will lead to tenure and promotion...."

Roen's concern—the reason he tries to dissuade his students—is that writing program administration is undervalued and inappropriately evaluated at many colleges and universities. That concerns me, too, as does the reason Roen's students seldom heed his advice.

Recall the typical telephone conversation: "They really need me to direct composition." Those words suggest a lot about awareness, and acceptance, of professional responsibility—the same responsibility I've seen writing directors across the country accept—to try to move current theory and research into college writing instruction. If my experience with graduate students is typical, this sense of responsibility grows from student encounters with the field's expanding range of exciting theories and approaches and from their efforts to reflect such things in the classes they are teaching—and those they imagine teaching in the future.

Without consciously trying to, departments foster this sense of responsibility by having graduate students teach writing classes while they are reading, discussing, and writing about the scholarship of composition studies. This encourages a desirable professional fusion of interest in "theory" and "practice." But this fusion centers on the individual teacher and his or her classes and students. And it's clear (in the Council of Writing Program Administrators' 1992 guidelines, for instance) that this is only part of what is needed to be

34

a writing program administrator. So Thomas Hilgers and Joy Marsella say in *Making Your Writing Program Work* that "training as researchers and theorists provides few writing specialists with the knowledge and expertise they need to find work in program administration immediately congenial" (8–9).

With this situation in mind, Michael Pemberton has written about "Underpreparation in Graduate Composition Programs":

> [A] graduate program that concerns itself solely with immersing students in the details of critical theory, social construction, cognitivism, and empirical research is fulfilling only a part of its educational mission….Since program administration will undoubtedly comprise a part of their future job duties, courses in program administration should, logically, be an integral part of the major. (164)

Pemberton's response is a substantial graduate course dealing with theoretical backgrounds, institutional missions, and practical administrative details of "the three forms of writing administration composition specialists are likely to become involved with in their careers: first-year composition programs, writing centers, and WAC programs"(167–68; see 171–73 for a course outline). A course in writing program administration makes a lot of sense in doctoral composition programs, which is why I've taught such courses and will again. Still, I'm troubled by the inferences students may draw from such courses: that the complexities of writing administration can be packed into a semester   a week for WAC, two for tutoring and writing centers, another for assessment—and that, if they can, writing program leadership really can't be too significant. Too often, English department faculty and personnel committees dismiss the work of writing directors as administrative management rather than as the educational leadership that may "in some respects, be viewed as the purest possible expression of theoretical principles in composition" (Pemberton 164). So I've come to believe that among the important things a doctoral rhetoric program should provide students—whether with an administration course, discussions and assignments in other courses, or assistantships or graduate administrative assignments such as those described by Holberg and Taylor in a recent issue of *Composition Chronicle*. But it's equally important for students to be made aware that administration of a writing program goes beyond paper pushing; **administration is macrolevel teaching.**

Individual teachers (including writing directors, in their own courses) select materials and approaches, make assignments, respond to writing, evaluate student performance, and so on. On the other hand, program administrators (except in their own classes) work behind the scenes and may be largely invisible to students. If, as Kenneth Eble put it in *The Craft of Teaching*, "teaching is a presence of mind and person and body in relation to another mind and person and body, a complex array of mental, spiritual, and physical acts affecting others"(10), then the teacher's mind and person and body relate to the minds, persons, and bodies of students, while the writing director's major and direct relationships are with the teachers on her staff. (This paragraph recasts from a closely related context a passage in Gebhardt 45.)

Rather than select the books for her own couple of classes, the writing director may select books (or shape a process for selecting books) for dozens or hundreds of sections. Rather than try to understand and adjust for instructional problems involving her own students, she works daily with graduate assistants and others worried about such things in their classes. Rather than jump into trial-and-error innovation to shape her own sections around a promising scholarly trend, she may study how the trend might work with many sections and teachers and seek to locate resources for the staff development and public relations efforts to adjust the curriculum of her program.

In such activities, a writing director is a teacher who works with students, not directly but through policies, committees, staff members, programs of training and supervision, appeals procedures, and the like. And the writing director's many "managerial" activities (developing and working within budgets, completing reports, keeping the writing center staffed and copiers running, etc.) are tools for macrolevel teaching, not the heart or soul of program administration.

This idea of writing administration as growing out of the teacher's curricular and instructional roles can help graduate students evolve the conceptions of teaching upon which they will begin their careers. For instance, when they discover in their graduate courses or dissertation research ideas that change the way they think about their classes or the writing of their students, the macro-teaching concept may prompt useful reflection about how those ideas could work across a writing program. When they find themselves depressed or outraged after a student conference, they may begin—however informally and intuitively—to evolve ways to talk about such charged moments with their staff members in the future.

Such reflections—and rhetoric Ph.D. students have myriad opportunities for them—promote the fusion of interest in "theory" and "practice" I mentioned earlier. But they extend the fusion beyond the individual teacher and his or her classes and students and into the broader realm of writing instruction in which composition specialists work as program directors.

WORKS CITED

Council of Writing Program Administrators. "Guidelines for Writing Program Administrator (WPA) Positions." *WPA: Writing Program Administration* 16.1–2 (Fall–Winter 1992): 89–94.

Eble, Kenneth. *The Craft of Teaching: A Guide to Mastering the Professor's Art.* 2nd ed. San Francisco: Jossey, 1988.

Gebhardt, Richard C. "The Department Chair's Role in Enhancing Teaching." *ADE Bulletin* No. 100 (Winter 1991): 45–48.

Hilgers, Thomas L., and Joy Marsella. *Making Your Writing Program Work: A Guide to Good Practice.* Newbury Park, CA: Sage, 1992.

Holberg, Jennifer, and Marcy M. Taylor. "Apprenticeship versus Partnership: Graduate Students as Administrators." *Composition Chronicle* 8:9 (January 1996): 6–8.

Pemberton, Michael A. "Tales Too Terrible to Tell: Unstated Truths and Underpreparation in Graduate Composition Programs." *Writing Ourselves Into the Story.* Ed. Sheryl I. Fontaine and Susan Hunter. Carbondale: Southern Illinois UP, 1993. 154–73.

Roen, Duane H. "Writing Administration as Scholarship and Teaching." *Academic Advancement in Composition Studies: Scholarship, Publication, Promotion, Tenure.* Ed. Richard C. Gebhardt and Barbara Genelle Smith Gebhardt. Mahwah, NJ: Lawrence Erlbaum, forthcoming. 43–55.

Gebhardt, Richard, "Administration as Focus for Understanding the Teaching of Writing." *Composition Chronicle* 1996 (Oct) 5-6. Reprinted by permission of author.

Working Outside of English

Barry M. Maid
Arizona State University—East

It may come as a surprise for many new or aspiring WPAs to discover that the program they will administer does not comfortably reside within an English department. Some would have us believe that this is a new phenomenon, but historically this has never really been the case. The department of rhetoric at the St. Paul campus of the University of Minnesota, for example, dates back to 1909. This is not the place to argue about whether writing programs belong in English departments but rather simply to give some descriptions of how programs that reside outside of English departments might be structured as well as how the significant issues that confront all WPAs might be different as a function of those different structures. Once we survey different potential organizational issues, we can then turn to the independent program's perspective of the specific issues that are important to all writing programs: faculty, curriculum, and budget.

The first organizational issue to address is that of reporting lines. If there's a question about reporting lines, it should be easily cleared up by looking at the institution's organizational chart. However, the information presented there doesn't always reflect the total reality. While it's clear that the director of an independent program might report to a dean or a provost, that director's tenure home may still remain in English. A condition like this, while not necessarily causing a "conflict of interest," can easily lead to difficult situations.

In order to better understand the variety of reporting lines a director of an independent writing program might see, let's begin by looking at what the "normal" reporting line would be if the program were housed within a traditional English department. In this situation, the director would have some kind of administrative or quasi-administrative title and report to the department chair or head. This structure is clean, straightforward, and easily understood by faculty. Once outside of departmental structures, however, the program director might report to a dean, an associate dean, a provost, an associate provost, or perhaps some other administrative entity. Part of the determination of the reporting line will depend on the nature of the program itself.

For example, a writing center whose mission is viewed as being a "support" rather than an "academic" service might report through student affairs rather than academic affairs.

Independent writing units come in more flavors than you can find at Baskin-Robbins. There are independent first-year comp programs, independent basic writing units, independent writing centers, and independent WAC units. There are full-fledged academic departments that offer degrees. In some ways, units like my former Department of Rhetoric and Writing at the University of Arkansas at Little Rock or the Department of Rhetoric and Communication at Mt. Saint Mary's in Maryland are less interesting; WPA issues that are purely administrative in nature (budget, schedules) tend to emulate the same patterns as within English departments—with the significant difference that once in a writing department, WPA issues that are discipline-based (curriculum, pedagogy) are more readily understood by the entire faculty. Some units look like departments but don't offer degrees. One of the best examples is the Division of Rhetoric and Composition (DRC) at the University of Texas at Austin. It is a division because it offers no degrees, and its faculty, who teach in the well-respected Ph.D. program in rhetoric and composition, do so in the English department, where the program resides. All of these offer differing options for the status of the program, the program's staff (the teaching staff of independent programs is not always considered faculty), and the program's curriculum.

STATUS AND THE ACADEMIC

Academics don't like to talk much about status. Indeed, many of them vehemently object to being labeled "status conscious." The truth, however, is that academics, like all humans, seem to be obsessed with status. We just ascribe status in different ways than do others. Clearly, in the American academy, units that grant degrees have more status than units that don't. And to continue in our status-conscious world, units that grant graduate degrees (especially Ph.D.s) have more status than units that grant undergraduate degrees only. There are actually some good reasons for this. Funding often follows numbers of majors and graduates. Funding is greater for graduate students than for undergraduate students. Because of this, in the best of all possible worlds, an independent writing unit would be a full-fledged academic department that would grant degrees (whether they would be graduate and undergraduate or only undergraduate would depend on the mission of the institution). If the unit is a fully acknowledged academic department, it will most likely be led by a chair or head and, because of the nature of writing programs, have several other subadministrators who report to the chair.

Depending on the campus structure, it may be possible to have a department without offering a degree. The next best thing to offering a degree is to offer a minor—that is, an important piece of someone else's degree. In fact, at the postconvention workshop on independent writing programs held at the Nashville Conference on College Composition and Communication (CCCC) in 1994, the idea of building a minor was deemed the best first step for any independent program not yet in the degree business.

Beyond degree programs, the most commonly found independent units (though admittedly these are not inclusive) are first-year writing programs, basic writing programs, writing centers, and writing-across-the-curriculum or writing-in-the-disciplines programs. Sometimes some of these programs are clustered. Basic writing might be housed within first-year composition. However, on some campuses all developmental courses are housed in a developmental studies unit (usually comprised of writing, reading and/or study skills, and math). Until this past academic year (1999–2000), Georgia State University was an institution with such a unit. These units are as likely as not to report either to a college of education or even to student services as they are to a provost. Writing centers and WAC programs (which are sometimes combined) are also positioned outside of the English department. Again, writing centers may find themselves as part of a larger learning center. They also may find themselves reporting to student services. When coupled with a campuswide WAC program, the likelihood is greater that they will report through academic affairs. One of the most interesting placements of programs of this nature is at the University of Wyoming, where the writing center and WAC program are housed in the Center for Teaching Excellence. At Wyoming, the director of WAC/writing center is paid through the Center for Teaching Excellence and reports to its director.

This position might simply be considered interesting in and of itself. However, the organizational reporting line of an independent writing unit can be the determining factor in the status of the director and the staff. In the just cited example of Wyoming, while the director is clearly outside of English, her staff comes from English, creating an interesting symbiotic relationship. In a similar kind of program but with different direct reporting lines, the University Toledo has a writing center/WAC director who reports directly to the provost; however, she holds tenure in English. The status and cooperation an independent program might find within the academic structure of an institution may be partly determined by reporting lines. In order for the staff of an independent writing program to work effectively across campus, that staff must be perceived by the campus faculty at large as having viable academic status within academic affairs. The quickest, easiest, and surest way for that to happen is to have the program staffed by tenured or tenure-track faculty. Whether it is a wise decision or not, faculty are simply more likely to work cooperatively with faculty than with professional staff. This is not to say that faculty won't or can't work with professional staff but simply that in the academic pecking order, professional staff are beneath faculty. There are, of course, many particular instances where the professional staff has a strong and cooperative working relationship with the faculty. However, that usually is more of a function of the personality of the individual staff and faculty at particular institutions than of a general institutional culture pattern. In fact, when personalities change, relationships between programs and faculty can change as well.

Finally, in terms of organizational issues is the matter of tenure. If the director of an independent program is a tenure-track faculty member, the question arises, Where is the tenure home of the director? In most instances it is not in the program but rather in a traditional academic department. For directors of writing programs that traditional academic department is usually an English department. Again, this potentially causes all kinds of problems. If tenure-track faculty members are hired to direct writing programs outside of their tenure home and are evaluated outside of the department as well as inside, the tenure process itself can be problematic. It is quite possible for individuals to be hired to direct a program; to do so in exemplary fashion; to receive high evaluations from students, peers, and administrators; and then be denied tenure because they did not perform like traditional English faculty members—even though they were specifically hired not to be traditional English faculty members. Clearly, the easy answer is to place only tenured faculty in these positions. In many places, however, though philosophically a good idea, this is not practical. In other instances it creates a class of permanent associate professors, faculty who by the very nature of their administrative work are doomed to do the kind of work that is not promotable, though their work may clearly be more in line with meeting the mission of the institution than the work of the traditional faculty.

FACULTY

Who are the faculty in independent writing units? Are they different from the faculty in traditional English departments? Obviously, the answer to that last question is going to be yes and no. Once again, the nature of the institution and the unit is going to help determine who staffs the independent unit. If the unit is a full-blown program or department, the likelihood is greater that it will be staffed by people with faculty status. If the unit is a writing center, it might be staffed by someone with the title of professional staff rather than faculty. What's the difference between being professional staff rather than a faculty appointment? I suspect that it mainly lies in the area of salary and institutional status. Faculty make more money than professional staff. Faculty also carry more local status than staff. (Actually, the local nature of status is quite interesting. Once individuals move beyond the arena of their own campus—whether by publishing or presenting at professional meetings—the profession in general seems to care little about the terms of appointment, being more concerned about the quality of work. There is more to say about this in the area of credentials.)

However, to get a clearer picture of who might staff the unit, let's look at some different units with their staffing possibilities. First of all, the full-fledged academic department will have staff that most mirrors traditional departments. The faculty will have at least some tenured or tenure-track members. There may be nontenure-track faculty. There is the potential that adjuncts and/or graduate students will do some of the teaching. The unit might also employ some professional staff in a variety of positions.

In most instances the tenure-track faculty will possess doctoral degrees; however, not necessarily the Ph.D. In fact, the number of recognizable names in rhetoric and composition followed by Ed.D. or even D.A. is noteworthy. It is reasonable to expect that new tenure-track hires will have specialties in rhetoric and composition, technical communication, or something similar. The days of the literary retreads (like me) seem to be long past—unless an individual shows some serious retraining and professional development. However, the credentials of nontenure-track faculty, adjuncts, and professional staff remain very much a local issue. Sometimes institutions and programs hire at the professional staff level so that they don't have to hire someone with a doctoral degree. Sometimes they hire doctoral-degree people as professional staff. Again, it's important to remember that professional staff costs less than faculty. Likewise, nontenure-track faculty costs less than tenure-track faculty. More often than not, the staffing of a writing program is an economic, *not* an academic issue. Unfortunately, this appears as though it will remain frustratingly so whether the program resides inside or outside an English department. We can see this is true in English departments where literary specialists, often with little training and less interest in composition, teach required composition courses as part of their load. The reason for this is economic. At schools where literature faculty teach half their teaching load in composition, to not have them teach composition would mean that the school would need half the number of literature faculty and significantly more writing faculty. (This relates to what is becoming an interesting emerging phenomenon in full-fledged writing departments. Many times, the assumption, especially on the part of central administration, is that in a full writing department the staffing of first-year composition will be done by full-time faculty. Yet when that unit has to staff upper-level and, perhaps, graduate classes so that students can receive their degrees in that area in a timely fashion, the full-time faculty find themselves doing more work with undergraduate majors and graduate students than with first-year students. As a result, once again TAs and adjuncts staff first-year composition.)

All of this becomes even more complicated if the unit is *not* a full-fledged academic department. One of the potential configurations of an independent program is for a first-year composition program to be freestanding. In situations like this, it is not uncommon for the program director to be a tenured or tenure-track member of the English department who teaches some courses in English but whose primary responsibility is to the first-year program. Nontenure-track faculty staffs some of these programs, some are staffed primarily by adjuncts, and other programs use graduate assistants. The no longer existing program at the University of Minnesota looked something like that. The former director and four faculty members were from English, though there was the potential that they could draw on faculty from other departments. The director reported directly to the dean.

In all cases, but especially in these independent programs, who does the hiring and what they look at for faculty to be hired tends to be local and can greatly determine the nature of the program. Clearly, the most stable model is to have permanent full- time faculty. In freestanding units, this usually means nontenure-track faculty. Most faculty members, and many institutions, seem to think that any faculty member who has received a contract for a seventh year has *de facto* tenure. This may be true if it is written in an institution's policies or if there is a union contract with a faculty union, but in most instances, this remains part of the mythology of higher education. Indeed, such a policy ensures continued instability in nontenure-track faculty. Programs who use term appointment faculty will never have faculty with a real investment in the program. Term appointment faculty members are, understandably, more interested in where their next job will be than in program development.

If the program uses adjuncts, it's common for the director to make those hires. Depending on the local market conditions, the director can determine credential qualifications. A master's degree is usually the basic criterion. Whether the adjunct has real training/experience in composition is another story.

Finally, if the program uses graduate assistants, the hiring may be problematic. Ideally, we might expect the director of the program to choose the graduate assistants, but in many instances a graduate committee or a graduate director—usually in English—chooses the graduate assistants for the director. As a result, those chosen to teach in the composition program (tutor in the writing center) are not necessarily the best choices or the choice of the WPA. Since the influence a WPA can have on who is eligible to be a TA is often made more difficult the farther the WPA is from the graduate students' unit, WPAs of independent programs might find themselves with a group of potential TAs in whose selection they had no say.

All of these staffing problems can be mitigated with preservice training and ongoing professional development. However, much of that is a function of budgetary constraints.

Beyond the freestanding first-year composition program, we can see the freestanding writing center or WAC program. Both of these tend to be one-person operations—though the director may hire some staff. In the writing center the staff usually consists of tutors—both graduate and undergraduate. One of the most interesting exceptions to this is at Mt. Saint Mary's College in Maryland, where the degree-granting department of rhetoric and communication emerged from the independent writing center and where tenured faculty members still teach in the writing center. More common is the scenario where the writing center director holds a professional staff position. That is possible, but less likely, for a WAC director. In all likelihood a WAC director will hold a doctorate; it's next to impossible to work with faculty across the curriculum with a lower degree. The writing center director might hold a doctorate or a master's degree. The decision, once again, is usually determined locally and is, more often than not, a matter of economics rather than academics. People with master's degrees cost less than those with doctorates.

BUDGET

One of the first things Jeanne Simpson, Former Assistant Vice President for Academic Affairs at Eastern Illinois University and one of the most respected voices on WCenter—the writing center listserv—says when talking about administrative issues is, "It's always the money." When running writing programs, however, the issue of money goes beyond how much? (It's never enough.) Where the money comes from and who controls it are of equal concern. The best situation is, of course, when the budget is hard money (institutionally funded and expected to be continuing) and the WPA has control of the budget. However, this is not always the case—even in independent units. There are often strings attached to dollars, and quite often dollars are soft (generated by grants or fees and therefore not likely to be around in the future or not in the same amounts). Here's another issue where reporting lines become important to understand. Deans, provosts, and vice provosts who fund independent programs may also have some say in how the money is to be spent. Are dollars for TAs and/or adjuncts included in the base budget, or does the WPA have to go ask, negotiate, grovel for more funds just to get needed classes taught? Is there funding for adequate support for classroom activities like copying? Do all faculty members—including TAs and adjuncts—have adequate office space, telephones, and computer access? Is there realistic and meaningful budget planning? For example, if a full-time faculty is hired on a new line, is there more budget support for the unit, or is the unit simply supposed to absorb the costs? When extra adjuncts are hired at the last minute, do they have office space? Is it adequate?

The other issue of knowing where the money comes from has to do with whom you're competing with. The unfortunate reality is that university budgets are made up of a finite number of dollars. Money that goes to your program doesn't go to another program. That other program's director will then probably feel shortchanged. Being independent means that WPAs will have the advantage of making their own case for increased funding at budget time. (That's an axiom. We always ask for more and always spend every penny.) The disadvantage independent programs face is that they don't usually have institutional history and culture on their side. Interestingly enough, both of those can be powerful factors in making budgetary determinations. What is usually most effective for WPAs of independent programs is to base their arguments on institutional mission—usually putting a strong emphasis on teaching. One of the real advantages WPAs have at budget time is that their work really is student-centered and their primary emphasis is on teaching. These are issues, when articulated clearly and backed up with both statistical and anecdotal evidence, which actually may make a difference at funding time. Central administrators, including those who make funding decisions are driven, to a point, by student issues.

Though central administrators do seem sensitive to student issues, academic culture works against areas seen as "service areas." Almost all writing programs—especially independent programs—are seen as service units. There is a kind of irony in this. As I have stated multiple times and in multiple places, the professoriate is a service profession in denial. In order to maintain the act of denial, service functions such as first-year composition, writing centers, and WAC programs need to be devalued. There is probably no way the director of any writing program can single-handedly change campus culture; however, it is possible to be aware of political factors both internal and external to help build a case at budget time. For the past several years (and it looks as if it will be in the foreseeable future) the buzzwords are *accountability* and *retention*. Knowing this, WPAs whose programs have a strong assessment plan and who, by using that assessment strategy, can demonstrate, through multiple measures that their programs are helping with student retention in the institution might just be rewarded at budget time.

CURRICULUM

In some ways the most important thing we, as faculty, do is to develop and deliver curriculum. In most areas it's crucial that the faculty teaching the courses are completely involved in curricular decisions. This is not always the case with writing programs—especially not with independent programs. All campuses have curricular processes where faculty can develop courses. Before going through college- and universitywide approval processes, curriculum is usually scrutinized most closely at the department level. Obviously, this creates all kinds of potential problems if the program does not reside in a department. Though curricular issues can prove difficult for both independent WAC programs and writing centers, independent first-year composition programs may have the most potential problems as they, by definition, offer courses. The first real issue is, Who owns the course? If the courses still have an ENG prefix, all curricular decisions go through the English department. If the courses, themselves, are freestanding, the question is, Who determines the curriculum? Where programs have few permanent full-time faculty, the curriculum, for good or ill, can be the work of one person—the director. Clearly, that might appear appealing to some who have found needed curricular changes blocked or detoured by literary colleagues. Still, it's a model that is ultimately very limiting. No program can survive around one person's vision.

This whole issue of curriculum and academic credit becomes even cloudier when looking at units that don't necessarily offer classes but might. Writing centers offer a good example of this. It's possible for a writing center to train and use peer tutors without offering academic credit. However, it's common for writing centers to expect their tutors to take a course in peer tutoring either before they begin or during their first semester of tutor work.

When the writing center is outside of a department, where does the credit come from? Again, looking at the University of Toledo, the director of the independent writing center offers a class in writing theory, originally only for tutors but now open to everyone, through the English department.

FINALLY, WHAT DOES IT ALL MEAN?

The thought of running an independent program might seem frightening or liberating to a WPA. In many ways, both emotions are valid. While there is no doubt that not having to answer to colleagues who really don't understand what you do is a liberating feeling, what should be clear in what I've presented is that unless your program is a completely autonomous, institutionalized unit (and that includes offering credit classes and tenure), you will, in some very important ways, still remain tied to an academic unit—usually English. That means that though on a day-to-day level you may report to a dean or a provost, you will retain some crucial ties with the old structures. Understanding where the true independence exists and where the old links remain (and this will vary), becomes one of your most important jobs.

PART II

ADMINISTERING, MANAGING, LEADING

Developing Healthy Management and Leadership Styles: Surviving the WPA's "Inside Game"

Irene Ward
Kansas State University

> *The interaction of work and worker poses the great societal paradox: we create social institutions and in turn are created by them.*
> —Daniel Katz, Robert L. Kahn, and J. Stacy Adams

Much of the preparation for becoming a writing program administrator (WPA) involves expertise in content areas. Many graduate programs offer a course at the Ph.D. level to help prepare prospective WPAs for entry-level jobs. One area that I feel is neglected in this training is management and leadership. Because of this, I feel that WPAs are often not prepared for some of the more challenging aspects of their jobs. Moreover, much of WPA work may set them up for job "burnout." Coping skills developed in graduate school or as a faculty member may not be the ones that will lead to an effective, satisfying, and healthy adjustment to WPA work, especially for the young and untenured. Developing coping and leadership skills early can help ensure that WPAs remain healthy and effective in the position of WPA. The first part of this essay defines "burnout." The second part establishes that many of the previous circumstances, or antecedents, to burnout are present in WPA work and the people who may do this kind of work. The third part proposes strategies that can mitigate some aspects of burnout—for instance, by learning to involve others and delegate, by taking control and avoiding feeling like a victim, and by maintaining a balance between work and the rest of your life and finding ways to recharge and renew your energy. The last part suggests some useful sources for a self-investigation of issues of leadership that can help

WPAs develop daily practices that will enable them to thrive on the job even in times of adversity.

Developing coping skills in advance of stressful times can help WPAs avoid the kind of stress that can lead to job burnout. Occupational health research is currently finding more evidence (because they are finding better ways to measure it) that job stress and burnout cause ill health. So, as much as burnout will lessen your ability to be effective in your WPA position, more important, it can cause other serious health risks and it can cause illness. I hope that this essay will help WPAs make informed and healthy choices about how they will approach the work of administering a writing program—work that I have many times found worthwhile, rewarding, challenging, and downright fun and at others, frustrating, draining, repetitive, and downright drudgery. I will outline some specific examples of how certain simple principles can enhance WPAs' effectiveness while allowing them to maintain their health and happiness. I have come to conceive of leadership as a matter of daily practice—a practice that has sustained me in times of conflict and nourished me in times of calm.

WHAT IS BURNOUT?

Much of what psychologists know about burnout comes from studying people in helping professions: police officers, health care professionals, and teachers. Christina Maslach, a prolific researcher in this area, describes the "prevailing norms" in these professions:

> Within such occupations, the prevailing norms are to be selfless and put others' needs first; to work long hours and do whatever it takes to help a client, patient or student; to go the extra mile and to give one's all. Moreover, the organizational environments for these jobs are shaped by various social, political, and economic factors (such as funding cutbacks or policy restrictions) that result in work settings that are high in demands and low in resources. (68)

Charles Schuster has delightfully provided a literary analogy for how these norms play themselves out in the working lives of many WPAs by comparing WPAs to Boxer the horse in Orwell's *Animal Farm* (see pages 331–342 in this volume).

In a major summary of burnout research, Cynthia L. Cordes and Thomas W. Dougherty define burnout and characterize it as having three components

1. *Emotional exhaustion,* a tendency to treat others in a "depersonalized" and "dehumanizing" manner, and a sense of "diminished personal accomplishment." The emotional exhaustion, or "compassion fatigue," is often accompanied by burnout sufferers' frustration that they are unable to "continue to give of themselves or be as responsible for clients as they have been in the past." Another symptom of emotional exhaustion is

dread of going to work. Work that previously energized them —that they did with passion and joy—now depletes their energies for work *and* life.

2. *Depersonalization of clients,* which can be demonstrated when, for example, a health care worker refers to patients by their ailments instead of using their names: "the broken leg at the end of the hall" or "the gallstones in 205." In WPA offices sometimes students become "the losers out there." It becomes easy to dismiss students' concerns and problems and to be inadvertently callous to the student whose family member really did die. Students for whom the system works rarely drop by your office to tell how happy they are with their writing classes. Emotionally exhausted workers become "detached" and often attempt to "compartmentalize" their professional life or increasingly to "intellectualize" it. Others retreat into highly rule-bound behaviors, insisting that things be done by the book, instead of trying to find the best solution for a particular client's needs. Others retreat into longer breaks and social conversations with coworkers; and absenteeism will often increase. Most researchers agree that this detachment and depersonalization of clients could be a way of coping and deflecting the emotional pain of the situation.

3. *Feelings of diminished personal accomplishment,* which occur as burnout sufferers begin to lose self-esteem, often accompanied by feelings of hopelessness or powerlessness. As workers see the same problems year after year and observe clients making little progress in spite of all the resources provided to them, it becomes increasingly difficult for them to see the big picture and how their actions make any difference (623–24).

Burnout is now classed as a particular kind of workplace stress associated with jobs that include "high levels of interpersonal contact," and its symptoms are not found in other kinds of stress. What is important to note is that burnout is "a prolonged response to chronic *interpersonal* stressors on the job" (Maslach 68: emphasis added). Although burnout shares some symptoms with depression, it is not synonymous with it. According to Maslach, "burnout is a problem that is specific to the work context, in contrast to depression that tends to pervade every domain of a person's life" (79). Maslach argues for a more refined theory of burnout and groups its antecedents into two major groups: degree of "engagement" and "job-person mismatches" (discussed at length below). In the process, she refines the definition of burnout: "Burnout is one end of a continuum in the relationship people establish with their jobs" (73); she places "engagement" at the other end (see figure below).

Burnout ◄─────────────────────────────────────► Engagement
exhaustion, cynicism, ineffectiveness   energy, involvement, efficacy

Engagement is the mirror image of burnout: "engagement consists of a state of high *energy* (rather than exhaustion), strong *involvement* (rather than cyniçism), and a sense of *efficacy* (rather than a reduced sense of accomplishment)" (73). Not only does Maslach's refinement help illuminate the complexity of "burnout," it also may point to strategies for reducing the risk of burnout and even preventing it (81)—strategies I will discuss in the third section of this essay.

ANTECEDENTS OF BURNOUT
AND THE WPA'S DUTIES

Cordes and Dougherty also summarize the research on the antecedents of burnout. A number of factors in the workplace, as well as certain personal characteristics can contribute to burnout. They categorize these characteristics in three areas: role characteristics, including "role overload, ambiguity, and conflict"; "organizational characteristics," including "job context and contingency of rewards and punishments"; and personal characteristics, including job expectations, perception of career progress, and certain demographic characteristics. According to these researchers, the most significant antecedent is "the nature of the employee-client relationship," a factor that I will discuss at length below (632). Other factors such as perception of "uncertainty" and perceived "importance of outcomes" also play a role (625). Maslach, in more recent research, further documents the role of job mismatch in contributing to job burnout and provides "six areas in which the mismatch can take place" (74). A number of these characteristics and mismatches are often present in a writing program administrator's working environment and in the kinds of people who may find themselves doing or seeking this kind of work. Kahn and Maslach disagree about the role of personal characteristics in the development of burnout, with Maslach claiming that "situational variables are more strongly predictive of burnout than are personal ones" (76), and Kahn claims that personal characteristics can increase the risk for burnout. In the next section, I will describe what I see as some burnout antecedents (workplace and personal characteristics) that may, in particular, set up WPAs for burnout. Please keep in mind while reading the next section that I'm not trying to paint a negative picture of WPA work and cause anyone to turn down a potentially good job or to run to the department head's office and resign. I hope to be realistic about what WPAs might be facing and help them start out with or move toward a sound healthy approach to their work that will sustain them over the long term. If WPAs find that their jobs have any of these characteristics, I hope that this information can help them negotiate the kinds of working conditions that promote their health and the health of their programs.

The Employee-Client Relationship

The most significant antecedent, or prior condition, to worker burnout, according to Cordes and Dougherty, is the nature of the employee-client relationship. However, before talking about the WPA's client relationships it is necessary to define "clients." As examples, for health care workers, clients are the patients they care for; for police officers, clients are the "perpetrators" and the perpetrators' victims; for teachers, clients are the students. Who are the clients for WPAs? The answer to this will differ depending on the nature of the writing program administrator's position. I am going to follow Cordes and Dougherty, who broaden the definition of "client" to include "any individual, internal or external, with whom one interacts on a professional basis" (628). For WPAs, clients could then include students in the classes in a particular writing program, the faculty members and instructors who teach in the program, and the graduate teaching assistants whom they are often charged with training. If the WPA runs the writing center, add the tutors and their students. WAC {writing across the curriculum} WPAs clients include the faculty members who participate in writing across the curriculum. Add to all of these one's colleagues, inside and outside the home department, and a number of other lateral and higher administrators, including but not limited to the registrar, head of student services, enrollment managers, and academic assistance personnel, any number of deans and associate deans, and, sometimes, the parents of the undergraduate students enrolled in writing courses. I could go on, but even this incomplete list clearly shows that WPA duties involve a great deal of "people work." The research on burnout clearly indicates that "[c]lient interactions that are more direct, frequent, or of longer duration, for example, or client problems that are chronic (versus acute) are associated with higher levels of burnout" (Cordes and Dougherty 628).

Many WPAs' job descriptions include dealing with student complaints and problems; in short, required duties entail a great deal of interaction with students. Often, WPA-student interaction can be rather routine; the student needs some adjustment to a class schedule or evaluation of a transcript. Many of these interactions can be positive. However, the WPA also sees many students with problems that, in reality, might be equally routine, but are accompanied by anxiety, anger, and sometimes even aggression by the student. Some students look for a place to vent frustrations with what they perceive are difficult circumstances. If the stance taken by the client is "aggressive, passive-dependent, or defensive" and the stance of the WPA is that "he or she alone is responsible for ensuring the future well-being of the [student]," then the WPA can perceive this part of the job as "an awesome and exhausting burden." The risk of burnout increases as the number, intensity, and duration of these types of interactions increase (Cordes and Dougherty 629).

Since many departments offer many more sections of writing than all the other literature courses combined, even a small percentage of these students having real or perceived difficulties can be a significant drain of time and emotional energy on the WPA. If the WPA is also charged with faculty development and training, then add sometimes anxious, inexperienced teachers who, rightfully, need support in dealing with their instructional duties and the students in their classrooms. To draw an example from my own experience as a WPA, I found that students presented a limited range of problems, but that these problems affected a significant number students who would then show up at my door. Although, most of the time these issues were relatively easy to resolve (mostly enrollment red tape), they often caused the students a high degree of anxiety, which played itself out in stressful ways in my interactions with them. Although I could advocate for change, I did not have the power to enforce change in the enrollment procedures that brought the students to my door in large numbers. Several times a semester, WPA-student interactions can intensify the stress, causing a more intense emotional situation: a threat of violence (real or perceived) in a classroom, instances of verbal abuse between students and instructors, students who have lost emotional control, and, sometimes, irate parents. The sheer repetition of these stressful interactions over years can be draining; moreover, the stress is compounded when others will not or cannot support ways to alleviate problems and the resultant anxiety. So either directly, by seeing students in one's own office, or indirectly, by advising new teachers on how do deal with student issues in their classroom, it is easy to see how WPA-student and WPA-faculty interactions could make WPAs vulnerable to burnout.

Yet another interesting finding in the research on burnout is that managers who perform "boundary spanning functions"—that is, whose jobs entail providing service functions among departments—were much more likely to suffer from burnout than, say, production managers who deal more consistently with people in their sector (Cordes and Dougherty 632). In writing programs where writing courses "serve" the majors of other departments, WPAs act as boundary spanners. As noted above, a WPA's client list is often extensive and includes a number of interactions with people in other areas. Sometimes WPAs can even perform boundary-spanning functions with their own colleagues in literature. Typically, WPAs are far more visible in their institutions than most of the English department faculty; as an untenured faculty member, I regularly talked with faculty members from other departments, advisers from various colleges, associate deans, and deans from around the university. WPAs often have to coordinate with tutoring programs, basic writing programs, ESL programs for foreign students, student services, and the athletic department, just to name a few. This visibility can be daunting for an untenured WPA. Even a tenured WPA can find it difficult to deal with so many demands and expectations on the program's limited resources. Clearly, WPA work spans a number of boundaries, adding yet another aspect of this work that makes WPAs vulnerable to burnout.

Role Conflict, Ambiguity, and Overload

Other major stressors found to contribute to burnout are role conflict, role ambiguity, and role overload. Role conflict occurs when one's expectations about one's role are incompatible or incongruous with those who have assigned the role or have the power to assess one's success in the role. Conflict also can occur when one aspect of one's duties makes it difficult to perform another, or when one's values are in conflict with the expectations of the assigned role. Role ambiguity can arise when there is some uncertainty or unpredictability in one's work environment—for example, when one is uncertain about the "criteria for performance evaluations" in a tenure and promotion review. Role overload can occur when a person "lacks the information to accomplish required duties" (Cordes and Dougherty 630) or when a person has to "do too much in too little time and with too few resources" (Maslach 75).

It seems that a strong case can be made that WPA work, especially when performed by an untenured person, is fraught with both role conflict and role ambiguity. First, I'll explore ways that WPA work can involve role conflict. One possible source of conflict can be personal values and ethics (Maslach 76). For instance, a WPA may be uncomfortable in the role of leader and manager. Academics may hold negative stereotypes of leaders. Because academics are trained to be critical thinkers, we also mistrust leadership and the power it often garners and, with reason, carry around negative stereotypes of leadership. Looking around in our home institutions, we don't often find models of leadership that attract us. I've heard faculty members say things like "If she (or he) *wants* to be chair then we don't want her (or him)." Our mistrust seems to be justified by those institutions and individuals who don't "walk the talk"—whose stated mission and actions are incompatible. Moreover, our scholarly discourse often involves the critique of power structures that disadvantage and privilege but that rarely serve the needs of all that seek access. We can recognize leadership and power gone astray. Even if we accept the need for leadership, we are not trained how to use power responsibly or to be positive leaders. Because we come up through a hierarchical system of education in which it often seems that we have little or no power we sometimes fear power and have no strategies for dealing with it. Ambivalence toward leadership and its related power can diffuse both one's energy and effectiveness. (See White "Use It or Lose It," reprinted in this part.) Without some sort of resolution to their conflicts about power and leadership, WPAs set themselves up for a great deal of discomfort in doing the job and possibly cut off the possibility of being effective.

There may be conflicts between one's stated responsibilities and one's real work. For instance, a WPA may have stated job responsibilities of 50 percent teaching, 30 percent service, and 20 percent research. However, research time may conflict with the latest crisis in the program or the latest round of meetings on enrollment management, and so on and so on. You may come to the office to prepare for your classes or a conference paper, only to find a line of people at your door. Also, there is an unpredictable nature to these "emergencies." One good example of this occurred at the end of a summer term, when classes had ceased but grades had not been turned in. It appeared that I would have two quiet days in my office to write. About an hour after I arrived, an irate parent, trailing his son, entered my office intent on intimidating me into changing his son's failing grade before the term grades were turned in. The department head was on vacation, as was the dean of the college and the dean of student life—I was it. This very intense interpersonal encounter lasted about 45 minutes with him shouting in my office and then at the departmental office staff and then at me again—until we found an assistant dean to talk to him (by then he had worn himself out). I had remained outwardly calm and had followed university policy; nonetheless, I was emotionally drained and unable to concentrate for the rest of the day. While I was a WPA, few of my planned retreats into writing were interruption-free. These types of outbreaks of WPA work into the other required aspects of the job, both teaching and research, create conflicts that are difficult to resolve. In this case I was not really in a position to tell the parent, "Go away. I had planned to write today."

Lack of control over ones' resources and work can cause role conflict. Maslach describes this lack of control as occurring when people "have little control over the work they do, either because of rigid policies and tight monitoring or because of chaotic job conditions. Such lack of control prevents people from being able to solve problems, make choices, and have some input into the achievement of the outcomes for which they will be held accountable" (75). The WPA literature is full of accounts of WPAs trying to deal with lack of power and control over the programs they are charged with administering. Both White (reprinted here) and Olson are good examples to review in this area. For instance, if the director of graduate studies (DGS) awards teaching assistantships on the basis of academic merit alone, often without even consulting the WPA, then the WPA has little control over who teaches in the program. It may be difficult to remove TAs who are poor or incompetent in the classroom due to this same DGS who is sometimes the person vested with the authority to take away assistantships. At the very least, even when the WPA has the authority to fire, if not hire, the DGS may be resistant to cut off a good student's financial aid. Few department heads are willing to give WPAs any budget oversight, preferring to hold that authority themselves. So while the WPA is held responsible for the quality of the program, he or she often has difficulty controlling the very factors that will ensure its success: continued funding and competent, motivated, well-trained teachers.

Role ambiguity functions in the process of evaluating and valuing WPA work for tenure and promotion, both to assistant and to full. Even though one's employment agreement may call for WPA work to be counted in tenure and promotion reviews and decisions, we still have few cases to rely on at institutions with heavy research and publication demands. This uncertainty can place an added burden on WPAs to meet, even exceed, the more traditional expectations for tenure and promotion in their departments and colleges.

The example of the unexpected visit by the irate parent serves to demonstrate one way that role overload can be part of a WPA's work. Few WPAs have had any training in dealing with conflict resolution or in dealing with "difficult" students or in effective supervising. What in a WPA's academic training prepares him or her to deal with anxious and irate people? What in WPA training equips the administrator to make the move from being a GTA to training and supervising GTAs? In this area of WPA work, the administrator can experience role overload if he or she doesn't have the skills at hand to deal effectively with many of the intense personal interactions that occur regularly in our work (Cordes and Dougherty 631). Incompetence in dealing fairly and firmly with student complaints can sometimes even cause student complaints to increase if word gets around that the WPA is inconsistent (and hence, in students' eyes, "unfair") or if the WPA is perceived to be a "soft touch"; in the latter case, even more students may come and test the system to see what the real limits are.

Another aspect of "role overload" is sometimes just that: an overload of duties to perform (Kahn 425; Maslach 75). We have all seen the long "wish" list of skills and responsibilities in job advertisements for WPAs, demonstrating poor understanding by some English departments of what WPA work entails (Hourigan and Sun, forthcoming). Moreover, a WPA's job duties can innocently swell to meet new challenges and demands within his or her institution, because writing programs change, as do the institutions that house them. The potential for a WPA's job description to become "overloaded" is something that WPAs need to guard against continually.

Still other factors contribute to WPA burnout. However, not all WPAs burn out, just as not all nurses, teachers, or police officers burn out. Some people cope day after day, year after year with such stressors and remain productive and happy. Cordes and Dougherty and Robert L. Kahn have identified personal characteristics that, along with work environment, contribute to the possibility of burnout. For instance, people in any of these demographic groups were found to be at higher risk: young, single, and childless. Those who seemed to experience less burnout were likely to be older, experienced employees, to be married, and to have children (Cordes and Dougherty 633). A second significant personal characteristic that contributes to burnout is "high" and "unmet" expectations about the organization or the job (Cordes and Dougherty 636). Both expectations about what the person will be able to achieve and about the nature of the "professional system in general" can make a significant contribution to burnout. If a person finds that being a WPA is nothing like what he expected, or if he had hopes of significant reform that never happened, then chances increase that he may suffer symptoms of burnout. Individuals who are likely to be successful in this competitive job market are inclined to have high expectations both for themselves and for the institutions and departments that they are joining. If the new WPA's expectations are not realistic, he may be setting himself up for stress and eventual burnout. Third, individuals who have had career success experience less burnout (Cordes and Dougherty 637). If a WPA's work environment does not contribute to the real or perceived progress toward tenure and promotion or comes to interfere with other career goals, this might contribute to that third component of burnout: perceived lack of personal achievement.

In another group of studies specifically looking at conflict, ambiguity, and overload in "job stress" (not specifically defined as burnout), three other personal characteristics seemed to help predict if a person will suffer from job stress: being "anxiety prone," introverted, or flexible. Of course, we have no data to say if WPAs are more or less "anxiety prone," but if researchers are right (keep in mind, Maslach says they are not) and these personal characteristics increase one's risk for burnout, then care needs to be taken in matching personal characteristics to the demands of the job (Kahn 423).

The last personal characteristic turns out to be a significant buffer against the effects of the stressors that cause burnout, if one has lots of it. All the research suggests that having social support lessens or "buffers" the risk of burnout (Cordes and Dougherty 633; French 450, Maslach 75). This is probably why people who are married and have children seem to be less likely to suffer negatively from job stress.

Let's look at how lack of social support could be a major stressor for WPAs. I've pulled together some typical personal characteristics to form a hypothetical profile of a new Ph.D. applying for an entry-level WPA position. This new WPA is young, single, inexperienced (first job), new to town, and the only writing specialist in the department. She won't have an extensive social support system. Moreover, if this new WPA, who is close in age and social affinity to the GTAs, draws too heavily for such support from this group, the more senior faculty may have trouble seeing her as a true colleague. The profession has long argued that doing WPA work puts the assistant professor at risk for tenure and promotion; now, in addition, we can see that it also may place unhealthy job stress on her as well. It would be essential for any WPA to develop or have in place a network of social support, to have healthy professional and personal relationships.

In the face of all these stressors, what is one to do? Interestingly enough there is currently little in the occupational health research that can help us. Maslach suggests that while looking for avenues to prevent or lessen the effects of the stressors that lead to job burnout, we should also be looking for ways to increase the avenues for positive and healthy "engagement," the mirror image of the negative, unhealthy job burnout. The rest of this essay discusses how WPAs might go about protecting themselves while advocating for the reforms that will alleviate the potentially dangerous effects of job burnout.

Some of the changes to WPA work environment will cost departmental resources, and so will take time and diligence to get into place. In the meantime, here are some things that you can do to promote your success and health.

- *Obtain a reasonable job description and have an annual review with your chair.* In Part V Jeanne Gunner writes about the importance of negotiating a reasonable job description before one even takes a position. However, writing programs are affected by changes in other programs or in response to new conditions. At such times, the WPA can find that such changes cause him to make shifts in the program that may affect his duties. For instance, during my tenure as WPA, the university added a new support program for students "at risk" that had an impact on the writing program in a number of ways; but, most important, this change added a new "client" to my list and different enrollment procedures for these students. A large change or a number of smaller changes outside a writing program can innocently swell a WPA's duties and tasks. Keep records of each of these changes and discuss the impact they have on your job with your head or chair at your annual review. Each new task either takes time away from other assigned duties in service, teaching, and research or decreases the time left for a life away from work. Moreover, adjusting to any change takes time and emotional energy. Any changes a WPA may initiate should be carefully thought out, considering what additional personal resources, time, and energy it will require on their part. These steps would be positive in avoiding the role-overload stressor.

- *Involve others and build teams.* Being an effective administrator means being able to draw on staff, committees, and teachers to get the work done effectively. Increasing the involvement of those who work in the program develops a sense of ownership, fosters initiative, and improves teamwork. Yes, getting staff and instructors involved requires initial time and effort; however, it pays off in the future with reduced time on your part to do what they can do. Learn to delegate and develop a style of leadership that empowers others to act effectively. One of the best examples of how this might work is described in Lynn Meeks and Christine Hult's "A Co-Mentoring Model of Administration," which is part of an entire issue of *WPA: Writing Program Administration* on collaborative models of writing program administration ([21, 2/3] Spring 1998).

- *Seek out positive role models.* WPAs are fortunate to have supportive colleagues. Many current and former WPAs who did not burn out and have even gone on to higher administration are a generous lot, eager to share successes and mistakes. These folks regularly attend the Conference on College Composition and Communication Convention and the WPA Summer Workshop and Conference. Join these associations, attend the meetings, and subscribe to *WPA Journal* and *WPA-L*. In your institution, there are successful administrators who manage all aspects of their jobs without suffering burnout. Seek them out and ask for their advice.

- *Negotiate for the training you need: supervisory skills, leadership, and management.* Training in writing pedagogy, rhetoric, and composition theory do not necessarily equip a person to be an effective supervisor, manager, and leader. If you do not have experience in these areas, identify ways to get this training and the resources to support them. There may be academic courses you can audit or continuing education courses you can take to increase your knowledge and skill base. Ask your dean and head about support for attending leadership and administrative workshops for higher education. Several reputable companies offer one- or two-day seminars in many aspects of leadership and management. See the end of this essay for a list of such companies.

- *Develop realistic expectations about what can be accomplished.* Institutional change rarely takes place quickly. What is more likely to happen is that it will take small incremental steps and even setbacks before changes can be implemented. For a good example of what this incremental change looks like, see Kristine Hansen's account of improving the working conditions and pay for the part-time instructors in her program. Charles Schuster gives useful advice about using the art of "crisis creation" to help bring about program reform while also cautioning not to create more than one a year, because it will cost you "a lot of a person's time and erode a great deal of equanimity" (Foreword xiv). I would add that each of these crises will cost you in emotional energy as well. Carefully choose which battles you wish to fight and plan that when you do you will lose time and energy in other areas. This is where having realistic expectations about what can be accomplished will help guide you to find battles that you are likely to win.

- *Discover ways to cut down on interruptions that interfere with your other duties, especially the intensely emotional ones.* Some faculty members are able to work feasibly at home, but few English departments will be able to duplicate your telephone, copier, and computer resources in your home; however, you might negotiate for a portable computer so that you can be more flexible in where you can get substantive work done. Check to see if your library has carrels that could become a quiet workspace away from your administrative office. Ask your head and dean for help in finding alternative office space or even desk space. If you have a writing committee, see if each member could take a turn being "on call" during busy times at the beginning and end of semesters to help students. Most universities require that student complaints and grievances be initiated in writing. Devise a form that students can fill out on the spot or take away with them. Insisting that students adhere to this policy allows you to address these issues at a time you choose each week rather than randomly all week long. Moreover, it cuts down on the number of anxious and emotionally charged interpersonal encounters you engage in, saving emotional energy and reducing stress. Sometimes you can delegate this part of the job, but keep in mind that anyone who handles these often emotionally charged interpersonal interactions will be at risk for eventual burnout too.

- *Balance your life and outside interests with your work.* One thing that occupational health specialists agree on is that those with healthy, functional social support systems outside the workplace seem to be less likely to suffer from burnout. In order to maintain these social support systems, be it your family or some other social group, you need to give them time and energy. More important, these relationships can nourish, restore, and actually increase your energy for your job.

Balancing home and social life with work will also help avoid burnout. The law of diminishing returns applies to WPAs. Coming in early and leaving late is acceptable for the crunch times; however, few can remain productive under these conditions for months on end. Try to figure out what is the most productive number of hours you can work per week. How much can you work and still feel focused, calm, and alert? Some people can work 50 hours a week comfortably, others only 40. When you establish your comfort level, try to stick to it unless you have clear reasons not to. Try not to drift into staying late or coming in on weekends unless you have a deadline. You really are more productive in your 40 hours when you rest and renew yourself.

- *Stop thinking you are a victim; take control.* Even when all around you may be chaotic, try to remain focused on your responsibilities and doing the best you can with the resources you have. There will always be a shortage, of money, time, and personnel. You could always do a better job if you had more of each, but until then work realistically with what is available. This doesn't mean that you should not ask for what you need; sometimes you will get it, and at other times you won't. Learn to say no, calmly and without anger, when you are asked to do what can't be done with the resources available; but whenever possible, try to offer alternative solutions that may solve the problem without adding new resources or increasing the stresses on the you and the program. Learn the art of the "trade off." When given major new responsibilities that can't be realistically integrated with current ones, say to your boss, "If we do what you ask, we won't be able to continue to do….Which do you think is most important for us to do, since we can't do both?" In this manner, you are acting responsibly both to your institution and to yourself. Always keep in mind that the only aspect of your job that you really have control over is your own reactions and behavior. Most important, let go of what is not open to change at this time.

- *Create a list of deal breakers.* Take some time to think about those conditions that would make your job so difficult or disagreeable that you wouldn't want to continue. For instance, one of my deal breakers was increasing class sizes. My predecessor and a number of GTAs had fought a difficult battle with the dean over this issue the year before I arrived, resulting in additional office space for GTAs and assurances that the writing program would not be asked to raise enrollments above 22 students per section. Once I was almost tested on this issue. An associate dean had raised the caps to 23 during summer orientation in response to demand for more seats; evidently parents were pounding on desks in the dean's office. The next morning I came in and simply lowered the caps again to 22, and nothing more was said. This could have been a risky thing to do (I was untenured), but because I knew that it was a deal breaker, I was able to act decisively. I also avoided a long period of possible stressful indecision by having an idea where the boundaries were in advance. However, unless you mean it, it is not a good strategy to threaten to resign. Your credibility may be irretrievably damaged.

This list gives you some tips on managing your career as a WPA and remaining happy and productive. What follows, I think, is the key to the inverse of burnout: energy, involvement, and efficacy, helping WPAs move toward the engagement end of Maslach's continuum of burnout and engagement.

HOW PRACTICING LEADERSHIP MAY HELP AVOID BURNOUT

A traditional and simple definition of leadership is "the process of inducing others to take actions toward a common goal" (Locke 2). Notice that leadership is a process, not a product. It is something that is ongoing over time. Leadership is sometimes distinguished from management, while acknowledging that such a distinction is difficult to make:

> The key function of a *leader* is to establish the basic vision (purpose, mission, overarching goal, or agenda) of the organization. The leader specifies the end as well as the overarching strategy for reaching it (Kotter 1990). The key function of a *manager* is to implement the vision. The manager and subordinates act in ways that constitute the means to achieving the stated end. (Locke 4)

Leading and managing activities bleed into each other in most instances, and they certainly do for most WPAs. We are leaders in our programs if we are responsible for curriculum and faculty development. We are managers also because we are charged with implementing a certain amount of university and departmental policy, like student grievance and honesty policies. For instance, in the program I administered, my vision of the *how* and the *what* about writing instruction guided the program, although I realize that the degree to which this is true for others varies greatly. Nevertheless, as WPAs, we clearly lead and manage.

Lynn Bloom helps us see that WPAs both lead and manage, but she names these two aspects of WPA work differently. She calls the managerial aspects of the job the "literal" approach, metaphorically described as "straight lines," and the leadership aspect of the job as the "creative" approach, described as "butterflies." She is worth quoting at length here:

> For administration of writing programs, as of any other complicated system, represents a balance between the straight lines and the butterflies—bureaucracy and creativity, the preordained, the pragmatic, and the precedent-setting. Some aspects of administration are boring—endless forms to fill out, memos to circulate, meetings to call, details to follow up on and follow up on. Other aspects are downright unpleasant, dealing with malcontents, malevolence, and—because WPAs are among the chronically fiscally challenged—budgets and the priorities and hard choices these impose. Together these constitute program administration's dark straight slashes, necessary but not fun. *The administrator needs always to envision the butterflies beneath and beyond these confining boundaries if writing program administration is to make a significant difference to the people and program it affects.* (73; emphasis added)

Bloom identifies teacher training, influencing undergraduate and graduate education, and establishing an institution's reputation in composition and rhetoric as areas where WPA work is creative and, in Bloom's terms, provides avenues for healthy leadership that can energize and nurture your career as a WPA.

Notice that Bloom locates the butterflies "beneath and beyond." She does this because the danger is that WPAs become bogged down in the day-to-day managerial aspects of the work and lose sight of the possibilities for constructive leadership that the position offers. In short, I'm claming that increasing the leadership aspects of the job and balancing them with the managerial aspects can lessen the risk of burnout that some aspects of WPA work entails. Several of these leadership roles are clearly outlined in Bloom's essay, and each program and institution will offer various other opportunities for the WPA to enhance his or her leadership role.

But how does a WPA acquire and use leadership and power in positive and productive ways? Recently management and leadership scholars have posited theories of leadership that are more comprehensive, less mechanistic, and healthier (and they have more and more data to suggest that these alternatives are more effective). These theories do not focus on the "great man" but shift the emphasis from a single influential person to productive interpersonal relationships that empower all to succeed. The new leaders are not merely charismatic; they don't enforce a personal vision to which others must adhere or leave. They are vehicles of empowerment and agency in those whom "*they serve.*" They are about "creating success for others" (Belasco 189). These leaders are facilitators and coalition builders. They are keepers of the vision, but the vision is not theirs alone; the vision is subject to revision, can be challenged, reimagined, and adjusted as circumstances change.

As I noted above, sometimes taking an administrative and leadership role can cause some conflicts because of our suspicions of leaders and the assumed power that comes with the territory of administration. Moreover, leadership is often difficult territory for women to negotiate. Hildy Miller provides a productive discussion of WPA leadership and administration from a feminist point of view (reprinted in this part), and her essay echoes many of the leadership principles that I will use in this essay. Also, she covers many of the traps and pitfalls women administrators need to be aware of, especially if you opt to use a leadership style that as of yet is sometimes poorly understood.

People are suspicious of power, as well they should be, but coming to terms with power is essential to using it well. As WPA you have some power—probably more than you think. In an important study of how people have derived power in social situations, French and Raven found that power comes from several distinct sources. The first three kinds of power—legitimate, reward, and coercive power—are rather limited for the WPA. The source of legitimate power comes from recognition that someone has the "*right* to lead others." Elected officials have this kind of power, as do corporate executive officers appointed by boards of directors. WPAs have some legitimate power, but this often varies greatly from institution to institution. With little control over traditional sources of reward, like raises and promotions, WPAs often have little reward power (Saal and Knight 339–43; see also Olson and Moxley). Coercive power for most WPAs is limited; for example, some WPAs may have the power to remove an incompetent TA or instructor from the classroom, but does not have coercive power over a faculty member who is underperforming. Coercive power arises from fear; the WPA can take away the job that is supporting a TA's graduate study, and this kind of fear is only marginally useful in leadership that seeks to empower others toward excellence (Saal and Knight 340). It turns out that the most effective sources of power—those that have the most positive effects on organizations—are the sources of power to which WPAs have the most access: expert power and referent power.

Expert power comes from the perception that someone has the requisite knowledge to get the job done. If you have academic credentials in the area of composition and rhetoric, this could be a source of power. What is important is that others perceive that you are knowledgeable (Saal and Knight). In most departments expert power is demonstrated by publications and presentations in scholarly venues, which is why it is important for department heads to be perceived as at least competent scholars. In the same way, it will most likely be important that WPAs continue to publish and remain current in the scholarly activity in composition and rhetoric. Outside the department, expert power is visible by how the program runs, by other administrators' perception of the program, and by how credibly a WPA presents him or herself when representing the program. Being able to explain the soundness of the practices and policies of the program to faculty members, to other administrators, and often to the dean earns a WPA a reputation as knowledgeable.

The last kind of power, what French and Raven call referent power, is derived from what kind of person you are—in rhetorical terms, your *ethos*. Everyone assumes you will treat them in the manner they have observed you treat others. If students in one of your classes observe you being dismissive of another student's ideas, they will hesitate to risk sharing their thoughts with you. The same is true when TAs find you gossiping about others in the mailroom; they assume that you will also talk about them behind their backs, and you've lost an opportunity to gain their trust. You have access to an enormous amount of referent power, but you have to be mindful of it and earn it over time.

Many of the leadership and management theories of the "new economy" and "the information age" will resonate with WPAs. This kind of leadership starts from within each person and is not imposed from above or from without. Its buzzwords are "respect, understanding, acceptance, and appreciation" (Ghandhi 218). These leadership theorists write about concepts like "interconnectedness" "interdependence" and "fellowship" (Belesco 189, 197). They speak of leadership as teaching and learning. Since WPAs are often learners and teachers first, they should find that many of the values and skills of classroom leadership apply to being an administrative leader as well.

Earning a reputation as a leader, learning confidence in your own leadership, gaining a voice that others are willing to listen to, having allies in place to help—these are the practices of leadership that will help when things get tough. Becoming a leader in your position also has several other positive side effects, such as reminding you that your job is more than the last student complaint you handled, more than the last form you filled out, more than the last time you repeated the same policy for the millionth time. The practice of leadership, I hope, will provide the needed balance between creativity and getting the job done and the needed perspective when you're feeling beleaguered.

There are many rewarding things about being a WPA. But if these jobs include elements that can cause job burnout, we need to be aware and take care or avoid this possibly debilitating effect of our work. We need to be able to understand how this happens, if it is present in our work, and then begin to work for healthier working conditions. We have to have ways to discuss these issues with department heads and deans that don't look like mere whining about having too much work to do. It is not in anyone's best interest to burn out WPAs. The institution and the profession need to nurture and maintain our current and future leaders.

Most important, WPAs have a right to jobs that are humane and that foster good heath and emotional well-being. We have a right to healthy relationships in our families and communities that balance our working lives. However, we have to teach the university how to treat us. I hope that this essay will also inspire WPAs to speak up for themselves when they need to. We need to prepare WPAs for facing challenges of the job: the professional, and political, and even the personal. WPAs can withstand most of these challenges, learning that there are ways to win, and learning that sometimes you lose as well—and you often get a chance to fight the good fight on another day in another way. We have to know when what's going on is really out of our control—and so, when to let go. This is part of any responsible job. With a clearer understanding of what to expect and what the danger signs might be, many can find WPA work energizing, fulfilling, and effective.

WORKS CITED

Belesco, Jim. "Creating Success for Others." Hasselbein, Goldsmith, and Summerville 189–97.

Bloom, Lynn. "Making a Difference: Writing Program Administration as a Creative Process." Janangelo and Hansen. 73–81.

Cordes, Cynthia L., and Thomas W. Dougherty. "A Review and an Integration of Research on Job Burnout." *Academy of Management Review* 18.4 (1993): 621–56.

French, John R. P. "Person-Role Fit." Katz, Kahn, and Adams 444–50.

Ghandhi, Arun. "The Four Cardinal Principles of Leadership." Hasselbein, Goldsmith, and Summerville 217–24.

Hansen, Kristine. "Face to Face with Part-Timers: Ethics and the Professionalization of Writing Facilities." Janangelo and Hansen 23–45

Hesselbein, Frances, Marshall Goldsmith, and Iain Summerville, eds. *Leading Beyond the Walls*. Drucker Foundation Wisdom to Action Series. San Francisco: Jossey, 1999.

C. H. Sun, Lulu and Maureen M. Hourigan. "The 'MLA Job Information List': The Perils of Not Paying Attention." *M/MLA: The Journal of the Midwest Modern Language Association* 33.2 (2000). 79–93.

Janangelo, Joseph, and Kristine Hansen, eds. *Resituating Writing: Constructing and Administering Writing Programs.* Cross Currents. Portsmouth: Boynton, 1995.

Kahn, Robert L. "Conflict, Ambiguity, and Overload: Three Elements in Job Stress. Katz, Kahn, and Adams 418–28

Katz, Daniel, Robert L. Kahn, and J. Stacy Adams. *The Study of Organizations.* San Francisco: Jossey, 1982.

Locke, Edwin A. *The Essence of Leadership: The Four Keys to Leading Successfully.* New York: Lexington, 1991.

Maslach, Christina. "A Multidimensional Theory of Burnout." *Theories of Organizational Stress.* Ed. Cary L. Cooper. New York: Oxford UP, 1998. 68–85.

Olson, Gary A., and Joseph M. Moxley. "Directing Freshman Composition: The Limits of Authority." *College Composition and Communication* 40 (1989): 51–60.

Saal, Frank E., and Patrick A. Knight. *Industrial Organizational Psychology: Science and Practice.* Pacific Grove: Brooks, 1988.

Schuster, Charles I. Foreword. Janangelo and Hansen ix–xiv.

———. "The Politics of Promotion." *The Politics of Writing Instruction: Postsecondary.* Ed. Richard Bullock and John Trimbur. Portsmouth: Boyton, 1991. 85–95.

White, Edward M. "Use It or Lose It: Power and the Writing Program Administrator." *WPA: Writing Program Administration* 15.1–2 (1991): 3–12.

Recommended Books on Leadership and Management

This is just a sampling of the books available in the category of higher education and leadership. There are new books published often. Also, the literature on leadership is voluminous. Check your library and search your favorite web bookseller for more titles.

Bogue, E. Grady. *Leadership by Design: Strengthening Integrity in Higher Education. Higher and Adult Education.* San Francisco: Jossey, 1994.

Benisom, Estela Mara, Anna Neumann, and Robert Birnbaum, eds. *Making Sense of Administrative Leadership: The L Word in Higher Education.* Ashe-Eric Higher Education Report. 1989.

———, and Anna Neumann. *Redesigning Collegiate Leadership: Teams and Teamwork in Higher Education.* Baltimore: Johns Hopkins UP, 1994.

Bowen, William G., and Harold T. Shapiro, eds. *Universities and Their Leadership.* Princeton: Princeton UP, 1998.

Dickenson, Robert C., and Stanley O. Ikenberry. *Prioritizing Academic Programs and Services: Reallocating Resources to Achieve Strategic Balance.* Higher and Adult Education. San Francisco: Jossey, 1999.

Fife, Jonathan D., and Michael D. Brown, eds. *Higher Leadership: An Analysis of the Gender Gap.* Ashe-Eric Higher Education Report. 1995.

Fisher, Roger, and Alan Sharp. *Getting It Done: How To Lead When You're Not In Charge.* New York: Harper, 1998.

Hartman, Mary S., ed. *Talking Leadership: Conversations with Powerful Women.* New Brunswick, NJ: Rutgers UP, 1999.

Hecht, Irene W. *The Department Chair as Academic Leader.* Phoenix: Oryx P, 1998.

Henry, David D., Lloyd C. Elam, James G. March, and Hanna Holborn Gray, eds. *Values, Leadership and Quality: The Administration of Higher Education: David D. Henry Lectures, 1979–5*. Urbana: U of Illinois P, 1991

Lucas, Ann F., and Ann E. Lucas. *Strengthening Departmental Leadership: A Team-Building Guide for Chairs in Colleges and Universities*. Higher and Adult Education. San Francisco: Jossey, 1994.

McDade, Sharon A., and Phyllis H. Lewis, eds. *Developing Administrative Excellence: Creating a Culture of Leadership*. New Directions for Higher Education 87. San Francisco: Jossey-Bass, 1994.

Outcalt, Charles L., Shannon K. Faris, and Kathleen McMahon. *Developing Non-Hierarchical Leadership on Campus: Case Studies and Best Practices in Higher Education*. Greenwood Educators' Reference. Glenview, IL: Greenwood P, 2000.

Prichard, Craig. *Making Managers in Universities and Colleges*. Houston: Open U P, 2000.

Ramsden, Paul. *Learning to Lead in Higher Education*. New York: Routledge, 1998.

Seagren, Alan T., Daniel W. Wheeler, John W. Creswell, Michael T. Miller. *Academic Leadership in Community Colleges*. Lincoln: U of Nebraska P, 1994.

Schick, Edgar B., Richard J. Novak, and James A. Norton. *Shared Visions of Public Higher Education Governance: Structures and Leadership Styles That Work*. Washington: American Assn. of State Colleges and Universities, 1992.

White, Barnetta M. *Leadership Training for Women in Higher Education*. New York: Irvington, 1983.

Resources for Additional Training in Management and Leadership

Summer Institute for Women in Higher Education
Bryn Mawr College
101 North Marion Avenue
Bryn Mawr, PA 19010–2899
610 526–7325

Fred Prior Career Track
Offers one-day seminars and online training in everything from computer skills to management, leadership, and conflict resolution. See their web site for a schedule of seminars near you. ⟨www.pryor.com⟩

American Association for Higher Education (AAHE)
One Dupont Circle NW, Suite 360
Washington, DC 20036
Phone: 202 293–6440
Fax: 202 293–0073
[www.aahe.org]

The Administrative Audience:
A Rhetorical Problem

Joyce Kinkead
Utah State University

Jeanne Simpson
Emeritus, Eastern Illinois University

Satires about life in the academy—Jane Smiley's *Moo*, Richard Russo's *Straight Man*—typically skewer members of central administration. On Jon Hassler's fictional campus, the president believes that a good motto for his northern Minnesota state school is "Paul Bunyan's alma mater," and wonders what Bunyan's fee might be when a faculty member facetiously suggests him for the commencement speaker. Robert Grudin in his biting *Book* defines administrators as [one] who fulfill[s] the *timeworn obligations of his profession: bullying his subordinates and cringing before his superiors, stifling talent and rewarding mediocrity, promoting faddishness and punishing integrity, rejecting the most impassioned and justified individual plea yet acquiescing to every whim of political interest;...shirking decisions and articulating such decisions as had to be made in memos so vague, oblique and circumnavigational as barely to deserve the name language. (10)*

Traditionally, administrators of writing programs have joined in the president-as-buffoon conversation, probably without reflecting much on the implications of doing so. Writing Program Administrators tend to continue to regard themselves primarily as faculty, perhaps without understanding the implications of the administrative role they have undertaken. We encourage WPAs to find the common ground they share with other administrators—to reckon with them.

As administrators ourselves—one at the college level and one in central administration—we would like to share what we have learned about the administrative audience, what we wish we had known when we were directors of writing centers and writing programs. Had we been more savvy about administrative rhetoric, we believe we could have negotiated more dollars, more space, more options for expanding and improving services. We naively assumed that because we directed programs that we saw as intrinsically "good" and ethical that support should flow to them from university coffers.

Rather than work against the institution, we need to acknowledge that we are part of the institution and can be effective change agents. Our success in writing programs can translate to success for the university at large. By communicating well with the administrative culture in the terminology of administration, we stand to gain resources and respect. For our purposes here, we will assume that the usual administrator is reasonable (we recognize that Darth Administrator does exist, but rarely) and also has funds that could be allocated to a writing program. As Diana George notes, administrators are "more interested in the workings of writing centers [and writing programs] than we think they are. Many are enlightened. Many want to work with us" (38).

How do we work with them? The first step is to understand administrative *culture*. WPAs know how to administer, how to "walk the walk," but they may not achieve their rhetorical goals because they do not know how to "talk the talk." The perception of WPAs as lacking administrative skill or experience may stem from their ignorance of the frames of reference higher level administrators use. To move closer to solving this problem, it is helpful to know some of the key terms that pepper a typical provost's meeting. The following glossary includes the most important of these terms. Each institution will have others, often in the form of acronyms to be deciphered, that refer to processes and units unique to that place. Using this common language in reports and proposals written by the WPA is part of finding common ground. Following the glossary, we'll talk how to use these terms as well as other strategies.

The term *FTE* may be applied to *faculty full-time equivalents*; for instance, someone who teaches half-time is considered .50 FTE faculty. A faculty member who teaches 24–27 credit hours (approximately 3 or 4 courses per semester) over the academic year might be defined as one FTE; thus if the writing program needs someone to teach 12 credit hours, a .50 FTE would be requested. Using the term faculty FTE encourages more efficient thinking about staffing needs than counting individual people. The cost per faculty FTE is the "exchange rate" in the economy of staffing plans. This approach is not intended to dehumanize faculty, though it may be perceived that way. Ultimately, all academic issues boil down to budget decisions, and if the goal is to encourage a beneficial decision, the first step is to use the language of budgets.

Understanding this terminology will help a WPA to see how the economics of the institution work. Some institutions distribute funds according to the number of student credit hours (SCH) generated so that a department that opts for teaching large-enrollment sections of courses may be rewarded financially while a writing program that maintains relatively small class sizes needs to look elsewhere for funding justification. One alternative "currency" is contact hours between faculty and students. However, in a standard, three-semester hour writing class, there is no particular advantage to using this measure of faculty productivity. A WPA may need to consider carefully which measure to use to present the writing program in the most advantageous way. Fortunately, for most institutions, courses that teach good communication skills are bedrock foundation courses. Given that institutions know that employers seek not only graduates with good communication skills but also those who are problem solvers and computer literate, writing programs should be in the catbird seat. Another rationale for supporting writing programs is that composition courses may be the only small class a first-year student enrolls in—the one class in which a student does not feel lost in an uncaring, anonymous lecture hall— which has a direct effect on retention rates.

On occasion, an administrator may believe that money could be saved by cutting required writing courses, thinking, "Just look at all of the graduate teaching assistants and part-time instructors funded to staff this program." In point of fact, the writing program is one of the least expensive programs to fund, since TA and part-time salaries tend to be lower than the average salary of a full-time, tenure-line faculty member. Or, conversely, an administrator might look at the relatively small number of seats in the average first-year writing course and wonder how the department can afford such a luxury. Using full-time, tenure-line faculty might indeed be beyond the department's reach, but using temporary faculty with no obligation for research and service makes the small class size cost-effective. A tenure-line FTE costs upwards of $35,000 (not including an additional 35 percent for benefits) while a temporary faculty FTE might cost $28,000 or less. We are not arguing that this kind of calculation is always appropriate, especially at a significant sacrifice of quality. However, a WPA needs to understand how this equation works and why it appeals to central administration. To make the case for an alternative staffing plan, a WPA needs to be able to demonstrate how a similar— or at least acceptable—cost-to-benefit ratio can be achieved in other ways. The WPA needs to realize the administrator up the line is going to ask, "Why shouldn't I just hire a batch of part-timers?" And the WPA needs to have an answer framed in terms the administrator understands and uses.

Productivity is a legitimate concern for central administrators as public institutions feel pressure from funding agencies to produce the most students (which may be defined as completed degrees or as student credit hours) for the least cost. Productivity is often figured as SCH plus tuition plus faculty load. The institutional data officer will also calculate cost per SCH for each program, a calculation by which the writing program turns out to be a bargain. Legislators tend to care more about teaching than scholarship or research, not least because teaching loads are more easily quantified than research or service activities. They scrutinize faculty workload, also derived from FTE and SCH numbers. It is common these days for the media to report research taking a beating on the floor of state congress as a member asks, "Why is our faculty spending time on researching the digestive system of bottle flies when they could be teaching more classes?" While productivity may have a factory connotation offensive to some faculty, the input-output construct is a fact of life for administrators answerable to external constituents and agencies.

Mission statement defines the goals of the institution. A land-grant institution, for instance, generally has an outreach or extension mission, which means providing service to the state at large, while universities created under the normal school banner have a teacher education mission. Tying writing program goals to the mission statement is a savvy way to demonstrate that the program supports institutional goals. An institution's general education program may feature its own mission statement (also supporting the larger statement), and its goals usually are integral to those of the writing program. In fact, the WPA is a logical person to sit on any general education oversight committee. Taking a page from other units, it is wise for the writing program itself to have its own mission statement as administrators will immediately recognize this familiar concept. If possible, a WPA also should draw on language from the region's accreditation handbook. (For example, the writing program "identifies student competencies, sequences its courses, provides synthesis of learning, and assesses learning outcomes." From *Commission on Colleges Accreditation Handbook*, Northwest region.)

Assessment is required for accreditation by regional and national bodies. The WPA organization has been clever to establish its own review and campus visit protocol—again, a recognizable process valued by administrators.

The larger institution has a plethora of assessment data to gather; however, writing programs are responsible primarily for *program review*—in brief, Is the program achieving its goals and objectives? This means that the WPA and any governing committee are responsible for defining program objectives, putting them in place, reviewing effectiveness, and then revising as needed.

Assessment is typically one of the weak points of writing programs. Numerical assessments of student writing skills are notoriously crude, and qualitative methods may be perceived as too subjective. Even so, central administrations frequently experience strong pressure to use assessment to document "value added" or "productivity." The demand for assessment of programs means that WPAs must consider how they will address assessment issues.

Accreditation teams that visit a campus determine if there is evidence that students who take required writing courses or engage in writing across the curriculum (WAC) programs really are better writers at mid-career and end-of-career. If there is no WAC program, then students might show gains in writing skill from first year to mid-career and then show losses in skill by graduation. Administrators may be surprised to learn that writing courses do not inoculate the student for the entire undergraduate career and that writing skills may actually atrophy if not reinforced and expanded to include disciplinary discourse conventions. In fact, administrators may blame the writing program for declining writing skills among students unless they understand this concept.

According to accreditation standards, the responsibility for program development and assessment is vested in the faculty, but the WPA has the responsibility to see that these tasks get done. Knowing the assessment methods and formats used in the rest of the institution, and especially by central administration, can help the WPA to guide the process and prevent faculty from pursuing dead ends. The unique assessment problems of writing programs should be made clear but with due attention as well to the institution's common assessment models.

Accountability refers to reports to off-campus authorities or stakeholders, such as the institution's governing board, the state governing body, the commissioner for higher education, the governor, or the legislature. Given the erosion in public trust and respect for universities, accountability receives increasing emphasis. The WPA can join in the cause to regain public trust by contributing information and narratives about successes. This activity may vary from "hometown news" releases about students who win writing awards to public readings of stellar first-year essays, from bulleted reports to the department chair and dean to invited presentations before governing boards. Administrators use these terms frequently. Their meanings are well-understood and so embedded that, as with a nation's currency, everyone is expected to know how to use them and how they relate to each other.

WORDS IN ACTION

Using a vocabulary recognizable by administrators is one part of solving the rhetorical problem of communicating with administrators. WPAs need to study the data, politics and protocols of their institutions. Giving evidence of being an uninformed amateur can end your efforts to get support suddenly and prematurely. Another way to fail is to submit a document blotched with errors; writing professionals are held to a higher standard of correctness. In brief, proofread carefully. Likewise, be sure to calculate your own data accurately, drawing on institutional planning and research facilities. Make friends with the chief information officer (at least know the correct title and the name of the incumbent); obtain a copy of the university's annual data report—a volume too often unfamiliar to faculty. Educate yourself about budget lines and the rules regarding them. Be aware of any constraints such as freeze dates or rules about transferring from one budget category to another. (Some universities offer primers about institutional rules, perhaps in a code, in a department head handbook, or through on-site workshops. Harvard and Higher Education Resource Services [HERS]—an organization that promotes women in administrative roles—offer summer workshops focused on understanding institutional finances for those interested in administrative careers. Yearlong fellowships in administration that encourage a macro view of the institution are sponsored by the American Council on Education.)

An isolated WPA is a WPA ineffective at getting resources and support. Find out who is doing what on your campus that might dovetail with the writing program in order to combine efforts with others and avoid duplication of efforts. For instance, if your department seeks an undergraduate major in writing, a likely question will be "how does this duplicate what the Communication department is already doing" or "how is this similar to the corporate communications major in Business." Making friends with colleagues in other departments also means finding allies who will support proposals when they come before institutional curriculum committees.

Perhaps the most important advice for getting what you want as a WPA addresses the format of documents you send forward. Consider that 80 percent of an administrator's day is scheduled, which leaves precious little time for reading. As a result, administrators value proposals—not essays or editorials—that are short, communicate effectively, use graphs, figures, and lists. The subtext of the proposal is "I am a team player; we can help each other; we have mutual goals." Data should be pictured graphically; for instance, a writing center that wants to expand its funding sources might use one pie chart to demonstrate that majors using its services come from Arts & Sciences (40 percent), Education (30 percent), Technology (20 percent), and Business (10 percent) while in a second chart, funding sources are defined as Arts & Sciences (85 percent) and all others (15 percent). Clearly the message here is that the writing center serves a university-wide audience and should receive funds from central allocation. Or, a retention bar chart might demonstrate that students who use the writing center are more likely to stay in college than those who do not.

The proposal should be worded in such a way that administrators have reasons to say "yes" to the request. Any project that results in tangible success stories—bragging rights for them—has a greater likelihood of being funded. Consider that a president, provost, or dean spends considerable time in fund-raising activities and needs academic "stories" and big dreams to share with potential donors. It's the WPA's job to provide content for these stories and dreams to the administrator and give her the opportunity to make the school and the program look good. If the administrator cannot say yes at the moment, then she may be able to say yes later if the proposal includes a plan for stages of development, including seed money for year one, increasing over a five-year period. Or, the plan might include viable alternatives, offering three options so that the administrator may choose the one most attractive or most fundable at the moment.

Even if the proposal does not earn a yes the first time, a WPA should not give up a good idea. Not being able to say yes is not the same as saying a final, definitive no. A good proposal should be kept "on the table" with regular revision and submission.

We often find that administrators have neither time nor patience to read beyond page one, but if a report must be longer than that, then it is wise to begin with an executive summary (again, no longer than one page). Bullet points (e.g.,)

- the writing program introduced on-line instruction

offer essential kernels of information not to be overlooked. Headings provide signposts for the reader and make the document easy to follow. Likewise, the title should be written in such a way to make the document easy to file—and then easy to find. The focus of a document should be simple, especially if it is a request for funds. A request for money buried in a 20-page document is unlikely to be fulfilled. Exact figures for funds should be used whenever possible, and relevant institutional policies and reports should be cited with date and page.

WPAs particularly should be sensitive to the issue of *chain of command.* Making "end runs" is frowned upon in the academy, and on some campuses is a "capital" offense. Thus, any report or proposal may pass through departmental curriculum committees, department chairs/heads, deans, college curriculum committees, provosts/vice-presidents. Not only does this process follow the communication links, it also builds support for the request as each group or body approves. Knowing the chain of command helps the WPA identify the persons who need to be lobbied for support. Not following chain of command can have disastrous results. One dean told us the story of a faculty member who went around him to make a request of the provost, a request that did not fit in college priorities but was funded centrally; as the dean ended the story, he added, "Doesn't he know that I can hurt him?" The perils of end runs.

This group of committees and administrators will include a variety of audiences with multiple interests and priorities. They should be kept in mind as you collect data, process it, and then write it up. What do they not know? Why should they support your ideas and requests? Does any of them have a vested interest in NOT supporting your proposal? Why? How could you change the situation to make it more advantageous?

Given the chain of command, a proposal may take some time to travel through this process, so planning ahead and knowing dates for requests are also important. For instance, on some campuses, annual budget requests for the fiscal year following the upcoming one are made in March; yes, that's a two-year lead time for requests for state funds. Last minute or late budget requests generally go to the bottom of the priority list, and being late or untimely with requests creates a negative impression. And a realistic understanding of the budget process allows a WPA to do effective planning.

College-level administrators typically need ideas for budget requests, especially for programmatic requests. The format for proposals may be rigid, but models should be available in departmental or college offices. Keep in mind that *new* programs are more likely to be funded than ongoing programs, and no administrator wants to sink money into a weak or dying enterprise, so the language should always focus on how a program is strong or adds value to the institution or to the curriculum.

As you prepare proposals, think big and for the long term as well as considering immediate, smaller scale needs. Nickel-and-dime requests often disappear in the shadow of more glamorous, big-ticket items. A good rule of thumb is to ask for everything you want, know what is not really essential so you can revise your plan quickly, and then take what you can get and build on it. Have some proposals ready to revise up or down quickly.

TRAINING YOUR STAFF TO USE "ADMIN-SPEAK"

Using cases with program staff and committees or in the graduate courses offered to doctoral students looking to careers in writing program administration can help identify problems, avenues for resolution, and routes for requests. Rather than waiting for the next request to come along, by discussing cases, the staff can anticipate problems, share solutions, and plan for improved writing program practice. The efficacy of cases allows staff to exchange ideas and also rehearse administrative talk. Cases may range from how to deal with ethical situations (e.g., plagiarism, harassment) to how to position the program for fund-raising. We offer the following case—a request for technology proposals asap—for discussion in staff meetings. In doing so, we use the term *staff* rather loosely, acknowledging that a center's staff may vary from undergraduate to graduate students, from paraprofessionals to volunteers. Consequently, appropriate topics for the case depend on the type of staff. And, in fact, members of the staff may write cases at year's end for use in future meetings.

As WPA at Upstate Tech University (UTU), you are frustrated to see funding and overhead monies lavished on the engineering and science colleges as they get cutting-edge equipment. Meanwhile, your writing program/center has a dozen outdated computers whose drives go "clunk, whirr, sputter." What you would really like is increased space with more and newer computer stations so that the students enrolled in writing courses could use word processing, e-mail, software that promotes classroom interchanges and oral presentations. Your department head has just heard that UTU will receive some one-time monies from the state legislature earmarked for technology. Of course, the deans of science and engineering assume that they will come their way. As WPA, how do you go about getting part of the technology pie? At the college level—your department is housed within the College of Liberal Arts—the dean determines how the college allotment will be parceled out while the provost divides the funds among the colleges. In an emergency writing staff meeting, you ask your colleagues how to position the writing program to channel part of the funds to the long-dreamed-of computer addition.

When we have used this case with our own staffs, they have enthusiastically brainstormed, coming up with the following ideas:

- if a foundation has not already been laid to establish university allies, it may be fruitless to apply; have interdepartmental alliances been formed?
- read and review the legislative document and use its language in any request;
- use key words from the institution's strategic plan (e.g., retention, computer literacy);
- structure the request so it is clear that it is not only the writing program that will benefit from the new computer addition but that it will also have an impact university-wide;

- stress the benefits of a new writing computer room to engineering and science colleges;
- suggest that a student from science or engineering will be employed as technical support;
- provide data with a breakdown of student majors enrolled in the writing program;
- demonstrate that an electronic classroom could help the university overall with desktop publishing applications;
- survey faculty computer needs and assess student need by working with director of computer services;
- demonstrate how this request will provide seed funding that allows the writing program to seek additional extramural funds;
- bring in outside consultants to help develop a vision statement for the program;
- compare the program to "peer" institutions to demonstrate we are falling behind our competitors; or, conversely, show how the program has national status but is in danger of losing that if new program is not approved;
- show that this is a cost-efficient plan—that the committee has discarded more expensive proposals;
- if the department or college is financially able, suggest matching funds;
- draw on national studies or alumni surveys that show computer skills need to be emphasized;
- gather statistics on the writing program (e.g., SCHs) and develop a multi year plan;
- avoid whining.

The brainstorming approach developed a strong selection of options for our imaginary WPA while providing practice in honing "admin-speak." The same process can be used for actual circumstances, allowing the WPA to draft written requests built on the suggestions generated once the group understands the administrative audience.

THE COMMON GROUND: STABLE OR VOLATILE?

At any one time, states vary in their financial stability; some institutions may be downsizing (or "right-sizing" as it is euphemistically termed) while others are facing enrollment surges. Still others are changing institutional personality and philosophy, some turning to a corporatization of academe. For the WPA, it is important, in flush times or hard times, to report consistently on the writing program's work and to make requests for support. Even in financially difficult times, unforeseen opportunities may arise.

Harold Shapiro, president of Princeton, believes that the central administration exists to "serve and to lead," freeing the faculty of "administrative chores" (74). He recalls, though, President (of Princeton) Woodrow Wilson's analysis of college faculties as "sometimes touched with as much sensitiveness and personal jealousy as church choirs" (82). In other words, satires of faculty and faculty life can be as biting as those of administrators. The tension between the two worlds exists, in part, because of a language barrier. WPAs stand on the boundary between them, often implementing administration policy and transmitting faculty concerns, and therefore have a significant opportunity to improve communication and to diminish the stereotypes and perceptions that cause so much frustration. We suggest that WPAs need to be translators and mediators, and to do so, they need to know the terminology and values of administration as well as those of faculty.

Even when faculty present rhetorically savvy requests, additional funding may not be forthcoming. A WPA may do everything right and still not get needed support—even if the administrator is sympathetic. Perhaps it is the year that the chemistry program needs federally mandated safety equipment or health insurance costs skyrocket. The university must respond to multiple needs simultaneously.

When do we know that the WPA has been an effective communicator? When the provost supports funding for a new communication across the curriculum program. When the department head understands that the new writing center director must be a tenure-track position, not a staff position. When the computers in the writing lab are upgraded or replaced every four years. When the faculty senate supports an increased writing requirement in general education. When the president invites the WPA to make a presentation at the governing board meeting. When the development officer offers a naming opportunity for the writing program. When the dean turns down a new writing position request regretfully.

As WPAs we have the opportunity to shape and reshape the institution in ways that matter. We share with presidents and vice presidents the responsibility to "serve and lead."

WORKS CITED

George, Diana. "Talking to the Boss: A Preface." *Writing Center Journal* 9.1 (1988): 37–44.

Grudin, Robert. *Book.* New York: Penguin, 1993.

Hassler, Jon. *Dean's List.* New York: Random, 1997.

Hassler, Jon. *Rookery Blues.* New York: Random, 1995.

Riley, Richard. *Straight Man.* New York: Vintage, 1998.

Shapiro, Harold T. "University Presidents—Then and Now." *Universities and Their Leadership.* Ed. William G. Bowen and Harold T. Shapiro. Princeton: Princeton UP, 1998.

Simpson, Jeanne. "Perceptions, Realities, and Possibilities: Central Administration and Writing Centers." *Writing Center Perspectives.* Ed. Byron Stay, Christina Murphy, and Eric Hobson. Emmitsburg: NWCA P, 1995.

Smiley, Jane. *Moo.* New York: Random, 1995.

Postmasculinist Directions in Writing Program Administration

Hildy Miller
University of Minnesota

While I have practiced feminist teaching for many years, it was not until my first administrative job helping direct a writing program in a Ph.D. granting department that I began to consider how to transfer feminist principles to an administrative domain. The challenge has been a formidable one. It is one thing to be a practicing feminist in the classroom—a context comparatively set apart from institutional ideologies. But it is another problem altogether to transfer these principles to the administrative domain, embedded as deeply as it is within masculinist traditions of department and academy.[1]

For nearly a decade we have mulled over the implications of feminism within the instructional context (Caywood and Overing; Gabriel and Smithson). Generally, such teaching has come to be associated with strategies for ameliorating the power differential between instructor and students. Its hallmarks include collaboration, supportiveness, and an emphasis on process. By most accounts, the feminist classroom emerged in tandem with the student centered class. As Miller, Flynn (423) and others have pointed out, composition studies is in many ways inherently a feminized field. Yet even as we continue to explore all the positive implications of this approach, we have also recognized its conflicts. The political reality for most students is that within the academy they may never again encounter the sorts of cooperative classrooms we create. Nor may they again encounter our process-oriented rhetorical contexts. And as instructors we may struggle to balance nonauthoritarian forms of leadership with institutional conventions, such as assigning grades, that run counter to our own guiding ideologies. These tensions have been apparent for quite some time.

But we have only just begun to see the conflicts in applying similar feminist principles to administration. As was the case with feminist teaching, feminist administration seems to be emerging first from practice, and only now, tentatively, is it being theorized. Not surprisingly, the move to articulate feminist administration is occurring simultaneously with our recognition of the more general need to theorize administrative practices (Pemberton). Yet if feminist teaching is at odds with the larger masculinist academic structure, feminist administration is doubly so. WPAs are struggling as it is to establish and wield power and to oversee administrative structures that are often fragile and fragmented. At every turn, established authoritarian forms of leadership threaten to destroy nascent programmatic philosophies that would cooperatively guide such concerns as teacher training, mentoring, and curriculum development.

I want to focus, then, on this administrative intersection where ideological realities collide by considering some basic questions. First of all, what does "feminist directing" look like in actual practice? Secondly, in what ways does a delivery system informed by feminist ideology clash with the masculinist administrative structures in which it is embedded? And, finally, how can two such seemingly incompatible systems be made to mesh into a "postmasculinist" approach?

SOME CAVEATS ABOUT GENDERED TERMS

Feminist directing, like feminist teaching, surely implies such approaches as cooperation, collaboration, shared leadership, and the integration of the cognitive and the affective (Schniedewind). Yet I know that to label such an enterprise "feminist" is risky, for it may sound essentialist. Worse yet, when contrasted with "masculinist" directing, it may seem to reinforce patriarchal epistemologies that characteristically dichotomize reality. That is to say, from years of immersion in masculinist discourse, we habitually adopt a critical stance that assumes "either or" rather than the more feminist "both and." The delimiting role of dichotomy on masculinist discourse has been discussed extensively by many feminists (Schaef; Cixous and Clement; Lloyd). More recently, the problem of inappropriately continuing to apply dichotomous assumptions to pluralistic sociopolitical realities has also been recognized (Gates). So I should say at the outset that within the flawed language and epistemology that we have, I am using the term "feminist" only as a very general designator meaning an orientation, an inclination, a way of seeing and speaking and leading that is probably influenced by gender. It arises from those attitudes and behaviors which in the dominant culture are most associated with women. But it is not practiced exclusively by women or, indeed, found at all in some women.

A second point about feminist directing that I should make is that I am not touting it as an approach superior to masculinist administration. The inherent problems in assuming that matriarchal approaches to directing should replace the patriarchal, thereby substituting one limited modus operandi for another, have arisen in previous discussions of the issue (Dickson 145). In fact, alternatives put forward by American feminists have a long history, dating back to the nineteenth century, of foundering because of these very claims—and fears—that new ideas necessarily extinguish the old. Given these assumptions, I know I risk being trapped/trapping myself in an "either or" mind-set that dictates we must have one or the other but not both. One approach is automatically assumed to be thought better than another.

With these caveats, I am going to go ahead and use the terms "feminist" and "masculinist" to describe conflicting administrative ideologies. Similar approaches go by other names in American business. "Horizontal business organization," "shop floor and consumer participation management," and "cooperative management" are just a few of the terms used in describing egalitarian rather than top-down hierarchical structures.

These approaches, like those suggested by feminist administration, also stem from multicultural awareness, with most new models adapted from Japanese management strategies. Writing directors Burnham and Nims have drawn on this tradition in using the business term Total Quality Management (TQM) to describe their participatory program. Though such terms are more neutral, and thereby help to avoid essentializing, dichotomizing, and hierarchizing, I am not convinced that it is particularly useful to transfer the language of management to the academic setting. After all, the terms "masculinist" and "feminist" aptly describe the ideological conflict within the academy as I see it from my perspective as a woman and as a feminist. Within our field too, they perhaps best describe the sorts of political connections we are making between classroom and administrative structures. And finally, such terminology is consistent with the way in which feminist theory has been overtly named in its transformation of the academic enterprise at so many other levels—changing research methodologies, pedagogy, and scholarly writing—to name a few. However, recognizing both the real and perceived shortcomings of using this language, I will periodically weave in reminders that I am using the terms more as crude designators than as absolute and opposing categories. In the end, I will also suggest the term "postmasculinist" for the combination of "masculinist" and "feminist" approaches, which may help to lead us beyond linguistic-epistemological-administrative polarization. By taking a closer look at the implications of feminist directing and the nature of the ideological conflicts it encounters, the most significant issues revolve around different conceptions of leadership and administrative structures.

FEMINIST LEADERSHIP
AND ADMINISTRATIVE POWER

The exercise of personal power on the part of writing program administrators has become an issue in itself lately for several reasons. It is generally agreed that many administrators feel a sense of powerlessness, more specifically, a sense of having enormous responsibilities without accompanying power. Actual powers are, in fact, limited. Olson and Moxley, for example, in their survey of writing programs, discovered limits in the ability of directors to establish policy in hiring decisions, to set course directions, develop new programs, and handle political problems (53–54). Without such powers, they conclude, WPAs function more as coordinators than as directors. In addition, the lines of responsibility and the boundaries of territory are often blurred. When boundaries overlap, writing administrator concerns are often outweighed by those of department or institution. In a Ph.D. granting department, for example, teaching assistantships may be used to further the aims of the department in attracting the best graduate students rather than in addressing the concerns of a writing director for hiring the best teachers. Other considerations complicating the allotment of power include the untenured status of many WPAs (Janangelo 61) and the underling position of composition in relation to English studies (Miller). It is no wonder that, in hierarchical terms, many writing directors feel like figurehead monarchs of make-believe realms.

With our institutional authority so compromised, recent discussion has centered on how writing directors can exercise personal authority in a way that not only mitigates our sense of powerlessness but matches our growing sense of professionalism. The underlying premise of this discussion is that seeing is believing. That is, if one looks and acts the part, then this persona can compensate for the actual uncertainty of one's position. For many who are struggling with this issue, the model of personal power being advanced is unmistakably a masculinist one. So, for example, a writing director may be like a general in recognizing adversaries and courting allies (White). Or a director may be statesmanlike: "In interacting with people, prospective WPAs should display confidence, diplomacy, a strong will, and the rhetorical skill and vocal capacity to speak forcefully" (Thomas 43). Certainly, most writing administrators would recognize the utility of this model of leadership.

Nevertheless, a feminist vision of personal power is likely to be quite different. It represents a different way of exercising power because it is based on a different notion of what power is. At base, power is seen as a limitless rather than finite quantity. Therefore, power cannot be subject to a zero-sum game in which we are led to believe that increasing one person's power necessarily diminishes another's. Ideally, as Lamb has said, power can be "mutually enabling" (21). Rather than cultivating "power over," an effective leader focuses on "being peer" (Schaef 104). Gunner, for example, repudiates the field's internal statements on professional status for advocating a "WPA-centric model" rather than a "decentered" one (10). She says:

> In the ideal program...the intellectual agenda and authority would come from a synthesis of informal instructors and the program they develop—it would be a group, or collaborative, entity in need of a spokesperson or liaison, perhaps, but not a single position assigned total curricular responsibility or autocratic power. (13)

Without such internal participation, she warns, programs tend to stagnate and alienate. Howard and her colleagues envision themselves not as White's "warriors" seeking power over others but rather as Cixous's "flying mice" who empower themselves (qtd. in Howard 39). To lead, then, is not to dominate but rather to facilitate, to share power, and to enable both self and others to contribute.

Such behavior makes sense within the feminist epistemological stance of "both/and" rather than "either/or." Masculinist epistemologies imply that one must either promote one's own interests or forgo these to further someone else's. In reference to administrative conflict, White operates on this assumption in observing: "… when friendship or even professional loyalty and self-interest conflict, self-interest always wins" (4). However, feminist McNaron provides a counter-example of how such an administrative dynamic can be seen as "both self and others." In this anecdote she speaks of the collegial relationship she enjoys with two other faculty members:

> Once a chairman tried to exploit our connection. As usual, he had failed to award us our deserved merit points for the year and we had written letters of protest. One day, I received a note asking me to stop by his office. He was prepared to grant me additional points, but when I asked about Shirley and Mimi, he said that his original calculations stood. Without missing a beat, I looked him squarely in the eye and said, "Well, then, don't give me any more, since it would be unfair; they had even better years than I." His expression was of someone hearing a language totally foreign to his ear. Unable to believe me, he offered again, only to hear me refuse again. I walked out feeling like the winner; I had spoken from a position of unity and love in response to his meager ground of money and competition. (190)

To apply such a feminist approach to power in writing program administration, suggests, as Mielke did in describing a feminist model, "the inevitable need for reliance on networking, appealing to the web of human connection rather than personal power …." (175) Leadership is therefore characterized as relational. Personal authority may appear as being receptive, cooperative, willing to promote discussion, listen to divergent views, and look for common interests. In feminist directing, as Dickson (144) and Bishop and Crossley (70) assert, communicative functions appear as a significant source of power.

My administrative experience contains many examples of applying this approach. I recall facilitating a meeting with three graduate student assistants that took the form of a "think tank" to share ideas for developing a teacher education seminar. I probably talked the least and listened the most in order to encourage the tentative observations and plans that strengthened the resulting class. During the same week I also headed off a potentially time-consuming grievance by an angry mother whose son had failed a composition course. While my investigation indicated that her accusations against the instructor were groundless, I also reached out to her personally to suggest constructive solutions based on our joint concern for her son. Testimonials like these are typical of success stories associated with feminist exercise of power.

However, this approach cannot be used consistently in an administrative situation comprised of conflicting ideologies. I have found that, ironically, within the institution "being peer" works best when I am "one up" in masculinist terms. My interactions with actual peers during the same week reveals a different side of the story. On the same day that I employed feminist leadership with graduate students, I had to change to a masculinist style at a meeting held immediately afterwards. The conciliatory talk with the mother was followed by a friendly argument over policy with a colleague who prefers this masculinist mode of problem-solving. In the bi-epistemological institution, personas have to change with context.

But such a balancing act can quickly go awry. Because of ideological conflict, feminist approaches are likely to be misinterpreted from a masculinist point of view. Leadership can appear weak if receptivity is mistaken for passivity; affective responses such as laughter for lack of seriousness; and the sharing of power for looking to others for direction. When boundaries of administrative responsibility blur, cooperative approaches to resolving conflicts may be mistaken for encroachment into territory, thereby turning mild adversarial responses into pitched battles. Such responses are familiar to anyone who has practiced feminist teaching. Sometimes one or two students comment on course evaluations that they are uncomfortable with a feminist style. As one said recently to me, "I'm not used to this." In administration too, changing the game can make others profoundly uneasy. WPAs may be convinced of the value of feminist approaches but have to proceed cautiously given the risks associated with not playing the game. In this light, the general or the statesman may appear as much safer roles to play because they are better understood by others.

For women administrators working in a feminist way, the problems are compounded, since women's authority is still problematic in academic culture. This quandary has been apparent for some time in teaching. As Friedman points out, "Both students and ourselves are socialized to believe…that any kind of authority is incompatible with the feminine" (207). As a female teacher, establishing authority can be difficult; as a female administrator, it is even more challenging. Students, colleagues across the institution, and members of the community are still likely to doubt women's credentials (Eichhorn, Farris, Hayes, Hernandez, Jarratt, Stubbs, and Sciachitano 299). I vividly recall such an encounter after a meeting in which I had represented my department as an administrator. Someone said to me incredulously: "*You* are a professor?" Then, adding insult to injury, "Tenure track?"

Of course, most women academics have learned to take such comments in stride, but they are reminders of our outsider status. If we add to this position an outsider persona and a "different voiced" leadership style, it may exacerbate the problems. On the other hand, as studies have shown, when women adopt more masculinist personas, other difficulties may develop. Positive qualities such as assertiveness in men can be seen negatively as domineering behavior in women. The challenge for feminist administrators, particularly if we are women, is much the same as that Aisenberg and Harrington point to for women throughout the academy:

> The problem, then, for women [and WPAs generally] who reject the prevailing model for professional discourse is to find a countermodel that commands

respect. How can women become insiders and acquire an insider's voice of authority while questioning insider values? Where is the model for new forms of discourse? Not readily available, is the predictable answer (78).

Yet we must surely attempt to articulate new forms of leadership in administration, just as we have in the classroom.

UNDOING HIERARCHIC STRUCTURES AND FEMINIST ADMINISTRATION

Feminist administrative structures are also likely to be different from masculinist systems established in the academy. In general, the concept of community in which leadership is shared can be substituted for the notion of hierarchy. With the self seen as inter-relational and personal power enhanced by empowering others, such a community is marked by collaboration and cooperation. Rather than striving to develop uniform and universalized rules, feminist communities tend to produce flexible decisions arising from experiential contexts. Ideas are tentative, and thus subject to alteration as contextual needs change. While not all members of a community need to agree on all details, there is generally basic consensus on important points.

In our writing program we have put in place feminist structures insofar as we can.[2] With the staff, which consists largely of graduate students and adjunct faculty, we collaborate to set course goals and share class materials. Instructors gather twice a year at the beginning of each semester to exchange ideas. Throughout the year teachers also contribute ideas to a resource file for our two freshman courses that everyone can consult and use. By sharing information in this way, course structures can develop organically from instructors themselves rather than from the more masculinist approach of a top-down edict dictating content. New directions for courses emerge gradually as teachers respond to the changing needs of students and ongoing shifts in pedagogical applications of composition theory.

Such feminist innovations have been successful in both this composition program and others. However, each WPA also inherits a delivery system determined in part by the department, the institution, and the accrediting system to which the program belongs. Since most are informed by masculinist ideology, they tend to be structured hierarchically. Herein lies the source of contradiction and conflict. In my writing program, for example, hierarchy is embedded in the way that teacher education is structured as a seminar taught by the composition director for which a student is graded. No doubt when this course was originally developed, it followed the convention that imparting knowledge about teaching was a one-person, top-down enterprise. In this masculinist model, only the director designs and teaches the course. Now, however, we have feminized the approach by collaborating with instructor volunteers who offer pedagogical presentations and lead small group discussions. Such a model introduces new instructors immediately to the sort of teaching collaborative that structures the writing program. Yet this informal feminist collaboration continues paradoxically within the formal masculinist system of a traditional seminar, an accrediting convention unlikely to change.

Whereas in this case we had to modify an existing structure, in other cases we have had to supplement one. An inherited mentor system for new teaching assistants, similar to that of many programs, is permanently in place. Though it serves many useful functions, it too is based on a hierarchical scheme in which a faculty member "supervises" a new teacher. Here we have supplemented with the more feminist notion of mentor groups that provide "support" rather than "supervision." In these groups new instructors meet regularly with other new and experienced teachers, including faculty or graduate student administrators, throughout the first year. Group members discuss pedagogical issues and take turns visiting one another's classes. In many ways, the two mentoring systems are successful in providing double support and/or supervision for new instructors. Still, the burden of shifting between the different ideologies on which the two systems are based falls on new instructors. In one mentor group, for example, I described a protocol for observing another teacher's class, stressing the notion of observing rather than judging and of working collaboratively with the observed teacher in providing feedback. One member of my group asked, "Is this the approach to class observations that our faculty mentors will use?" Of course, in many cases, it was not. They were more likely to construct the purpose of the visits in hierarchical terms of judging a teacher's competency. At times like these, new instructors feel buffeted between feminist and masculinist ideologies.

Overall, such examples suggest that masculinist and feminist delivery systems can be successfully—if lopsidedly—blended. The result may be a better admixture or an awkward compromise. However, this overlay of ideologies is unlikely to be perceived as comprised of equal contributions. Instead, within the more established ideologies of department and institution, it is probably only hierarchical administrative structure that counts. In such a system, lines of accountability are viewed as all-important. One person at the top must function as a figure to take both credit and blame. As a result, just as feminist directors must alternate feminist and masculinist personas to cope with double ideologies, we also need to design collaborative administrative structures that can be translated hierarchically.

Whether feminist systems masquerade as masculinist systems or are openly apparent, they are still subject to misunderstanding. The seeming lack of centralized mono-authority is often perceived as chaos. Such misperception probably arises from the masculinist epistemological perspective in which an organizational structure is assumed to be either hierarchical or chaotic. Understandably, since this long established system has claimed universality for itself, it is difficult for those of us conditioned by it to recognize an alternative organizing principle. Fears of administrative chaos sound familiar since they parallel similar reactions to decentered feminist teaching that we have been aware of for a long time. Therefore, the challenge for feminist directors is not only to figure out how to blend actual delivery systems but how to assuage fears. For, as Howard asserts, directors must not only figure out how to develop such structures but how to maintain them—"to function as a collective within the hierarchy....(47).

COMBINING FEMINIST AND MASCULINIST ADMINISTRATION

Though I have no formulas for dissolving all the tensions between the two systems, I do have some suggestions for WPAs introducing feminist approaches. Above all, it is essential to communicate attempts to reinvent the game. Explain the philosophy that undergirds new methods, if possible, before rather than after the fact in order to prepare others for the differences. Afterwards, draw attention to any positive outcomes. Model different kinds of leadership and different delivery systems. Time and again, I have seen the need for such clarification. I think, for example, of a recent "think tank" collaborative effort in which a latecomer mistook it for a leaderless group and began trying to dominate. I think of a colleague from another department for whom we develop special composition courses who was concerned that the courses we offered did not look alike, not seeing the common course goals that underlay them. Therefore, the more explicit we are about specific applications, the more comfortable everyone will become, and the easier it will be for others to generalize this way of working to other parts of the program.

However, do not expect communication to resolve all resistance easily. Just as students often resist the unfamiliar tenets of the feminist classroom, so too many people will find feminist directing a threat. When seen through the lenses of masculinist assumptions, as I have suggested, leadership may look weak and the delivery system chaotic. Communicating the rationale and modeling the alternative can surely help. But as many marginalized groups have learned, resistance to new approaches can in itself be quite resistant to attempts at explanation. As Lorde warned early on, being put in a position of constantly explaining, justifying, and defending new perspectives may lead to a "diversion of energies," which eventually becomes depleting (100). Schaef's rule of thumb for dealing with this sort of resistance is to explain new concepts only twice (55). Thus it is important to communicate and then act rather than to bog down perpetually explaining.

Secondly, provide some focal points for communication. Since the focus of authority is decentered, tangible mechanisms can not only facilitate collaboration but help to eliminate confusion. My colleague Dennis Hall began a composition newsletter produced by the administrative staff each week. It advertises ongoing activities in the program—courses, meetings, and workshops, along with items of professional interest such as calls for papers and acknowledgments of the professional activities of our staff. The newsletter communicates not only to those in the program but to other faculty and administrators throughout the English department and university who receive it. Other mechanisms facilitate communication among teachers. Course units contributed by instructors are collected in a resource file to which everyone has access. The best of the group has been assembled into a copy center packet complete with unit overviews, readings, journal entries, and ideas for class activities. Such collections formalize the informal exchange of teaching ideas that we encourage. Each year we also distribute a "Who's Using What" list of texts currently used by instructors, along with textbook reviews, so that teachers can contact others either using the same texts or ones they would like to try. These and other mechanisms provide tangible points of reference.

Finally, begin developing appropriate language for feminist directing. As rhetoricians we understand the extent to which language shapes reality. In fact, a large part of the feminist enterprise has been to invent terms for concepts and experiences unacknowledged by the dominant culture. With feminist administration too, we need to develop new descriptive terms that reflect systemic change. In my own case, I refer to our staff of graduate teaching assistants and adjunct faculty as a "teaching collaborative" and to small support groups as "mentor groups." More recently, in a letter to new teaching assistants, I coined the term "web of support," drawing unconsciously on Gilligan's work, as a way of describing our program.

Other more traditional terms suggesting hierarchy have simply been replaced. Instead of "teaching assistants," we use "teachers" or "instructors." After all, as a colleague once pointed out, they actually are assisting no one but are instead running their own classes. We have also adopted the current term "teacher education" instead of the more traditional expression "teacher training," which has implications of running lesser beings through a prescribed set of paces on command rather than providing adults with materials with which to make informed decisions. None of the terms I have developed is wildly imaginative, but they make a start at rectifying the conflict between hierarchical language and feminist approaches. Ultimately, changed language will reinforce changed ways of working.

In keeping with the notion that language reflects and reinforces change, I would like to suggest the term "postmasculinist" for the kind of approach that is likely to evolve as feminist and masculinist orientations to administration are combined. From a philosophical standpoint, the principle of "both/and" indicates that these divergent perspectives can at least be made congruent. As a matter of practicality, the two must merge. After all, masculinist assumptions about power, leadership, and administrative structure permeate the academy, affecting feminist approaches at every turn. Merging the two requires a WPA to take a bi-epistemological stance. As a marginalized group, women have historically learned to function in two worlds. Compositionists who apply feminist principles in the classroom do the same. Thus it is not surprising that WPAs would also need to employ these strategies.

Outsiders of all sorts are singularly adept at playing two games: we play both the established game even as we attempt to reinvent the game. Or as Mielke says flatly, "The marginal should employ marginal strategies" (175). The postmasculinist, then, is not just a matter of replacing masculinist with feminist, but rather of somehow doing both or creating a space for one to exist within the other.

At least in my institution, thus far, such an approach is working—awkward, ungainly, and self-contradictory though it may be. And in other schools, for the moment, the ideological conflicts seem to be meshing similarly. Howard and her colleagues, for example, have been so successful at playing both games that they have managed to create an ideologically workable space for themselves. She explains her strategy:

> Those in the outer circle who wish to change an institution have a much higher probability of success if what they propose is depicted as an enhancement of the status quo and if those who propose it depict themselves as the equal rather than the superior or inferior of those to whom they propose it (38).

From this bi-epistemological stance, they have been able not "to win a higher place in the established order" but rather "to shape [their] own place, a place of power-sharing collectivity and liberatory pedagogy" (39). She explains their "both and" approach: "I can only say that although we have recognized and participated in the hierarchical structures endemic to academic bureaucracy, we have at the same time striven to level or avert hierarchy, or at least to devise an alternative to it" (44–45).

I am not claiming, of course, that such an approach resolves all problems. In reading Howard's account, I infer that at her institution, as at mine, there is basic underlying support for the aims and methods of the composition program, despite profound ideological conflicts. Certainly, the situation is different elsewhere. Bishop and Crossley conclude, in describing their recent situation, that some sort of ideological clash is inevitable. For, they say, "Understandings of our field are built on defining *against* mainstream academic values more than anything else" (77). Bishop found herself seemingly forced to choose between masculinist "fiscal realities" that higher administration decreed would enlarge her program and her feminist concern for protecting the quality of the program she had worked so hard to establish. One reviewer read her story in masculinist terms as a classic dichotomy, in which her feminist concern was morally superior but practically unworkable—resulting in a battle that was unwinnable. The other reviewer, however, offered a more feminist reading of a Gilligan-esque dilemma of competing responsibilities, suggesting that she collaborate with the chair in figuring out how to increase resources to handle the heavier load (73–74). I cannot know, of course, whether this was really a workable solution in Bishop's specific case given the differences from one institution to another. But it is a response in keeping with the sort of bi-epistemological stance that characterizes a postmasculinist approach.

It is resolving conflict from a "both and" rather than "either or" position, and exercising power from a position of equality. Certainly. Bishop's resignation calls attention to the serious repercussions of ideological conflicts. As we continue gravitating toward—even endorsing—feminist approaches to administration, it is urgent that, in postmasculinist fashion, we find ways to accommodate both masculinist and feminist models.

NOTES

1. I wish to thank Sherrie Gradin and Amber Dahlin for their helpful comments on an early draft of this piece, along with the *WPA* reviewers for their responses to a later draft.
2. In developing approaches to feminist directing, I am indebted to Robert Brown, director of the composition program at the University of Minnesota during my early years as a graduate student there. A pioneer in feminist administration, he produced an unusually innovative writing program. My own efforts have roots in his model.

WORKS CITED

Aisenberg, Nadya, and Mona Harrington. *Women of Academe: Outsiders in the Sacred Grove*. Amherst: U of Massachusetts P, 1988.

Bishop, Wendy, and Gay Lynn Crossley. "How to Tell a Story of Stopping: The Complexities of Narrating a WPA's Experience." *WPA: Writing Program Administration* 20.3 (1996): 70–79.

Burnham, Christopher C., and Cheryl Nims. "Closing the Circle: Outcomes Assessment, TQM and the WPA." *WPA: Writing Program Administration* 19.1–2 (1995): 50–65.

Caywood, Cynthia L., and Gillian R. Overing, eds. *Teaching Writing: Pedagogy, Gender, and Equity*. Albany: State U of New York P, 1987.

Cixous, Helene, and Catherine Clement. *The Newly Born Woman*. Trans. Betsy Wing. *The Theory and History of Literature* 24. Minneapolis: U of Minnesota P, 1986.

Dickson, Marcia. "Directing Without Power: Adventures in Constructing a Model of Feminist Writing Programs Administration." Fontaine and Hunter 140–53.

Eichhorn, Jill, Sara Farris, Karen Hayes, Adriana Hernandez, Susan C. Jarratt, Karen Powers-Stubbs, and Marian M. Sciachitano. "A Symposium on Feminist Experiences in the Composition Classroom." *College Composition and Communication* 43 (1992): 297–322.

Flynn, Elizabeth A. "Composing as a Woman." *College Composition and Communication* 39 (1988): 423–35.

Fontaine, Sheryl I., and Susan Hunter, eds. *Writing Ourselves into the Story*. Carbondale: Southern Illinois UP, 1993.

Frey, Olivia. "Equity and Peace in the New Writing Class." Caywood and Overing 93–106.

Friedman, Susan Stanford. "Authority in the Feminist Classroom: A Contradiction in Terms?" *Gendered Subjects: The Dynamics of Feminist Teaching*. Ed. Margo Culley and Catherine Portuges. Boston: Routledge, 1985. 203–07.

Gabriel, Susan L., and Isaiah Smithson, ed. *Gender in the Classroom: Power and Pedagogy*. Chicago: U of Illinois P, 1990.

Gates, Henry Louis. "A Pretty Good Society." *Time* 16 November 1992: 84–86.

Gilligan, Carol. *In a Different Voice.* Cambridge, MA: Harvard UP, 1982.

Gunner, Jeanne. "Decentering the WPA." *WPA: Writing Program Administration* 18.1–2 (1994): 8–15.

Hall, Dennis. "*Compost:* A Writing Program Newsletter and Its Rationale." *WPA: Writing Program Administration* 17.1–2 (1993): 75–82.

Howard, Rebecca Moore. "Power Revisited; Or, How We Became a Department." *WPA: Writing Program Administration* 16.3 (1993): 37–49.

Janangelo, Joseph. "Somewhere Between Disparity and Despair: Writing Program Administrators, Image Problems, and the MLA Job List." *WPA: Writing Program Administration* 15.1–2 (1991): 60–66.

Lamb, Catherine E. "Beyond Argument in Feminist Composition." *College Composition and Communication* 42 (1991): 11–24.

Lloyd, Genevieve. *The Man of Reason: "Male" and "Female" in Western Philosophy.* Minneapolis: U of Minnesota P, 1984.

Lorde, Audre. "The Master's Tools Will Never Dismantle the Master's House." *This Bridge Called My Back.* Ed. Cherrie Moraga and Gloria Anzaldua. 2nd ed. Latham: Kitchen Table, Women of Color P, 1983. 98–106.

McNaron, Toni. *I Dwell in Possibility.* The Cross-Cultural Memoir Series. New York: Feminist P, 1992.

Mielke, Robert. "Revisionist Theory on Moral Development and Its Impact Upon Pedagogical and Departmental Practice." Caywood and Overing 172–183.

Miller, Susan. *Textual Carnivals: The Politics of Composition.* Carbondale: Southern Illinois UP, 1991.

Olson, Gary A., and Joseph M. Moxley. "Directing Freshman Composition: The Limits of Authority." *College Composition and Communication* 40 (1989): 51–60.

Pemberton, Michael. "Tales Too Terrible to Tell: Unstated Truths and Underpreparation in Graduate Composition Programs." Fontaine and Hunter 154–173.

Schaef, Anne Wilson. *Women's Reality: An Emerging Female System White Male Society.* Minneapolis: Winston, 1981.

Schniedewind, Nancy. "Feminist Values: Guidelines for Teaching Methodology in Women's Studies." *Freire for the Classroom.* Ed. Ira Shor. Portsmouth, NH: Heinemann, 1987. 170–79.

Thomas, Trudelle. "The Graduate Student as Apprentice WPA: Experiencing the Future." *WPA: Writing Program Adaministration:* 14.3 (1991): 41–51.

White, Edward M. "Use it or Lose it: Power and the WPA." *WPA: Writing Program Administration* 15.1–2 (1991): 3–12.

WPA Work at the Small College or University: Re-Imagining Power and Making the Small School Visible

Thomas Amorose
Seattle Pacific University

Within the growing discourse of writing program administration, the work of Writing Program Administrators at small colleges and universities goes under-reported and generally unaddressed. Disciplinary efforts to piece together who and what the WPA is—ranging from recent statements of the WPA's intellectual work to more general descriptions of the health and wealth of the collective WPA enterprise—continually omit the material conditions of small-school WPAs, the nature of composition programs at small institutions, and the small-school contribution to the growing WPA culture. This gradual process of collective erasure may have started as early as the turn of the century when the universal first-year composition course became a common feature at large institutions (Brereton). Certainly the invisibility of small-school WPA work grew with the rise of large composition programs at these institutions, their flowering in the 1960s, and the growth of organizations such as College Composition and Communication, established to provide a forum to discuss the needs of big-university programs. What has become known as the "period of professionalization" of our field, which began shortly thereafter and has continued into the present, seems to have eclipsed almost entirely the small-school composition scene.[1] I want to claim here that this erasure has proven detrimental to small- and large-institution WPAs alike. Not only have small-school WPAs been thus under-served, through this erasure, by the discourse on WPA work; large-university WPAs have also lost out, missing ways to enlarge their vision of their work and strengthen their role within their institutions.

This is not to say that differences between small-and large-school writing programs have gone unnoticed. Some of the writing-program surveys that began appearing in the 1980s found that the type and size of the institution in which a writing program is situated can affect that program's fundamental nature. Generally, these studies find that campus environment—more than professional standards, graduate preparation, or other such external factors—determines to a surprising degree the effectiveness and content of writing programs. For example, in their 1981 report, Stephen P. Witte et al. conclude that, while programs differ dramatically from institution to institution, they "are each designed to address primarily the local needs of the institution, the department, and the student body" (120). Following up on this observation, Carol Hartzog, in her 1986 study of writing programs at diverse institutions, says that "the forces closest to home seem to be the strongest," with each program "being tailored to or resulting from its particular circumstances" (9, 14). Among local forces exerting such definitive pressure on programs, Hartzog cites "a tradition of liberal education" at some campuses and quotes writing directors who claim that the fact that their institutions are "small" or "committed to a humanistic education" (a feature of most small institutions) affects their programs in a major way (9). Edward M. White is even more comprehensive about the small/big difference. Reviewing studies earlier than his own, White reports that "campus size" is a factor "in determining what takes place in classrooms and who is doing the teaching," and that there exists "a relationship between campus size and staffing patterns," with "small colleges" tending to hire differently than large ones (*Developing* 19, 20). Citing at one point the findings of Stephen P. Witte and Lester Faigley's *Evaluating College Writing Programs*, White states that disparities even in faculty development opportunities "are in part related to the size of the institution" (23). Finally, Linda G. Polin and Edward M. White's findings on institutional goals and faculty retraining indicate that "the smaller the size of the staff" of a writing program, "the more readily they can be affected by composition program decisions" (25). Moreover, Polin and White find that, as staff-size increases, "the role of the writing program administrator changes" (25). Difference in size, then, corresponds to a panoply of qualitative differences in a writing program and its administrator's material conditions. To the extent that small programs are most often found at correspondingly small institutions, these and other differences from the practices common at large universities are most pronounced at the small school.

It is therefore all the more puzzling that such differences from the usual pattern of large-school WPA work go generally unreported in the WPA literature that has blossomed over the last decade or so. Although small-school WPAs do represent a portion of those who ought to be served by that literature, as we shall see in at least one crucial area of discussion, the literature may actually provide a disservice to the WPA at the small institution.[2] Perhaps more importantly, failure to include and examine in the literature the story of small-school writing programs may inadvertently imply that these programs have not participated in the progress that the emerging narrative of WPA work chronicles. Whatever the reason, the omission renders incomplete that narrative and prevents the WPA discourse community from seeing the small-school minority in its midst.

Since only one example of this unconscious omission and inadvertent disservice can be examined in the limited space of this essay, I will focus here on the way that the dominance of large-school culture within the more recent WPA record has resulted in the over-valorizing of power as a tool for the WPA. I will argue that this over-valuation has led to inexact description of the concept of WPA power in the record and, as importantly, has overshadowed other political instruments available to the program administrator. As it turns out, power, accurately described or not, proves of limited use to the WPA at the small college or university, while those political instruments neglected in the WPA record prove to be the essential tools of the small-school WPA. So, to the degree that these instruments are rendered invisible by an over-emphasis on power, small-school WPA work is rendered, in this crucial area at least, invisible also. Perhaps worse, the small-school WPA feels written out of the record, the growth of which ought to strengthen her purpose and role, not diminish it. Absent more articulate discussion of other political instruments than power, the WPA record is made that much less applicable, and useful, to the small-school WPA.

This is only one, though a critical, example of the discursive neglect of the small-school WPA in our profession, so I am using it "merely" as a window onto the small-school WPA's political culture, which is different from the majority WPA culture in countless other ways as well. In other words, my purpose here is not to summarize all differences between these cultures in such short space but to crack open this covered-over dissonance. My hope is that this opening will urge others to investigate more fully the world of small-school programs and their differentness from the large-school programs whose presence dominates the WPA record. Movement is already underway to investigate this "smaller" culture and its unique features. Along with colleagues at other small institutions, I have created a CCC Special Interest Group on composition in the small college/university, which held its first meeting at the 1999 Atlanta conference. I have also created a listserv ⟨small-comp@spu.edu⟩ to encourage small-school compositionists to support one another and begin gaining a larger voice in the profession. My intention in doing these things is not to be divisive. In fact, it is just the opposite: I wish to enlarge the record to include small-school programs and their WPAs not just to benefit small-school WPAs but to help their counterparts at large institutions as well. In the specific case at hand here, I hope to show that recording the small-school WPA's use of political tools other than power will enlarge the repertoire of instruments available to all WPAs for addressing their political scene. All WPAs stand to gain any time the current excellent record on WPA work expands to reflect the diversity of WPA work, since with this diversity comes a multiplicity of new options for doing our work well, regardless of our institution's size.

POWER AS THEME IN WPA "ADVICE" LITERATURE

A dominant concern in the WPA record is the political marginalization and general diminution in status of the WPA within the structure of institutions and in the teaching profession generally. Prime expressions of this concern are contained in the "statements" over the last decade or so, ranging from the Wyoming and Portland Resolutions to the CCC's "Principles and Standards," and, more specific to the case here, the WPA's own "Evaluating the Intellectual Work of Writing Program Administrators." Developing alongside these statements and, in many respects, elucidating them, a body of literature has grown up to advise the writing administrator on how to claim and use power to offset threats and dangers to her program. Perhaps this emphasis on power has resulted from the hostile institutional climate that has historically faced WPAs at most colleges and universities, large and small, and the quite understandable need for this literature to show WPAs how to get hold of the biggest, heaviest weapon they can, just so they can survive. Or perhaps it results from the development, within composition as a field, of a more valued and fully explicated identity of writing program administrator. (For example, Christine Hult finds scholarship on "power and the WPA" to be a good gauge of the healthy growth of the WPA status on campus and within the profession at large ["Scholarship" 126].) Whatever the reason, this emphasis is not particularly helpful for the small-school WPA, given the cultural conditions under which she works. Power is not the primary instrument of her political success, and exertion of power in the small-school setting may often be counter-productive, leading to the erosion of the WPA's effectiveness. The problem is exacerbated by the way the "advice literature" uses the term "power" to mean "influence" and "authority" as well. Often, the three terms are used interchangeably, leading to inexactness and definitional confusion but, more problematically, to the overlooking of influence and authority as political instruments for WPAs.

This confusion of influence and authority with power may derive from the prominent status in composition studies of Michel Foucault's claims about power's broad reach, as evidenced in, among other texts, *The Archeology of Knowledge*. While not wishing to challenge these claims on a systemic level or their general value until now to WPAs, I find more helpful, for the issue at hand at least, David V. J. Bell's articulation of the differences among power, influence, and authority, a differentiation which effectively allows for these terms' more discriminating application to the political conditions of WPAs. We can therefore use Bell to build upon the work-to-date on WPA power. Although, as Bell indicates, "in everyday speech, their meanings overlap" and "the terms are sometimes used interchangeably," power, influence and authority "each consists of a special, distinct form of communication" (15, 12). Power is based on "communications which involve either threats or promises" and "rests on the ability to manipulate positive or negative sanctions" (21, 26). It expresses itself as a hypothetical proposition: If you do (or don't do) X, I will do (or won't do) Y.

According to Bell, authority and influence operate quite differently from power. Authority relies not on threats and promises but on tradition and social institutions. Persons in authority, says Bell, resort (and need to resort) to power only when authority fails. Power, as understood in this distinction, may be direct and overt, but authority seems far "cleaner" and in some sense superior to power, especially when it rests not on the potential for violence or reward ("political authority") but on expertise ("expert authority") (Bell 40). In order to bolster its effectiveness, says Bell, authority "surrounds itself with symbols designed to inspire admiration and awe" (36). Further, authority relies on "credenda"—"things to be believed"—that stand behind and legitimize it (42). Authority's ease of use (with it, one can sometimes simply decree what one wants to have happen), its basis in deeply held, pre-existent beliefs, and its ongoing support by symbols may make it a better instrument than power for establishing the legitimacy of a position, from which benefits (including power) can then flow.

Influence (here in Bell's rendering at least) is, like power, propositional in nature, but the proposition is quite different: If you do (or don't do) X, you— and not I—will (or won't) experience Y. Influence, in other words, uses persuasion, in this case persuading people of the benefits that could accrue from their own acts. According to Bell, influence is the attempt to "affect the action" of someone "in the absence of sanctions (i.e., threats or promises)"—in other words, in the absence of power (24). It may take the form of advice, encouragement or even warning. Like authority, influence has the advantage of resting on pre-existent bases: prestige (either personal, positional, or a blend of the two) and obligation, a kind of debt (though not the threat of debt, which would be the effect of power) to which the influencer can appeal as she seeks to persuade. While none of this is to say that power lacks its uses, nuancing the discussion of WPA politics by including the subtler and perhaps more long-lasting tools of authority and influence can only enhance the repertoire of a writing administrator.

With these distinctions in hand, we can turn now to seeing how the advice literature, in its perhaps historically necessary emphasis on power, inadvertently may overlook or muddle the value to the WPA of authority and influence. Advice essays seem to fall into three categories. The first category contains essays that urge the WPA to seek power overtly. In doing so, however, they expand the definition of power until it engulfs the definitions of influence and authority. As a result, authors in this genre end up talking about influence or authority when they think they are describing power, or vice versa. For example, White [see next essay], in urging WPAs to overcome their resistance to power and begin using it against the "enemies" laying "siege" to their writing programs, recommends what he says are "three basic weapons" of power: "good arguments, good data, and good allies" ("Use It" 6, 7). But where is the threat of punishment or promise of reward (Bell's essentials for the exercise of power) in offering arguments or data? Aren't these really the tools of influence, and not weapons at all? Similarly, Gary A. Olson and Joseph M. Moxley advise WPAs to "remain sensitive to the subtle transactions of power...so that they can take actions to prevent the erosion of their authority" and "influence such things as budget allocations, commission reports, and legislation" (58–59). While we certainly could imagine taking separately any of these pieces of advice, the question that they together beg is how the terms relate to one another. When am I supposed to assert authority rather than power, power rather than influence? What's the difference between the terms anyway? A similar muddling exists in Rebecca Moore Howard's advice on how to exert "institution changing power" by developing the ability to communicate orally and in writing, and the knack for knowing when to use one or the other (37). But aren't these in fact the tools of influence? Then Howard says that no one except the WPA will carry out responsibilities in the writing program "unless you hound her into doing so, but find polite, cheerful, even indirect ways of hounding" (41). This statement inadvertently combines power and influence by using a metaphor of power—hounds threatening a prey—to describe an act of influence: polite, cheerful and indirect urging.

The second category in this literature features articles advising the WPA to share her power with others in the program. But since these articles, like those in the first category, dwell on WPA power, they undervalue, misunderstand or ignore the authority and influence that, along with power, are available to the WPA. For instance, Barbara L. Cambridge and Ben W. McClelland argue for a WPA role that is the opposite of campus "icon," to use David Bartholomae's term (quoted in Cambridge and McClelland 157). In recommending that the WPA become a partner instead of an icon, Cambridge and McClelland would have the WPA share power with others under a "federalist model" and serve only as the "center" and the "cultural glue" of the program (155, 157). But will true "federalism" occur when power and only power is distributed, while program authority might still reside mainly with the WPA, whether she wants it or not? Or does renouncing the role of icon mean giving up authority as well as power? Might it be beneficial to remain the writing icon while sharing power with "partners," since iconic status gives the WPA authority through supplying her with Bell's "credenda" and symbols of expertise? Such authority might make the WPA a more effective "cultural glue." Moreover, what is the role of influence—for rhetoricians like us, perhaps the most valuable political instrument—in the life of WPA-as-hub? As helpful as its idea of power-sharing may be, the Cambridge/McClelland model, by encouraging the WPA to disperse her power without considering the potential roles authority and influence can play in her effective leadership, might inadvertently leave the WPA without political tools. She could then end up being not the center of campus writing efforts but a peripheral functionary, her program vulnerable to political assaults from outside.

Other authors in this power-sharing category also help the WPA deal with the problematics of power but may prove less helpful in determining power's exact relationship to other political tools. Jeanne Gunner writes that, in a "truly professional program,...authority would come from a synthesis of informed instructors and the program they develop" and not from "a single person assigned...autocratic power" (13). A welcomed way of describing a good program, but some questions nevertheless arise. Does distribution of authority lead automatically to distribution of power? While the ideas of sharing authority and sharing power have real value for a program, how does this casual equation of authority and power help the WPA understand the precise natures and specific uses of these very different political instruments? Hult also recommends the dispersal of power as she argues, using political systems as analogy, that the best form of a writing program is a "constitutional democracy" populated by a staff of "well-trained, professional writing experts" for whom the WPA is a "representative" ("Politics" 48). This WPA seems neither "icon" nor "partner," so it is difficult to say exactly what relationship exists between distributed power and authority. Note also that, all matters of authority aside, neither Gunner nor Hult conceives of a role for influence and its relation to either power or authority. Once again, a quite natural preoccupation with power (here casually blended with authority) muddles examination of all the political tools available to a WPA and how they might work together.

The final category of advice literature, characterized as feminist or "post-masculinist" by its authors, recommends giving power away entirely, with little if any reference to the benefits or drawbacks of authority and influence. It rejects the Olson/Moxley "patriarchal/bureaucratic model because it [the model] emphasizes control rather than collaboration" and instead urges the feminist WPA to forgo "the illusion of control" (Dickson 144, 148). In this construction of writing program administration, "faculties should collaboratively direct writing programs themselves," and "the concept of community in which leadership is shared can be substituted for the notion of hierarchy" in a writing program (Dickson 140; Miller 55). Ironically, in its preoccupation with power—if only to stand over against it—the feminist/post-masculinist political model provides helpful antidotes to the abuse of power but seemingly fails to imagine other political tools, and specifically the tool of influence, that might be more attractive than power to a non-patriarchal, non-hierarchical WPA. It also seems to overlook the possibilities inherent in the authority stemming from a WPA's iconic status. Would a feminist WPA, by definition, need to renounce authority along with power, or could she develop a new and exciting kind of program authority, based on WPA as icon of post-masculinist administrative methods? Absent authority and influence and having renounced power, does the feminist WPA become, from an institutional standpoint at least, thoroughly de-politicized? The way out of this win-but-lose dilemma may reside in examining small-school political practices with reference to the political instruments under discussion here.

SMALL-CAMPUS POLITICAL CULTURE AND THE WPA'S ROLE

In its assumption of general applicability, the advice literature has come to stand as totalizing statement of the WPA's political condition. At this point, it is helpful to recall, however, that the earlier-cited program surveys from the 1980s noted how programs vary in dramatic ways according to their size and the size of their institution. This being the case, we should focus on the small campus and its WPA in order to enlarge the WPA record. In the process, we can offer a potential corrective to that record's inscribing of power as the predominant, if not sole political instrument available to the program administrator. Once we focus on the small-school milieu, we see that the importance of and availability to the small-school WPA of power, authority, and influence runs in reverse of this ordering. The three also relate to one another in complex ways. Of the three, influence is easily the most necessary to the small-school WPA, while authority may be the most available. The solo exertion of power when it is available, which isn't often, can prove problematic and even dangerous. Understanding the political culture of small institutions can thus deepen and enrich general understanding of the WPA position.

AUTHORITY

The first difference between small-school composition programs and those inscribed in the majority of WPA narratives relates to the political status of the small-school WPA. As much as some small-school WPAs, like their large-school counterparts, might like to rid themselves of it, there seems no way for the small-school WPA to abjure the role of writing "icon" or composition's symbolic authority on her campus. But, perhaps unlike the large-school WPA, the small-school program administrator can benefit enormously from willingly accepting this position rather than resisting it, as the advice literature recommends. For composition can be far less marginalized in the small institution—particularly if the institution is based in the liberal-arts tradition—than in the large research university because its image, its symbolic presence (if not its pedagogical reality) remains part of the way that smaller institutions continually discover how to mean and to affirm what they are. That is, writing instruction is often so enmeshed in the small school's self-enacting discourse—from its marketing and admissions materials to its claims of "certifying" graduates as "writing-proficient"—that its sacredness as part of the institution's mission is unquestioned. So to be an icon (the religious nature of the metaphor is appropriate here) of such an invested enterprise as the teaching of writing and administration of writing programs is also to become potentially a venerable symbol (but not merely a symbol) in and of oneself, if one wishes to be. This status can then secure the trappings that, as noted by Bell, support authority. In turn, the WPA can use this authority and its trappings to her advantage.

However, it is important to be clear about the WPA's iconic authority on the small campus. Like the cherishing of writing instruction that underlies it, this authority may be primarily, or even exclusively, symbolic, which makes it different from the authority based in power discussed in the advice literature. At a recent CCCC (Conference on College Composition and Communication) panel on the small-campus compositionist, one small-school WPA introduced himself as his campus's director of composition, only to add that his is largely a titular position, in that he does not actually "direct" anything. This status might seem ridiculous to someone used to WPA work at a large institution, but at a small one it indicates that composition is valued sufficiently that faculty and administration feel a need to personify it, to make composition the charge of a "keeper of the flame," even if that charge brings with it little real power and diminished direct authority. But this case also reveals that the position carries with it significant moral authority (Bell's authority based in expertise). This latter kind of authority gets exercised not in the hiring and training of TAs or adjuncts, the operating of an office solely dedicated to composition, or any of the other functions or arrangements that indicate hierarchical authority, although many small-school WPAs may have some of these duties assigned them. Rather, this kind of authority gets exercised at those junctures in the cultural life of the institution where issues or plans essential to how the institution defines itself are being considered. Because small schools are, well, small and therefore smaller than the program type embodied in WPA literature, the WPA can play a larger role in this cultural life; it is a matter both of mission and of scale. Given her iconic status, the small-school WPA is more frequently asked to be involved—indeed, expected to be involved—in this bigger sphere than is her large-institution counterpart. For this reason, the moral authority possessed by the small-school WPA can be enormous compared to the direct authority of a large-school WPA, precisely because the small-school WPA operates not in a bureaucratic structure of offices and TAs, but at pivotal points in institutional life, remaining detached perhaps from significant, direct programmatic power (the desideratum of Olson/Moxley and the bane of Dickson/Miller) and therefore able to appeal to higher institutional values than "turf." This also means that authority can be potentially long-lasting, the WPA less subject to the threat-and-promise marketplace of power.

INFLUENCE

The influence—that term most neglected in the advice literature—the small-campus WPA possesses can also be long-lasting, and is the WPA's most effective tool. The reasons that influence is so valuable to the small-school WPA range from the obvious to the complex. First, we should note that influence, if it is to be successful, relies on opportunities for persuading or convincing. The greater the number of occasions for persuading, the likelier the possibility of successful influence. A corollary to this observation also holds true: the more frequent the occasions for persuading, the greater the likelihood that influence—not power or authority—will be expected or required. So, on the simplest level, influence assumes a greater role than power or authority in the small-school WPA's role because the campus's size creates more occasions for interactions with colleagues and administrators than does the larger campus. Many small colleges or universities are located in small communities (e.g., college towns), and, even when this is not the case, many small schools become their own small communities. Colleagues from many disciplines may be neighbors, either literal or figurative, or close friends of the WPA, may belong to some of the same civic organizations, churches or temples, and perhaps share the same small locker room or work-out class. Even moral authority can only go so far in these situations, where familiarity demystifies even the most cherished iconography. The small-school WPA is as likely to talk to his college's president as his large-university counterpart is to talk to her dean. The president may even be, as has been the case at one point in my career, a friend, precisely because (among other things) the small-campus climate allowed him to see my work in building a composition program. The opportunities for influence (within the bounds of friendship) were therefore enormous. The use of what little power I possessed—by making threats or promises—would have been shallow and ineffective, and certainly would have ended a productive relationship. Of course, the use and abuse of power is a daily occurrence on small as well as large campuses. But when, on a day-to-day, relational basis, one must face colleagues she has just threatened or to whom she has just promised reward, the stakes and risks of power plays grow exceedingly high. And institutional memory tends to be far more durable on small than on large college campuses, in part because small-school players tend to remain in place far longer than do their counterparts at larger institutions. To sum up: if we wanted to adapt White's article to the small-college WPA's situation, it would need to be re-titled, "Very Limited Power: Use It Often, and You'll Lose It." Influence, on the other hand, seems a near-limitless and longer-lasting political resource.

Perhaps influence's effectiveness at the small institution derives ultimately from the more uniform and more consolidated campus culture found there, a culture arising frequently from historical roots in, and the ongoing valuing of, liberal-arts education. This consolidation around core liberal-arts values leads to fewer struggles about the fundamentals than one might find on the larger, more mission-diverse campus. However, since nearly everyone on a small campus is invested in these values, there are likely to be more struggles around translating them into practices. The small-school WPA, the first-year composition program in particular, and the writing program in general can become either victim or beneficiary of this reversal of what might seem the typical large-school situation, depending upon how well the small-school WPA reads her scene and uses influence effectively. For example, the idea that teaching first-year writing is central to the small-school enterprise is generally not worth disputing on many small-college campuses because such teaching is regarded as embodying a fundamental campus value. If an abolitionist were to try to dismantle first-year writing at many of these institutions, she would likely find no one interested even in struggling over such a (rightly or wrongly) uncontested good, and would get nowhere fast. But if the WPA seeks to make changes to the first-year program, then she may actually face a struggle because so many institutional players are invested in the program as an expression of deep institutional values. Paradoxically, the same campus-cultural investment in the first-year program that may provide the WPA with iconic authority also limits her power. (Note how the marginalization about which many large-institution WPAs might complain is not, for the small-school WPA, the source of powerlessness; it is the exact opposite, the centrality of her institutional role, that diminishes her power.) Perhaps this situation results from first-year composition's function, within the small school, as the place where students are expected to "invent the university" to a degree that Bartholomae probably did not imagine when he made this observation about the purpose of the first-year writing course (134). The situation shows how crucial it is for you, as the small-school WPA, to resist the advice literature's recommendations about seizing power and acknowledge that uniformity in institutional values renders you powerless in crucial areas. But you must also realize that all this attention to writing instruction as a fundamental good gives you a position from which you can influence all sorts of key players to assist and support you.

The same pattern applies to small-school WAC programs, which can seem both more feasible and more difficult to administer than their counterparts at larger institutions. Again, depending on how this administrative responsibility is played, a small-school WAC administrator can reap the benefits or inherit a perennial burden. Certainly, writing's centrality requires that the WAC administrator accept a greater level of campus exposure and perhaps higher personal expectations from others than her large-school counterpart is required to accept. This fact, coupled with two features of the small-school environment mentioned earlier—its relatively "flat" organization and smaller number of players, many of whom work in intimate settings with the WPA—makes the art of influence all the more important in WAC work. Calling on moral authority and citing the value of writing instruction is a start, but the success and survival of small-school WAC lies in the WPA's ability to accept "givens" about small-school writing programs and then shape, by using influence, the way colleagues and administrators invest in them.

WHY THE SMALL-SCHOOL NARRATIVE MATTERS TO COMPOSITION AT LARGE

All of these observations about the political practices of small-campus writing programs and their differentness from their large-campus counterparts do more, however, than point out an area where the literature's advice proves inapplicable to small-college composition. They also point to the many potential benefits of incorporating small-school composition's ethos into WPA practices and the small-school narrative into the WPA record that inscribes those practices. As stated early in this essay, the most obvious benefit is that our literature will become more accurately representative of all WPAs and thereby reflect the diversity of practices that come under the heading of WPA work. The fuller the record, the greater its richness and utility. Besides aiding current WPAs, "large" and "small," this enlarged awareness of what constitutes the WPA role and milieu may in turn enlarge the scope of graduate preparation received by future WPAs (many of whom may get jobs as small-school WPAs).

An equally important benefit comes in the way this move toward greater inclusion can interrogate large-school assumptions about WPA work. Taking the above discussion of WPA power as example, the small-school narrative might deconstruct the discourse of power found in the majority record. Simply put, one comes to wonder what the over-emphasis on issues of power tells us about the professional culture of WPAs. Are we unempowered liberatory pedagogists trying to improve our programs (the attractive self-portrait we frequently invoke), or are we really "boss compositionists" fixated on the means for strengthening our positions (Sledd 5)? Or even when we recommend sharing/giving away power, do we really just want to get rid of it because the idea of being powerful goes against this liberatory self-image, and not because we genuinely want to empower others? Our own discursive preoccupations may disguise our intentions superficially but reveal them on a profounder level. Tempering our power-talk with observations about authority and influence might instigate a profound cultural shift in our work. Greater attention, by all WPAs, to iconic "expert" authority and especially to influence could not only make us more effective in our positions by complementing our awareness of power's role; it could also make us potential agents in a larger political sea-change in our institutions. Instead of accumulating power or even distributing it among those we choose, we could try to transcend the marketplace of threats and promises altogether and rely on "expert" authority and influence to get our work done. Using these far more equitable and participatory political instruments might help make the politics of our programs and institutions, in turn, more equitable and participatory. Moreover, discussion of the values related to the liberal-arts orientation frequently associated with small-school composition might counteract tendencies in composition/rhetoric to acquiesce in literacy education aimed merely at preparing students for the world of work. I have in mind here the approach to literacy training that assumes it is egalitarian because it helps students gain an employment skill which, in turn, supposedly enables them to participate more fully in the world at large. The underpinnings of this approach often go ideologically unexamined in the discipline (cf. Crowley). No doubt, to someone advocating this purpose for literacy training, a liberal-arts approach to teaching writing could feel the opposite of egalitarian: elitist and impractical, in the original sense of the word. What Gee, Hull and Lankshear show, however, is that students, whatever their preparation, are going to be entering a "new work order" that is hardly an egalitarian place to live or labor and looks more like a place where the possession of skills merely guarantees life-long exploitation (xi). Given this new "order," literacy training that is de facto vocational may unwittingly cooperate in students' oppression. In contrast, writing instruction with a liberal-arts orientation—which, like all liberal-arts practices, is founded in critique—could prepare students to offer resistance to newly emerging oppressive labor configurations and contribute strongly to a liberatory pedagogy. All these visions or re-visions of dominant assumptions in our work, then, might not just stop our profession from believing that large programs are the norm and their practices therefore normal; they also might aid the WPA, "large" or "small," in creating institutional political cultures and pedagogical practices that model a truly just public sphere, one in which critique, influential persuasion, and appeals to reliable authority help all of us resist the raw exercise of power and avoid becoming inadvertent agents of the oppression we claim to despise.

Nor should we overlook the benefits to small-school WPAs and their programs that this newly enlarged disciplinary record might provide. Unlike many of their colleagues at research institutions, most small-college professionals receive only modest support for research and publication. Yet, increasingly, they are expected to undertake a full program of research and active engagement with the profession. Given the fact that most small-school WPAs must still carry heavy teaching loads, full committee assignments, and advising responsibilities—all on top of writing-program duties—the material conditions of their employment often conflict with these increased research expectations, and small-school WPAs can feel pulled in too many directions at once—even more so than their large-school counterparts. The unfortunate result of this over-multiplication of tasks may be denial of tenure or promotion, and the compiling of a record of achievements in areas honored and valued at one's home institution (e.g., "service") but of diminished value on the job market, even when applying for openings at other small institutions. This situation needs public airing at professional meetings and in the profession's journals; it may well be one of the greatest difficulties in material conditions extant in the field, yet it remains discursively unexamined. Needless to say, increased receptivity at those meetings and in those journals to scholarship based in the small-school setting would both inspire small-college WPAs and provide them with ready-made avenues of research to enter. Writing the small school into the WPA record will benefit both the profession and all its diverse members.

NOTES

1. I realize that "small school" is an easily contested term. I am using it here to identify four-year institutions that offer undergraduate education primarily, if not exclusively, and therefore rarely employ teaching assistants in large composition programs overseen by the WPA. Instead, small schools frequently use full-time tenured or tenure-track faculty (including literature faculty) to teach composition on the first-year as well as other levels, using only a small pool of adjuncts (though

this practice is changing). These institutions often adhere to some ethos associated with being small or relatively small in size—e.g., a teaching (vs. research) orientation, a liberal-arts mission, individualized student attention. Typically, they enroll 2,000–3,000 students, though some "small" regional universities may have as many as 5,000 undergraduates. No single Carnegie Foundation category captures entirely the diverse small-college/university cohort as I and others conceive of it, however, and small schools range in ranking from "elite" to "non-competitive" in student selection. In any case, the institutions I am describing here all regard their smallness as a feature tied centrally to their identity. So, in essence, I am considering an institution "small" if it considers itself so, and acts according to practices it associates with its small size. A working definition only!

2. Determining just how many small-school writing programs exist is difficult if not impossible, given current data. In the Modern Language Association's most recent survey of English departments, 243 of the 524 departments responding to the survey, or 46 percent, were departments in institutions with enrollments under 5,000, which qualifies them as "small" as defined in note 1. However, since 30 percent of respondents to the survey were departments in two-year institutions, it is impossible to determine how many of the 243 small institutions are four-year colleges/universities—the subject of this essay. The MLA survey goes on to report that over 95 percent of all four-year institutions offer courses in "English composition." For what it is worth, then, it is safe to assume that nearly all small colleges/universities have writing programs (and most of these a WPA?), whatever the actual number of those programs may be (Huber 37).

WORKS CITED

Bartholomae, David. "Inventing the University." *When a Writer Can't Write and Other Composing Problems.* Ed. Mike Rose. New York: Guilford, 1995: 134–65.

Bell, David V. J. *Power, Influence and Authority: An Essay in Political Linguistics.* New York: Oxford UP, 1975.

Brereton, John C., ed. *The Origins of Composition Studies in the American College, 1875–1925: A Documentary History.* Pittsburgh: U Pittsburgh P, 1995.

Cambridge, Barbara L., and Ben W. McClelland. "From Icon to Partner: Repositioning the Writing Program Administrator." *Resituating Writing: Constructing and Administering Writing Programs.* Ed. Joseph Janangelo and Kristine Hansen. Portsmouth, NH: Heinemann, 1995. 151–59.

Carnegie Foundation for the Advancement of Teaching. "Carnegie Foundation's Classification of 3,600 Institutions of Higher Education." *Chronicle of Higher Education* 6 Apr. 1994: A18.

Conference on College Composition and Communication. "Statement of Principles and Standards for the Postsecondary Teaching of Writing." *College Composition and Communication* 40 (October 1989): 329–36.

Crowley, Sharon. *Composition in the University: Historical and Polemical Essays.* Pittsburgh: U Pittsburgh P, 1998.

Dickson, Marcia. "Directing Without Power: Adventures in Constructing a Model of Feminist Writing Program Administration." *Writing Ourselves Into the Story: Unheard Voices from Composition Studies.* Ed. Sheryl I. Fontaine and Susan Hunter. Carbondale: Southern Illinois UP, 1995: 140–53.

Foucault, Michel. *The Archeology of Knowledge*. Trans. A. M. Sheridan Smith. New York: Random, 1972.

Gee, James Paul, Glynda Hull, and Colin Lankshear. *The New Work Order: Behind the Language of the New Capitalism*. Boulder: Westview, 1996.

Gunner, Jeanne. "Decentering the WPA." *WPA: Writing Program Administration:* 18 (1994): 8–15.

Hartzog, Carol. *Composition in the Academy: A Study of Writing Program Administration.* New York: MLA, 1986.

Howard, Rebecca Moore. "Power Revisited: Or, How We Became a Department." *WPA: Writing Program Administration:* 16 (1993): 37–49.

Huber, Bettina J. "Undergraduate English Programs: Findings from an MLA Survey of the 1991–92 Academic Year." *ADE Bulletin* 115 (1996): 34–73.

Hult, Christine. "Politics Redux: The Organization and Administration of Writing Programs." *WPA: Writing Program Administration:* 18 (1995): 44–52.

———. "The Scholarship of Administration." *Resituating Writing: Constructing and Administering Writing Programs*. Ed. Joseph Janangelo and Kristine Hansen. Portsmouth, NH: Heinemann, 1995: 119–31.

———,and the Portland Resolution Committee. "The Portland Resolution." *WPA: Writing Program Administration:* 16 (1992): 88–94.

Miller, Hildy. "Postmaculinist Directions in Writing Program Administration." *WPA: Writing Program Administration* 20 (1996): 49–61.[See previous essay]

Olson, Gary A., and Joseph M. Moxley. "Directing Freshman Composition: The Limits of Authority." *College Composition and Communication* 40 (1989): 51–60.

Polin, Linda G., and Edward M. White. "Speaking Frankly: Writing Program Administrators Look at Instructional Goals and Faculty Retraining." *WPA: Writing Program Administration:* 9 (1985): 19–30.

Robertson, Linda, Sharon Crowley, and Frank Lentricchia. "The Wyoming Conference Resolution Opposing Unfair Salaries and Working Conditions for Post-Secondary Teachers of Writing." *College English* 49 (1987): 274–80.

Sledd, James. "Why the Wyoming Resolution Had to Be Emasculated: A History and a Quixotism." *Journal of Advanced Composition Online* 11.2 (1991). 23 Jul. 1999 ⟨http://nosferatu.cas.usf.edu/JAC/112/sledd.html⟩.

White, Edward M. *Developing Successful College Writing Programs*. San Francisco: Jossey, 1989.

———. "Use It or Lose It: Power and the WPA." *WPA: Writing Program Administration* 15 (1991): 3–12. [See next essay.]

Witte, Stephen P., and Lester Faigley. *Evaluating College Writing Programs*. Carbondale: Southern Illinois UP, 1983.

Witte, Stephen P., Paul R. Meyer, and Thomas P. Miller. "A National Survey of College and University Writing Program Directors." *Writing Program Assessment Project Technical Report 2*. Austin: U Texas, 1981.

WPA Executive Committee. "Evaluating the Intellectual Work of Writing Program Administrators: A Draft." *WPA: Writing Program Administration:* 20.1–2 (1996): 92–103.

Use It or Lose It: Power and the WPA

Edward M. White
University of Arizona

Fortunately, the first time I encountered truly naked power as a WPA I was ready for it. Not consciously, I must add. But I had already been an English department chair for nine years, and then a statewide administrator in halls where nobody pretended (as they do on campus) that everyone is powerless. So I had absorbed from the atmosphere certain lessons: recognize the fact that all administration deals in power; power games demand aggressive players; assert that you have power (even if you don't) and you can often wield it.

I was now back on campus, coordinating a large-scale Writing-Across-the-Curriculum (WAC) program, with a wide range of responsibilities. And the Dean of Humanities had just let me know that I would be losing all assigned time, all clerical support, all faculty development money, even the pittance of a Xerox budget that had been part of the deal when I took the job. Without these funds, the program would fragment and then disappear.

"You can't do that!" I protested. "The budget for the program was designated by the university and can't be used for other things."

The dean was practiced. He knew that WPAs are normally powerless and that the WAC program (since it is outside of the departmental power structure) had no real way to fight back. He also knew that he was the administrator who was supposed to fight for my program, and he was knifing me in the back.

"I knew you'd be upset," he went on soothingly. "But this was all decided at the Chairs' Meeting. With every department growing and the budget holding still, the chairs decided that they needed that budget more than you did."

Another fact of power (in universities as well as in foreign relations) is that its most arbitrary use is always presented as if it were the most reasonable and logical consequence of facts out of anyone's control. In addition, the power stroke is supposed to have overwhelming support as a *fait accompli*. Despite myself, I had to admire the skill with which the dean was closing down all routes of opposition.

Like most WAC programs, ours was kept at some distance from the English department so that we could demonstrate that writing was the concern of the whole faculty. But my good friend the English Department Chair was still supposed to keep an eye out to protect WAC. That was, however, another lesson I had picked up: when friendship or even professional loyalty and self-interest conflict, self-interest always wins. I wondered briefly what she would say, soothingly, to me when I next saw her. Meanwhile, I was very angry with the dean.

"Does that mean you lied to me when you said that Humanities would look after the WAC program?" I said.

"Don't fly off the handle, now," he replied, turning away. "I said I'd do all I could to support the program. And I have."

The problem was clear. The University had funneled its support for the WAC program in the most logical direction, through the School of Humanities. The School had both autonomy and democracy in allocating its funds. But all power resided with the deans and the department chairs, and every chair's principal allegiance was to his or her department, so programs that were outside of departments simply had no say in how resources got spent. The problem was not really personal, though I felt aggrieved and angry at the dean and the chair; it was institutional. There was no way to fight back within the school, but institutional problems are the main business of central administration. I started calling central administrators.

I hit pay dirt on my second call. We had a new dean of undergraduate studies, a clever and ambitious fellow who was ready to talk. I went right over.

"Here you are," I said, after a few opening pleasantries, "a dean of undergraduate studies, without an undergraduate study to your name. How would you like to take our WAC program under your wing?"

I saw a glint in his eye. The only budget he had at the time was for his own office, and he was looking for ways to expand his role in the university. I told him the sad tale of what the dean of Humanities and the chairs in the school had done to WAC.

"It was inevitable," I went on. "How can the WAC program compete with the Art department for funds? Or even with the German department? We need to get out of the departmental competition altogether. Your office is the natural one."

He agreed, and set up an appointment for us with the Academic Vice President on the spot. Two days later, the WAC program was transferred, with its budget intact, out of Humanities to the Office of Undergraduate Studies. During the course of that year, incidentally, that Office gathered unto itself the Learning Center (from Student Affairs), the Advising Center (a new program), the moribund Honors program, and a handful of other programs that needed a strong administrative advocate and a safe haven for their funds. Support for WAC has since continued to grow. That dean thanks me for helping his empire expand, and he is the steady advocate of WAC in administrative circles that the program must have. My Humanities dean wasn't soothing or very friendly for some time. (He has since departed; shrewd and unscrupulous deans rise rapidly.) But he never attacked the writing program again; I was happier with his respect than I was with his useless soothing patronization.

This experience has important general implications. When I listen to new WPAs at the WPA summer workshops, I realize that power and the various uses of power are centrally important to most WPAs—but most of them are not only unaware of that fact, but resistant to it. We are writers, almost by definition against the establishment, hostile to the powers that be, opposed to that dread monster, "the Administration." Yet, as WPAs, we somehow find ourselves part of what we abhor: hiring and firing, evaluating and scheduling, fobbing off student complaints, and doing a hundred other administrative jobs, including the manipulation of power to protect our programs. Sometimes it seems better not to think about it, about power, about our own place in the power structure. Better just to stay with a conviction of our own powerlessness, amply affirmed by the deans and department chairs who (it appears) have *real* power.

But my campus experience made inescapable the fact that my job as WPA included being canny with power; the WAC program would have been doomed if I had not fought back against that "real power" and defeated it. I had discovered a kind of power that does not appear in flow charts, power that most WPAs have, and I was able to use it to save the program. What I did was to refuse to accept the condition of powerlessness. As a program director, I was figuratively able to pick up the WAC program, rescue it from dean abuse, and place it in a new home. In fact, I had more power than the dean of Humanities, though none of it was official. I had, appropriately enough for a writing teacher, empowered myself (a move Olson and Moxley propose for all WPAs).

Of course, it helped to be a tenured professor who knew the ropes. But I am convinced that any WPA could have done what I did. We must empower ourselves in order to do our jobs.

WPAs in general live schizophrenically, hating power yet wielding it, devoid of official power (for the most part) yet responsible for large and complex programs. Many are appointed for rotating terms by English department chairs who, as Olson and Moxley have shown, appreciate us principally for our accessibility and ability to communicate, that is, for our ability to keep things nicely under control without exerting any real authority. But the situation of most WPAs is one more or less under siege, and we had better take stock of the power arrayed against us, the power we have to fight for our programs, or we will not be doing our jobs. If we really don't want to deal in power, we had better step aside, or we will be doing more harm than good.

To understand our situations, we need to assess where the enemies of our program lurk, what their motives and weapons are, and how we can marshal forces to combat them. We also need to see where our allies are and find out ways to strengthen them and to keep them friendly. If these metaphors sound overly military and Machiavellian, you are either new to administration, or you act instinctively in ways that you prefer not to recognize.

THE ENEMIES OF WRITING PROGRAMS

We can divide the enemies of writing programs into two groups: the natural antagonists of any program that uses scarce resources (that is to say, any department or school that does not see writing as essential to its own concerns), and the elitist opponents of writing in particular, those who as a matter of principle see the writing program as an inappropriate or low-priority use of resources. I much prefer to encounter the natural predators than the people of principle.

The natural antagonists of all programs other than their own are relatively easy to deal with; you need only be alert to the usual attacks on funds for writing: upon small class size, decent salaries for writing teachers, and the Xerox budget, and you can face them down. (My dean of Humanities was an extreme case of this kind.) This means, of course, that you need to have someone representing the interests of the writing program when the resource allocations are made, preferably someone whose self-interest has some stake in the writing program. (This is why I had to move our WAC program when it became clear that those who were supposed to represent our interests were more interested in dismembering than promoting the program.) A very few writing programs have their own budget lines and are recognized as financial entities, but most of us must depend upon English chairs and school deans to look after the program. A careful WPA will use the three basic weapons of bureaucracy to deal with these bureaucratic foes: good arguments, good data, and good allies, mixed with caution and cunning.

The good arguments come easily to WPAs: the historical value of writing and rhetoric, the dismal state of freshman writing skill, the need for writing reinforcement across the disciplines, the sheer difficulty of writing well, the relation of writing to reading and critical thinking, the role of writing in all active learning, the need for small classes so that writing can be assigned and responded to, and so on. The powerful arguments for writing programs will persuade (and persuade again—the battle is never won) most of the natural antagonists, who will turn their greedy eyes to less important programs. Those who will not be persuaded must be circumvented.

The need for good data is less obvious, but careful WPAs will have on hand the entrance or placement test scores of freshmen, the drop-out rates for freshmen taking regular or remedial writing, the number of visits a month to the Writing Center, the number of students affected by the WAC program, the amount of time spent responding to student papers by the average writing teacher, the amount of writing done on the job by graduates, and other handy numbers. And I have already spoken to the crucial importance of good allies, particularly in the administrative chain of command. Routine bureaucratic weapons will usually prevail in routine bureaucratic skirmishes.

But the second group of enemies, those who oppose college writing instruction on principle, is much more difficult to handle. They have a view of writing as mechanics (or something equally elementary), or as a gift of the muse (or something equally mystical). In either case, for them, arguments, data, and allies are irrelevant; these are elitists or others living in a fantasy world, and they believe deeply that writing programs are not a proper part of higher education. Often (but by no means always) housed in English departments, they have an equal contempt for pedagogy and for composition, and their motives are sometimes obscured, even from themselves. Their perceived calling is for higher things, and they have no intention of debasing themselves by learning anything about composition, which they avoid teaching to the equal relief of the students and themselves. For this group (and I have encountered them on high school as well as on college campuses), any money spent on writing is a diversion from the serious nature of teaching—which has no very clear relation to learning.

Against such foes, only one answer will work: sheer power. It is futile to argue with them, for you cannot pierce to the hidden sources of their beliefs. The most difficult part of being a WPA is combating those who have only scorn for our enterprise, for that means assessing and using the forces at our disposal.

Since many WPAs these days remain untenured, sometimes not even on tenure track, the paths to personal power often seem blocked and risky. (This is an important argument for appointing only tenured WPAs, a trend that appears to be developing as rhetoric and composition gain prestige as scholarly fields.) The best solution to this problem is to avoid placing oneself in a weak situation; every prospective WPA must recognize that occasions are sure to occur that require the use of power. As the promised faculty shortage emerges in the 1990s, untenured faculty should avoid becoming WPAs until their positions become more secure. But this emerging policy will not help present WPAs already in weak positions. (This smacks of Will Rogers' advice on how to become rich in the stock market: buy stock when it is cheap and sell it after it has gone way up in price; if it doesn't go up, don't buy it.) Nonetheless, the first rule of administration is to avoid placing yourself in a position that is untenable, that is, in a position with large, unmanageable responsibilities but very little authority (read Power).

When the position of WPA is defined as one without power, it becomes a trap. Olson and Moxley, in their survey of English department chairs, turned up a classic definition from an unusually honest chair:

> Our director is not a faculty member. He is an underpaid lecturer without tenure! At one time, the freshman English Director was always a regular member of the faculty, usually an assistant professor. In recent years, we have appointed a Ph.D., who is *not* a member of the standing faculty. This has worked well, since it does not destroy the career of an assistant professor. The only slight negative is that the Freshman Director may not have quite the authority in the department that a member of the regular faculty would have. (55)

As the demand for specialists in rhetoric and composition increases, such demeaning positions will become harder and harder to fill by qualified faculty. Those who are willing to have their careers destroyed by taking such a job will have to find ways to fight out of an almost impenetrable wall of restrictions.

WIELDING POWER

But let us assume that the WPA has done reasonable negotiation before undertaking the position. What are the power issues he or she faces in relation to the writing staff, the English department, and the administration?

As every WPA knows to his or her discomfort, the staff tend to view the WPA as the boss, no matter how little power the position may in fact hold. Of course, some WPAs *are* the boss, with the power and the burdens that the term suggests; but most have only the responsibility of recommending hiring and changes of status. But the major power that comes with being perceived as the boss is the opportunity to improve the teaching of writing. A mere collection of syllabuses (not even the tenured full professor can fuss about that), followed by a meeting about them, can focus attention upon the best teaching going on. The same can be said of a collection of writing assignments, followed by a meeting during which teachers can explain the context and purpose of the best ones, including the role of revision and grading. Some WPAs also have direct power over texts and syllabuses, but most have only indirect power over these, achieved by focusing upon goals for the program and preferred ways of meeting them. Certainly, the most important aspect of the WPA's job (after survival) is the improvement of instruction. And most WPAs have substantial real and perceived power to accomplish that end.

One important exception to that last statement must be added, however: few WPAs can do very much with the tenured faculty who, on many campuses, still teach writing courses. Some of these tenured faculty do teach writing very badly, but I am convinced that most of them do better than rumor allows. They may use some old-fashioned techniques, but some research shows that older faculty are more receptive to new ideas than are the less secure beginners (White and Polin, I, 321–23). WPAs are often frustrated by the tenured teachers, who resist the instruction of workshops and seminars and, most of all, the newfangled ideas of the new hot-shot WPA. But more often than not, these teachers are giving good assignments and spending time with their students. Experienced WPAs tend to do relatively little with the tenured faculty; they will enlist them as mentors for the newer faculty (who may have something to teach their mentors), and waste no more time trying to tame the untamable.

Power in relation to the English department is another matter, one tangled hopelessly in the dispute over the professional status of rhetoric and composition as a field. If the department is aware of this field, or willing to consider the possibility of it as a field, the WPA gains power as any other faculty member gains power, usually through publication and other professional activity. Both CCCC and the ADE have published statements arguing that professional activity for composition faculty and administrators may include joint authorship of articles, textbooks, administration, workshops, and the like; it is important early on to seek a statement in writing that the English department (if that is where the WPA's future lies) will recognize such work. If not, the WPA must either find a department that will or will prepare to publish in the field of literature. In four-year colleges and universities, faculty power is still very much a matter of publication that "counts." Personal power in the department usually comes from off campus, from books, articles, and positions in national organizations. Two-year colleges are more ready to accept excellent teaching and superheroic administration as sufficient.

Some WPAs do not have to deal with English departments, which is both a good and a bad arrangement. It is a great relief to apply for tenure without having to prove literary scholarship, if you are focused entirely upon rhetoric and composition. But it is also lonely and dangerous to be out there on your own, with no department to protect you, dealing directly with the deans and vice-presidents. In either case, the trickiest power relation that any WPA must maintain is with the administration, which returns me to my opening anecdote. If you have developed some personal power, through tenure and professional recognition, and institutional power, through administration of a good writing program, you can manipulate the administration to the degree your political savvy allows. But, while most WPAs have not yet gained that degree of security, the power game must still be played.

A survey by the National Center for Research to Improve Postsecondary Teaching and Learning (NCRIPTAL) discovered that administrators "view faculty members as much more powerful than faculty members view themselves. This discrepancy suggests that either administrators overestimate the power of faculty or that faculty are unaware of the influence they actually possess" (4). This administrative perception of power is doubly true for those faculty administering academic programs; most administrators simply cannot conceive how powerless most WPAs feel themselves to be. However powerless the WPA may feel, the administration often feels otherwise, and it is essential for the writing program that the WPA foster this illusion as much as possible. And it is not wholly an illusion, since power is ultimately a matter of perception.

The WPA has much power inherent in the position. A well-run composition program is a power base, since it frees administrators from what they fear most: constant harassment from discontented students and faculty. Furthermore, the writing ability that WPAs usually possess is, as we tell our students, an instrument of power. Some WPAs are fearsome memo writers, aware of the value of crucial copies to key people (the "cc" at the bottom), and are spared depredations from terror of their pens and keyboards. Others are quick draws at a survey; they know that few faculty are happy with the writing skills of their students, and they can always come up with fresh data to demonstrate the value of their work (and, incidentally, drum up support at the same time).

Another source of power for the WPA comes from the profession itself. Many WPAs have fostered networks locally, or even nationally, upon which they can draw for help: letters of support or evaluation, evidence of practice elsewhere, statements of professional standards, and the like. The summer seminar for WPAs sponsored by WPA is a rich source of contacts for professional power. Another act of power is to call for an evaluation of the writing program by the consultant/evaluator panel of WPA itself; a team of well-known outside evaluators taking the writing program seriously represents the kind of power that administrators are accustomed to listening to carefully.

The final source of all administrative power is risky: the power to resign. However indispensable you may feel yourself to be, never make that threat unless you are really prepared to do it, for the odds are that your resignation will be accepted, regretfully, but with some internal rejoicing. A resignation is like war, a failure of diplomacy, and a threat to resign is like a threat to declare war. And like war, a resignation in pique leaves a real mess for someone else to clean up. Nonetheless, sometimes this last resort is the only way to get the attention of the people who hold funds. The next WPA is the one to profit from a resignation, a tactic only the tenured are likely to contemplate.

This paper is, I notice, governed by military metaphors, not the kind of thing we are used to reading in these polite pages about writing and teaching. But I remember a brief conversation about power at the 1989 WPA Summer Workshop which keeps convincing me that these issues need to be brought to the surface. One member of the group said, "If we have learned anything at all from the Women's Movement, we ought to have learned that we can gain power by simply asserting that we have it."

"In some cases, yes," replied a veteran. "But we have also learned that if you assert power you don't have, you can be slapped down pretty quickly. Power games really *matter* at work, just as they do at home."

Power is in some ways like money or sex; it is only of pressing importance if you have none. But those with official power wield it so naturally and, often, so skillfully, that those on the receiving end never know what hit them. Administrators, including WPAs, cannot afford the luxury of powerlessness. The only way to do the job of a WPA is to be aware of the power relationships we necessarily conduct, and to use the considerable power we have for the good of our program.

WORKS CITED

NCRIPTAL. *Update*. 2 1989–90.

Olson, Gary A., and Joseph M. Moxley. "Directing Freshman Composition: The Limits of Authority." *College Composition and Communication* 40 (1989): 51–59.

White, Edward M., and Linda Polin. *Research in Effective Teaching of Writing: Final Report*. (2 vols.) Washington: NIE, 1986. ERIC Document ED 275 007.

PART III

TEACHING ASSISTANT TRAINING AND STAFF DEVELOPMENT

A Selection of Strategies for Training Teaching Assistants

Irene Ward
Kansas State University

Merry Perry
University of South Florida

What are the most current theories about effective teaching assistant (TA) training? What are some of the best TA training practices? How can I train TAs with limited financial and faculty support? What topics should I include in a TA training program? What do TAs need to know before they enter the classroom? How will enhancing TA training alleviate my job stress?

These and similar questions continue to challenge writing program administrators (WPAs) who supervise graduate TAs. If you seek answers to one or more of these questions, then this overview of relevant issues and practices will be of special interest to you. First, we suggest that you conceptualize this training as a learning process related to and influenced by the material, psychological, and social circumstances of TAs. Next we provide program evaluation questions and describe what to do with this information. Then we offer two important lists: recommended minimum practices—a basic template for training—and suggestions to improve an existing program. Finally, we suggest various ways to enhance the professional development of TAs. We also include a useful bibliography for TA training, teacher education, and composition instruction. We don't pretend to have all or even most of the answers on how to conduct successful training; instead, our goal is to supplement the existing literature by providing a useful resource to which you can repeatedly refer as you create, develop, or enhance your training program.

INTRODUCTION

TA training programs, like the writing programs they serve, have evolved to meet the needs of particular programs and institutions. We are all familiar with the nationwide increase in undergraduate enrollment, the increasing number of part-time instructors employed by academic institutions, and the financial challenges associated with these circumstances. As the children of baby boomers reach college age over the next ten years, university enrollments will increase exponentially. Who is going to teach these new students?

English departments can hire either four part-timers—TAs and adjuncts—or one full-time faculty member (assuming a full-time line is available). Few institutions can afford to staff all of their courses with full-timers, so part-time workers are needed to get the job done. (This situation is not new; part-timers have been part of the academic workforce since the early twentieth century.) Moreover, part-time instructors often teach a large percentage of an English department's writing courses, especially first-year composition. According to the "Final Report of the MLA Committee on Professional Employment," a sample of English departments in 1996–97 revealed that in Ph.D.-granting departments, TAs taught 63 percent and part-timers 19 percent of first-year writing courses. In MA-granting departments, TAs taught 11 percent and part-timers 42 percent (29). These statistics reveal the widespread use of TAs and part-time instructors in postsecondary writing courses across the nation.

In 1989, Jody Nyquist, Robert Abbott, and Donald Wulff called upon universities to develop TA training programs or face the fact that "the 500,000 new professors who will be needed by 2014 will probably not be prepared to teach undergraduates" (9). As of this writing (June 2000), the field of English studies is still dealing with a glut of new Ph.D.s, largely because many departments depend on graduate students to teach lower-division writing courses. Thus, the question remains unanswered: are we training the new professoriate or are we training inexpensive temporary workers who eventually will have to find work in areas outside academia? Whatever the answer may be, the simple fact remains: TAs need training both before and during their stint as instructors. Therefore, you will want to provide TAs with the best possible training so that they learn how to accomplish their jobs in an efficient manner, enhance undergraduate education at your institution, and make your job as WPA easier.

As a current or future supervisor of TAs, you are probably concerned about the increasing number of TAs used to staff writing courses at your institution. While some critics may bemoan the "corporatization" of the university and the "exploitation" of graduate students as writing instructors, you have a more immediate problem at hand: how to provide quality training to TAs in the least expensive and most efficient manner possible. Before we discuss some of the most effective ways to train TAs, we'd like you to consider how you conceptualize training.

CONCEPTUALIZING TA TRAINING

According to Nyquist, Abbott, and Wulff, instead of assuming that TAs "can directly apply whatever instructional skills or information we give them," we need to conceptualize TA training as a process that focuses on and seeks to understand the multiple and interrelated dimensions of the TA experience (11). Some of these important dimensions include the individual characteristics and needs of TAs, the relationships TAs have with one another, the demands of undergraduate students, the "expectations of supervisors and administrators, and, sometimes, the requirements of instructional developers" (11). This final dimension has become increasingly important in computerized learning environments that are often designed by someone other than the instructor. In short, the most effective conceptualization of TA training considers the multiple subject positions that TAs inhabit; the relationships between TAs, students, administrators, and supervisors; and the circumstances of a particular writing program.

Whether or not TAs will become future professors or move on to other fields, they are both teachers and students while working in your writing program. Just like anyone who begins a new job, TAs need to acquire a range of new abilities and skills. David Bartholomae describes how undergraduates learn to "invent the university" whenever they sit down to write an academic paper. He defines this process as learning to "speak our language, to speak as we do, to try on the peculiar ways of knowing, selecting, evaluating, reporting, concluding, and arguing that define the discourse of our community" (134). This description of what successful writing students do can also be applied to TAs who must adopt the role of teacher and learn an entirely new discourse. Bartholomae's list of "knowing, selecting, evaluating, reporting, concluding, and arguing" describes some of the activities that teachers are called upon to perform.

Most new TAs need to learn to see themselves in an entirely new way—as teachers. Thomas Recchio offers an insightful comparison between new graduate students and first-year students when he suggests that "both are trying to navigate in what seems to be a new discursive world where language is used in unfamiliar ways, where the demands for attentive reading, detailed analysis, and critical response seem to be increasing tenfold" (58). Recchio's analysis is useful; however, we should give TAs credit for their ongoing engagement with—and success in—graduate study. In order to assist new graduate students—many of whom become TAs almost immediately after acceptance into a program—we should treat them "like junior colleagues who are given all the support and help the institution can muster in order to succeed at their chosen profession" (McLeod and Schwarzbach 86).

TAs walk a tightrope between several subject positions: student, teacher, and scholar. Many readers will remember the disorienting effect of being treated as a student in one arena and then having to switch to being a teacher in charge of one's own classes. Brian Bly explains how GTAs "face a fundamental conflict between the position of authority they possess as composition professors and the lack of authority inherent in their roles as students in a graduate program" (2). Although this conflict is unavoidable, Bly contends that English departments can bolster TAs' sense of authority in the classroom by "recognizing the implications of their physical work environment; providing closer assistance from experienced faculty members, such as workshops on evaluating student writing; and inculcating a respect for graduate instructors as colleagues in the department" (2). As they learn what is expected of them, TAs inevitably face new challenges in both roles. A TA's first semester can be a challenging experience, and even those with teaching experience often find the balancing act they face overwhelming at times. Because some institutions pay paltry stipends, some TAs must become "freeway fliers" or "roads scholars," commuting between various teaching positions just to pay the bills (White 161).

In addition to teaching responsibilities, TAs must complete the course requirements of their academic institution. (Some universities now require nine or even twelve hours of classes per semester in order to maintain eligibility for financial aid.) Many composition instructors are familiar with the responsibility of teaching and grading the work of 2, 3, or even 4 classes of approximately 25 students per week. Add to this challenging situation the fact that many—if not most—new TAs feel ill-prepared to do their jobs, and you've created a stress-filled situation that would challenge even the best of us.

Many first-year TAs come to graduate school and their first teaching jobs with a great deal of anxiety about their performance in both their new coursework and new teaching duties. This anxiety can soon translate into low morale if TAs are not supported with workable strategies for handling the increased demands on their intellect and time. Effective training and mentoring should shift their focus from feeling overwhelmed to feeling excited about their newly acquired skills. This shift in focus will keep TAs challenged and interested, preventing them from sinking into paralyzing despair over their perceived lack of control in their new surroundings. As their abilities increase, TAs will become more confident and successful in their teaching and learning environments. By focusing on the positive aspects of TAs' experiences and abilities, WPAs can help TAs fashion themselves into successful members of the academy.

In contrast, focusing on TAs' anxieties may result in lower levels of functioning. As writing program director, you need to determine whether a TA is merely anxious about his or her performance or whether a problem exists in the administration of the program. Learning how to tell the difference between a complaint and a legitimate problem will save time and keep you focused productively on the program. When TAs come to your office with a concern about their workloads (and it would be normal for anyone in their situation to be concerned), listen attentively. Many TAs are sincerely concerned about their ability to do a good job. They may have been very successful in their previous educational and work experiences, but now graduate school and teaching are challenging them in unfamiliar ways. Clearly, some TAs have not yet developed reliable strategies for coping with new trials. They may set high standards for personal performance in many areas of their lives; thus, they are unfamiliar with the necessity of making choices that they may perceive as compromising those standards. One of the most important ways that WPAs or teaching mentors can assist TAs is to help them find ways to meet both personal and institutional performance expectations without becoming overwhelmingly frustrated by time constraints. In *Working Effectively with Graduate Students,* Nyquist and Wulff offer clear guidelines for the development of a planned, comprehensive assessment program (104–26). We believe that both ongoing training and assessment will help TAs learn how to negotiate all the demands of their experience.

Many professions place strenuous demands on personal time. Anxiety in any area—teaching, coursework, or scholarship—will affect the other areas due to the dynamic tensions among multiple demands. Our experience has taught us that TAs function better when they are challenged to deal with issues and given the ongoing support—practical information and positive reinforcement—they need. Often, you can alleviate TA anxiety by offering "how to" advice about specific teaching practices: responding to students' papers in less time, decreasing the chances that plagiarism will occur, dealing with difficult students, conducting successful peer-editing sessions, and motivating students. In addition, it is critical that the department provide a united front and support for what TAs feel are conflicting demands on their time and energy. A supportive director of graduate studies is a great help in being able to reassure students that "Yes, you are expected to do well in both areas" and "yes, you can do it." However, when faced with concrete evidence (such as poor student evaluations) that the demands of teaching in the writing program are in some way harming a significant number of TAs (and undergraduates), the WPA needs to review and perhaps reform administrative or training structures. (See Meek and Hult for a discussion of problem TAs.)

To be effective, the administrative and training structures of a writing program should help TAs reach a high standard of teaching effectiveness while supporting them in their roles as students. Fortunately for most writing program directors, many new TAs are creative and have internalized good teaching strategies by observing their former instructors. (Unfortunately, the reverse is sometimes true.) Thus, much of what a WPA does is help them make that tacit knowledge explicit by encouraging them to use and build upon already-known effective teaching strategies. One of the greatest joys in training new TAs has been the mutual learning process that occurs. For example, we present a practice unit that fits the goals of the program, talk about its rationale and pitfalls, give them the tips we've learned from teaching this assignment, and show them some possible classroom activities. During later classroom observations, we are impressed by the creative and effective ways the new teachers have built upon the bare bones we provided and have devised even richer classroom experiences for their students. In turn, we learn from watching them and gain improved practices to hand on to the next group of new teachers.

EVALUATING YOUR CURRENT WRITING PROGRAM

In order to build a TA training program that fits your particular institutional needs and circumstances, you need to conduct a thorough evaluation of your current writing program. Then you will be better prepared to make informed choices about which TA training practices might be appropriate, which practices could be instituted immediately, and which practices could be considered in the future. The questions listed below will help you to gather important information for designing your training program and assist in your evaluation of what is and is not working. (Also, see White's self-evaluation exercise, 209–19.) We also recommend an evaluatory visit from writing program consultants, if possible.

Questions for Evaluating the Contexts and Constraints of Your Training Program

Time: How much time do TAs realistically have for training? How much time do trainers have to spend with TAs? How much time do you have to make TAs "classroom ready"? How long does the training program last? Do you offer both preliminary and ongoing training sessions?

Space: What are the space restrictions for your TA training program? Can you acquire additional space for TA training?

Personnel: Who is available to help? Who could be made available?

Resources: Is there money to fund a summer training session? Can you locate money to fund extensive training prior to placing TAs in the classroom? Is there faculty release time for mentoring new teachers? How are *faculty* members and TAs compensated for mentoring and training? Is this compensation adequate? What other incentives might you offer for help with training?

Institutional expectations: How much program assessment are you expected to do and at what intervals? What is the reputation of the program? Are your courses required? Who does the program serve? Who are the stakeholders in the program— students, parents, other programs, and so on?

Students: What skills do they bring with them? What percentage of them are non-native English speakers? How many language groups do they represent? What kinds of computer skills do they have? Do they live on campus or commute? Are they traditional-aged students (18–22), or are they adults returning to school?

Structure and pedagogical goal of your writing program: Is there an exit exam? How can you help ensure that the course material and the assessment match up? Does your program have stated or even unstated expectations about what students should be able to do when they successfully complete a course in the program? What do you think the program teaches—general literacy skills, academic discourse, writing about literature? How does the program accomplish this mission?

The purpose of the preceding fact-gathering exercise is to help you gain a clearer understanding of your writing program's particular practices and expectations. After carefully considering your answers, you can begin to plan ways to improve your TA training program. (Also, this information might be useful when you attempt to obtain money, personnel, or other resources for training.) By comparing your current writing program and training practices to the two lists of TA training ideas that appear later in this chapter, you will get an idea of what you need to do to initiate your desired reforms.

In next section, we begin by considering the Wyoming Resolution's call for improved TA training. Then we offer our definition of minimum training practices, following it with a list of suggestions for enhancing an existing program.

THE WYOMING RESOLUTION AND TA TRAINING

Since the Conference on College Composition and Communication (CCCC) published the final draft of the Wyoming Resolution in October 1989, there has been a movement to improve working conditions and training for TAs following the guidelines set forth in that document: "Each institution should provide *adequate* training and supervision of graduate writing instructors, and this training should be conducted by someone with appropriate preparation or experience in rhetoric or composition" (CCCC Executive Committee 332; emphasis added). Unfortunately, the Wyoming Resolution doesn't offer specific suggestions for how universities can enact its resolutions, nor does it define adequate training. (Wyche-Smith and Rose.)

In contrast to the language used in the Wyoming Resolution, in 1998 the *ADE Bulletin* published this call to improve graduate education: "Departments and institutions should reexamine graduate programs to ensure that they offer the *highest quality* training in analysis and pedagogical methods and that they are responsive to curricular trends and available positions" ("Statement" 23; emphasis added). In what follows, we respond to these two different ways of describing GTA training by first suggesting practices that might define an adequate TA training program. We have not created this definition in order to denigrate those writing programs that fail to meet these standards. Instead, we offer this definition as a template that you can use to compare where your program is to where you'd like it to go. We follow our discussion of minimum requirements with a variety of suggestions for improving an existing program and offering the highest quality training.

Clearly, each WPA's ability to institute these TA training recommendations will depend on the particular circumstances of her or his writing program: financial and personnel resources, level of institutional support, and departmental support. We believe that WPAs who are dedicated to improving TA training at their institution can and should attempt to find creative ways to provide training and support. Not all of these suggestions require financial support; many of them simply require time and determination to implement. Finally, these descriptions are the result of a variety of ideas obtained from our own training as TAs; discussions in practica that we have taught; suggestions from various writing programs across the nation; and conversations with numerous TAs, writing instructors, and administrators.

In *New Methods in College Writing Programs,* Paul Connolly and Teresa Vilardi offer descriptions of 28 programs. (Also see Jollifee and Gibaldi and Mirollo for more descriptions of training programs.) Some of the elements common to these—and many other—training programs require TAs to:

1. Take a composition theory and pedagogy course at an academic institution sometime during their stints as writing teachers.

2. Attend a training seminar—ranging in length from a few days to two weeks—prior to teaching.

3. Be assigned to a faculty mentor who will observe and evaluate them several times during their first semester of teaching.

4. Attend a weekly three-hour teaching practicum that provides practical advice on how to be an effective teacher.

These four elements constitute the most basic requirements for a TA training program. However, we have expanded these elements to develop the following list of suggested minimum requirements for TA training.

Suggested Minimum Requirements for a TA Training Program

Prior to teaching, new TAs (and adjuncts) should:

- Receive course assignment(s), textbook(s), a sample departmental course syllabus, and a TA handbook (with both institutional and departmental information necessary for effective teaching) at least one month prior to the first day of classes.

- Attend an intensive TA training course (see Figure 3.1).

- Receive or have access to a first-year composition resource folder or bound packet that contains materials from experienced TAs. This material should contain sample exercises, class assignments, essay assignment sheets, quizzes on required readings, library exercise sheets, descriptions of successful activities, and other materials compiled from former first-year writing instructors.

During the first semester of teaching, TAs should:

- Attend a TA practicum once per week. In this course, discussion topics might include practical suggestions for teaching writing, various in-class writing activities, practice grading sessions, and methods for dealing with problems (see Appendix A for other suggestions). Also, students could

Topics Suitable for TA Training Prior to Teaching	Topics Suitable for Prior to Teaching, for Workshops and Ongoing Training	Topics Suitable for TA Workshops and Ongoing Training
• TA's Roles and Responsibilities • Institutional and Program Policies • Syllabus and Course Policy Design • The First Day of Class	• Fulfilling Course Objectives • Motivating Student Learning • Time Management: Being a Successful TA *and* Graduate Student • Classroom Management: Relating to Students and Dealing with Difficult Students • Explaining the Process Approach to Writing • Assessing Students' Work: Establishing Grading Standards and Responding to Students' Writing • Methods of Teaching Writing: Lectures and Presentations, Classroom Discussion, Peer Editing, Group work/Collaborative Learning, and Active Learning • Diverse Student Populations • Plagiarism/Academic Dishonesty • Conferencing with Students • Introduction to Local Library and Research Tools	• Teaching Multiculturism • Balancing Current Expectations/Responsibilities and Future Career Demands • Creating a Professional Teaching Portfolio • Composing a Teaching Philosophy • Teaching Problem-Solving Methods • Teaching with Technology (computers, listservs, email, web pages) • Using Media to Enhance Teaching (videos, slides, television, transparencies, etc.) • Teaching Students to Conduct Library Research • Measuring and Evaluating Student Learning • Learning Styles and How to Accommodate Them in the Classroom • Peer Mentoring • Professionalizing Issues • Assessing/Evaluating Teaching Effectiveness

Figure 3.1 Table of TA Training Topics
This Table is intended as an heuristic and can be altered and added to as needed to your training program

be required to present at least one ten-minute lesson appropriate for first-year composition (Baker and Kinkead).

• Be observed and evaluated by an experienced composition faculty member during the semester.

In response to the Wyoming Resolution and to the field's increased awareness of writing as a process, most TA training programs probably fulfill these minimum requirements. However, our goal as WPAs should be to transform adequate TA training programs into outstanding programs that combine useful composition theory with effective teacher training to create writing teachers who have a high degree of expertise. We believe that TAs should be viewed as apprentice teachers; thus, their experiences both as graduate students and as first-year instructors should provide them numerous opportunities to learn about teaching from effective teachers.

Suggestions for Improving an Existing TA Training Program

Prior to teaching, new TAs could:

* *Participate in extensive summer TA workshop sessions prior to the beginning of fall classes.* Depending on your resources and time, there are several ways to accomplish this goal. Some institutions begin TAs' pay schedule one month prior to the first day of fall classes. TAs are then required to attend a one- to four- week training session (we suggest incorporating most, if not all, of the suggestions listed in Appendix A). Or, if it's impossible to modify the TA pay schedule at your institution, you could offer a graduate course during the summer with a title such as "Teaching Composition to Undergraduates." Then, you might make successful completion of the course a prerequisite for TA employment. Richard Bullock describes a useful scenario for giving TAs supervised teaching experience prior to teaching their own classes. At Wright State University, an "Introduction to College Writing Workshop" is held four mornings during the week before fall classes begin. Any student accepted into ENG 101 is encouraged to attend, and "about eighty students attend each year" (11). New TAs attend training sessions; then, they work with experienced TAs to coteach this writing workshop to undergraduates.

* *Take two required courses: one in composition theory and one in composition pedagogy.* The theory course could provide the necessary theoretical background for the teaching methods modeled in the pedagogy course. Also, these two courses should be taught as often as possible by a rhetoric and composition specialist who is an experienced writing instructor.

* *Observe and evaluate experienced writing instructors—including faculty, adjuncts, and TAs.*

* *Participate in a full-semester internship with an experienced first-year writing instructor.* This will require some training of supervising instructors, but experienced TAs should welcome the experience and the vita line. Under the supervision of the writing program director, future TAs could be paired with experienced TAs and assist in teaching a first-year writing course throughout an entire semester. (The number of sections offered would depend on the number of new TAs teaching the following semes-

ter). Credit for this internship could be provided by a credit course titled something like "Practice in Teaching First-Year Composition."

- *Participate in a full-semester teaching internship with an experienced faculty member.* For example, the University of South Florida offers a graduate course entitled "Practice in Teaching Composition," where one or two senior TAs coteach an upper-level writing course with a full-time faculty member. Also, this same opportunity exists for literature students who wish to enroll in the course "Practice in Teaching Literature." This coteaching experience offers an invaluable opportunity for TAs to learn from experienced English faculty.

- *Participate in one-on-one mentoring/teaching relationships, observing and assisting experienced TAs and faculty.*

- *Meet with mentor TAs once per week to discuss any issues or concerns.*

Both prior to and during the first year of teaching, new TAs should:

- *Take numerous workshops on a variety of topics relevant to composition instruction.* For example, a committee of experienced first-year writing instructors (TAs, adjuncts, and faculty) could develop, design, and teach these workshops (see Figure 3.1 for workshop suggestions). For example, every semester the University of South Florida offers different optional graduate courses to enhance teaching abilities. Recent course offerings include "Master Class in Composition Theory," "Teaching Composition," Teaching with Computers," and "Teaching Literature."

- *Participate in a faculty-mentor program.* Assign each new TA to a faculty mentor who teaches writing courses. New TAs should observe faculty members teaching classes and offer constructive feedback. Then, faculty mentors could observe new TAs and provide suggestions for improvement. New TAs need numerous opportunities to observe writing classes taught by full-time faculty, adjuncts, and TAs. Also, this practice of observation and feedback should be constructed as a reciprocal, rather than evaluative, relationship in which novices and experienced teachers offer each other assistance.

- *Participate in a peer coaching program similar to the one initiated by Arizona State University in the fall of 1989.* In this program, groups of three new TAs first met to share "ideas to improve their lesson planning, classroom performance, and grading proficiency" (Cooper and Kehl 29). After collaboratively creating lesson plans and writing specific outlines that described "the goals for student behavior and the teaching strategies that would be used to accomplish those goals," group members visited one another's' classes twice and wrote descriptive narratives of what they had observed (32). A similar type of program called "cooperative observation" is practiced at the University of Washington. (According to William Irmscher, this program is "adapted from a program used at Indiana University under Michael Flanigan" [33]). In the fall semester new TAs are paired together; in the spring, new and experienced TAs form pairs. The three stages of the program consist of:

1. A "preobservation conference" where TAs define their goals for a particular class and "indicate any particular things they would like the other [TA] to observe"
2. A postobservation meeting where TAs discuss their observations in a descriptive, rather than judgmental, form
3. A final report to the director in which each TA describes the "value of the experience" (Irmscher 33–34). We suggest that this report be limited to a one- to two-page description.
4. *Become a member of a TA teaching team.* According to the size of a program, TA teams—composed of small groups of instructors who teach the same course—could form and meet to share ideas about successful pedagogical techniques. This pool of shared knowledge, teaching methods, and activities would be collected in the program's first-year composition resource folder (described above) and provide an ongoing way to introduce fresh ideas to classrooms.
5. *Participate in a TA mentor program.* Experienced TA mentors are paired with novice TAs. This provides an opportunity for new TAs to observe experienced writing instructors and gain assistance in developing creative classroom activities.
6. *Read a special packet of materials similar to what TAs receive at the University of Colorado at Denver.* Richard P. Van DeWeghe explains how "TAs receive our booklet, 'Notes Toward a Definition/Description of the Writing Program and Courses,' explaining the theoretical and research foundations for our program" (37–38). TAs need to understand each writing course's particular objectives. Also, a workshop could be developed wherein the packet material is discussed and analyzed. This might contribute to program unity.
7. *Create a professional (or teaching) portfolio.* When they first begin teaching, TAs should be given a list of materials to compile and save for their portfolio. This list might include the following items:

- personal teaching philosophy
- list of courses taught
- student evaluations—both typed prose evaluations and numerical evaluations
- vita
- letters of recommendation
- teaching evaluations from peers and supervisors
- list of honors and awards
- syllabi from all courses taught
- sample student papers

- evidence of teacher training (certificates from workshops, special training courses, computer training, etc.)
- evidence of professional activities
- documentation of service to the department, institution, and the field

This portfolio would serve several useful purposes. First, in the early years of graduate school, the portfolio would encourage TAs to reflect on and evaluate their teaching, scholarship, and service activities and accomplishments. Training workshops in portfolio preparation and revision could be offered every semester. Also, WPAs and/or teacher mentors could periodically review each portfolio, then meet with individual TAs to discuss their progress. Thus, this portfolio could provide a concrete and documented method of providing ongoing supervision and evaluation of teaching effectiveness. Moreover, the creation of a teaching portfolio would offer TAs the opportunity to engage in self-reflection and self-evaluation, while providing an invaluable tool when applying for scholarships, fellowships, teaching awards, and future teaching assistantships and positions.

- *Guest-teach one session of an experienced instructor's class.* Under the supervision of a trained instructor (faculty or experienced TA), new TAs could guest-teach one session of another instructor's class. In addition to providing useful teaching experience for the novice TA, this teaching session would allow the experienced instructor to observe, evaluate, and offer suggestions for improvement.

- *Create a teaching video by recording themselves teaching a class.* Then, TAs could exchange videotapes and make suggestions for improvement or conduct a self-evaluation. This practice can be a useful way to evaluate ongoing improvement in teaching abilities. (Keep in mind that the session being videotaped is performative in nature and may not reflect the everyday teaching practices of the TA.) When, and if, the TA eventually goes out onto the academic job market, this video might enhance marketability by providing further evidence of teaching excellence. Some universities offer videotaping services to faculty members as part of faculty development. Check to see if your institution has such services available.

- *Assist writing program directors.* Experienced and trained TAs can do this in numerous ways. Trudelle Thomas suggests involving "experienced TAs in training programs for new teaching assistants and faculty members (such as fall orientation or an ongoing teaching practicum for new teachers), perhaps by inviting outstanding teaching assistants to help plan the program, give guest lectures on some aspect of teaching at which they excel, or take part in a panel presentation" (48). All these activities also provide useful professional development opportunities to TAs.

These suggestions for enhancing an existing TA training program provide numerous opportunities for ongoing training, supervision, and evaluation of new TAs during their employment at your institution. TAs who prove to be outstanding teachers can be recruited as peer mentors for novice TAs. This cycle can be self-renewing as novices develop into experienced instructors and valued members of your department. Most TAs do an admirable job teaching first-year writing, especially considering their lack of extensive teacher training and the ongoing demands of graduate school. Also, many TAs bring a variety of creative teaching methods to the classroom. By enhancing your institution's training program, you can assist TAs in two important ways: reduce their stress, and increase their ability to be exemplary educators.

Besides alleviating stress and improving teaching abilities, enhanced TA training might make your job as a WPA easier. By educating TAs, you may end up avoiding many undergraduate students' complaints before they occur. The most common complaints that WPAs receive from undergraduate students include TA incompetence, grade discrepancies, and personality conflicts between students and their instructors. Many inappropriate teaching practices are a result of inexperience or lack of knowledge. (Of course, we all know exceptions to this rule.) By educating novice TAs about grading standards and the importance of keeping accurate records, and by conducting practice grading sessions that include new TAs and experienced first-year writing instructors, many grading complaints may be avoided.

MENTORING TAs

According to Carol Hartzog, "training graduate assistants to teach strengthens the program, at the same time preparing them for their own professional careers" (48). Besides assisting TAs in their ongoing development as writing teachers, WPAs (and all faculty) can and should mentor TAs (and all graduate students) by offering numerous opportunities for professional development. Below, we offer a list of suggestions for mentoring TAs. (Most of these suggestions also apply to graduate students who do not teach.)

Research/publications

- Offer graduate research assistant (GRA) positions—editing, proofreading, and/or research.
- Create a departmental newsletter and offer editing opportunities for TAs.
- Offer a professional seminar course on how to succeed in the job market. Possible topics might include: creating a vita, letter of application, and dossier; successful interviewing techniques; and improving professional development.
- Offer both a scholarly writing for composition and a scholarly writing for literature course.
- Encourage TAs to write papers for both conference presentation and publication.
- Offer to proofread/edit TAs' scholarly submissions.

Service

- Recommend TAs for university and departmental committee work. Offer these opportunities to as many TAs as possible.
- Recommend TAs for positions as editorial assistants, readers, and/or reviewers for journals.

Awards and honors

- Create departmental TA awards to be presented at an annual awards ceremony.
- Recommend TAs for departmental and university awards and scholarships.

As with being a TA, serving as WPA is a frequently challenging, periodically disheartening, and often satisfying job. The challenge of TA training in the twenty-first century is to view it as an ongoing process; like the writing process, it's in constant need of revision. We hope that this essay will help you and all writing program directors make the experience of training TAs a mutually satisfying experience for everyone involved. After all, we have a duty to all of our students—both undergraduate and graduate—to provide them with an outstanding education and a positive academic experience.

WORKS CITED

Baker, Mark A., and Joyce A. Kinkead. "Using Microteaching to Evaluate Teaching Assistants in a Writing Program." *Evaluating Teachers of Writing*. Ed. Christine A. Hult. Urbana: NCTE, 1994. 108–19.

Bartholomae, David. "Inventing the University." *When a Writer Can't Write: Studies in Writer's Block and Other Composing-Process Problems*. Ed. Mike Rose. New York: Guilford, 1985. 134–65.

Bly, Brain K. "Uneasy Transitions: The Graduate Teaching Assistant in the Composition Program." *In Our Own Voice: Graduate Students Teach Writing*. Ed. Tina Lavonne Good and Leanne B. Warshauer. Boston: Allyn & Bacon, 2000. 2–9.

Bullock, Richard. "In Pursuit of Competence: Preparing New Graduate Teaching Assistants for the Classroom." *Administrative Problem-Solving for Writing Programs and Writing Centers: Scenarios in Effective Program Management*. Ed. Linda Myers-Breslin. Urbana: NCTE, 1999. 3–13.

CCCC Executive Committee. "Statement of Principles and Standards for the Postsecondary Teaching of Writing." *College Composition and Communication* 40 (1989): 329–36.

Connolly, Paul, and Teresa Vilardi, Ed. *New Methods in College Writing Programs: Theories in Practice*. New York: MLA, 1986.

Cooper, Allene, and D. G. Kehl. "Development of Composition Instruction Through Peer Coaching." *WPA: Writing Program Administration* 14.3 (1991): 27–39. "Final Report of the MLA Committee on Professional Employment." *ADE Bulletin* 119 (1998): 27–45.

Gibaldi, Joseph, and James V. Mirollo, Ed. *The Teaching Apprentice Program in Language and Literature*. New York: MLA, 1981.

Hartzog, Carol P. "Faculty and Teaching Assistants." *Composition and the Academy: A Study of Writing Program Administration*. New York: MLA, 1986. 44–53.

Irmscher, William F. "TA Training: A Period of Discovery." *Training the New Teacher of College Composition*. Ed. Charles W. Bridges. Urbana: NCTE, 1986. 27–36.

Jolliffe, David A., ed. "Programs of Note in English and Composition." *Preparing Graduate Students to Teach: A Guide to Programs That Improve Undergraduate Education and Develop Tomorrow's Faculty*. Ed. Leo M. Lambert and Stacey Lane Tice. Washington DC: American Association for Higher Education, 1993. 77–85.

McLeod, Susan H., and Fred S. Schwarzbach. "What About the TAs? Making the Wyoming Resolution a Reality for Graduate Students." *WPA: Writing Program Administration* 17.1–2 (1993): 83–87.

Meeks, Lynn Langer, and Christine A. Hult. "The Problem Graduate Instructor." *Administrative Problem-Solving for Writing Programs and Writing Centers: Scenarios in Effective Program Management*. Ed. Linda Myers-Breslin. Urbana: NCTE, 1999. 30–43.

Nyquist, Jody D., Robert D. Abbott, and Donald H. Wulff. "The Challenge of TA Training in the 1990s." *Teaching Assistant Training in the 1990s: New Directions for Teaching and Learning*. Ed. Jody D. Nyquist, Robert D. Abbott, and Donald H. Wulff. San Francisco: Jossey, 1989. 7–14.

Nyquist, Jody D., and Donald H. Wulff. *Working Effectively With Graduate Assistants*. Thousand Oaks: Sage, 1996.

Recchio, Thomas E. "Parallel Academic Lives: Affinities of Teaching Assistants and Freshman Writers." *WPA: Writing Program Administration* 15.3 (1992): 57–61.

"Statement from the Conference on the Growing Use of Part-Time and Adjunct Faculty." *ADE Bulletin* 119 (1998): 19–26.

Thomas, Trudelle. "The Graduate Student as Apprentice WPA: Experiencing the Future." *WPA: Writing Program Administration* 14.3 (1991): 41–51.

VanDeWeghe, Richard P. "Linking Pedagogy to Purpose for Teaching Assistants in Basic Writing." *Training the New Teacher of College Composition*. Ed. Charles W. Bridges. Urbana: NCTE, 1986. 37–46.

White, Edward M. *Developing Successful College Writing Programs*. San Francisco: Jossey-Bass, 1989.

Wyche-Smith, Susan, and Shirley K. Rose. "One Hundred Ways to Make the Wyoming Resolution a Reality: A Guide to Personal and Political Action." *College Composition and Communication* 41 (1990): 318–21.

Additional Resources for TA Training

(This list of resources is designed as a supplement to the excellent bibliography appearing in this part's essay by Timothy Catalano et al.)

TA Training

Allen, R. R., and Theodore Reuter. *Teaching Assistant Strategies: An Introduction to College Teaching*. Dubuque: Kendall/Hunt, 1990.

Andrews, John D. W., ed. *Strengthening the Teaching Assistant Faculty*. San Francisco: Jossey, 1985.

Anson, Chris M., David A. Jolliffe, and Nancy Shapiro. "Stories to Teach By: Using Narrative Cases in TA and Faculty Development." *WPA: Writing Program Administration* 19.1–2 (1995): 24–37.

Anson, Chris M., and Carol Rutz. "Graduate Students, Writing Programs, and Consensus-Based Management: Collaboration in the Face of Disciplinary Ideology." *WPA: Writing Program Administration* 21.2–3 (1998): 106–20.

Bailey, Kathleen M., Frank Pialorsi, and Jean Zukowski/Faust, Ed. *Foreign Teaching Assistants in U.S. Universities*. Washington: National Association for Foreign Student Affairs, 1984.

Baiocco, Sharon A., and Jamie N. DeWaters. "We're Talking About a Revolution: The Need for Reform in Faculty Preparation and Development." *Successful College Teaching: Problem-Solving Strategies of Distinguished Professors*. Boston: Allyn, 1998. 31–52.

Baird, Leonard L. "Helping Graduate Students: A Graduate Adviser's View." Student Services for the Changing Graduate Student Population. Ed. Anne S. Pruitt-Logan and Paul D. Isaac. San Francisco: Jossey, 1995. 25–32.

Bishop, Wendy. "Attitudes and Expectations: How Theory in the Graduate Student (Teacher) Complicates the English Curriculum." *Teaching Lives: Essays and Stories*. Logan: Utah State UP, 1997. 192–207.

Black, Beverly. "TA Training: Making a Difference in Undergraduate Education." Seldin and Associates, Improving 65–76.

Bloom, Lynn Z. "Making a Difference: Writing Program Administration as a Creative Process." *Composition* 229–37.

———, with Thomas Recchio. "Initiation Rites, Initiation Rights." *Composition* 223–28.

Boardman, Kathleen A. "A Usable Past: Functions of Stories Among New TAs." *WPA: Writing Program Administration* 18.1–2 (1994): 29–36.

Bordonaro, T. "Improving the Performance of Teaching Assistants through the Development and Interpretation of Informal Evaluations." *Journal of Graduate Teaching Assistant Development* 3.1 (1995–96): 21–26.

Boyer, Ernest L. "A New Generation of Scholars." *Scholarship Reconsidered: Priorities of the Professoriate*. Princeton: Carnegie Foundation for the Advancement of Teaching, 1990. 65–74.

Brock, Mary Anne Browder, and Janet Ellerby. "Out of Control: TA Training and Liberation Pedagogy." *Sharing Pedagogies: Students and Teachers Write About Dialogic Practices*. Ed. Gail Tayko and John Paul Tassoni. Portsmouth: Boynton, 1997. 114–28.

Champagne, David W. "Your Role as Teacher Trainer of the Next Generation of College Teachers." *Champagne* 187–90.

Christensen, Francis. "The Course in Advanced Composition for Teachers." *College Composition and Communication* 24 (1975): 163–70.

Coles, William E., Jr. "Teaching the Teaching of Composition: Evolving a Style." *College Composition and Communication* 28 (1977): 268–70.

Comprone, Joseph J. "Preparing the New Composition Teacher." *College Composition and Communication* 25 (1974): 49–51.

Crowley, Sharon. "Terms of Employment: Rhetoric Slaves and Lesser Men." Composition in the University: Historical and Polemical Essays. Pittsburgh: U of Pittsburgh P, 1998. 118–31.

Curzan, Anne, and Lisa Damour. *First Day to Final Grade: A Graduate Student's Guide to Teaching*. Ann Arbor: U of Michigan P, 2000.

Davis, Charles A. *Handbook for New College Teachers and Teaching Assistants*. Kalamazoo: Western Michigan UP, 1992.

Donovan, Timothy R., Patricia Sprouse, and Patricia Williams. "How TAs Teach Themselves." *Training the New Teacher of College Composition.* Ed. Charles W. Bridges. Urbana: NCTE, 1986. 139–47.

Duba-Biedermann, L. "Graduate Assistant Development: Problems of Role Ambiguity and Faculty Supervision." *Journal of Graduate Teaching Assistant Development* 1.3 (1995): 119–25.

Eble, Kenneth E. "Preparing College Teachers." *The Craft of Teaching: A Guide to Mastering the Professor's Art.* 2nd ed. San Francisco: Jossey, 1988. 197–213.

Eison, James, and Ellen Stevens. "Faculty Development Workshops and Institutes." Wright and Associates 206–27.

Eison, James, and Marsha Vanderford. "Enhancing GTA Training in Academic Departments: Some Self-Assessment Guidelines." Center for Teaching and Learning Services, U of Minnesota. 〈http://www1.umn.edu/ohr/teachlearn/tasuper/enhance.html〉.

Gage, John T. "The Uses of a Handbook for Teachers." *WPA: Writing Program Administration* 13.3 (1990): 5–15.

Gale, Irene. "Conflicting Paradigms: Theoretical and Administrative Tensions in Writing Program Administration." *WPA: Writing Program Administration* 14.1–2 (1990): 41–50.

Gebhardt, Richard C. "Balancing Theory with Practice in the Training of Writing Teachers." *College Composition and Communication* 24 (1973): 134–40.

Good, Tina Lavonne, and Leanne B. Warshauer, Ed. *In Our Own Voice: Graduate Students Teach Writing.* Boston: Allyn, 2000. Graham, Margaret Baker, and Carol David. "What's Up on Monday Morning? TA Training and Freshman English." *Writing on the Edge* 7.2 (1996): 59–72.

Hairston, Maxine. "Training Teaching Assistants in English." *College Composition and Communication* 25 (1974): 52–55.

Hattenhauer, Darryl, and Mary Ellen Shaw. "The Teaching Assistant as Apprentice." *College Composition and Communication* 33 (1982): 452–54.

"How to Succeed as a New Teacher: A Handbook for Teaching Assistants." New Rochelle: Change Magazine P, 1978.

Jarvis, Donald K. "Improving Junior Faculty Teaching." *Junior Faculty Development: A Handbook.* New York: MLA, 1991. 57–70.

Katz, Seth R. "Graduate Programs and Job Training." Showalter et al. 121–30.

Kennedy, Mary M. "Does Teacher Education Make a Difference?" *Learning to Teach Writing: Does Teacher Education Make a Difference?* New York: Teachers College P, 1998. 166–88.

Knapp, James F. "Graduate Education and the Preparation of New Faculty Members." *ADE Bulletin* 112 (1995): 7–10.

Krupa, Gene H. "Helping New Teachers of Writing: Book, Model, and Mirror." *College Composition and Communication* 33 (1982): 442–45.

Lambert, Leo M., Stacey Lane Tice, and Patricia H. Featherstone. *University Teaching: A Guide for Graduate Students.* Syracuse: Syracuse UP, 1996.

Leverenz, Carrie Shively, and Amy Goodburn. "Professionalizing TA Training: Commitment to Teaching or Rhetorical Response to Market Crisis?" *WPA: Writing Program Administration* 22.1–2 (1998): 9–32.

Lewis, Karron G. "Training Focused on Postgsraduate Assistants: The North American Model." 10 Aug 2000 <http://www.ntlf.com/html/lib/bib/lewis.htm>.

Madden, Carolyn G., and Cynthia L. Myers, Ed. *Discourse and Performance of International Teaching Assistants.* Alexandria: TESOL, 1994.

Meyers, S. A. "Enhancing Relationships Between Instructors and Teaching Assistants." *Journal of Graduate Teaching Assistant Development* 2.3 (1995): 107–12.

Nemanich, Donald. "Preparing the Composition Teacher." *College Composition and Communication* 25 (1974): 46–48. Nilson, Linda B. "Course Coordination Between Faculty and TAs." Nilson 23–28.

Nyquist, Jody, Robert D. Abbott, Donald H. Wulff, and Jo Sprague, Ed. *Preparing the Professoriate of Tomorrow to Teach: Selected Readings in TA Training.* Dubuque: Kendall/Hunt, 1991.

Parker, Jo Ellen. "Fostering Excellence" *ADE Bulletin* 118 (1997): 22–27.

Pemberton, Michael A. "Tales Too Terrible to Tell: Unstated Truths and Underpreparation in Graduate Composition Programs." Ed. Sheryl I. Fontaine and Susan Hunter. *Writing Ourselves into the Story: Unheard Stories from Composition Studies.* Carbondale: Southern Illinois UP, 1993. 154–73.

Potts, Maureen, and David Schwalm. "A Training Program for Teaching Assistants in Freshman English." *WPA: Writing Program Administration* 7.1–2 (1983): 47–54.

Richlin, Laurie. "Preparing the Faculty of the Future to Teach." Wright and Associates 255–82.

———. "Graduate Education and the U.S. Faculty." Richlin, ed. 3–14.

Ronkowski, Shirley A. "Scholarly Teaching: Developmental Stages of Pedagogical Scholarship. Richlin, ed. 79–90.

Rose, Shirley K., and Margaret J. Finders. "Learning from Experience: Using Situated Performances in Writing Teacher Development." *WPA: Writing Program Administration* 22.1–2 (1998): 33–52.

Schell, Eileen E. "Teaching Under Unusual Conditions: Graduate Teaching Assistants and the CCCC's 'Progress Report.'" *College Composition and Communication* 43 (1992): 164–67.

Schuster, Jack H. "Preparing the Next Generation of Faculty: The Graduate School's Opportunity." Richlin, ed. 27–38.

Shannon, David M. "TA Teaching Effectiveness: The Impact of Training and Teaching Experience." *Journal of Higher Education* 69.4 (1998): 440–66.

Showalter, Elaine. "The Risks of Good Teaching: How 1 Professor and 9 T.A.s Plunged into Pedagogy." *Chronicle of Higher Education* 9 (July 1999): B4–6.

Smith, Jan, Colleen M. Meyers, and Amy J. Burkhalter. *Communicate: Strategies For International Teaching Assistants.* Englewood Cliffs: Prentice, 1992.

Swyt, Wendi. "Teacher Training in the Contact Zone." *WPA: Writing Program Administration* 19.3 (1996): 24–35.

Weiser, Irwin. "Teaching Assistants as Collaborators in Their Preparation and Evaluation." Ed. Christine A. Hult. Urbana: NCTE. 133–46.

Vesilind, P. Aarne. *So You Want to Be a Professor? A Handbook for Graduate Students.* Thousand Oaks: Sage, 2000.

Teaching Composition

Anson, Chris M., Joan Graham, David A. Jolliffe, Nancy Shapiro, and Carolyn H. Smith. *Scenarios for Teaching Writing: Contexts for Discussion and Reflective Practice.* Urbana: NCTE, 1993.

Bloom, Lynn Z. *Composition Studies as a Creative Art: Teaching, Writing, Scholarship, Administration.* Logan: Utah State UP, 1998.

Connors, Robert, and Cheryl Glenn. *The New St. Martin's Guide to Teaching Writing.* Boston: Bedford, 1999.

Corbett, Edward P. J., Nancy Myers, and Gary Tate, Ed. *The Writing Teacher's Sourcebook.* 4th ed. New York: Oxford UP, 2000.

Dethier, Brock. *The Composition Instructor's Survival Guide*: Portsmouth: Boynton, 1999.

Foster, David. *A Primer for Writing Teachers: Theories, Theorists, Issues, Problems.* 2nd ed. Portsmouth: Boynton, 1992.

Parker, Robert P. "Writing Courses for Teachers: From Practice to Theory." *College Composition and Communication* 33 (1982): 411–19.

Rankin, Elizabeth. *Seeing Yourself as a Teacher: Conversations With Five New Teachers in a University Writing Program.* Urbana: NCTE, 1994.

Tate, Gary, and Edward P. J. Corbett. *Teaching Freshman Composition.* New York: Oxford UP, 1967.

College Teaching: Tips, Strategies, and Methods

Adams, Maurianne, ed. *Promoting Diversity in College Classrooms: Innovative Responses for the Curriculum, Faculty, and Institutions.* San Francisco: Jossey, 1992.

Angelo, Thomas A., and K. Patricia Cross, Ed. *Classroom Assessment Techniques: A Handbook for College Teachers.* 2nd ed. San Francisco: Jossey, 1993.

Banta, Trudy W., et al., Ed. *Assessment in Practice: Putting Principles to Work on College Campuses.* San Francisco: Jossey, 1996.

Barnes, Louis B., C. Roland Christensen, and Abby J. Hansen. *Teaching and the Case Method: Text, Cases, and Readings.* 3rd ed. Boston: Harvard Business School P, 1994.

Bean, John C. *Engaging Ideas: The Professor's Guide to Integrating Writing, Critical Thinking, and Active Learning in the Classroom.* San Francisco: Jossey, 1996.

Blythe, Hal, and Charlie Sweet. *It Works for Me: Shared Tips for Teaching.* Stillwater: New Forums, 1998.

Boice, Robert. *Advice for New Faculty Members: Nihil Nimus.* Boston: Allyn, 2000.

Bonwell, Charles C., and James A. Eison. *Active Learning: Creating Excitement in the Classroom.* ASHE-ERIC Higher Education Report No. 1. Washington: George Washington U School of Education and Human Development, 1991.

Brinkley, Alan, et al. *The Chicago Handbook for Teachers: A Practical Guide to the College Classroom.* Chicago: U of Chicago P, 1999.

Brookfield, Stephen D. *Becoming a Critically Reflective Teacher.* San Francisco: Jossey, 1995.

Brown, George, and Madeleine Atkins. *Effective Teaching in Higher Education.* London: Methuen, 1988.

Champagne, David W. *The Intelligent Professor's Guide to Teaching.* Pittsburgh: Interactive Teaching-Learning Systems, 1995.

Civikly, Jean M. *Classroom Communication: Principles and Practice.* Dubuque: Brown, 1992.

Dantonio, Marylou. *Collegial Teaching: Inquiry into the Teaching Self.* Bloomington: Phi Delta Kappa, 1995.

Davis, Barbara Gross. *Tools for Teaching.* San Francisco: Jossey, 1993.

Eble, Kenneth E. *The Aims of College Teaching.* San Francisco: Jossey, 1983.

Erickson, Bette LaSere, and Diane Weltner Strommer. *Teaching College Freshmen.* San Francisco: Jossey, 1991.

Fisch, Linc. *The Chalk Dust Collection: Thoughts and Reflections on Teaching in Colleges and Universities.* Stillwater: New Forums, 1996.

Frye, Bill J., ed. *Teaching in College: A Resource for College Teachers.* 3rd ed. Cleveland: Info-Tec, 1994.

Huba, Mary E., and Jann E. Freed. *Learner-Centered Assessment on College Campuses: Shifting the Focus from Teaching to Learning.* Boston: Allyn, 2000.

Lowman, Joseph. *Mastering the Techniques of Teaching.* 2nd ed. San Francisco: Jossey, 1995.

Lyons, Richard E., Marcella L. Kysilka, and George E. Pawlas. *The Adjunct Professor's Guide to Success: Surviving and Thriving in the College Classroom.* Boston: Allyn, 1999.

McKeachie, Wilbert J. *Teaching Tips: Strategies, Research, and Theory for College and University Teachers.* 10th ed. Boston: Houghton, 1999.

Meyers, Chet, and Thomas B. Jones. *Promoting Active Learning: Strategies for the College Classroom.* San Francisco: Jossey, 1993.

Miller, W. R., and Marie F. Miller. *Handbook for College Teaching.* Sautee-Nacoochee: PineCrest, 1997.

Nilson, Linda B. *Teaching at Its Best: A Research-Based Resource for College Instructors.* Bolton: Anker, 1998.

Powers, Bob. *Instructor Excellence: Mastering the Delivery of Training.* San Francisco: Jossey, 1992.

Ralph, Edwin G. *Motivating Teaching in Higher Education: A Manual for Faculty Development.* Stillwater: New Forums, 1998.

Ramsden, Paul. *Learning to Teach in Higher Education.* New York: Routledge, 1992.

Royse, David D. *Teaching Tips for College and University Instructors: A Practical Guide.* Boston: Allyn, 2000.

Seldin, Peter, and Associates. *How Administrators Can Improve Teaching: Moving from Talk to Action in Higher Education.* San Francisco: Jossey, 1990.

———. *Improving College Teaching.* Bolton: Anker, 1995.

Seldin, Peter, Linda F. Annis, and John Zubizarreta. "Using the Teaching Portfolio to Improve Instruction." Wright and Associates 237–54.

Stocking, S. Holly, et al., Ed. *More Quick Hits: Successful Strategies by Award-Winning Teachers.* Bloomington: Indiana UP, 1998.

Taylor, Vernon L. Teaching Tips for Part-Time Teachers. 2nd ed. Middletown: Key, 1984.

Theall, Michael, and Jennifer Franklin, Ed. *Effective Practices for Improving Teaching.* San Francisco: Jossey, 1991.

Weimer, Maryellen. *Improving Your Classroom Teaching.* Newbury Park: Sage, 1993.

Wright, W. Alan, and Associates. *Teaching Improvement Practices: Successful Strategies for Higher Education.* Bolton: Anker, 1995.

Mentoring

Enos, Theresa. "Mentoring—and (Wo)mentoring—in Composition Studies." *Academic Advancement in Composition Studies: Scholarship, Publication, Promotion, Tenure.* Ed. Richard C. Gebhardt and Barbara Genelle Smith Gebhardt. Mahwah, NJ: Erlbaum, 1997. 137–45.

Lagowski, Jeanne M., and James W. Vick. "Faculty as Mentors." *Teaching Through Academic Advising: A Faculty Perspective.* San Francisco: Jossey, 1995. 79–85.

Malderez, Angi, and Caroline Bodòczky. *Mentor Courses: A Resource Book for Teacher-Trainers.* Cambridge, Eng.: Cambridge UP, 1999.

Wunsch, Marie A., ed. *Mentoring Revisited: Making an Impact on Individuals and Institutions.* San Francisco: Jossey, 1994.

TA Training Videos

In a Class by Themselves: Graduate Student Instructors Teaching at UC Berkeley. Videocassette. Berkeley: Regents of the U of California, 1995.

Becoming an Effective Teaching Assistant. Videocassette. Santa Cruz: Social Sciences Media Lab, U of California, 1988.

The Truth about Teachers. Videocassette. Santa Monica: Pyramid, 1989.

The Scholarship of Teaching and Learning: Implications for Undergraduate and Graduate Instruction. Videocassette. Seattle: U of Washington, 1999.

Enabling Teaching Assistants. Videocassette. Santa Monica: Pyramid Media, 1995.

60 minutes: Get Real. Videocassette. CBS, 1995.

The Good, the Bad, and the Ugliest of Graduate Student Instructing. Videocassette. Berkeley: U of California, Office of Media Services, 1990.

Issues on Campus: A View from the Laboratory. Videocassette. Santa Barbara: U of California, Instructional Development, 1988.

Teaching Assistants: Agents of Change Orientation Video. Videocassette. Chico: California State U, Office of Professional Development, 1991.

Preparing the Professoriate of Tomorrow for Teaching: Enhancing the TA Experience. Eight videocassettes. Seattle: U of Washington, Instructional Media Services, 1990.

Teaching Assistant Communication Strategies. Videocassette. Ames: Media Resources Center, Iowa State U, 1989.

Selected Web Sources

Bonwell, Charles C. "Active Learning Site Home Page." 15 Aug. 2000. ⟨http://www.active-learning-site.com/index.htm⟩

Center for Learning and Teaching. "Bibliography: What Is Good/Effective Teaching." Cornell U. 15 Aug. 2000 ⟨http://www.clt.cornell/resources/biblio/biblioteach.html⟩

Center for Teaching Excellence. "C.T.E. T.A. Cyber-Handbook." Tufts U. 15 Aug. 2000. ⟨http://ase.tufts.edu/cte/search_pages/tasearch/htm⟩

Eberly Center. "Additional Resources for Faculty and TAs." Carnegie Melon U. 15 Aug. 2000. ⟨http://www.cmu.edu/provost/teaching/bibliography.htm⟩

Indiana U. "Scholarship of Teaching and Learning." 15 Aug. 2000. ⟨http://www.indiana.edu/~deanfac/sotl/links.html⟩

TA Training and Development Program. "TA Developers' Network." U of Guelph. 15 Aug. 2000. ⟨http://www.tss.uogelph.ca/ta/tanetwork.html⟩

Teaching Effectiveness Program. "Faculty Development Centers Around the World." U of Oregon. 15 Aug. ⟨http://darkwing.uoregon.edu/~tep/links/index.html⟩

Training the Workforce: Overview of GTA Education Curricula

Catherine G. Latterell

Pennsylvania State University—Altoona

Teacher-training programs for graduate teaching assistants (GTAs) serve several important roles in rhetoric and composition studies. They hold historical significance because training workshops and pedagogy courses were often the only graduate-level composition courses offered in many English departments during the first 50 years of this century. Additionally, courses in teaching writing currently are required for graduate students who teach any course (regardless of their disciplinary specialization) in nearly all graduate programs in departments of English.[1] Thus, not only do these courses serve as an introduction or gateway to rhetoric and composition studies for most graduate students, but they are also the only site in a majority of graduate programs in English studies concerned with preparing teachers. Consequently, they play a significant part in preparing future scholars and teachers in rhetoric and composition and in preparing graduate students to assume the particular teaching tasks of an individual English department.

As a discipline we know very little about the general assumptions underlying GTA education programs. I, therefore, surveyed WPAs to learn the kinds and ranges of writing pedagogy courses required for teaching assistants.[2] Scholars writing about WPA issues or about the history of teaching college writing often claim that the training of teaching assistants has vastly improved over the last 20 to 30 years (cf., Bridges; Donovan and McClelland; Gere; Hartzog). Corbett's description of his preparation for teaching writing illustrates how most people describe training in writing instruction before such improvements:

> The English teachers of my generation were mainly, if not exclusively, trained to take over a literature class....But for the teaching of writing, which supported their graduate studies, usually the only training they got was in a rather desultory practicum, which met once a week and which dealt chiefly with the nuts-and-bolts aspects of the writing course (445).

Now, Corbett and others say, our GTA education programs are much improved. For instance, Paul Connolly and Teresa Vilardi, in their 1986 study of college writing programs, note that graduate teaching assistants "are more thoroughly trained and supervised than in the past, through courses, staff meetings, and classroom observation" (3). Certainly, they are right. Given the recent growth in rhetoric and composition graduate programs and the vitality of many teachers and scholars in this field, we can generally claim that GTA education programs are doing more and are doing a better job. What I sought to learn, however, is how we specifically approach GTA education: What patterns, if any, can be discerned in the primary instructional goals of required pedagogy courses at different institutions. From this overview emerges a set of concerns or challenges that GTA educators and writing program administrators need to consider as our curriculum and sense of the discipline continue to evolve.

BACKGROUND

To examine how we commonly prepare GTAs as writing teachers, I solicited a number of documents from writing program administrators working in graduate programs that grant doctoral degrees in rhetoric and composition. In determining which programs to contact, I relied on the survey of the field published in the spring 1994 issue of *Rhetoric Review* titled "Doctoral Programs in Rhetoric and Composition: A Catalog of the Profession." This survey reports that, as of 1993, 72 doctoral programs in English studies offer a specialization in rhetoric and composition (Brown et al. 240). From these 72 programs, I requested the following information regarding their GTA education curricula:

- descriptions of courses that form the GTA education curriculum, including goal or purpose statements of the program;
- orientation and course materials (e.g., policy statements and syllabi) from required teaching practica or pedagogy courses;
- a copy of the TA handbook, if one existed.

In all, writing program administrators from 36 institutions provided some or all of the information I requested, which represents 50 percent of those programs included in Brown et al.'s "Catalog of the Profession" (see Figure 3.2.)

Importantly, my purpose in conducting this research was not to account for and describe every possible approach to preparing GTAs for teaching writing. Each program administrator inevitably develops practices and procedures unique to the specific needs and constraints of the composition curriculum existing in their institution. Rather, I was interested in broadly examining the kinds and ranges of approaches to GTA education that we are currently employing, and in identifying common perspectives on how we represent the activity of teaching writing to the newest members of the rhetoric and composition field—GTAs.

Institution	Name of Ph.D. Offered
U Arizona	English, concent. in Rhetoric, Composition & Teaching of Writing
Arizona U	English, concent. in Rhetoric & Composition
Ball SU	English, concent. in Composition
Bowling Green SU	English, concent. in Rhetoric & Writing
U Cincinnati	English
U Connecticut	English
East Texas SU	Ed.D. in College Teaching of English
Florida SU	English
U Illinois, Chicago	English, spec. in Language, Literacy & Rhetoric
Illinois SU	D.A. in English
U Kansas	English
Louisiana SU	English, option in Rhetoric, Composition & Linguistics
U Louisville	Rhetoric & Composition
U Maryland, College Park	English
U Massachusetts, Amherst	English, emphasis in Writing & the Teaching of Writing
U Miami (Ohio)	English, concent. in Rhetoric & Composition
Michigan Tech U	Rhetoric & Technical Communication
U Minnesota, Twin Cities	English, spec. In Composition Studies
U Minnesota, Twin Cities	Rhetoric, Scientific & Technical Communication
U Nebraska, Lincoln	English, concent. in Composition Practice & Theory
New Mexico SU, Las Cruces	Rhetoric & Professional Communication
U North Carolina, Greensboro	English, spec. in Rhetoric & Composition
U Oregon	English
Pennsylvania SU, Univ Park	English, concent. in Rhetoric & Composition
U Southern California	Rhetoric & Composition
U Southern Mississippi	English, spec. in Rhetoric & Composition
Syracuse U	English, minor in Composition & Cultural Rhetoric
U Tennessee, Knoxville	English
U Texas, Arlington	Humanities, concent. in Rhetoric, Composition & Criticism
U Texas, Austin	English, concent. in Rhetoric & Composition
Texas A&M U	English, concent. in Rhetoric, Composition & Discourse Studies
U Utah	English (Communication or Educational Studies), emphasis in Rhetoric & Composition
U Washington	English, concent. in Rhetoric & Composition
Washington SU	English, concent. in Rhetoric & Composition
U Waterloo (Canada)	Literature & Rhetoric
U Wisconsin, Milwaukee	English, concent. in Rhetoric & Composition

Figure 3.2 Institutions of Faculty Responding to Survey (All offer a degree in rhetoric and composition)

AN OVERVIEW OF GTA EDUCATION CURRICULA

What is immediately noticeable about the descriptions of GTA education programs I received is their rough similarity given a wide range of programmatic possibilities. Of the 36 programs represented in this survey, 23 locate their teacher-preparation program in a single course, which may or may not be repeated throughout each term of a GTA's initial year of teaching. Another seven programs have developed a combination of courses which fulfill their teacher preparation requirements, and two more have developed extensive mentoring programs in combination with a course requirement. Four programs offer some combination of apprenticeships and/or workshops in place of formal course offerings. Mentoring programs which involve experienced GTAs, part-time instructors, and/or full-time faculty members in the professional development of first-year GTAs exist in varying degrees in all programs. Additionally, nearly all the programs (32) reported that they require a fall orientation for new GTAs: One program stated that it holds no orientation and three did not answer this question. Of the 32 programs requiring an orientation, half stated that it lasted five days or more—with two programs reporting that GTAs enroll in required writing pedagogy courses during the summer. Five programs operate a one-day orientation. Moreover, many of the courses comprising these GTA education programs evaluate GTAs on similar tasks and writing assignments—the most common of which is a teaching portfolio frequently required as a final project.

The following discussion concentrates on the course descriptions and rationales comprising the core of most GTA education programs. In order to examine the range of curricular approaches in these programs, I categorized courses according to their primary instructional goals. Although other ways of categorizing these courses exist, this approach allowed me to focus on common pedagogical methods and curricular strategies. Using this scheme, most courses fell along a continuum which, as it moves from left to right, becomes more theoretical and removed from the first-year writing classroom (see figure below).

Apprenticeships—Practica—Teaching Methods courses—Theory seminars

This continuum represents a general method of categorization. Clearly, discussion of writing theory does happen in many of the practica described, just as practical issues arise in theory seminars. However, generally speaking, the priority of a practicum is practical and immediate training in teaching strategies, and the priority of a theory seminar is to explore historical contexts and philosophical issues related to writing instruction. Also, many GTA education programs offered several courses and/or implemented mentoring programs, thus developing their own continuums for dealing with complex issues of practice and theory within its GTA education programs.

Finally, I must stress that these course descriptions represent snapshots of how each program executed their GTA training in a particular term or year. Many writing program administrators willingly shared these materials so that we might glimpse the range of writing pedagogy existing in GTA education programs nationally. Their generosity provides us with an opportunity to freeze-frame an on-going, ever-evolving activity of the field.

Apprenticeships

Apprenticeship, or preceptorship, programs vary based on a number a factors. Perhaps the most important factor shaping the design of such programs is how apprenticeships relate to, and are positioned within, a broader pedagogical curriculum. At the University of Oregon and the University of Tennessee-Knoxville (UTK), for instance, prospective teaching assistants, or teaching fellows as they are called at Oregon, participate in a year-long apprenticeship program prior to teaching their own classes. At both institutions, this apprenticeship program is integrated into a GTA education program that includes coursework in writing instruction. In both programs, new graduate students work individually with a teacher experienced in the program, spending a set amount of time observing the supervising teacher's class and meeting together outside of class, thereby gaining practical experience prior to teaching.

Other institutions use an apprenticeship program with GTAs who are teaching immediately in their first term—offering this experience as the primary source of pedagogical information. The writing program at the University of Arizona operates a preceptorship program in which first-year GTAs are assigned a teaching adviser with whom they meet in small groups and individually on a regular basis. The University of Massachusetts at Amherst similarly places teaching associates in instructional teams which are led by a course director who is a member of the writing program staff and/or a member of the English faculty. The program handbook from UMass-Amherst states that during these meetings, "the team discusses various aspects of teaching as well as various issues that arise in class: for example, conducting peer-response sessions and student conferences, presenting the 'documented essay,' setting appropriate goals, and evaluating student writing." At the University of Waterloo, graduate students are apprenticed in their first year of support to a faculty member who is teaching a large undergraduate writing course. The duties of the apprentice in this program commonly include "leading tutorials, responding to students' writing, grading students' writing, conferring with students, attending course lectures, and compiling final marks."

Methods of evaluating the performance of GTAs in apprenticeship programs are best exemplified by the following description provided by the GTA educator at the University of Arizona.

Preceptorship Requirements

   a. Submit to your TEAD [Teaching Adviser]:
      1. syllabus and course policy
      2. assignment sheet for each essay
      3. copies of all class handouts
      4. two sets of graded papers (1 before midsemester, 1 after)
      5. midsemester self-evaluation of teaching
      6. semester grades
   b. Attend all preceptorship and colloquium meetings called by TEAD, course director, and composition director.
   c. Respond promptly to all memos.

How Your TEAD Will Evaluate You

   a. Visit 2 classes (announced);

b. Review 2 sets of graded papers;

c. Confer with you after each visit and paper review;

d. Respond in writing to self-evaluation;

e. Write semester evaluation.

The purpose of these apprenticeship programs is often stated in practical terms. Apprenticeships provide GTAs with a support person, someone experienced in the teaching of writing and knowledgeable about the particular institution and writing program. For example, the purpose of the apprenticeship program in the English department at the University of Tennessee-Knoxville is "to introduce the graduate assistants to the specific philosophy— and a variety of methods for teaching in—UTK's composition program, as well as give them first-hand experience working with UTK [first-year students]." Similarly, the composition teachers' handbook from the University of Oregon states that the goal of the apprenticeship is to provide "practical experience in every aspect of teaching." It adds that apprenticeships provide supervising teachers (themselves often also graduate teaching fellows) "the opportunity to discuss their class and teaching methods with an eager student and to receive constructive criticism." In addition, therefore, GTA educators stress that apprenticeships can be rewarding learning experiences, given their highly individual character. These programs smooth first-year GTAs' transition into a writing program and their role as teachers.

Practica

Many titles are given to the type of course I categorize as a practicum. Workshop, proseminar, colloquium, and staff meeting are all descriptions used in GTA education materials. The primary instructional focus of these courses is to provide practical support for GTAs in their first term (and sometimes repeated through their first year) of teaching. Although within this grouping some courses are more practical than others, their common denominator is that a majority of time in these classes is spent dealing with the immediate questions and concerns new GTAs have regarding their current teaching. Courses in this category constitute the largest group within the continuum of GTA education curricula. Although several programs combine a practicum with teaching methods courses or writing theory seminars (e.g., Illinois State, Florida State, and the University of Nebraska at Lincoln), many rely on a practicum as the primary source of pedagogical instruction for GTAs.

Within this category, courses range from those described as support groups and staff meetings to those in which GTAs are asked to develop teaching philosophies grounded in current writing pedagogy. In those programs where this course is offered in consecutive terms during GTAs' first year of teaching, the character of the course frequently changes during second and third terms to concentrate on rhetoric and composition theory (e.g., Michigan Tech, Penn State).

Because these courses range in their level of practicality, let me begin by describing those which specialize in providing GTAs with weekly practical assistance. One educator of such a course described it as a teacher community where GTAs can "trade stories as well as share problems, strategies, and plans." Not all first-year GTAs may be required to attend these practica, only those who have not taken a pedagogy course at another institution. As another GTA educator wrote, "Theory is not emphasized in these courses." These practica frequently focus on problem-solving and idea-sharing, as descriptions from GTA educators at Illinois State, the University of Kansas at Lawrence, and Syracuse University respectively illustrate:

- The proseminar meets "weekly for 50 minutes to answer questions, address problems, share strategies, and in general try to meet practical teaching needs."

- "This course...normally consists of weekly meetings, directed by a senior faculty member, at which relevant pedagogical matters—from disciplinary problems and grading standards to assignment topics and rhetorical theory—are discussed."

- "Teaching Practicum requires that you attend and participate in two-hour, small-group meetings each week throughout the semester....You will be able to talk about what to do in the classroom, develop course plans, share ideas with other first-year and experienced teachers, and work out whatever problems or questions you might have on weekly basis."

Also, in this type of course, GTA educators may organize the practicum syllabus to follow the standard syllabus used by GTAs in their first-year writing classes, often keeping just ahead of it. Syllabi from two such courses state that together the GTAs and their instructor will prepare assignments, read students' drafts, grade papers, "practice techniques of evaluation and peer-editing," and discuss teaching problems when they occur. When time permits, more general issues of the teaching of writing are addressed. And, as a final activity, one program invites first-year students "into the seminar to tell us what we've done right or wrong."

Those courses that present introductions to rhetoric and composition studies, while still remaining primarily focused on providing GTAs with immediate practical assistance, close the gap along the continuum of curricula between the most practical practica and those courses which address teaching methods. The Composition Instructors' Workshop at Bowling Green State University, which addresses ways new instructors might "integrate current rhetoric and composition theory in the classroom," as well as courses at Texas A&M and the University of Louisville, exemplify versions of this kind of practicum. While explaining that the course will discuss "some composition theory, but not much," course materials from Texas A&M state the following goals:

1. learn to teach English in a college environment;

2. understand issues that affect the teaching of English in college;

3. become a better writer yourself;

4. manage your teaching and your students so that you and your students benefit from your semester together.

Similarly, a course offered at the University of Louisville provides "a very brief overview of traditional and contemporary rhetoric and of current research in composition theory and pedagogy, all illustrated with reference to English 101 and 102 at the University of Louisville." This approach allows GTAs to address the practical issues of syllabus design, assignment writing, commenting on students' writing, and leading class discussions with some reference to broader theoretical contexts.

Methods of evaluating GTAs in these types of courses combine classroom observations, examining sets of graded papers, peer observations, participation, and teaching journals or notebooks. The following list of requirements is used for a course taught in the writing program at Michigan Tech:

1. *A teaching notebook* in which you not only record but reflect upon your teaching practice—this includes reflection on planning or on articles you have read or discussions you have had about practice or that somehow inform your teaching.

2. *A portfolio of your work this term*—including syllabus, assignment sheets, at least three student papers that represent a range of abilities and include your responses, and a final statement on your teaching for the quarter.

3. At least *two peer observations* and a follow-up conference with me.

4. *Participation* in the seminar in terms of leading discussions, being prepared for discussions, and bringing student writing (or other work) in as assigned.

Teaching Methods Courses

Courses grouped into this category form a bridge between practica, which concentrate on immediate teaching questions and concerns, and theory seminars, which concentrate on historical contexts and exploring rhetoric and composition theories. Teaching methods courses are full-credit courses (as opposed to one-credit or partial-credit practica) and often consciously mimic methods courses taught in education departments. The primary instructional goal of these courses is to immerse GTAs in the language and methods of a program's writing pedagogy. These courses seek to imbue GTAs with practical teaching strategies, pedagogical texts, and most of all, a language for talking about teaching. In a teaching methods course, new teachers approach teaching from a number of perspectives. They engage in a variety of writing activities designed to model practices they will use in their own classrooms. They read and discuss not only student papers but also the professional literature of composition theory and writing pedagogy, becoming familiar with a language of teaching and the contexts out of which it developed. They observe teachers—even apprentice to them—help grade papers, conference with students, and may teach a class session. They work in writing centers tutoring first-year students for a limited number of hours. They engage in teacher research and produce (often collaborative) final projects for the course.

The theory presented in these courses is specifically pedagogical in nature and supports programmatic imperatives. For example, a course taught at Washington State University titled "Seminar in the Teaching of Writing: The Methodology of Composition" is organized to help GTAs "study, evaluate, and practice methods currently used in the teaching of composition, methods such as conferencing, heuristics, collaboration, peer-group critique, writing across the curriculum, epistemics, free writing, and others." Another course, offered at Ball State University, lists the following goals:

Students will attempt to

- Become acquainted with the history and current aims of composition teaching;
- Become familiar with the special demands of the Ball State Writing Program; and
- Learn about problems in composition pedagogy and explore possible solutions.

Those also in the Teaching Preparation Program will

- Study course organization and assignments in detail;
- Become acquainted with methods of experienced teachers; and
- Learn design issues and procedures for a typical composition course.

Both of Florida State's required summer courses, Teaching English as a Guided Study and Teaching English in College, with their focus on helping GTAs develop both specific teaching practices and teaching philosophies grounded in current composition theory, demonstrate the immersion of GTAs in both hands-on training and pedagogical discussion that characterizes teaching methods courses. Course materials from Teaching English in College state that GTAs will examine composition theory, "especially cognitive, developmental, and process approaches within the dynamics of social and expressivist theories of language," in order to help them develop a statement of teaching philosophy as well as the course materials they will use to teach their first classes in the fall. In addition to seminar discussions and writing workshops, GTAs also intern with instructors who are teaching summer-term writing courses.

Materials from Teaching English as a Guided Study, the second required course at Florida State, describe a course that examines three issues in tutoring and teaching: response, revision, and evaluation/grading. The primary instructional goals of this course include helping GTAs "develop a theory-based set of response, revision, and evaluation practices;" providing GTAs with experience in a writing workshop classroom by "participating in activities similar to those experienced by first-year writing students;" and obtaining "practical tutoring experience by tutoring two hours a week in the FSU Reading/Writing Center."

Theory Seminars

At the farthest right end of the continuum are those courses which most closely resemble a graduate seminar, asking GTAs to explore the reaches and possibilities of theory's influence on teaching philosophies and practices. In all cases, these courses represent the second in a series of required courses within a program's GTA education curriculum. These types of courses differ from practica in central ways: although practical issues may be addressed, they concentrate on theoretical debates and on broadly historicizing the teaching of composition.

Moreover, these types of courses differ from teaching methods courses: theory seminars do not provide many moments for practical application, instead inviting GTAs into dialogue with contrasting theoretical perspectives. These courses range broadly over rhetorical and composition theories which may not all be directly pedagogical in nature or directly applied to teaching practices in class discussion. Importantly, the theories discussed in these courses are not limited to composition or rhetorical theories. As courses offered at the University of Nebraska-Lincoln, the University of Wisconsin-Milwaukee, and Illinois State demonstrate, theory seminars frequently include reading from other traditions such as psychology, education, linguistics, philosophy, feminist theory, critical theory, and politics.

Some courses within this category bring local concerns into dialogue with broader issues in theory important to writing instruction. Such a course, taught at the University of Nebraska-Lincoln, brings into dialogue local and national contexts of writing instruction: "This course serves two purposes....The first purpose is to introduce you to the philosophy and practice of composition teaching at UNL. The other purpose is to provide an introduction and overview of the field of composition and rhetoric, to invite you into some of the debates that energize the field, and to explore connections between the teaching of writing and the discipline of English as a whole." Similarly, a course at the University of Connecticut also stresses a double emphasis on theory and practice:

> On the one hand, the course is designed to provide a grounding in the day to day practice of teaching writing, and on the other hand, in order for such a practice to be meaningful and dynamic, the course requires critical reflection on teaching practice; in short, one assumption behind the course is that practice and theory are not dichotomous.

These courses typically ask GTAs to consider the following: (1) the ways in which writing teachers inflect their instruction with philosophical/theoretical biases; and (2) what consequences such biases have on the nature of learning in the classroom. One GTA educator explained that the goal of this course is to explore "what philosophies tacitly or overtly underlie certain teaching practices and what theories we can consciously use to strengthen our own teaching and writing." Another GTA educator, from the University of Wisconsin-Milwaukee, writes that "the goal of the course, quite simply, is to cultivate critical and reflective practice. To that end, the course addresses theoretical issues and questions—where did college composition come from? What is its mission?—as well as practical ones—How do we respond productively to student writing? How do we go about preparing students to work in peer response groups?" Yet another GTA educator writes even more strongly that

> As teachers, I think, we always feel a centripetal pressure that centers our attention on the mechanics of the classroom. What should we assign today?…What should we ask our students to write about? By what objective standard should we grade our students' work? But when we consider the context—institutional, disciplinary, social, and personal—of our students and ourselves, we feel a range of centrifugal pressures that complicate what at first glance seems to be the safely enclosed world of the classroom. Those centrifugal pressures make it impossible to see the classroom as a neutral site of learning where the key questions are about the effective presentation and objective evaluation of material. The classroom is not a safe haven; it is a contested site where learning results from an active process of questioning, dialogue, and negotiation.

This type of course presents a particular challenge to new writing teachers—asking them, as a GTA educator from East Texas State University puts it, "to make what is known about composition an integral part of their own approach to teaching writing." Also, however, some of these courses extend beyond this concern, asking GTAs to consider the ways in which their practices are embedded in cultural contexts that texture the learning experiences of their students.

Not surprisingly, the methods of evaluating GTAs in these courses resemble evaluation methods commonly used in graduate seminars. Class presentations, short papers (often responses to or reflections on the assigned readings), and a single formal research paper constitute the most common methods of evaluating GTAs. Often, writing assignments are collected in teaching portfolios at the end of a term, and one of the most common types of writing assignments included in this portfolio is a statement of teaching philosophy.

THE MOST TYPICAL CURRICULAR
REQUIREMENTS—AND THREE CONCERNS

While this continuum presents the range of course types that constitute GTA education programs across the country, it also illustrates that most programs (three fourths of those represented in this overview) rely on a practicum to prepare new teachers of writing. To summarize the common characteristics of a practicum, the following comprise a typical GTA education program in rhetoric and composition studies:

- One course that meets once a week, sometimes repeated each term of a GTA's first year of teaching but more often not, totaling an average of three credit-hours.
- Taught by the director of the writing program or another member of the writing program committee.
- Focuses on the immediate needs and concerns of GTAs who are teaching in the program for the first time. Provides new teachers with discussion-leading strategies, guidelines for writing assignments and responding to student writing, as well as space for problem-solving and idea-sharing.
- Presents a brief overview of composition and rhetorical theories.
- Requires very minimal reading, focusing instead on first-year writing course materials and samples of first-year students' writing.
- Requires attendance, and participation is graded.
- Requires GTAs to keep a journal or teacher's notebook in which they record and reflect on lesson plans, assignments, and their students' progress.
- Requires GTAs to be observed by the Practicum instructor, and possibly also to observe another instructor's class.
- Requires GTAs to turn in all teaching materials as well as sets of graded papers or a selective sample of graded papers for evaluation by the Practicum instructor.

Based on these characteristics, the primary approach to preparing new teachers of writing is to supply a structure within which they can productively operate. That structure typically provides new teachers with standardized teaching materials, supervised practice in responding to and evaluating student writing, and practical guidance in the day-to-day procedures of classroom instruction. Given the distress many graduate students experience when faced with their first teaching assignments, as well as the concomitant concerns of GTA educators/WPAs to maintain consistent standards in all writing classes, this approach to preparing GTAs is understandable and necessary.

In fact, such practical instruction has a number of advantages. First, it provides an immediate program of action for inexperienced teachers, a way of behaving as a teacher. Second, this kind of course helps GTA educators assert a defining influence over the instructional goals and pedagogical philosophy of a writing program. Third, practical training, a kind of "Here's how I do it" approach, can lay the groundwork for incorporating coaching and learning by doing approaches in GTA education (see, for example, Donald Schön's work on educating the reflective practitioner). Finally, given the multiple strains on the time and energy of both WPAs and GTAs, practical training appeals to their needs to both give and receive concrete guidance.

However, despite the usefulness of this approach to GTA education, it raises some important questions. The prevalence of this type of course may suggest that the rhetoric and composition field teaches teachers within a pedagogical model that relies on translation-based approaches to theory and writing instruction and on one-way modes of communication: GTA educator to GTAs, GTAs to first-year students. This presents at least three concerns.

First, by relying primarily on practica that are skills-based, we are encouraging a notion that writing courses are contentless and that teaching writing requires minimal expertise. If writing "happens" and the most we can do is provide the best environment for it and the right kind of encouragement, then a skills-based curriculum for GTAs makes some sense. However, compositionists and literacy theorists have recently questioned the contentless argument, contending that it reinforces class divisions by privileging those students who are already familiar with the literate practices they are expected to acquire in these courses (cf. Faigley, Miller, Delpit, Shor). Moreover, there is a danger that these practica devolve writing pedagogy from a critical practice with an epistemological grounding to sets of lesson plans and activities disconnected from a teaching philosophy.

Second, this type of teacher preparation perpetuates traditional administrative power structures that may neutralize the discipline's efforts to redefine teaching and administrative activities for tenure and promotion cases as well as for the professionalizing of the discipline. Several programs participating in the survey encourage the active involvement of tenured, tenure-track, and part-time professional faculty; however, most rely on a single writing program administrator to deal with GTAs. An assumption of such an approach may be that centralizing a writing program in one position helps departments designate an established resource for dealing with writing issues. However, Jeanne Gunner has suggested such WPA-centric models maintain "a troubling degree of division" between WPAs and the writing instructors and GTAs who constitute their writing programs (8). She argues that such an "anti-democratic" division of authority disconnects writing teachers from the curriculum they teach, undermining their skills and helping departments justify "using literature graduate students and faculty to do a composition job" (13). WPA-centric programs striate authority in a top-heavy fashion and fix communication channels as one-way: top-down. Although, as Gunner argues, one person cannot simply transmit knowledge to others "via a prescribed syllabus, a preselected textbook" (13) and a set of teaching strategies, these are prominent characteristics of GTA education curricula.

Third, the emphasis on skills training in the majority of GTA education programs may encourage a perception compositionists have long battled: Teaching writing is not valued, even by the rhetoric and composition field. By dispensing "training" in one- to two-hour doses once a week for one (possibly two) terms, this model encourages the passing out of class activities and other quick-fixes—an inoculation method of GTA education. We need to examine the message we are sending GTAs and our other colleagues in English studies by maintaining such practices.

Countering these concerns will require GTA educators and WPAs to build pedagogy courses and education programs that are more balanced, nested in teaching communities, and extended beyond the participation of first-year GTAs and a single faculty member.

STRIKING A BALANCE BETWEEN PRACTICAL AND THEORETICAL FRAMEWORKS

GTA education curricula should strike a balance between providing GTAs with practical skills and advice and helping them understand the writing theory and pedagogy grounding those skills. It would be a serious mistake to completely discontinue providing first-year GTAs with concrete and practical advice for teaching writing. What we need, then, is to find ways to balance these "whats" with "whys": We need to contextualize that advice by providing GTAs with the theoretical frameworks shaping them. Certainly, one step toward producing this balance includes a re-consideration of the kinds of reading (or lack of it) we require for GTAs in these courses.

Balancing these needs is the difference between providing GTAs with a vocabulary of key words and teaching them a language. For instance, teaching GTAs how to help students work through different stages of writing as they draft a single essay gives GTAs a set of process-based practices and key words from which they can teach. It gives them a vocabulary they can use with their students and with each other. It's a useful starting place. In addition, however, pedagogy courses need to help GTAs develop a language for teaching writing, which means contextualizing these key words within the discussions in rhetoric and composition studies about the goals and purposes of writing process approaches to teaching, about the debates over what that means, and about the evolution of those concepts. Bringing this kind of context into pedagogy courses helps new teachers gain an understanding of the complexity of writing instruction. It will help many of them fight the urge to dismiss students (or their own abilities) when an assignment or a class activity goes awry. What's more, grounding the teaching strategies shared in a practicum in a broader theoretical framework gives GTAs more tools for thinking about what's happening in their classrooms and for arriving at their own solutions to problems.

Incorporating discussion of and reflection on writing theory and pedagogy essays or texts is an important step in preparing GTAs to become professional teachers. By engaging in dialogues with a body of literature and with other composition specialists, GTAs can begin to develop a language to articulate why they grade papers in a certain way or why they believe in certain kinds of assignments and not others. By promoting such dialogues, we prepare GTAs for the future when they will need to know how to find answers to concerns we cannot predict during a practicum.

Developing Teaching Communities

Those GTA education programs that seem most impressive introduce first-year teachers to their writing pedagogy from multiple perspectives. They combat the damaging notion that teaching is an isolated activity—a private act between students and teachers occurring behind closed doors—by promoting community-building activities among new GTAs, advanced GTAs, instructors, and tenure-track faculty. On a grand scale are those programs in which GTAs participate in apprenticeship programs, tutor in writing centers, and enroll in pedagogy courses. These programs cultivate teaching communities in which first-year GTAs are immersed in multiple forums and conversations about teaching. Although developing such an extensive GTA education curriculum may not be possible in many programs, it should be our goal to develop an atmosphere where teaching or pedagogy is not viewed as the lowly concern of one administrator or one group of brand-new teachers.

Writing programs can cultivate teaching communities, in part, by multiplying the places and the people GTAs interact with as they develop their own teaching practices and philosophies. Some programs pair new and advanced GTAs together, asking them to visit each other's classes for a term and meet to discuss them. Some programs require GTAs, at some point in their first year, to work in a writing center tutoring students. Some programs organize regular grading workshops for small groups of faculty, part-time instructors, and GTAs. Some programs use the fall orientation as a place to showcase experienced teachers' talents by encouraging them to develop workshops or lead discussion sessions. Some programs have developed task forces consisting of writing teachers of all levels to advise the GTA educator and/or WPA on particular curriculum issues. Some programs encourage first-year and advanced GTAs to develop research groups, team-teach, draft conference abstracts and presentations, develop and run colloquia, and participate formally in the writing program by sitting on committees or acting as assistants to the writing program administrator.

By introducing GTAs to writing pedagogy and practice from many avenues and many people's perspectives, they learn to view teaching as a vibrant, constantly evolving, and valued practice. Additionally, GTA education programs that are anchored in such communities promote on-going teacher education which extends well beyond a GTA's first term or year of teaching.

Engaging More Teachers in Pedagogy and GTA Education

More than anything else, and before much else can happen, GTA education programs will need the support and active involvement of many more people than this overview indicates are involved in preparing graduate teaching assistants. Tenured faculty, advanced GTAs, writing center professionals, instructors, and undergraduate students are under-utilized resources in most GTA education programs. Moreover, current administrative structures which, in many cases, place too many administrative burdens on one person—the

WPA—will need rethinking. Some programs have split this position, creating a separate GTA educator position, having both positions held by tenured or tenure-track faculty. Some programs require all tenured or tenure-track faculty members in rhetoric and composition studies to rotate writing program responsibilities—including teaching or team-teaching required writing pedagogy courses. Unless or until pedagogy is a part of the regular conversations of many people in a department, instead of only one WPA and one group of new GTAs, writing teachers will struggle to combat their isolation and education programs will continue to over-emphasize skills-based models of writing instruction.

Although current curricula for educating GTAs ranges from apprenticeships and practica to combinations of methods and theory courses, the majority of writing programs continue to rely on one course—the practicum—for preparing graduate students to teach writing. Maintaining this primarily skills-based approach to educating GTAs helps ensure that the first-year students in their classes receive similar writing instruction, meeting or at least approaching programmatic standards. However, such a curriculum raises concerns regarding the shape and direction of writing pedagogy in rhetoric and composition studies and the long-term preparation of GTAs as professional teachers. By offering this overview as well as these three challenge areas, I hope to promote on-going discussions about what we are and are not achieving in our efforts to prepare new writing teachers and to introduce graduate students to rhetoric and composition studies.[3]

NOTES

1. How many English departments require GTAs to complete courses in writing instruction? According to Carol Hartzog's 1986 study, 83 percent of schools responding to her study require such training programs and another 10 percent answered that courses in writing instruction were optional (Hartzog 48–49). More recently, in a 1994 study titled, "Doctoral Programs in Rhetoric and Composition: A Catalog of the Profession," 56 percent of the 72 programs listed a writing pedagogy course as a "core or required course"—this despite the authors' contention that they found little consistency in core requirements among the programs (Brown et al.).

2. This article is a condensed version of the second chapter of my dissertation, "The Politics of GTA Education in Rhetoric and Composition Studies." This larger project constructs a portrait of GTA education in rhetoric and composition studies and complicates common approaches to preparing GTAs by outlining a set of initiatives for broadening the field's writing pedagogy. The dissertation's central argument is that GTA education programs are an important site of disciplinary formation and have much to tell the field about the processes through which writing pedagogies are produced. Methodologically, it relies on a variety of interpretative and qualitative approaches. Beyond Chapter Two which is represented here, Chapter Three examines commonplace narratives which emerge from a review of the professional discourse on GTA education. Chapter Four analyzes

course materials, writing program materials, and in-depth interviews with four GTA educators and generates a series of principles and practices which constitute alternatives for preparing graduate students as writing teachers and as members of the rhetoric and composition field. Finally, Chapter Five articulates a number of programmatic challenges that remain constant for GTA educators.

3. I would like to thank Chris Burnham, Rebecca Moore Howard, Marilyn Cooper, and Diana George for their helpful responses to drafts of this essay. Also, I thank Cynthia Selfe and Stuart Selber—my mentors, teachers, and friends—for their generosity and support of this project.

WORKS CITED

Bridges, Charles W., ed. *Training the New Teacher of College Composition.* Urbana: NCTE, 1986.

Brown, Stuart C., et al. "Doctoral Programs in Rhetoric and Composition: A Catalog of the Profession." *Rhetoric Review* 12 (1994): 240–389.

Connolly, Paul and Teresa Vilardi. *New Methods in College Writing Programs.* New York: MLA, 1986.

Corbett, Edward P. J. "Teaching Composition: Where We've Been and Where We're Going." *College English* 38 (1987): 444–52.

Delpit, Lisa. D. "The Silenced Dialogue: Power and Pedagogy in Educating Other People's Children." *Harvard Educational Review* 58 (Aug. 1988): 280–98.

Donovan, Timothy R. and Ben McClelland. *Eight Approaches to Teaching Composition.* Urbana: NCTE, 1980.

Faigley, Lester. *Fragments of Rationality: Postmodernity and the Subject of Composition.* Pittsburgh: U of Pittsburgh P, 1992.

Gere, Anne Ruggles. "Teaching Writing Teachers." Rev. of *Rhetoric and Composition,* by Richard Graves. *College English* 47 (1985): 58–65.

Gunner, Jeanne. "Decentering the WPA." *WPA: Writing Program Administration* 18 (Fall/Winter 1994): 8–15.

Hartzog, Carol P. *Composition and the Academy: A Study of Writing Program Administration.* New York: MLA, 1986.

Miller, Susan. *Textual Carnivals: The Politics of Composition.* Carbondale: Southern Illinois U P, 1991.

Schön, Donald A. *Educating the Reflective Practitioner: Toward a New Design for Teaching and Learning in the Professions.* San Francisco: Jossey, 1987.

Shor, Ira. *Empowering Education: Critical Teaching for Social Change.* Chicago: U of Chicago P, 1992.

Professional Development
for Writing Program Staff

William J. Carpenter
Lafayette College

Given the usually hybrid nature of many writing program faculties, the concept of professional development for these populations can prove difficult to define and realize. One can imagine, for example, the many different notions of professional development that exist among first-year TAs, tenth-year adjuncts, and fifth-year assistant professors facing tenure reviews. Even within faculties not quite this diverse, different ideas among staff members about what it means to "develop as a professional" probably exist.

And so they should. Professional responsibilities are not the same for everybody, nor are professional interests. We know that careers are personal things, as are the decisions made concerning them. And often these decisions require considering a multitude of factors, including personal goals, family obligations, and economic status. Each individual's combination of factors is both unique and fluid, changing with each experience and decision and affecting the person's understanding of and interest in his or her professional status (Caffarella). But this diversity should not preclude the need to discuss what professional development means to faculties and writing programs. Such discussions can encourage faculty members to analyze and critique the conventions and expectations of their fields, thus promoting a critical awareness of their professional positions.

In this essay I define professional development for writing programs, explore some of the general ideas that can inform those initiatives, and offer some recommendations for activities and meetings. My purpose here is to help WPAs begin and nurture conversations among their staffs about working in a professional field or discipline. I believe that these types of conversations can help faculty members make better-informed decisions about their careers. Armed with both practical knowledge and critical awareness, faculty members can interact with their chosen fields as informed participants, ready and able to engage in professional activities in ways that respond to their own interests and goals.

DEFINING PROFESSIONAL DEVELOPMENT

In this section, I distinguish professional development from other types of development or training programs. I look to establish a space within the crowded terrain of writing programs for discussing issues related to professional life. Such discussions, I argue, can benefit the local writing program and the fields that compose English studies. By inviting faculty members to analyze the discourse and expectations of their disciplines, professional development programs invite them to become critical participants in the conversations that shape their fields. Local programs gain faculty members who enjoy a sense of purpose and place in their fields, and the fields gain faculty members who bring with them experience and knowledge.

Professional development is perhaps best understood as a component of "faculty development," a term that refers to programs and activities designed to improve the overall quality of college and university teaching staffs. The Professional and Organizational Development Network in Higher Education (POD) states that good faculty development programs combine three main areas of focus, each concerned with improving the individual faculty member's ability to perform his or her duties in productive and rewarding ways. By concentrating on the faculty member as a teacher, a person, and a professional, these programs help the member develop and improve the skills necessary to survive and succeed in higher education and, perhaps, elsewhere. (For more information about POD, visit its web site ⟨www.podnetwork.org⟩.)

The first two types of faculty development listed above might best be termed teacher and personal development, and they both prove important in fostering and maintaining a productive, healthy writing program staff. These two areas, however, probably already receive a great deal of attention from WPAs and faculty members because of their importance to one of the primary purposes of the program—to teach writing courses well. Activities such as new teacher orientations, classroom visits, teaching workshops, grading sessions, and one-on-one conferences between individual members and the WPA provide faculty members with support and feedback concerning their teaching practices and personal concerns. During these activities, faculty members receive training in meeting program requirements, information about new classroom strategies, and advice on topics ranging from first-day jitters to time management. This information helps the faculty members stay focused on the goals of the program, while also providing them with the tools and strategies for dealing with their daily job duties. By necessity, these types of faculty development activities occur routinely within writing programs. Factor in the continual turnover within many writing program staffs, as well as the different levels of training and experience among the members, and we can imagine how planning and performing these types of activities consume much of a WPA's time, energy, and budget.

While development programs aimed at the faculty member as teacher and person do prove vital to the pedagogical and mental health of the program, they do not necessarily address the larger issues of professionalism within the faculty members' chosen fields and areas of interest. In other words, teacher and personal development initiatives usually focus on the local context, the particular program within the particular institution. The advice and information created within these initiatives can be generalized to some extent, but its primary purpose is to maintain and improve the local faculty members and program. Professional development initiatives, on the other hand, have as their primary purpose introducing the faculty members to the knowledge and methods of the larger professional communities found within higher education. They seek to enhance faculty members' understanding of the ways in which professionals present themselves and their knowledge to others in their field. Professional development promotes interest and participation in the conversations beyond the walls of a particular program or institution; it encourages faculty members to see themselves as members of both local programs and larger, more diverse communities of professionals.

Let me offer, then, this definition:

> Professional development programs enhance an individual's knowledge of a discipline's or field's expectations of its members. They assist the individual in developing the skills necessary for presenting him- or herself as a rightful member of a professional community, one who is capable of participating in and shaping the conversations and activities that define the community and its members. In addition, they offer opportunities to analyze and critique the community and the actions of its members.

This definition stresses the point that professional development enhances the individual's understanding of the expectations—beyond the teaching-related—a professional field or discipline has for its members.

Professional development programs introduce the individual to the practices and methods employed by the members of a discipline or field. For most of us, "discipline" refers to English studies, and "field" refers to a particular area of study within the discipline, such as composition and rhetoric, literary studies, and creative writing. Members of a field participate in ritualisticlike communiqués, structured interactions designed to establish and maintain professional identities for both the field itself and the individuals who create them. The most public (and most celebrated) of these interactions are, of course, publications and conference presentations, through which members communicate their ideas and define their professional interests. But a field has other ways of establishing and maintaining professional identities, and in many instances, these other means prove more difficult for new members to understand and produce than the more scholarly counterparts. For instance, think about the roles documents such as curriculum vitae, grant proposals, teaching philosophies and portfolios, job application letters, committee reports, budget requests, letters of recommendation, and course proposals play in the different fields of English studies. To be successful, professionals must learn to present themselves and their ideas through these types of channels as well.

I am not arguing that professional development entails only learning the forms used by members of the fields. Rather, I want to suggest that such development should lead to a better understanding of how these methods of communication represent the practices, values, and expectations of the fields themselves. The professional culture of a field of study is maintained and transmitted through the methods of communication to which the field subscribes; understanding the culture requires understanding the means by which it reproduces itself. At its base, professional development is an enculturation device, an introduction to the ways and means of a field, so to speak. Effective professional development initiatives combine practical training with critical analysis; they encourage members to learn how the fields maintain themselves, as well as why they do so in their particular ways. By combining the practical with the critical, professional development encourages faculty members to analyze their own positions in the fields, as well as to consider the best strategies for accomplishing their career goals. It helps develop faculty members into thoughtful, critical members of their fields.

The definition offered above allows room for the diverse needs and expectations of a writing program staff. As I noted earlier, careers are personal things. The choices one makes depend on the level at which one chooses to participate in the conversations and activities that define the field. Professional development initiatives need to consider both the expectations of the faculty members and the differences among the fields within English studies. Unlike teaching and personal development initiatives, which focus mostly on local contexts and particular programmatic needs, professional development initiatives must focus on the discipline as a whole, thus serving as a resource for all interested members of the staff regardless of their particular fields of study.

RECOGNIZING SOME BASIC IDEAS
ABOUT PROFESSIONAL DEVELOPMENT

In the section above, I call professional development an enculturation device, a means by which the practices, values, and expectations of a discipline or its related fields can be communicated to and analyzed by individual members. To see it as such a device is to see it also as an agent for change within the writing program particularly and within the fields of English studies generally. While enculturation requires learning the appropriate channels for professional correspondence, it also creates opportunity for progressive responses to such requirements. Professional development should provide members with the knowledge and skills necessary to engage in their chosen fields in ways that benefit the individual and the larger communities. To do so, these initiatives must respond to the needs of the faculty members and the demands of the profession; they must consider their local and global contexts with the purpose of improving both.

On the local level, professional development can effect a great deal of change in members' perceptions of themselves and their fields. Any new understanding of the dynamics of a larger community prompts a change in individuals' awareness of their position within that community. This

...ss enables them to make better-informed decisions about ...d may encourage greater critical examination of the practices . On the global level, professional development creates a more ...geable workforce, one capable of recognizing, producing, critiquing, ...nanging the defining features of the discipline and its fields.

A sound theoretical framework for professional development programs is provided by research in the areas of adult education and staff development. In an article on reconceptualizing faculty development, Barbara L. Licklider, Carol Fulton, and Diane L. Schnelker construct an interactive model of faculty development based on these two areas of research, claiming that programs can be most effective when they recognize "faculty as colearners" who are willing and able to make sound decisions about their educational experiences (121). The authors outline clearly what should become the guiding principles behind professional development initiatives. WPAs will find the article doubly useful for its discussion of ways of improving undergraduate education through teacher, personal, and professional development.

Some adult education theory argues that adults respond best to educational programs that encourage self-directed and transformative learning, reflective practice, and participation in a community of similarly interested teachers and learners (Licklider et. al. 122). In terms of professional development, this means that faculty members will probably best respond to programs that invite them to "make their own decisions about what they want to learn and how learning should occur" (122). The opportunity to make one's own educational decisions promotes in the individual a greater sense of ownership toward the information learned and the program that presents it. Some faculty members will probably seek out programs that offer opportunities to reflect on their actions and to analyze the assumptions and beliefs that inform their practices. Adult learners often recognize the potential for personal change found within these activities and they participate in them when they see a possibility for self-improvement. Last, many adult learners prefer learning situations that are shaped by the interests and knowledge of the community's members. When faculty members bring their wide range of knowledge and abilities to any initiative, they recognize the individual's potential both to contribute to the group and to learn from it.

The adult education theory discussed by Licklider et. al. provides the foundation for all types of development programs in higher education; it presents "faculty as reflective practitioners," capable of creating the type of "conversation and community" they find productive and satisfying (123). The framework for such programs is informed by research on effective staff development. In summarizing this research, the authors explain that development programs are most effective when their contents, structures, and strategies respond to the faculty's interests, expectations, and learning styles. In terms of content, effective programs use members' self-described needs and interests as the bases for various activities. According to the authors, "Content is research-based, concrete, and skill-specific rather than solely conceptual"

(124). In other words, the activities should balance practical and theoretical knowledge, a strategy that encourages self-reflection and transformative learning. Effective programs center on "clear, specific goals and objectives which are established with the active involvement of participants" (124).Faculty members should determine the topics for development initiatives and they should play a lead role in shaping the types of activities within the programs. This type of ownership encourages members to analyze their needs and interests, as well as to direct their learning in ways that seem most beneficial to them. The research also shows that effective programs employ regular sessions that provide members with opportunities for nonthreatening, constructive feedback. The structure of a program should allow for faculty input, self-directed participation, and community-based conversation. Finally, the strategies for activities should be varied so as to encourage different types of participation among the members (124). Faculty members themselves can determine formats and discussion leaders or presenters, decisions that require communication and cooperation among members.

WPAs can use this information to generate some basic ideas for their programs' professional development initiatives. For starters, while WPAs should encourage such initiatives and perhaps begin the discussions that characterize them, the programs themselves should maintain a "grassroots" mentality. Professional development, as I've mentioned several times, must respond to the needs and interests of the faculty, and they must be the group that determines the content and structure of the programs. Without their guidance, the program risks appearing either as useless or as another mandate or task passed down from some authority, thus risking a backlash from people who do not want or need "another thing to do." Grassroots movements gain their power from the community working and learning together for the purpose of benefiting each individual and the group as a whole. Nobody knows their interests and needs, as well as how to respond to those things, better than the members themselves.

Professional development programs should receive steady attention from the WPA and participating faculty. Activities appearing at regular intervals during the year demonstrate both a continued commitment to the program and an interest in making such discussions an integral part of faculty life. The schedule for such activities should be staggered, allowing for greater participation from members with different daily routines. On a practical note, WPAs should offer to faculty members information on how to reserve rooms and audiovisual equipment, as well as provide access to photocopiers and bulletin board space. Such information and access would help faculty members plan, organize, and promote the activities themselves.

It is also important that programs and participants receive the acclaim and attention they deserve. WPAs could consider creating memos thanking members for their service. Participants could distribute summaries of the discussions. Effective examples of documents could be posted or distributed. These actions help programs maintain a high profile within the department, and they ensure that the information generated during the activities is disseminated to all members.

SOME SPECIFIC IDEAS
FOR PROFESSIONAL DEVELOPMENT

Here are a few suggestions for professional development activities. I want to stress that this list does not exhaust the possibilities, nor is it meant to promote a particular structure or agenda for a program. Professional development serves its purpose best when the activities and schedules result from conversations among faculty members and WPAs. These suggestions will, I hope, spark and inform those conversations.

I have divided the activities into three subgroups, each pertaining to a particular area of professional life: scholarship, professional involvement, and self-promotion. Faculty members and WPAs can determine how much attention from the programs each of these subgroups deserves.

Scholarship

Professional disciplines and fields are most overtly defined by the scholarship their members produce. Joining the professional conversations through publications and presentations requires learning the discourse expectations of the various communities. Professional development initiatives can provide faculty members with an introduction to these expectations, as well as with the feedback and encouragement crucial to successful scholarly endeavors. The following suggested activities can be easily shaped to meet the needs and expectations of a diverse faculty.

- *Discussion groups:* Meetings to discuss journal articles or scholarly books can provide members with regular opportunities to share their responses in a relaxed, unintimidating atmosphere. While WPAs can make suggestions, faculty members should choose what texts they read, thus allowing for the self-directed learning central to adult education. Discussion groups also promote community learning and reflective thinking.

- *Peer workshops:* Constructive feedback on papers, proposals, conference presentations, etc., can help faculty members improve their research and writing skills. Members can take turns submitting papers to the group. Not only do the members receive valuable feedback, they also have the opportunity to see what kind of work their colleagues are doing.

- *In-house conferences, colloquia, and special-interest presentations:* These activities offer faculty members the chance to present their ideas to their programs and departments. In-house conferences and regularly scheduled colloquia can provide practice in presenting papers to large groups. Special-interest presentations are a less formal means of interaction in which members with interest or expertise in a particular area lead group discussions.

Professional Involvement

Professionals involve themselves in their fields in more ways than through scholarship. Much of this participation, as crucial as it is to professional success, occurs with little or no fanfare, and graduate education does little to prepare faculty members for the behind-the-scenes work expected from professionals in the fields. Development programs that train faculty members for the common tasks and duties associated with their positions help them gain an awareness of other aspects of their jobs. They can also boost their confidence in their abilities to perform their jobs and raise their sense of involvement in their programs and fields. The list below suggests possible topics for activities.

- *Writing letters of recommendation and peer reviews:* Faculty members are often called upon to write letters of recommendation for students and peers. These documents often say as much about their authors as they do about their subjects, and instruction in writing these letters may help defuse some apprehension and nervousness among the faculty.

- *Becoming a textbook reviewer:* Large publishing companies are always looking for faculty members to review textbook manuscripts, editions, and proposals. Often these opportunities come with a small monetary bonus, but the real profit is in gaining a better understanding of the textbook business. Faculty members may also want to participate in focus groups and text comparisons. Publishers really do use the information they receive from these reviews, and participants should know that they are rendering a valuable service.

- *Serving on committees:* Depending on the structure of the program or department, writing-program faculty members may have the opportunity to serve on various committees, such as those that consider departmental award winners or curriculum changes. Development activities that focus on this type of service could describe the charges of the different committees, as well as the time and energy commitment each one requires. Committee service offers faculty members a voice in the governance of the program while introducing them to the primary method of departmental decision making.

Self-Promotion

Though the title of this subgroup may sound a bit crude, we should not underestimate the importance of documenting and communicating professional achievements. Landing a job, earning a raise, and being promoted depend not only on what one does in the workplace but also on how one presents those activities to others in the program and field. This focus for development can help members recognize their own positions as productive, knowledgeable members of their fields. The activities described below are designed to introduce faculty members to the discourse of self-promotion while also offering opportunities to reflect on their professional status.

- *Curriculum vitae and resumés:* No other document characterizes a professional as much as his or her C.V. or resumé. Too often, though, faculty members receive little help in constructing these documents. Session leaders could discuss the importance of these documents in job searches and promotion reviews, as well as the strategies involved in their layout and design. Faculty members may want to participate in peer workshops at which they could share ideas and receive feedback from others.

- *Teaching portfolios:* One way of documenting achievements as a teacher is through a teaching portfolio, a collection of texts designed to highlight the individual's strengths and talents as a teacher. Portfolios have become popular with job-search and promotion committees because they offer evidence of a teacher's performance in and perception of his position. Under normal circumstances, portfolios include a statement of teaching philosophy, self-evaluations, representative syllabi and assignments, samples from student evaluations, and examples of student papers. Development programs should plan informational meetings about the creation and use of portfolios, as well as workshops for teaching philosophies and self-evaluations.

- *Interview strategies:* Successful professionals recognize the importance of having sound interview skills. Development programs can organize mock-interviews and offer instructional sessions on performing in interviews. Colleges and universities often have job-placement centers that could be of help in this area.

Again, it is important that professional development programs encourage and respond to conversations between WPAs and faculty members. The structures and aims of these activities must be developed in relation to the programs' resources and faculty interests.

WHAT WPAs CAN DO

WPAs can initiate discussions on professional development by raising the issue with their staffs. Because WPAs are usually active members of their own professional fields, they have the skills and knowledge to serve as mentors and advisers to members who want to organize and participate in these types of programs. As mentors and advisers, WPAs can suggest possible activities and help members organize and conduct some of the meetings. WPAs should participate in as many activities as their schedules allow—not as leaders or supervisors but as peers and colleagues willing to share their knowledge and learn from others. Most important, WPAs should remember that the most successful professional development initiatives evolve in relation to faculty interests and concerns. The programs should be the property of the members; they should have the power to shape them.

WPAs do have a responsibility to provide faculty members with access to the resources of the program and department. Faculty members will need to make photocopies, reserve rooms, and use VCRs and laptop computers. They may also need funding for materials, as well as spaces to file their documents and handouts. As powerful allies in the battle for resources, WPAs should do what they can to make organizing and running these activities as easy and painless as possible. The benefit of doing so extends to the members, the programs, and the fields of English studies.

WORKS CITED

Caffarella, Rosemary S., and Lynn F. Zinn. "Professional Development for Faculty: A Conceptual Framework of Barriers and Supports." *Innovative Higher Education* 23.4 (1999): 241–54.

Graf, D. *POD Network*. 25 Oct. 2000 〈http://www.podnetwork.org〉.

Licklider, Barbara L., Carol Fulton, and Diane L. Schnelker. "Revisioning Faculty Development for Changing Times: The Foundation and Framework." *The Journal of Staff, Program and Organization Development* 15.3 (1997–98): 121–33.

TA Training in English:
An Annotated Bibliography

Timothy Catalano
Marietta College of Ohio

Will Clemens
University of Cincinatti

Julia Goodwin
Employee Relocation Council

Gary McMillin

Jeff White
Universtity of Alaska—Ancorage

Stephen Wilhoit
University of Dayton

In a recent national survey of writing program administrators employed by both private and public universities (*WPA: Writing Program Administration* 18.3 [1995]: 53–73), Sally Barr-Ebest found that 70–90 percent of the WPAs working at doctoral institutions were responsible for training graduate teaching assistants in their departments. At comprehensive universities (those offering masters degrees), 20–60 percent of the WPAs listed training TAs as one of their regular duties (56). Barr-Ebest also found that most WPAs received no formal training for their position; instead, they tended to learn on the job. Only 12 percent of the men and 3 percent of the women responding to the survey indicated that they relied on reading and research to learn how to perform their duties (54).

Perhaps one reason so few WPAs rely on reading and research to develop and refine the skills they need to perform their duties is the sheer difficulty of locating some material. While the *CCCC Bibliography* and various computer databases have made research in rhetoric and composition administration easier, material on TA training in English can still be hard to locate and obtain, as we found when we began compiling this bibliography almost two years ago. Prior to the 1980s, only a few books on TA training in English had been published; in reference works, articles could be indexed under a range of headings; and relevant book chapters often escaped indexing altogether.

Over the last ten to fifteen years, though, a number of important books have been published on TA training in English; TA training has been a popular topic for presentations at conferences such as CCCC, and an increasing number of important journals in the field have published work on the topic. This Bibliography includes many of the articles, book chapters, and conference presentations published on TA training since 1980 (plus a few older pieces), readings we found especially helpful as we reviewed and restructured our TA training program.

The annotations are purely descriptive; we have made no attempt to evaluate the quality of the material. For the sake of convenience, we have also grouped the readings under several headings: TA Training and Evaluation Techniques, Program Descriptions, Teaching Duties, Employment Issues, and History.

Readings under "TA Training and Evaluation Techniques" offer suggestions on how to train TAs and evaluate their performance. The material included under "Program Descriptions" addresses similar topics, but is more narrowly focused, offering in-depth discussions of training programs developed at particular institutions. Several readings located under these headings discuss how to structure TA training programs (Comley; D'Angelo; Gracie; Guinn; Humphries; Roberts; Weimer, Svinicki and Bauer; Weimer; Wilhoit, "Toward"), describe and categorize different types of programs currently in existence (Angelo and Cross; Haring-Smith), or discuss the results obtained from surveys of training programs across the country (Cooper and Kehl; Diamond and Gray; Puccio, "Graduate"; Ruszkiewicz, "Doing"). Most, though, address specific training and evaluation techniques, such as peer coaching (Cooper and Kehl; Hairston, "Training"; Puccio, "Graduate"), faculty mentorships (M. P. Baker; Hansen, Snyder, Davenport, and Stafford; Hayes), team teaching (Simpson), internships (Smith and Smith), videotaping classes (Baker and Kinkead; Puccio, "TAs"), role-playing (Strickland), and developing teaching portfolios (Webster). A few describe how to recognize and reward good teaching among TAs (Langford; Jackson), reduce anxiety about teaching (McBroom; Williams), address TA burnout (Hunt), encourage professional development among TAs (Davis), improve faculty-TA interaction (Dunn; Reagan, "Practicing"), conduct research (Angelo and Cross; Wilhoit, "Conducting"), and link training efforts with various stages of TA development (Staton and Darling; Tirrell).

Under the heading "Teaching Duties" are articles that suggest how to prepare TAs to teach courses other than introductory composition (Allen; Comprone; Cox) or work in a campus writing center (Blalock; Broder). Under the heading "Employment Issues" are articles that address TA stipends (Gething), taxes (M. J. Baker), workload (Gething), grievance procedures (M. J. Baker), and general working conditions (Minkel). Two address collective bargaining arrangements among TAs (Carlson; Craig, "University"). Finally, articles that examine training efforts of the past or discuss how current programs came to assume their present form are included under the heading "History of TA Training."

While reading and discussing this material on TA training, we have noted several trends. First, and not surprisingly, most of the readings offer practical advice on TA training: they discuss specific aspects of writing instruction TA supervisors should include in training programs and suggest how to cover that material. Only a few articles, most published in the mid- to late 80s, suggest that teacher training programs should also include instruction in composition theory (Haring-Smith; Hesse).

We also found surprising uniformity in the structure of the TA training programs described in the readings. Most involve preservice and in-service workshops, with support provided by more experienced TAs, faculty, or the TA supervisor. A few authors, though, have begun to question the theory and structure of TA training programs, raising a number of interesting questions: Who runs these programs? For what end? What is the role of the TA in these programs? What alternatives are available? (See, for example, Chism, Cano, and Pruitt; Cooper and Kehl; Dunn; Kelly et al.; Webster; Weimer, Svinicki, and Bauer; Weiser, "Teaching".)

We were also surprised by some almost uniform assumptions concerning the audience of these pieces. First, only a few articles addressed the role of WPAs at smaller, comprehensive universities (Foster; R. Smith). Barr-Ebest's survey found that many WPAs at these schools are responsible for TA training; their particular interests and concerns might not be getting adequate attention in the literature. Second, in almost every case, this material seems to be written by and addressed to WPAs or other interested faculty. Very few of the articles on TA training—even those examining employment issues—were written by or addressed to TAs themselves. While many of the pieces offer retrospective accounts of the author's experiences as a teaching assistant, very few works were written by currently employed TAs. Also, almost all of the articles narrowly focused on training new TAs to teach introductory composition courses. We ran across only a few articles that described other teaching duties or that examined how to prepare experienced TAs to teach introductory literature or advanced composition courses. Finally, only a few pieces seriously examined TA employment issues. WPAs hoping to find in the literature serious, varied discussions of TA workload, salaries, and benefits may be disappointed.

TA TRAINING AND EVALUATION TECHNIQUES

Abbott, Robert D., Donald H. Wulff, and C. Kati Szego. "Review of Research on TA Training." *Teaching Assistant Training in the 1990s.* Ed. Jody D. Nyquist, Robert D. Abbott, and Donald H. Wulff. San Francisco: Jossey, 1989. 111–124. Summarizes research on the components of TA training programs and the relationship between TA classroom behavior and student course evaluations. Concludes that the field needs more empirical study of TA training and offers suggestions for further research.

Angelo, Thomas A., and K. Patricia Cross. "Classroom Research for Teaching Assistants." *Teaching Assistant Training in the 1990s.* Ed. Jody D. Nyquist, Robert D. Abbott, and Donald H. Wulff. San Francisco: Jossey, 1989. 99–107. Contends that training programs can better prepare TAs for their future roles as college instructors by encouraging TAs to become teacher researchers. By closely studying their students' work and behavior in class, TAs learn to construct research projects as they improve their own teaching. Reviews how TA training programs are commonly structured.

Baker, Mark A., and Joyce A. Kinkead. "Using Microteaching to Evaluate Teaching Assistants in a Writing Program." *Evaluating Teachers of Writing.* Ed. Christine A. Hult. Urbana: NCTE, 1994. 108–119. Explains Utah State University's use of microteaching to evaluate TAs. After the TA and WPA discuss the skills the TA needs to teach a certain portion of a class, only that portion of the class is video-taped. The WPA reviews the tape with the TA to offer instruction, encouragement, and advice. Discusses problems with and advantages of this evaluation technique.

Baker, Moira P. "Mentoring as Teaching and Learning." Conference on College Composition and Communication. San Diego, 31 March–3 April 1993. ED 358 459. Provides personal narrative describing the need for good relationships between mentors and graduate teaching assistants. Focuses on aspects of this relationship at Radford University that improved both the TAs' and the mentors' teaching practices. Emphasizes that the benefits of such relationships will be felt in all courses, not just composition classes.

Border, Laura. "Producing a TA Newsletter." *Institutional Responsibilities and Responses in the Employment and Education of Teaching Assistants*. Ed. Nancy Van Note Chism. Columbus: Ohio State University Center for Teaching Excellence, 1987. 140–143. Discusses how a TA newsletter can improve communication among TAs and describes how to put together such a publication. Discusses content ideas including professional development as well as teacher training and support services.

Bridges, Charles W. "The Basics and the New Teacher in the College Composition Class." *Training the New Teacher of College Composition*. Ed. Charles W. Bridges. Urbana: NCTE, 1986. 13–26. Describes a training program which incorporates theory and practice in developing teachers capable of creating a "student-centered writing curriculum." Discusses five aspects of writing instruction which must be developed in new teachers (process vs. product, peer collaboration, assignment making, response vs. evaluation, and dealing with errors). Presents possible readings and assignments.

Chism, Nancy Van Note, Jamie Cano, and Anne S. Pruitt. "Teaching in a Diverse Environment: Knowledge and Skills Needed by TAs." *Teaching Assistant Training in the 1990s*. Ed. Jody D. Nyquist, Robert D. Abbott, and Donald H. Wulff. San Francisco: Jossey, 1989. 23–36. Argues that faculty members must take a leading role in preparing TAs to teach an increasingly diverse student body. Training programs should address how to teach ethnic minorities, returning adult students, students with disabilities, women, gay and lesbian students. Offers a number of ways TA training programs can be modified to meet these goals.

Comely, Nancy R. "The Teaching Seminar: Writing Isn't Just Rhetoric." *Training the New Teacher of College Composition*. Ed. Charles W. Bridges. Urbana: NCTE, 1986. 47–57. Argues that freshman composition teacher training programs should synthesize work in literary theory, creative writing, and composition rather than continue to separate these aspects of English studies. Discusses strategies and texts for combining reading and writing in the composition classroom and in teacher training programs.

Cooper, Allene, and D. G. Kehl. "Development of Composition Instruction through Peer Coaching." *WPA: Writing Program Administration* 14.3 (1991): 27–39. Advocates the use of collaborative coaching, especially for novice TAs who may feel a sense of isolation in the classroom. Maintains this isolation can be reduced through organized active cooperation among experienced TAs and newcomers. Presents results of a nationwide survey of TA training which indicated substantial interest in collaborative training techniques. Describes and evaluates the program developed at Arizona State University.

D'Angelo, Frank J. "Strategies for Involving Graduate Students in the Teaching of Composition." *ADE Bulletin* 54 (1977): 34–36. Suggests several strategies for helping TAs primarily trained in literary criticism use that knowledge to improve the writing instruction they offer: give TAs the historical context for modern composition instruction, focus on the study of form and structure in writing, demonstrate how literary criticism can inform composition instruction, demonstrate how composition theory can inform literary criticism.

Davis, William E. "TA Training: Professional Development for Future Faculty." *Institutional Responsibilities and Responses in the Employment and Education of Teaching Assistants*. Ed. Nancy Van Note Chism. Columbus: Ohio State University Center for Teaching Excellence, 1987. 129–131. Asserts that training programs do not adequately emphasize TA professional and career development. Claims that TAs respond more favorably to training programs that emphasize preparation for future careers in teaching. Discusses a professional development series offered at the University of California, Davis, and mentions possible directions for other professional development programs.

Diamond, Robert M., and Peter J. Gray. "A National Study of Teaching Assistants." *Institutional Responsibilities and Responses in the Employment and Education of Teaching Assistants*. Ed. Nancy Van Note Chism. Columbus: Ohio State University Center for Teaching Excellence, 1987. 80–82. Discusses results of research into the background, responsibilities, and preparation of TAs from research institutions across the country. Includes statistics from a five-part survey that consisted of questions on demographic information, teaching responsibilities and supervision, teaching preparation and support programs, training international TAs, and general comments and suggestions.

Dunn, Richard J. "Teaching Assistance, Not Teaching Assistants." *ADE Bulletin* 97 (1990): 47–50. Addresses a central contradiction in the treatment of TAs: on one hand, the institution considers graduate appointments a means of financial support; on the other hand, the graduate assistantship is a form of apprenticeship. Recommends departments do all they can to bridge the gaps between faculty members and TAs or administration and TAs. To accomplish these goals, suggests increasing pay, decreasing workload, integrating graduate studies and the TA position, and abolishing "post-doctoral" appointments.

Foster, David. "Training Writing Teachers in a Small Program." *WPA: Writing Program Administration* 10.1–2 (1986): 43–49. Maintains that larger composition programs should model their TA training practices on those commonly used in smaller programs which foster among TAs a sense of freedom, individuality, and collegiality. Suggests that larger composition programs allow TAs greater freedom in designing courses and selecting texts, organize small TA/faculty discussion groups, establish TA/faculty mentorships, and invite TA participation in department activities.

Gebhardt, Richard C. "Unifying Diversity in the Training of Writing Teachers." *Training the New Teacher of College Composition*. Ed. Charles W. Bridges. Urbana: NCTE, 1986. 1–12. Addresses training writing teachers in general, not just TAs. Suggests the diversity of needs among different client types within a training program can be overcome by emphasizing "unifying concepts." Explains three "unifying ideas" that should be addressed in teacher training programs. Acknowledges the need to balance theory and practice in training instructors.

Gracie, William J., Jr. "Serving Our Teaching Assistants and Our Profession: Teaching Graduate Students to Teach Composition." *Conference on College Composition and Communication*. San Francisco, March 1982. ED 214 170. Voices a concern that gains recently made in composition studies will be lost unless more attention is given to training TAs adequately. Good training programs should include sensitivity to the job market, course work in composition theory taken for credit, training in research methodologies, guest speakers, and teaching awards. Describes training program author developed at Miami University of Ohio.

Guinn, Dorothy Margaret. "Freshman Composition: Developing Teaching Assistant Teaching Potential." Conference on College Composition and Communication. San Francisco, March 1982. ED 215 359. Outlines some obstacles to teaching assistant training such as instructors' backgrounds in literary studies, little facility with teaching grammar, and lack of time for proper training. Discusses program at Southwestern University designed to address these problems through pre-service training in administrative concerns, classroom policies, evaluation procedures, and a one-semester graduate seminar and workshop to develop composition teaching skills by giving TAs a greater understanding of composition as a discipline.

Hairston, Maxine. "On Not Being a Composition Slave." *Training the New Teacher of College Composition.* Ed. Charles W. Bridges. Urbana: NCTE, 1986. 117–124. Discusses how contemporary theories of and guidelines for responding to student writing can help college composition teachers—especially TAs—avoid being overwhelmed when grading papers. Describes how to combine grading with student-teacher conferences.

Haring-Smith, Tori. "The Importance of Theory in the Training of Teaching Assistants." *ADE Bulletin* 82 (1985): 33–39. Divides TA training programs into three categories: (1) a Basic Training approach, (2) an Observation/Apprenticeship approach, and (3) an Advanced Writing Seminar approach. Describes how instruction in composition theory is omitted from all three approaches. Argues that a knowledge of theory helps TAs understand how the students in their classes compose essays, provides TAs with a meaningful framework in which to teach, alleviates TA burnout, and provides a means for effective TA self-evaluation.

Hesse, Douglas. "Teachers as Students, Reflecting Resistance." College Composition and Communication 44 (1993): 224–231. Examines why several students in a graduate composition theory course voiced frustration over theoretical readings. Argues that students may find some readings "difficult" because they lack sufficient knowledge of the field. Suggests that teachers ought to encourage their graduate students to reflect on why they find certain theorists difficult to understand and urge them not to reject new ideas out of hand. Claims that provocative theoretical texts encourage new and experienced instructors to confront their "commonsense" notions of teaching.

Hunt, Maurice. "Essay Evaluation as a Framework for Teaching Assistant Training." *Freshman English News* 14.2 (1985): 19–21. Stresses the need for emphasizing evaluation techniques in TA training workshops. Maintains that proper instruction in evaluation is central to effective training: to properly evaluate a paper is also to begin to learn how to help the student improve as a writer.

———. "Preventing Burn-out in Teaching Assistants." *Freshman English News* 15.1 (1986): 12–15. Describes the symptoms and causes of TA "burnout" then recommends several steps WPAs can take to help TAs manage their workload successfully. Suggestions include discussions of the importance of writing instruction, establishing faculty-TA mentorships, encouraging interactive pedagogy, and urging TAs to share their own work with their students.

Kelly, Kathleen Ann, et al. "To Have or Have Not: The Foucauldian Quandary of Control in Teacher-Training." *Conference on College Composition and Communication.* Cincinnati, March 1992. ED 348 674. Includes comments originally part of three talks on Foucauldian power/knowledge relationships. Suggests methods for encouraging teaching assistants to discuss openly and to question their pedagogical preferences.

Langford, Thomas A. "Recognizing Outstanding Teaching." Institutional Responsibilities and Responses in the Employment and Education of Teaching Assistants. Ed. Nancy Van Note Chism. Columbus: Ohio State University Center for Teaching Excellence, 1987. 132–33. Describes the TA recognition program designed to boost graduate student moral and enhance professional development at the Graduate School at Texas Tech. Discusses some of the program's benefits for TAs and the graduate school.

Larson, Richard L. "Making Assignments, Judging Writing, and Annotating Papers: Some Suggestions." *Training the New Teacher of College Composition.* Ed. Charles W. Bridges. Urbana: NCTE, 1986. 109–116. Provides suggestions on how new teachers of writing can develop their own assignments then evaluate and respond to their students' writing.

Lawrence, Joyce V. "Fostering and Monitoring TA Development: What Administrators Can Do." *Institutional Responsibilities and Responses in the Employment and Education of Teaching Assistants.* Ed. Nancy Van Note Chism. Columbus: Ohio State University Center for Teaching Excellence, 1987. 44–46. Discusses levels of interaction between graduate students and the university and how that relationship can become more positive through careful planning on the part of the graduate school. Examines the need for orientation, plans for performance evaluation, knowledge of graduate school's advocacy and support, and service assistance. Lists seven steps administrators can take to foster and monitor TA development.

Lunsford, Ronald F. "Planning for Spontaneity in the Writing Classroom and a Passel of Other Paradoxes." Training the New Teacher of College Composition. Ed. Charles W. Bridges. Urbana: NCTE, 1986. 95–108. Based on the author's own experience and study, suggests that the advantages of peer group editing outweigh the disadvantages, especially when the teacher acts as a consultant, moving from group to group, offering advice when called upon. Suggests short- and long-term training methods to prepare students to participate successfully in peer editing and revising.

McBroom, Geraldine L. "A New Crop of Teaching Assistants and How They Grew." *WPA: Writing Program Administration* 15.3 (1992): 62–68. Traces the development of a group of TAs from novices to "emerging teachers" based on comments they made in journals during their first year as instructors. Describes how these TAs overcame their initial anxiety about teaching by developing individual teaching styles, forming more realistic expectations about their jobs and their students, and learning about composition instruction from peers and faculty mentors.

Mauksch, Hans O. "The Context of Preparing Teaching Assistants." Institutional Responsibilities and Responses in the Employment and Education of Teaching Assistants. Ed. Nancy Van Note Chism. Columbus: Ohio State University Center for Teaching Excellence, 1987. 14–18. Says teaching becomes devalued for both professors and teaching assistants when too much emphasis is placed on natural talent rather than practice and work. Discusses several assumptions harmful to teachers, including the idea that the ability to teach is an innate gift.

Puccio, Paul M. "Graduate Instructor Representation in Writing Programs." Conference on College Composition and Communication. St. Louis, March 1988. ED 297 333. Presents the results of a survey of TA training techniques employed in 50 writing programs which revealed widespread interest in and reliance on peer support. Discusses the advantages and drawbacks of peer training and questions whether peers offer any insights not available from more experienced instructors.

Reagan, Sally Barr. "Practicing What We Preach." CEA Forum 20 (1990): 16–18. Suggests that TA training can be improved if supervisors move beyond the traditional instructional methods of reading, discussing, and lecturing. Offers as an alternative a training program that stresses practical experience and collaboration with faculty. Describes a program where new TAs observe and evaluate faculty-taught composition and literature courses which stress collaborative learning.

———. "Teaching TAs to Teach: Show, Don't Tell." *WPA: Writing Program Administration* 11.3 (1988): 41–51. Outlines a seven-step process developed at Drake University for showing TAs how to modify their classroom practices to meet the needs of different types of students. Describes how the TA supervisor used the Myers-Briggs Personality Inventory, interviews, course evaluations, and meetings to help TAs appreciate how different types of instruction affect different types of students. Provides results and caveats derived from the initial trial of the program.

Recchio, Thomas E. "Parallel Academic Lives: Affinities of Teaching Assistants and Freshman Writers." *WPA: Writing Program Administration* 15.3 (1992): 57–61. Argues that graduate teaching assistants have much in common with the students they teach. The transition one makes from undergraduate to graduate school is, in many ways, similar to the transition students make from high school to college. These similarities help TAs sympathize with the difficulties first-year students face in class as they are confronted by new information and critical concepts. Offers suggestions on how TAs may better understand their tasks as teachers of "critical consciousness."

Roberts, David D. "Survival Prosperity: TA Training Colloquia." Freshman English News 10.3 (1982): 4, 12–14. Identifies two goals often overlooked in TA training programs: TA prosperity and TA survival. In addition to stressing the theories behind rhetoric, organization, language acquisition, etc., training programs should also stress practical steps TAs should take to survive.

Ruszkiewicz, John J. "Doing What I Do: How New Teachers of Writing Compose." Conference on College Composition and Communication. Minneapolis, April 1979. ED 172 211. Presents the results of an informal survey of new TAs concerning their plans for teaching. Found that most TAs plan to base instruction in their composition classes on how they themselves compose essays and need to find better ways to cover pre-writing and grammar.

———. "The Great Commandment." Training the New Teacher of College Composition. Ed. Charles W. Bridges. Urbana: NCTE, 1986. 78–83. Suggests that, above all, writing teachers should teach writing. Emphasizes as goals for a writing course teaching invention, structure, style, audience analysis, assessment, and revision. Recognizes the difficult task TAs face and suggests they can overcome some problems by treating their students as apprentice writers.

Schenck, Mary Jane. "Writing Right Off: Strategies for Invention." Training the New Teacher of College Composition. Ed. Charles W. Bridges. Urbana: NCTE, 1986. 84–94. Argues that TAs' desire to maintain control in the classroom may limit their students' opportunity to explore certain invention techniques. Suggests that composition classes should use movies or current events to generate discussions in the classroom and should emphasize responding to and analyzing what students have read or seen. Urges TAs to consider using journals, free-writing, heuristics, and collaboration as invention activities.

Simpson, Isaiah. "Training and Evaluating Teaching Assistants through Team Teaching." Freshman English News 15.3 (1987): 4, 9–13. Argues that TAs are primarily teachers rather than assistants. Outlines the benefits of "team teaching"—having faculty members and TAs teach a course together. Discusses the strengths and weaknesses of such programs, explaining how they help train and evaluate new teaching assistants. Describes program developed at Southern Illinois University, Edwardsville, where faculty members work with TAs teaching one course a year.

Smith, Eugene, and Marilyn Smith. "A Graduate Internship in Teaching." Teaching English in the Two-year College 16 (1989): 197–200. Describes an internship program developed by the University of Washington and North Seattle Community College which places TAs at a two-year college to observe teaching practices and to provide basic assistance. Discusses benefits to the graduate students, faculty, and students. Provides a basic outline for instituting a similar program at other universities and two-year colleges.

Smith, Ron. "The Supervisor of In-service Training in Small Programs: A Basic Job Description." Conference on College Composition and Communication. Philadelphia, March 1976. ED 128 806. Argues that supervising TAs in smaller graduate programs differs from supervising them in larger programs. Suggests that supervisors in smaller programs must act as the TAs' manager, teacher, and friend, roles that sometimes conflict. Describes the qualifications effective TA supervisors must possess and outlines the primary duties and responsibilities they must meet.

Sprague, Jo, and Jody D. Nyquist. "TA Supervision." Teaching Assistant Training in the 1990s. Ed. Jody D. Nyquist, Robert D. Abbott, and Donald H. Wulff. San Francisco: Jossey, 1989. 37–53. Argues that TA supervisors must play several roles: manager, professional model, and mentor. Argues that supervisors can better succeed in these roles if they understand the changes TAs undergo as they move through several "phases" of development: senior learner, to colleague in training, to junior colleague. Suggests how TA supervisors can best help TAs at each stage of development.

Staton, Ann Q., and Ann L. Darling. "Socialization of Teaching Assistants." Teaching Assistant Training in the 1990s. Ed. Jody D. Nyquist, Robert D. Abbott, and Donald H. Wulff. San Francisco: Jossey, 1989. 15–22. Discusses the difficult position of TAs in the academy: being both student and teacher poses potential problems for new teaching assistants. Describes how TAs undergo both "role" and "cultural" socialization as they learn to work with their colleagues, succeed in graduate school, succeed as teachers, and advance in the academy. Suggests how training programs can facilitate successful socialization among TAs.

Strenski, Ellen. "Helping TAs Across the Curriculum Teach Writing: An Additional Use for the TA Handbook." WPA: Writing Program Administration 15.3 (1992): 68–73. Stresses the importance of a well-crafted TA handbook. Suggests that authors of TA handbooks are often too preoccupied with plagiarism and grading standards. Although these issues are important, other issues, such as time management, assignment design, and essay response should also be addressed in a TA handbook.

Strickland, Karen Syvrud. "Planning and Facilitating a Group Workshop." Conference on Employment and Education of Teaching Assistants. Columbus, OH, November 1986. ED 285 501. Discusses modeling and role-playing as tools for teaching new TAs. Suggests organizing informal gatherings to help TAs become familiar and willing to share ideas with one another.

Tirrell, Mary Kay. "Teaching Assistants as Teachers and Writers: Developmental Issues in TA Training." Writing Instructor 5 (1986): 51–56. Examines student and TA growth in light of the developmental theories expounded by Piaget, Vygotsky, Perry, and Bruner. Suggests that composition classes should be based on an understanding of students' cognitive and social growth. Explains how TA supervisors can use mentor programs, peer coaching, and journal writing to aid TA development.

Tremmel, Robert. "Beyond Self-criticism: Reflecting on Teacher Research and TA Education." Composition Studies 22.1 (1994): 44–64. Explores how work in "reflective practice" developed in teacher education programs can be used to improve TA training programs. Reviews efforts to improve TA training, noting relatively little attention has been given to the importance of "self-reflection" as a learning tool. Offers several suggestions on how to develop more reflective, self-critical TAs.

Webster, Janice Gohm. "Composition Teachers: No Experience Necessary?" ADE Bulletin 92 (1989): 41–42. Argues against having inexperienced TAs teach composition classes. Suggests instead that all tenured faculty members teach at least one composition class a term so TAs are free to take a course preparing them to be instructors.

Webster, John. "Great Expectations: Introducing Teaching Portfolios to a University Writing Program." National Council of Teachers of English Meeting. Louisville, November 1992. ED 361 748. Discusses how, at the University of Washington, a teaching portfolio system was implemented not only to assess and review the TAs' progress but also to help the TAs in the job market. Describes the content of the portfolios and the four-year process they followed to implement the program. Examines the strengths and limitations of portfolios and offers model criteria and assignments.

Weimer, Maryellen, Marilla D. Svinicki, and Gabriele Bauer. "Designing Programs to Prepare TAs to Teach." *Teaching Assistant Training in the 1990s*. Ed. Jody D. Nyquist, Robert D. Abbott, and Donald H. Wulff. San Francisco: Jossey, 1989. 57–70. Offers a series of questions that must be addressed by anyone beginning or evaluating a TA training program: (1) who should provide training; (2) if there are different providers, what should be the relationships among them; (3) how long should the program be and when should it occur; (4) what sorts of follow-up activities should be offered; (5) do international TAs need separate and more extensive preparation; (6) how should training be evaluated?

Weiser, Irwin. "Surveying New Teaching Assistants: Who They Are, What They Know, and What They Want to Know." *WPA: Writing Program Administration* 14.1–2 (1990): 63–71. Contends that TA training programs could be improved if supervisors gained a better understanding of the TAs' experiences, needs, concerns, and questions before they begin any orientation activities. Advocates sending a survey to all new TAs to gather this information and describes the findings resulting from a survey of new TAs at Purdue University. Includes a copy of the survey form.

———. "Teaching Assistants as Collaborators in Their Preparation and Evaluation." *Evaluating Teachers of Writing*. Ed. Christine A. Hult. Urbana: NCTE, 1994. 133–146. Argues that involving TAs in their preparation and evaluation contributes to their success in meeting the goals of a TA training program. Describes three ways TAs specifically contribute to their training and evaluation: they complete pre-orientation surveys, evaluate their mentors, and help choose which questions appear on the end-of-term student evaluations for the courses they teach.

Wilhoit, Stephen. "Conducting Research: An Essential Aspect of TA Training." *Kentucky English Bulletin* 39.1 (1989): 48–55. Outlines how TAs can join the teacher-research movement by conducting studies of their students. Suggests seven types of research projects TAs can undertake, examining the strengths and limitations of each. Argues that undertaking research projects is an important part of TA training.

———. "Toward a Comprehensive TA Training Program." *Kansas English* 78.2 (1993): 66–74. Argues that effective TA training programs must focus equal attention on teaching, graduate study, and professional development. Suggests specific skills TAs need to acquire to become successful teachers, students, and scholars.

Williams, Linda Stallworth. "The Effects of a Comprehensive Teaching Assistant Training Program on Teaching Anxiety and Effectiveness." *Research in Higher Education* 32 (1991): 585–598. Reports the results of a comprehensive study of how training programs affect TA anxiety. Twenty-seven TAs at the University of Oklahoma were divided into two groups: both participated in a pre-service training program and in-service theory and pedagogy course, but the experimental group also participated in a consultant observation and peer mentor program. TAs in the experimental group experienced lower levels of anxiety. Neither group, though, demonstrated an increase in teaching effectiveness ratings from students at the end of the term.

PROGRAM DESCRIPTIONS

Altman, Howard B. "TA Training at the University of Louisville: Creating a Climate." *Institutional Responsibilities and Responses in the Employment and Education of Teaching Assistants.* Ed. Nancy Van Note Chism. Columbus: Ohio State University Center for Teaching Excellence, 1987. 174–76. Describes the contents of the University of Louisville program's preacademic orientation for new TAs and the series of professional pedagogical seminars held twice a semester where TAs meet with outstanding faculty members to discuss pertinent issues. Evaluates the program by discussing the effectiveness or ineffectiveness of certain procedures and mentions future plans for training.

Bloom, Lynn Z. "Finding a Family, Finding a Voice: A Writing Teacher Teaches Writing Teachers." *Journal of Basic Writing* 9.2 (1990): 3–14. Discusses the circumstances which lead to changes in the TA training program at Virginia Commonwealth University. Stresses the importance of teaching writing instructors to focus on their own composing processes as a means of better understanding how to teach writing. Advocates forming a personal bond, a "community of writers," among professors and graduate students. Uses quotations from students' journals to illustrate the effectiveness of the program.

Diogenes, Marvin, Duane H. Roen, and C. Jan Swearingen. "Creating the Profession: The GAT Training Program at the University of Arizona." *WPA: Writing Program Administration* 10.1–2 (1986): 51–59. Describes the TA training program at the University of Arizona, which attempts to treat TAs as junior colleagues in the department by developing a sense of shared purpose. Includes information on Arizona's teaching handbook, class visitations, small group workshops, and successful TA/faculty collaborative publishing efforts.

Gefvert, Constance J. "An Apprenticeship for Teaching Assistants." *Freshman English News* 10.3 (1982): 16–19. Describes the TA apprenticeship program developed at Virginia Polytechnic Institute and State University. This program involves a reduced teaching load for new TAs so they can participate in an extensive pre-service workshop, complete course work in composition theory and pedagogy, participate in small advising groups led by faculty advisers, and work in at least one specialized setting (i.e., the Writing Center, a community college, etc.). Explains how the English Department obtained adequate institutional support for their program revisions.

Hairston, Maxine. "Training Teaching Assistants in English." College Composition and Communication 25 (1974): 52–55. Describes the TA training program at the University of Texas, Austin, and its extensive use of peer counselors. Explains how, because of the large number of new TAs entering the department each year, the program began forming 5 or 6 new TAs into peer support and training groups lead by experienced TAs. These "counselors" meet weekly with the new TAs to design course goals, answer questions, and discuss grading standards. Describes how the program benefits the department, new TAs, and the counselors themselves.

Hansen, Kristine, Phillip A. Snyder, Nancy Davenport, and Kimberli Stafford. "Collaborative Learning and Teaching: A Model for Mentoring TAs." *The TA Experience: Preparing for Multiple Roles*. Ed. Karron G. Lewis. Stillwater: New Forums Press, 1993. 251–259. Discusses the TA training program at Brigham Young University, which relies heavily on collaborative learning and faculty mentoring. After their initial training, TAs teach first-year composition courses then have the opportunity to team-teach large advanced writing courses with faculty. Other aspects of training include peer mentoring and class visitations. Provides assessment information suggesting the team-teaching model achieves good results.

Hayes, Darwin L. "Integrating Supervision, Evaluation, and Training: Graduate Student Internships in Teaching Composition." *Institutional Responsibilities and Responses in the Employment and Education of Teaching Assistants*. Ed. Nancy Van Note Chism. Columbus: Ohio State University Center for Teaching Excellence, 1987. 227–229. Describes the graduate student writing internship program at Brigham Young University. Students are prepared to teach upper-level English courses by being paired with faculty mentors, observing the faculty member teach the course before assuming sole responsibility for the class the following term. Maintains that the program improves the TAs' chances for employment and promotes collegiality.

Humphreys, W. Lee. "The TA Seminar and TA Support Services at the University of Tennessee, Knoxville." *Institutional Responsibilities and Responses in the Employment and Education of Teaching Assistants*. Ed. Nancy Van Note Chism. Columbus: Ohio State University Center for Teaching Excellence, 1987. 171–173. Describes the two main objectives of the TA training program at the University of Tennessee-Knoxville: to enhance the instruction offered on campus and to help TAs develop their professional skills for future university teaching jobs. Discusses the format and content of the training seminar and lists other support services.

Irmscher, William F. "TA Training: A Period of Discovery." *Training the New Teacher of College Composition*. Ed. Charles W. Bridges. Urbana: NCTE, 1986. 27–36. Describes the training program at the University of Washington. Argues that the similarities between the situations faced by new TAs and first-year students can be used to establish a sense of community in the classroom. Discusses the benefits of peer observation among TAs. Highlights the role of the director of training.

Jackson, William K. "Support Services for Graduate Teaching Assistants at the University of Georgia." *Institutional Responsibilities and Responses in the Employment and Education of Teaching Assistants.* Ed. Nancy Van Note Chism. Columbus: Ohio State University Center for Teaching Excellence, 1987. 158–59. Describes support services for TAs offered at the University of Georgia, such as a TA handbook, optional training program, international student screening for assistantships, and recognition of outstanding TA performance.

Puccio, Paul M. "TAs Help TAs: Peer Counseling and Mentoring." Conference on Employment and Education of Teaching Assistants. Columbus, November 1987. ED 285 502. Describes how the University of Massachusetts Resource Center provides experienced TAs as volunteer counselors for new TAs. Peer counselors use videotaping to make new TAs more aware of their teaching style. Suggests ways to train TA counselors so their relationship with new TAs remains friendly and productive.

Robinson, William S. "Teaching Composition Teachers How to Teach Writing." *Composition Chronicle* 3 (December 1990): 4–6. Describes the "Certificate in the Teaching of Composition" program at San Francisco State University. Focuses on the evolution of the program from a one-course seminar to a full-fledged MA degree. Argues that obtaining the certificate has helped students gain entrance into postgraduate programs and earn positions as writing program administrators.

Smith, Philip E., II. "A Pedagogy of Critical and Cultural Empowerment: What We Talk about in Graduate Teaching Seminars." Conference on College Composition and Communication. Seattle, March 1989. ED 307 617. Outlines the philosophy behind the University of Pittsburgh's graduate program and graduate teaching seminars. Describes content and emphasis of training seminars on teaching reading and writing, giving examples of readings employed. Includes excerpts of graduate student papers discussing teaching.

Smith, William L. "Using a College Writing Workshop in Training Future English Teachers." *English Education* 16.2 (1984): 76–82. Describes the University of Pittsburgh's Writing Workshop and the three-stage, highly structured internship program future writing teachers complete as a practical component to a required methods and theory course. Describes how the program gradually leads to the intern becoming an independent tutor before doing any actual classroom teaching. Lists five effects which the tutorial internship has been observed to have on interns' and former interns' teaching.

Van DeWeghe, Richard P. "Linking Pedagogy to Purpose for Teaching Assistants in Basic Writing." *Training the New Teacher of College Composition.* Ed. Charles W. Bridges. Urbana: NCTE, 1986. 37–46. Outlines the TA training some teaching assistants have when asked to teach technical writing courses. Attributes these fears to stereotypes and misconceptions concerning technical writing. Identifies and explores solutions to some of the problems TAs face when teaching these courses.

Employment Issues

Baker, Marilyn J. "Grievances and Taxes." *Institutional Responsibilities and Responses in the Employment and Education of Teaching Assistants.* Ed. Nancy Van Note Chism. Columbus: State University Center for Teaching Excellence, 1987. 49–52. Asserts that TAs need to be aware of grievance procedures and that those procedures should be tailored to the TAs' peculiar needs as both students and employees.

Outlines grievance procedures at the University of Southern California, discusses common complaints, and recommends specific measures to avoid them. Discusses tax laws and suggests ways to lessen their impact on TAs.

Carlson, Charles E. "A Negotiator's Perspective." *Institutional Responsibilities and Responses in the Employment and Education of Teaching Assistants.* Ed. Nancy Van Note Chism. Columbus: Ohio State University Center for Teaching Excellence, 1987. 60–64. Discusses future of collective bargaining for the University of Wisconsin-Madison, after legislation passed extending collective bargaining privileges to TAs. Gives background on his experience as a professional negotiator with the University of Wisconsin-Madison and the TAA (Teaching Assistant Association), discussing pros and cons of the arrangement. Elaborates on the difficulties TAs will encounter in bargaining with a state agency and discusses how the new legislation will affect all parties.

Craig, Judith S. "An Administrative Perspective." *Institutional Responsibilities and Responses in the Employment and Education of Teaching Assistants.* Ed. Nancy Van Note Chism. Columbus: Ohio State University Center for Teaching Excellence, 1987. 53–60. Gives background on what led to collective bargaining between the TAA (Teaching Assistant Association) and the administration at the University of Wisconsin-Madison, and discusses some of its consequences for graduate students and the university. Talks about common issues that surfaced during bargaining such as wages and benefits, workloads, evaluation processes, grievance procedures, course content and pedagogy, and jurisdiction. Lists advantages and disadvantages of collective bargaining.

———. "University-level Policies for TAs: Experience at the University of Wisconsin, Madison." *Institutional Responsibilities and Responses in the Employment and Education of Teaching Assistants.* Ed. Nancy Van Note Chism. Columbus: Ohio State University Center for Teaching Excellence, 1987. 38–43. Discusses origins, structures, problem areas, and strengths of teaching assistant policies at the University of Wisconsin-Madison.

Gething, Thomas. "Stipends and Workloads." *Institutional Responsibilities and Responses in the Employment and Education of Teaching Assistants.* Ed. Nancy Van Note Chism. Columbus: Ohio State University Center for Teaching Excellence, 1987. 47–49. Describes how the University of Hawaii handles TA stipends and workloads. Discusses five areas of concern for TAs and administrators: setting stipends, adjusting stipends, establishing variable rate stipends, deciding workloads and overloads, and obtaining comparative national data.

Minkel, C. W. "The Formulation of University Policy for Graduate Assistantship Administration." *Institutional Responsibilities and Responses in the Employment and Education of Teaching Assistants.* Ed. Nancy Van Note Chism. Columbus: Ohio State University Center for Teaching Excellence, 1987. 35–37. Presents results of a survey on teaching assistant conditions in 46 major universities based on those universities' policies and procedures. Recommends that universities use a "model policy" for graduate assistant administration that focuses on issues such as training, teaching goals, qualifications, outside employment, and academic standards.

Weiser, Irwin, and Karen Dwyer. "The CCCC's 'Statement of Principles and Standards for the Postsecondary Teaching of Writing': Implications for Writing Program Administrators and Teaching Assistants." *The TA Experience: Preparing for Multiple Roles.* Ed. Karron G. Lewis. Stillwater: New Forums Press, 1993. 19–24. Discusses the problems of applying standard, universal guidelines concerning the teaching of writing to particular institutions, using as an example the authors' efforts to apply the CCCC's guidelines to the writing program in place at Purdue University.

Special attention is given to the four guidelines that most directly apply to the role of graduate teaching assistants in the department. Argues that the CCCC's standards work best as guidelines, not as blueprints for program reform.

History of TA Training

Marting, Janet. "A Retrospective on Training Teaching Assistants." *WPA: Writing Program Administration* 11.1–2 (1987): 35–44. Traces similarities and differences among the concerns addressed in various discussions of TA training since 1930. Identifies historical shifts in opinion, especially on the question of whether academic or pedagogical preparation should be emphasized in training programs. Describes the fruitful mix of scholarship and pedagogy that characterizes the content of most current TA training programs.

Parrett, Joan L. "A Ten-Year Review of TA Training Programs: Trends, Patterns, and Common Practices." *Institutional Responsibilities and Responses in the Employment and Education of Teaching Assistants.* Ed. Nancy Van Note Chism. Columbus: Ohio State University Center for Teaching Excellence, 1987. 67–79. Describes a study of teaching-assistant training programs at the University of Colorado, describing both the theory-based orientation meeting and the more practical series of workshops held throughout the school year. Provides detailed descriptions of three sample workshops illustrating how they combine theory and practice.

Teaching Duties

Allen, O. Jane. "The Literature Major as Teacher of Technical Writing: A Bibliographical Orientation." *Training the New Teacher of College Composition.* Ed. Charles W. Bridges. Urbana: NCTE, 1986. 69–77. Asserts that in the future, TAs will likely teach lower-level technical writing classes which have become increasingly popular among students and increasingly hard to staff. Claims that if TAs are to succeed as teachers of technical writing, technical writing must be placed in the context of other types of writing. Provides bibliographic material on four points of emphasis: definition, audience analysis, visual aids, and collaboration. Concludes with suggestions for research in technical writing.

Blalock, Susan E. "The Tutor as Creative Teacher: Balancing Collaborative and Directive Teaching Styles." *The TA Experience: Preparing for Multiple Roles.* Ed. Karron G. Lewis. Stillwater: New Forums Press, 1993. 348–352. Describes how, at the University of Alaska-Fairbanks, graduate teaching assistants also work in the university writing center. Lessons learned working with students one-on-one in the writing center transfer to teaching strategies in the composition classroom and help TAs address the individual problems of students in their classes.

Broder, Peggy F. "Writing Centers and Teacher Training." *WPA: Writing Program Administration* 13.3 (1990): 37–45. Provides a general description of how working as tutors in writing centers can provide invaluable experience for prospective classroom teachers. Includes affirming comments from former tutors who have since become classroom teachers.

Comprone, Joseph J. "Managing Freshman English: Are We Really on the Right Track?" Conference on College Composition and Communication. Cincinnati, March 1992. ED 344 209. Questions whether TAs are best served by being put in charge of 25–30 students in a composition class of their own. Offers as an alternative having TAs meet with students in discussion sections of a much larger composition class taught by a professor. Describes how he designed such an experimental course at Michigan Technological University (113 first-year students, 9 TAs). Includes assessment techniques employed to evaluate the class, discusses student and TA response to the course, and suggests how schools can design similar courses.

Cox, Don R. "Fear and Loathing in the Classroom: Teaching Technical Writing for the First Time." *Training the New Teacher of College Composition.* Ed. Charles W. Bridges. Urbana: NCTE, 1986. 58–68. Examines the fears that centered on training program patterns, training methods, and training formats from 1976 to 1986 across academic disciplines at a number of institutions. Issues addressed include curricular planning, TA participation, professionalism, TA duties and problems, instructional aids, student learning patterns, and general education.

Pytlik, Betty P. "A Short History of Graduate Preparation of Writing Teachers." National Council of Teachers of English Meeting. Louisville, November 1992. ED 355 545. Sketches the history of writing-teacher education in the United States. Identifies several reasons why the 1950s was a decade of academic reform in English, emphasizing how it proved to be a crucial transition period that greatly affected the way graduate students were trained to teach.

———. "Teaching the Teacher of Writing: Whence and Wither?" Conference on College Composition and Communication. San Diego, March 1993. ED 355 541. Discusses some of the academic and administration changes brought about by World War II and the enactment of the G.I. Bill of Rights in 1944. Describes the freshman composition programs into which returning war veterans were placed. Describes, too, some of the few graduate methods courses offered during the forties, fifties, and sixties, as well as the typical training program for TAs entering the profession at that time.

———. "Teaching the Teachers of Writing: Evolving Theory." Conference on College Composition and Communication. Cincinnati, March 1992. ED 345 273. Discusses the culture-versus-efficiency debate that took place in the early decades of this century and from which TA training emerged. Identifies seven early twentieth-century assumptions about teacher preparation that still exist today.

PART IV

CURRICULUM DESIGN
AND ASSESSMENT

Curriculum Design for First-Year Writing Programs

David Smit

Kansas State University

For most of the fifty years that composition studies has been an academic field, the curriculum of first-year writing courses has been a matter of intense debate. Scholars in the field have argued about the kinds of writing that should be taught and the pedagogical strategies that should be used to teach writing from a wide range of perspectives and points of view, but no consensus has emerged about the "content" of introductory writing courses, except that they should require some amount of writing. The lack of such a consensus has existed since the beginning of the Conference on College Composition and Communication (CCCC) in 1949. In his inaugural article in *College Composition and Communication* in 1950, John C. Gerber, the first president of CCCC, lamented that the approximately nine thousand faculty members teaching college courses in composition and communication at the time shared the same problems and "the same general objectives," but that they had "for the most part gone [their] separate ways, experimenting here and improvising there" (12).

Forty-five years later, Denise David, Barbara Gordon, and Rita Pollard summarized the very different ways that writing was being taught in postsecondary institutions: as an introduction to the discourse of various disciplines, as a means of transforming social inequities, and as a way to talk about multiculturalism, literature, or other topics. In order to bring some coherence to these divergent views, David, Gordon, and Pollard proposed that composition studies get back to basics and rethink the fundamental question, "What do we mean when we call a course a writing course?" (524). To promote such reflection the group suggested that all writing courses should have the following characteristics:

1. The development of writing ability and metacognitive awareness its the primary objective of a writing course.

2. The students' writing is the privileged text in a writing course.

3. The subject of a writing course is writing." That is, what the students should spend most of their time thinking about and talking about is how they go about understanding themselves as writers, how they get ideas, how they compose in relation to various subjects, genres, and audiences, and how they respond to criticism of their work. (525–26)

To some scholars in the field this program may have seemed so uncontroversial as to be banal, but the article met with severe objections from two scholars with very different perspectives. On the one hand, Katherine Gottschalk argued that students have to write about particular subjects and therefore that writing instructors should devote class time to extensive discussion of that subject matter and to explorations of various points of view about those subjects. On the other hand, Phyllis Mentzell Ryder argued that writing is socially conditioned and therefore that writing instructors should spend considerable class time offering students "useful theoretical insights about language so that they can critically engage with the world around them" (601).

It would seem, then, that in fifty years as a profession and an academic field composition studies has few shared "premises and principles" for a first-year writing curriculum, except perhaps those articulated by Peter Elbow:

...that writing is the creating or constructing of meaning, not the transmission of meaning already worked out; that we need to work in whole discourse, not in bits and pieces progressing from word to sentence to paragraph to longer pieces, and that we need not start by learning grammar; that it's an essentially rhetorical enterprise such that we cannot put all emphasis on message and leave out audience or stance or voice; that we need to get students to write to more audiences than just to the teacher—for which it's helpful for them often to share their work with each other in small groups; indeed, that the construction of meaning tends to be a social enterprise as much as if not more than an individual one. (134–35)

In this bibliographic essay, I hope to provide new writing program administrators (WPAs), or more experienced WPAs contemplating a change in curriculum, a brief history of curricula in first-year writing courses so that they can make their curricular decisions in the larger context of what has gone before and what is being currently done. I will also offer a few theoretical and practical issues that WPAs should consider, if they have the opportunity and the means to design a new curriculum for their particular institutions.

A BRIEF HISTORY OF FIRST-YEAR WRITING CURRICULA

It strikes me that there have been three major periods in the way writing has been taught in introductory courses since World War II. The first was the "current-traditional" rhetoric that introductory writing courses inherited from the nineteenth century. The second was a result of the burst of creativity in discourse theory in the 1970s by the three Jameses—Kinneavy, Britton, and Moffett—and the rise of the "process approach" to teaching writing. This creativity produced a veritable chaos of new ways of thinking about first-year writing. The third was a result of the "social turn" in composition studies in the late 1980s and 1990s, which emphasized the contextual nature of meaning and the ways writing varies depending on genre and context. The turn toward the "social" resulted in courses that emphasized the nature of literacy, the many ways people use writing to accomplish various purposes in their lives, and the critical and theoretical knowledge necessary for writers to be active participants in a civic culture.

Current-Traditional Rhetoric

John Gerber was dismayed about the lack of consensus in writing instruction in 1950 despite the fact that at the time most writing was taught in what now seems a relatively unified way. Composition studies inherited a nineteenth-century tradition that writing was a generic ability best taught by training or disciplining the mind. In practice, this tenet of the faculty psychology of the period resulted in courses in which students simply wrote a large number of "themes" on various subjects, each "theme" a personal exploration of a topic assigned by the instructor. It was assumed that practice in writing themes on these topics trained students to organize any kind of writing on any subject, and it trained them to do so with a certain amount of eloquence and style.

Over time "theme writing" as the organizing principle of introductory writing courses evolved into what Richard Young has identified as "current traditional" rhetoric. The most common way to organize a course in current-traditional rhetoric was to assign students a series of themes or essays, which had to exemplify various modes of discourse: the descriptive essay, the definition essay, the comparison-and-contrast essay, the cause-and-effect essay, the explanatory essay, and the persuasive essay, to name the most popular. The rationale for organizing introductory courses this way was largely uninterrogated, and, we assume, primarily historical: that is, writing teachers tended to accept uncritically the notion that writing is a generic ability that could best be fostered by training the mind in certain basic organizational patterns. Once novice writers had learned these basic patterns they could apply them in new combinations in any genre and in any context.

As a result of this history, it is still common in the field to think of writing as just writing, as a comprehensive and unified set of knowledge and abilities, which can be taught in conjunction with any subject matter. Hence, the number of first-year writing courses which have been arbitrarily yoked with other subjects: writing about literature, writing arguments, writing and critical thinking, writing and multiculturalism, writing and cultural studies, and even versions of writing across the curriculum (WAC). Generally, the writing assigned in these courses follows the "content" of the course, and students are assigned to write only one genre, the personal essay. Often, the writing is used to evaluate how the students have understood the concepts and terms being taught in the course.

Curricula after the Dartmouth Conference and in the Age of Process

In 1966 the Dartmouth Conference met to discuss the teaching and learning of English. Participants came from both sides of the Atlantic. At the conference, John Dixon, James Moffett, and James Britton, among others, challenged the current-traditional paradigm and started a revolution in first-year writing curricula. Basically, the main point of the reformers was that writing is much more than the manipulation of a number of discourse conventions and that writing as a whole is much richer than the mere transmission of information. On the contrary, writing is based on the lived experience of writers and what they want to accomplish in particular social contexts. In addition, students develop writing abilities as a part of their cognitive and emotional development as a whole.

Soon after the Dartmouth Conference, James Moffett published his groundbreaking curriculum, *A Student-Centered Language Arts Curriculum, K–13: A Handbook for Teachers*, and its accompanying theoretical justification, *Teaching the Universe of Discourse* (1968). In these works, Moffett proposed that all writing is, in some sense, related to a particular subject matter and that all writing is, in some sense, rhetorical; that is, writers always write about a particular subject to a particular audience. And because writing abilities follow psychological development, Moffett argued that the English curriculum should be organized to develop the abilities of students in these two directions. The English curriculum should be based on students' increasing ability to move from concrete experience to abstract knowledge, and it should be based on students' increasing ability to move from immediate, personal audiences to more distant and abstract audiences.

Moffett's books were concerned primarily with the elementary and high school curriculum, so their influence on college-level writing programs was primarily theoretical. They provided composition specialists with an intellectual framework for thinking about the nature and sequence of the writing required in first-year writing courses.

Perhaps even more influential than Moffett's work was James Kinneavy's *A Theory of Discourse* (1971). Kinneavy argued strongly against the traditional modes as a way of classifying discourse and provided a much more rigorous and theoretically informed taxonomy. In Kinneavy's taxonomy, discourse is grouped in terms of four purposes or aims; expressive, referential, persuasive, and literary discourse. Kinneavy's work reinforced Moffett's and gave compositionists even more reason to think about the kind of writing that should be offered in first-year courses and how it should be taught: not according to preestablished conventions and formats but in ways that would help writers achieve their purposes.

Finally, in *The Development of Writing Abilities, 11–18* (1975), James Britton and his colleagues built on Moffett's work by elaborating on his concepts of discourse and audience. Britton and his coworkers developed an elaborate taxonomy of discourse that basically divided all of discourse into two main classes—the expressive and the transactional—and another taxonomy of possible audiences for students—the self, the teacher, and wider-known and unknown audiences.

This new emphasis on the range of discourse, the many ways writing can be done depending on its purpose, audience, and context was accompanied by a new interest in the "writing process," influenced most heavily by Janet Emig's book *The Composing Processes of Twelfth Graders.* In many ways, the specific conclusions Emig drew from her study of eight twelfth-graders have been less important than the mere fact that she insisted that composing processes were worth studying in the first place. Emig collected the writing her subjects did during the school year, conducted a number of intensive interviews, and required the students to compose several essays aloud. She developed a taxonomy of features for analyzing the composing process: planning, starting, composing aloud, hesitation and the tempo of composing, reformulation, and stopping and contemplating the product.

From these observations, Emig concluded that composing is recursive; it "does not occur as left-to-right, solid, uninterrupted activity with an even pace" (84). Rather, people compose according to their own individual rhythms, which start and stop, ebb and flow, according to what comes to mind as they try to juggle what they want to say in relation to what they have already said, their larger goal, and their accumulated experience of how writing should be done in the situation they find themselves. Emig's work resulted in a host of studies of the composing process, both theoretical and empirical, in the 70s and early 80s.

Designing Courses by Thematic and Rhetorical Sequences

In response to the creative theorizing about discourse and the intensive research into composing processes, many compositionists began to rethink the nature of first-year writing courses and offer rationales not about how writing could be taught as a collection of modes or as a way to promote a certain subject matter but about how writing could be taught as writing. The most innovative proposals emphasized that writing assignments should be tightly organized sequences which build on one another, thus taking into consideration, if only metaphorically, the developmental nature of learning to write and providing students with the opportunity to look back on what they have done and to reflect on the concepts highlighted by the assignment sequences.

For example, Moffett's curriculum was organized to reinforce the students' developing cognitive abilities. Students begin writing dialogues and letters about concrete subjects for familiar audiences as soon as they are able to put pencil to paper. Then, over the course of their elementary and high school careers, they write about increasingly abstract subjects to increasingly unknown or hostile audiences. Moffett devised an elaborate taxonomy of types of discourse that students might practice in school, beginning with dramatic dialogues and correspondence, proceeding through diaries, autobiographical narratives, memoirs, and various kinds of reportage, and culminating in what he calls "generalizing" and "theorizing": practice in making generalizations based on various particulars and conveying the results of research to audiences who might want or need to know the information.

Although Moffett's curriculum was designed mostly for elementary and high school language arts, it influenced a great many compositionists at the college level. For example, Gene Krupa designed a series of related assignments that requires students to use the same experience as the basis for writing for different purposes in different genres. In one such series Krupa invites his students to write about a job they have held. In the first assignment the students express how they feel about the job as if they were talking to a friend. In the second assignment they write a set of instructions to help others who work at the job overcome some problems associated with it. The third assignment is to write a letter of recommendation for someone who might want the job (*Situational* 30–35, 67–73, 116–22). The point of this series of assignments, of course, is to help students see that their knowledge and experience about a single subject can be the basis for many different kinds of writing, which use different genre conventions depending on the writer's purpose and audience, and to help them develop a strategy, a way of thinking, about the many aspects of writing they must control: a sense of style and voice, a sense of the variability of genre conventions, a sense of audience, what we might call rhetorical maturity.

Krupa also justifies these "rhetorically based" courses on the work of William Perry. In his book *Forms of Intellectual and Ethical Development* Perry argues that college students go through three stages of development. At first they tend to see the world entirely in terms of right and wrong. When confronted with much of what they learn in college they become increasingly relativistic and come to believe that "everyone is entitled to his own opinion, no matter what." Finally, they come to realize that people may hold a variety of positions for a variety of reasons, but that these reasons may or may not be adequately justified. In short, students come to realize that people have "multiple interpretations of reality" (Krupa, "Perry's" 19) but that some interpretations may be better justified than others. Krupa suggests that "rhetorically based" writing courses, those that are organized by assignment sequences that "maintain a common subject while varying the rhetorical situation, demonstrating the effect of audience and purpose on the way a writer sees and treats a subject," help students reach Perry's final stage of "perspectivism" ("Perry's" 19).

Krupa is on the faculty at the University of Iowa, so it is no coincidence that beginning in 1979 Iowa began to offer a series of summer NEH institutes on writing instruction, which promoted the thematic and rhetorical sequencing of assignments. Iowa's institutes were organized to help college teachers design and implement writing courses that were coherent and theoretically informed. Plans for the courses produced by the Iowa institutes have been collected in a volume entitled *Courses for Change in Writing*, edited by Carl Klaus and Nancy Jones. The content of these courses varies widely. Some investigate philosophical problems; some analyze literature; some are based on certain themes such as "Play and Work" or "Persons and Places." However, all of these courses have highly organized sequences of assignments designed to help students think through the implications of a problem, issue, or theme to their own personal satisfaction and then to help them think about how they might explain the result of their thinking to others in a variety of genres and contexts.

The "epistemic approach" to writing instruction promoted by Kenneth Dowst, who was also at Iowa for a time, continues Moffett's influence. However, for two of his fundamental premises, Dowst is also indebted to William James and John Dewey. Those premises are (1) that we know the world through the mediation of language and that (2) therefore our ability to self-consciously use and reflect on language has profound effects on what we in fact know. Dowst's curriculum is designed to help students "to see the extent to which their 'worlds' are determined by their language" and to give them practice in manipulating their language "in ways conducive to discovery and learning" (74). Dowst's assignments require students to think about the nature of writing. His first assignment invites students to reflect on the differences between good and bad prose. According to Dowst, this assignment often results in essays full of clichés and platitudes, so subsequent assignments, as many as twenty or more, invite students to reflect more deeply on the nature of clarity, the significance of editing, and other issues related to writing. One assignment calls for students to write as badly as possible, the kind of mechanical "themewriting" Dowst associates with current-traditional pedagogy. The course ends with a series of assignments in which students explore the implications of "naming" and "selecting" the ways in which we use language to order and interpret the world.

In many ways, William Coles has promoted courses similar to Dowst's. Influenced by a course he took from Theodore Baird at Amherst College, William Coles developed an elaborate thematic sequence of thirty assignments to help students explore the nature of language, learning, and teaching. Coles's first assignment calls for students to think on paper about what they want to learn while they are in college, how they intend to go about achieving these goals, and what they might do if how they are taught conflicts with what they want to learn. Further assignments explore the implications of teaching and learning by having the students read closely and respond to passages by Benjamin Franklin, D. H. Lawrence, and other writers, and by having them reflect on personal accounts of learning. The last paper for the course invites students to reflect on what the course itself has meant to them and what it might mean to say that teaching and learning is a metaphor for language. (For two other courses similar to those by Dowst and Coles, see Gibson, and Coles and Vopat.)

In addition, Ann Berthoff has organized a course around a highly structured series of invention exercises, what she calls "assisted invitations" to explore the world and how we perceive and understand it. Berthoff's exercises move from simple observations and "sensory knowing" through "seeing relationships" to "thinking about thinking." In designing her course this way, Berthoff hopes her students will learn that composing is a self-conscious and self-reflective process in which writers organically shape their perceptions and thoughts using the conventions of language and various forms of discourse.

The influence of thematic sequences of assignments continues in a currently well-known textbook, Donald Bartholomae and Anthony Petrosky's *Facts, Artifacts, and Counterfacts*. Bartholomae and Petrosky use the same principles of assignment sequencing but with a different purpose: to introduce students, especially basic writers, to academic discourse. Bartholomae and Petrosky assume that the fundamental problem for basic writers is that they are not familiar with the kinds of texts important to the university community and that they lack the social background to understand how the academic community goes about thinking and interpreting texts. Thus, *Facts, Artifacts, and Counterfacts* contains a range of readings on a variety of academic subjects, and many of the readings can used in connection with more than one subject. Bartholomae and Petrosky suggest that teachers organize their writing assignments in response to the readings, using prompts that will gradually make their students aware of how and why they read the way they do and how others might read differently from the way they do.

Of course, not all curricular ideas after Moffett, Kinneavy, and Britton use thematic and rhetorical sequences. Some promote the writing of certain kinds of discourse using the terms of the new taxonomies. For example, Peter Elbow and Don Steward are often associated—whether fairly or unfairly is a matter of debate—with the promotion of personal expressive writing. Other compositionists argue that first-year writing courses ought to focus on the kinds of referential and persuasive writing found in academic discourse.

Designing Courses According to Pedagogical Technique

In response to the emphasis on the writing process, two major ways of structuring class time became popular—workshops and conferences—both of which are still popular today. In fact, to many people, workshops are often what distinguish writing courses from other courses at the postsecondary level. Indeed, it seems that many writing programs organize their courses around getting ideas, planning, drafting, and revising, and that workshops are the primary way to implement these goals. In small groups, given certain prompts, students brainstorm ideas for papers, they comment on one another's plans, they share their drafts, and they offer suggestions for revision. Often, for these courses, it seems as if the kinds of writing students do is less important than the fact that they are working through the writing process. In his monumental work, *Research on Written Composition*, George Hillocks reviews the relevant empirical research on writing pedagogy and concludes that used in conjunction with clear objectives and focused instruction, small-group workshops that involve students actively in some aspect of the writing process or the acquisition of kinds of knowledge relevant to various kinds of writing are indeed the most effective means of teaching writing.

Of course, workshops can be conducted in many ways, and they can be used as the basis of writing courses in many ways. There is a large literature on writing workshops as part of the larger enterprise of collaborative learning. See, for example, Jeff Golub's edited collection of essays, *Focus on Collaborative Learning.*

Certain compositionists have gone so far as to recommend that most writing classes with their generic advice to large groups of students are less effective than meeting with students one-on-one to talk about their particular papers. Thus, Roger Garrison recommends that regular class meetings be abolished entirely in favor of weekly or biweekly conferences between the teacher and individual students. Thomas Carnicelli approves of Garrison's plan on principle but allows that certain things can be accomplished in regular classes, things such as having students read and respond to one another's papers so that they get more than one point of view about their writing. (For more on conferences, see Fisher and Murray.) As is true for those who advocate workshops, the proponents of conferences often seem to imply that what students write is less important than the fact that they write anything, so long as it is in close cooperation with a writing coach or mentor. This assumption was severely questioned when composition studies took a "social turn."

Curricula after the Social Turn

Practically from the very beginning of the emphasis on the process approach, certain composition scholars questioned its accuracy and its usefulness. This criticism was heavily influenced by the "spirit of the time." In disciplines as different as linguistics, anthropology, and literary theory there was a new interest in the social. In response to this social turn compositionists began to argue that an undue emphasis on the stages of a generic composing process ignored the larger social factors in which people write outside of the classroom and that an undue emphasis on generic skills ignored how much writing varies from genre to genre and context to context. However, this criticism did not reach critical mass until the early 1980s. An important and influential early essay was Patricia Bizzell's "Cognition, Context, and Certainty" (1982). In that piece Bizzell argued that the writing instruction of the time ignored the "hidden curriculum" by teaching generic formats and processes. What was hidden by generic instruction was any sense of the social context, the different discourse communities, in which all writing outside of classrooms occurs. As a result, Bizzell concluded, students were denied the opportunity to confront the political implications of why schools teach certain kinds of writing and not others. Bizzell recommended that writing courses focus on discourse analysis and the political implications of why various discourse communities use the language they use.

Then in 1984, Shirley Brice Heath published her pioneering work *Ways With Words*. Heath found that adult members of different social groups have very different ways of interacting with texts, especially narratives, and that as a result, they have very different ways of teaching their children how to use and interpret texts. These social differences have profound consequences in determining the degree to which children from various social groups are ready for the kind of instruction in reading and writing they will confront when they enter school (see especially 190–262).

In the same year that Heath published her groundbreaking work on the social aspects of literacy, Carolyn Miller published "Genre as Social Action" in which she reconceptualized genres not as sets of predetermined rules or conventions but as "typified rhetorical actions based on recurrent situations" (159). In other words, Miller conceived of genres as dynamic and evolving, their rules and conventions shaped, modified, and adapted by individuals in response to the demands of particular rhetorical situations. Both Heath's and Miller's work provided the impetus for a large amount of ethnographic research in the particular contexts in which writing takes place and the way social forces work to modify the received genre conventions (Berkenkotter and Huckin; Bazerman).

Equally groundbreaking for composition studies was the gradual circulation of the work of Lev Vygotsky and Mikhel Bakhtin. Vygotsky provided evidence that children learn language through social interaction with adults, that their ability to internalize thought, what he called "inner speech," was a process of internalizing the external dialogue with adult language users. In short, Vygotsky theorized that external dialogue and social relations were necessary for the development of internal language concepts. Bakhtin provided an even broader social theory for language. To Bakhtin, language is the result of many contributors, whose differing "voices" echo in the diction and structure of language and the conventions of various genres. As individuals then, we use the language we have been given in very particular social contexts, and what we think we mean and how other people understand us will always be a process of negotiating among the various voices inherent in the language and the differing perspectives of different audiences conditioned by different social circumstances.

Also influential was the work of Paulo Freire. In *Pedagogy of the Oppressed*, Freire argued against a banking concept of knowledge and education in which the dominant culture imposes its received wisdom and values. Freire promoted a form of education in which students are taught to analyze their own lives in terms of how they have been shaped by the larger culture. Through such analysis, critique, and conceptual development, students realize that they are responsible for their own learning, that they can become agents of change.

Many of the composition scholars influenced by the work of Vygotsky, Bakhtin, and Freire eventually became associated with two major movements in composition studies: cultural studies and critical pedagogy. James Berlin became an influential spokesman for cultural studies, and Ira Shor a major figure in critical pedagogy. Berlin's major text, written in conjunction with Michael Vivion, is *Cultural Studies in the English Classroom*. Shor's book *Critical Teaching and Everyday Life* is perhaps the most thorough application of Freire's ideas to writing instruction in America.

Building on the work of Vygotsky and Bakhtin and the genre theorists, a number of scholars in composition studies are also now thinking of writing as part of an "activity system," an "ongoing, object-directed, historically conditioned, dialectically structured, tool-mediated human interaction" (Russell, "Rethinking" 510). Activity systems may be such traditional social units as the family, religious organizations, schools, and professions, or they may also be ad hoc groups of people organized around common goals or common uses of media. Thus, the editors, contributors, and readers of a national magazine may constitute an activity system. So may a wide range of people committed to the study of a certain subject, such as cell biology, even though they may work in different institutions and participate at many different levels of expertise. Not only college professors of biology and researchers in industry make up an activity system in cell biology. Undergraduates who take cell biology courses, biology majors, and others who participate in the ongoing research and discussion of cell biology through individual laboratories, journals, and even the Internet also belong. Activity theory gives scholars a way to conceptualize the way writing fits into a large web of interaction among people and the way writing is both shaped by these interactions and in turn shapes them.

As a result of the social turn in composition studies, most current theories of writing are now what Martin Nystrand and his colleagues call functional, constructivist, contextual, and dialogic (301–12). These current theories have produced at least four new frameworks or ways of designing first-year writing courses: cultural studies and critical pedagogy frameworks, introduction to discourse frameworks, ethnographic framework, and service learning frameworks.

Cultural Studies/ Critical Pedagogy Frameworks

In one writing course focused on issues in cultural studies, Berlin argues in favor of writing courses that help students to examine "the cultural codes— the semiotic analysis—that are working themselves out in shaping consciousness in our students and ourselves" ("Poststructuralism, Semiotics" 146). Berlin invites students to analyze texts broadly conceived—print, film, television—in relation to "the key terms in the discourse and to situate these within the structure of meaning of which they form a part." One way of achieving these goals is by organizing a series of assignments in a two-step analysis. The first part of the analysis sets the key terms of the text "in relation to their binary opposites as suggested by the text itself"; the second part places the key terms "within the narrative structural forms suggested by the text, the culturally coded stories about patterns of behavior appropriate for people within certain situations. These codes deal with such social designations as race, class, gender, age, ethnicity, and the like" ("Poststructuralism, Semiotics" 146–47).

As part of the next step in his analysis Berlin asks his students to consider how key terms function in common "socially constructed narratives," and he encourage them to see similar behavior patterns in "capitalist economic narratives" and "their consequences for class, gender, and race relations and roles both in the workplace and elsewhere" (149). The ultimate point of this analysis is to get students to see that "texts—whether rhetorical or poetic—are ideologically invested in the construction of subjectivities within recommended economic, social and political arrangements" and to help students analyze their own experiences in these terms; to get them to see how their own subjectivities are influenced by given economic, social, and political roles and how they do not necessarily have to take on the roles assigned to them, that their roles can be negotiated and reshaped "to serve their own agendas" (150). To Berlin the implications of this analysis for composing should also become clear as students struggle to write essays analyzing various texts. They should also come to see that all writing "is situated within signifying practices and that learning to understand personal and social experience involves acts of discourse production and interpretation, the two acting interchangeably in reading and writing codes" (151).

Bruce McComisky also teaches from the perspective of cultural studies and critical pedagogy. In one of his courses, McComisky and his students choose a "socio-cultural 'institution'" to study, institutions such as "churches and religions, schools and systems of education, media technologies, family units, workplaces and unions, political parties and interest groups, etc." (32). In explaining his course, McComisky's major example is a course in which the students choose to investigate university life. The students begin by developing "critical position statements" in which they describe "their own positions on an issue while simultaneously critiquing a particular text" (33). For example, they work out a position on cultural literacy after reading E. D. Hirsch or a position on "problem posing" education after reading Paulo Freire. Then McComisky gives his students a number of paired writing assignments, "one critical and the other pragmatic." One assignment sequence asks students to write several critical essays evaluating their academic major at the university as an "elaborate rhetorical invention," and then to write a letter to the head of that department suggesting changes in the department's curriculum.

Introduction to Discourse Frameworks

David Russell has proposed that most college-level writing instruction be done through writing-across-the-curriculum (WAC)programs. What would be the function then of first-year writing courses? Russell believes that the primary function of first-year writing courses should be to introduce students to writing as an academic subject in the same way that beginning courses in linguistics introduce students to the systematic study of language. The goal of first-year writing courses should be to study writing from a variety of philosophical points of view and using a variety of research methods: those of rhetoric, linguistics, semiotics, education, communication, psychology, sociology, literary theory, and cultural studies. The primary goal of such a course would not be to improve the students' writing per se, although students might do a considerable amount of writing, but to make students more aware of "the role of writing in society and in their lives, to make more informed decisions about issues that involve it" ("Activity" 74).

Like Russell, Joseph Petraglia argues that most writing done outside of generic writing classes is so contextually and rhetorically determined that there is little that such classes can do to help novice writers adapt to different purposes, audiences, and contexts. Petraglia's solution is to get rid of any pretense that what he calls general writing skills instruction (GWSI) can promote such a wide range of rhetorical situations through hypothetical audiences and the role playing of rhetorical situations. Instead, Petraglia suggests that teachers should frankly acknowledge that they are the audience of "teacher-evaluators" to whom their students must address their writing and that the point of any writing assignment in a GWSI course is that students "demonstrate mastery over a disciplinary content" rather than "a mastery of rhetorical skills" (95). As a result, students should not be required to write persuasively, because they cannot learn enough about the content of any given course to be able to effectively persuade their only reader, the teacher. Petraglia recommends intensive reading in a particular subject matter as a way to introduce students to the "rhetoric" of the discipline or content area. In effect, he argues that first-year writing courses be organized primarily by content and that the primary way students will learn to write in these courses is by tacitly acquiring a knowledge of how to write about that content through reading. (For another argument for writing-intensive courses, see Brannon.)

Ethnographic Frameworks

Heath's work figured prominently at the English Coalition Conference, a meeting of representatives from a wide variety of constituencies in the teaching of English, from the elementary through the college level, during July 1987. As a result of its deliberations, the English Coalition Conference recommended instruction not just in writing but in all language in the context of the students' own social environments and the specific discourse communities in which students lived and worked. In its final report the Conference recommends that introductory writing courses at the college level be redesigned around "three basic principles: investigation or critical inquiry, collaboration, and conscious theorizing" (28). To put these pedagogical principles into practice, the Coalition recommends a "yearlong, entry-level course that will use current theory and research to focus on the uses of language; the value-laden nature of all such uses; and the ways we and our students use writing, reading, speaking, listening, and critical thinking to construct ourselves as individuals and as members of academic and other communities" (27). As a concrete example, the Coalition proposes a course with two focuses: one on personal identity and how students can shape their identity and how their identities are in turn shaped through language in particular social circumstances; the other on the language of a particular discourse community. For the first focus, the Coalition recommends that students "investigate the construct of self" by reading autobiographies, writing journals and narratives about their own experiences, that they "collect and analyze samples of their own ideolects," and that they share these findings with others in the class. Later the course would shift to a study of the language of particular workplaces, social groups, or academic disciplines. For this study of particular genres, students might take field notes based on observations of these discourse communities in action and read texts written for and about these communities, all of which might lead to a formal or critical analysis, either written or oral, of how language works in the community under study (27–28).

Courses similar to those recommended by the English Coalition have been implemented at the University of Massachusetts-Boston (Kuntz, Groden, and Zamel) and the University of Wisconsin-Madison (Weese, Fox, and Greene). At Massachusetts-Boston, first-year courses are based on the following principles:

- First-year courses should provide a "coherent framework" for students' "intellectual inquiry" into particular topics that are "challenging" and "of immediate importance" (85).

- First-year courses should provide students with "many opportunities to work with a variety of different forms of language use (group discussions; dialogues; interviews; lectures; debates; films; reading in book, periodicals, and popular literature; and, of course, writing)" (85).

- First-year courses should be interdisciplinary in nature.

- First-year courses should be multicultural.

- The work in first-year courses should be "linked to work outside the classroom" (85).

Service Learning Frameworks

Another way compositionists have responded to the social turn of the profession is through service learning, which introduces students to writing outside of the traditional classroom for community nonprofit and social service agencies. Such programs try to combine writing with an emphasis on social justice, in effect putting into practice the social goals articulated by Freire and his followers. However, the goals of these programs vary widely. Some programs place students in a service agency for an extended period of time and expect them to produce the sorts of documents used in that agency. Other programs study nonacademic settings and focus on reflecting and writing *about* these settings rather than writing the genres actually used in those settings. Still other programs divide their time and energy between the classroom and other service organizations where writing is done. Members of the class write the genres of the community organization they visit for short periods, but they also reflect on and write about their experiences in these community settings using school genres: journals, notebooks, personal essays, and research reports.

In an attempt to get the best of both the classroom experience and the writing experience in a community setting, both Stanford University and San Francisco State University offer two-course sequences. The first course initiates students into a service or community agency, for which they write school genres reflecting on their experiences; the second course offers students the opportunity to be "volunteer writers" for that community (Bacon). Often, for courses similar to Stanford's and San Francisco State's first semester, the curriculum consists of a series of guided reflections on what the students have learned by visiting and researching a particular service organization, which culminates in a research report. However, the curriculum for courses similar to the California school's second semester is entirely open and dependent on the kinds of writing needed by the service organizations the students work for. The writing in these settings varies widely. For David Cooper and Laura Julier's service learning course, for example, students "wrote public announcements for the Girl Scouts..., revised a job application manual for unemployed teens; wrote articles for newsletters for a senior care facility and homeless shelter; and created informational brochures for a public health clinic" (Julier 7).

Despite this rich history of curricular ideas for first-year writing courses, there is reason to believe that few have been very influential. After all, our professional books and journals publish new and innovative work; they do not necessarily publish what is popular or commonplace. Indeed, there is a certain amount of evidence that most writing courses are taught in fairly traditional ways. In his study of the writing programs in the California State system, Edward White found that writing is currently taught in one of six ways:

1. *The literature approach*, in which students primarily read literature anthologies and study prose models of writing.

2. *The peer workshop approach*, in which students engage in free writing, journal writing, or other invention techniques and participate in workshops in order to discuss or comment on one another's writing.

3. *The individualized writing lab approach*, in which students receive individualized instruction from an instructor or tutor.

4. *The text-based rhetoric approach*, in which students work through a rhetoric text, with or without a handbook, and practice various purposes or modes of writing, from description to persuasion.

5. *The basic skills approach*, in which students are taught grammar and usage and the basic units of prose, such as phrases, sentences, and paragraphs.

6. *The service course approach*, in which students practice writing "academic discourse," such as term papers, which will prepare them to write for other courses at the university (44–55).

It is noteworthy that with the exception of the peer workshop approach, and with the possible exception of certain text-based rhetoric approaches, these methods of teaching writing basically ignore much of the scholarship on curriculum published in the last fifty years.

SOME THINGS TO CONSIDER ABOUT DESIGNING FIRST-YEAR WRITING CURRICULA

Given such a long history and such a broad range of philosophies and pedagogies for first-year writing courses, what are WPAs to think, especially if they are in a position to influence the curriculum of a first-year writing program? It seems to me that thoughtful WPAs should begin with the basics. They should go back and reexamine their basic philosophies and presuppositions about writing. Then they should consider the practical implications of their ideas in their particular college and university contexts. Here are some things to think about.

Theoretical Issues about the Nature of Writing

- *What is writing?* Since the nineteenth century, writing has been considered a general and unified skill, the ability to manipulate syntax effectively and to edit properly in a range of rhetorical contexts. But genre theorists and activity theorists have called this assumption into question. Given that we use writing to accomplish many different purposes, that we use many different genre conventions in many different contexts, should we assume that learning how to write one genre in one context will necessarily transfer to other genres in other contexts? If we teach our students how to write personal essays, will they necessarily know how to write business letters?

   But if writing is not a general and unified skill, how can we characterize the kinds of knowledge and skill that various kinds of writing require? What knowledge and skills associated with writing, what genres and discourse conventions, should first-year courses promote, and why are these kinds of knowledge and skill privileged over others? Theoretical issues such as these are behind the often heated disagreements in composition studies about the content of first-year courses: whether they should focus on personal expressive writing, introduce students to the essentials of academic discourse, promote the writing of essays as a way to reflect critically on significant cultural issues, or a number of other goals.

- *How is writing learned?* Studies in literacy have confirmed that becoming literate is a long and arduous process. It often begins before children go to preschool and continues into adulthood. Often children from literate backgrounds learn to read and write with little instruction, and those from less literate backgrounds struggle even though they receive a great deal of instruction. All of this raises the question of the degree to which we acquire the ability to write much as we acquire the ability to speak, through reading and interaction with people in a literate environment, and the degree to which we learn the write in response to explicit instruction.

One of the main arguments in favor of the position that we largely acquire written language is that writing is too complex to learn through explicit rules, formats, and formulas; that most of what literate people do when they write was not explicitly taught them. All of this raises the question, out of all the things about writing that a first-year program could emphasize, of what should be left to students to acquire on their own and what should be explicitly taught. Or to put it in developmental terms, what can first-year courses provide that eighteen-year-old writers need at this point in their development?

- *Is there a single writing process, or are there many different writing processes?* It has often been acknowledged that one of the major contributions of contemporary scholarship in writing has been "process pedagogy," an emphasis on the writing process: teaching students explicitly to get ideas, plan, draft, revise, and edit, usually in that order. But now it is also generally accepted that accomplished writers write recursively, that the writing process is not linear, that in fact many expert writers engage in what Stephen Witte calls "pre text," planning and composing before drafting so that they do not seem to revise and edit at all.

  But if expert writers compose in many different ways and do not follow a single writing process, to what degree should we teach students to follow an explicit, linear writing process?

- *What basic form of instruction should be used?* George Hillocks has presented convincing evidence that instruction with explicit goals and limited foci, instruction with a great deal of interaction among students as they solve problems together, is significantly better than other kinds of instruction, such as lecturing, the close study of exemplary texts, or even an emphasis on the writing process.

- *How should writing in a course be evaluated?*

The Practical Implications of These Theoretical Issues

Having clarified their own positions—having decided on the specific knowledge and skills students should learn in first-year writing courses, the genres they should be taught, the basic pedagogical approaches to be implemented—WPAs are in a position to put their ideas into practice.

At the great majority of colleges and universities, first-year writing programs are housed in departments of English and directed by specialists in composition and rhetoric, but the courses are actually taught by instructors and graduate teaching assistants, many of whom have only minimal backgrounds, training, and experience in teaching writing. Often, only a small proportion of the regular English faculty teach introductory writing, if they teach introductory writing at all.

However, despite the fact that the actual teaching of writing is done by a limited number of people at the university, the number of people who feel they have a stake in the nature of the program and the way it is run is immense. Parents and alumni expect their children to be taught writing much as they themselves were taught when they were in school. Students expect to be taught to write in ways they are familiar with; that is, in ways they were taught in high school. In addition, instructors and GTAs expect to teach writing in ways they are familiar with; that is, using the pedagogical techniques and textbooks from their last teaching assignment or their last writing course in college. College and university administrators expect writing programs to promote the university's image as a place that supports students through small classes and a great deal of individual attention, the kind of attention students might not get in large sections of biology and introductory sociology. Administrators also expect first-year writing programs to promote useful, practical skills they can use to persuade state legislatures and boards of regents that the university is a good investment for tax dollars. Faculty across the university, including those in English departments, expect writing programs to prepare students to write for their courses so that they won't have to do so. And of course, prospective employers of graduating seniors and graduate faculty of master's and doctoral programs expect students to be prepared to write the kinds of discourse required of their particular workplace, profession, or discipline. In other words, the societal demands on first-year writing courses are impossibly wide and often contradictory.

How then should new WPAs proceed, especially if they wish to or have been invited to "revitalize," "update," or otherwise change a current writing program? Carefully. Very carefully. Here are some questions for WPAs to ponder as they consider implementing a new curriculum:

What is the traditional purpose or mission of the first-year writing courses in your institution? Is that purpose or mission generally well accepted? If so, will your proposed change be appropriate for that purpose or mission, and if you are proposing a significantly different purpose or mission, do you have the support of your department head, the English faculty, and your dean, should other stakeholders question what you are doing? If you do not have this support, what can you do to get it?

- *What background and experience in teaching writing have your instructors and graduate teaching assistants had?* Has this background and experience prepared them for teaching the kind of writing required in your curriculum, and has it prepared them to use the pedagogical methods appropriate for your curriculum? If not, how will you go about training your instructors and GTAs to teach your new curriculum?

- *Should you have materials in common?* Given the nature of your staff, should you have common textbooks, similar course plans and syllabi, common grading standards, and a method of promoting common grading standards, or should the staff be free to teach their courses as they see fit?

- *What background and experience in writing have your students had, and what sort of experience in writing do they expect from your courses?* What sort of experience in writing do they need? If your curriculum will require students to do things significantly different from what they expect from a writing course, what steps will you take to prepare students for the new curriculum and persuade the students of its effectiveness and appropriateness?

- *What will the other stakeholders in first-year writing think about your new curriculum?*—faculty across the university, parents, and public figures with an interest in higher education. If they might have objections, how will you attempt to assuage their fears and meet their objections?

- *Should first-year writing courses be required of all first-year students or only of those who "need" them?* And do you have the resources to provide writing instruction for all first-year students? For whatever reason, if you decide to not require first-year writing of all students, how will you go about determining who should take these courses and who should not?

- *What resources have you been given to develop a new curriculum?* Or to put it another way, what are your sources of support and are they sufficient for you to implement the curriculum you want?

One final practical consideration: While I believe that WPAs should begin with a vision of what their curriculum ought to be, a vision based on a coherent sense of what writing is and how it should be taught, there is also the practical matter of finding materials to use in class for others who may have to implement that vision. The practical issue is this: whether WPAs should use "found" textbooks and supporting materials or whether they should create their own materials. In the best of all possible worlds, I believe WPAs should receive enough support in both time and money to take at least several months off from regular teaching and other research, perhaps during the summer, to prepare the materials that instructors in their programs would need—readings, assignments, sample lessons. With the rise of customized course packets, it is easier than ever before for WPAs to design curricula and create materials that will put their vision into effect. However, I also realize that at many institutions money may be tight and those with a stake in the nature of the first-year writing program may have very determined but contrary visions of what first-year writing courses should be like. At such institutions all that a WPA may be able to do is to influence slightly the choice of textbooks that current instructors already use or other stakeholders approve of. I think WPAs should aim high to implement their vision, but I also think there is no shame in their accommodating themselves to reality.

Composition studies has a rich but contested history of what first-year writing curricula ought to be. It should be a source of inspiration for WPAs to join the history of this conversation and to make their mark on the way writing is taught to first-year students at American colleges and universities.

WORKS CITED

Bacon, Nora. "Community Service Writing: Problems, Challenges, Questions." *Writing the Community: Concepts and Models for Service-Learning in Composition*. Ed. Linda Adler-Kassner, Robert Crooks, and Ann Watters. Washington: AAHE, 1997. 39–55.

Bakhtin, Mikhel. *The Dialogic Imagination*. Austin: U of Texas P, 1981.

———. *Speech Genres and Other Late Essays*. Trans. V. W. McGee. Ed. C. Emerson and Michael Holquist. Austin: U of Texas P, 1986.

Bartholomae, David, and Anthony Petrosky, eds. *Facts, Artifacts, and Counterfacts: Theory and Method for a Reading and Writing Course*. Upper Montclair, NJ: Boynton, 1986.

Bazerman, Charles. *Shaping Written Knowledge*. Madison: U of Wisconsin P, 1988.

Berkenkotter, Carol, and Thomas N. Huckin. *Genre Knowledge in Disciplinary Communication*. Hillsdale, IL: Erlbaum, 1995.

Berlin, James. "Poststructuralism, Cultural Studies, and the Composition Classroom." *Rhetoric Review* 11 (Fall 1992): 16–33.

———. "Poststructuralism, Semiotics, and Social-Epistemic Rhetoric: Converging Agendas." *Defining the New Rhetorics*. Ed. Theresa Enos and Stuart C. Brown. Newbury Park, CA: Sage, 1993. 137–53.

Berlin, James, and Michael Vivion, eds. *Cultural Studies in the English Classroom*. Portsmouth: Boynton, 1992.

Berthoff, Ann E. *Forming/Thinking/Writing: The Composing Imagination*. Rochelle Park: Hayden, 1978.

———. *The Making of Meaning: Metaphors, Models and Maxims for Writing Teachers*. Upper Montclair, NJ: Boynton, 1981.

Bizzell, Patricia. "Cognition, Context, and Certainty." *PRE/TEXT* 3 (1982): 213–24.

Brannon, Lil. "(Dis)Missing Compulsory First-Year Composition." In Petraglia, 239–48.

Britton, James, et al. *The Development of Writing Abilities, 11–18*. London: Macmillan, 1975.

Carnicelli, Thomas A. "The Writing Conference: A One-to-One Conversation." Donovan and McClelland 101–31.

Coles, William E., Jr. *Teaching Composing*. Rochelle Park: Hayden, 1974.

———. *The Plural I: The Teaching of Writing*. New York: Holt, 1978; rpt. Upper Montclair, NJ: Boynton, 1988.

Coles, William E., Jr., and James Vopat. *What Makes Writing Good: A Multiperspective*. Lexington: Heath, 1985.

Dixon, John. Growth Through English. Reading, Eng.: National Association for the Teaching of English, 1967.

Donovan, Timothy R., and Ben W. McClelland, eds. *Eight Approaches to Teaching Composition*. Urbana: NCTE, 1980.

Dowst, Kenneth. "The Epistemic Approach: Writing, Knowing, and Learning." Donovan and McClellend 65–85.

Elbow, Peter. *What Is English?* New York: MLA/NCTE, 1990.

———. *Writing Without Teachers*. New York: Oxford UP, 1975.

Emig, Janet. *The Composing Processes of Twelfth Graders.* Urbana: NCTE, 1971.

Fisher, Lester, and Donald M. Murray. "Perhaps the Professor Should Cut Class." *College English* 35 (1973): 169–73.

Freire, Paulo. *Pedagogy of the Oppressed.* Trans. Myra Bergman Ramos. New York: Seabury,1968.

Garrison, Roger H. "One to One: Tutorial Instruction in Freshman Composition." *New Directions for Community Colleges.* San Francisco: Jossey, 1974. 55–83.

Gerber, John C. "The Conference on College Composition and Communication." *College Composition and Communication* 1.1 (March 1950): 12.

Gibson, Walker. *Seeing and Writing: Fifteen Exercises in Composing Experience.* 2nd ed. New York: McKay, 1974.

Golub, Jeff. *Focus on Collaborative Learning.* Urbana: NCTE, 1988.

Gottschalk, Katherine K. "Uncommon Grounds: What Are the Primary Traits of a Writing Course." *College Composition and Communication* 47.4 (December 1996): 594–99.

Hayes, John R., and Linda Flower. "Identifying the Organization of Writing Processes." *Cognitive Processes in Writing.* Ed. L. Gregg and E. Steinberg. Hillsdale, IL: Erlbaum, 1980. 3–30.

Hillocks, George, Jr. *Research on Written Composition.* Urbana: NCRE, 1986.

Julier, Laura. "Community Service Pedagogy." *Composition Pedagogies: A Bibliographic Guide.* Ed. Gary Tate, Amy Rupiper, and Kurt Schick. New York: Oxford UP, forthcoming.

Kinneavy, James. *A Theory of Discourse.* New York: Norton, 1971.

Kitzhaber, Albert. *Themes, Theories, and Therapy: The Teaching of Writing in College.* New York: McGraw, 1963.

Klaus, Carl H., and Nancy Jones. *Courses for Change in Writing.* Upper Montclair, NJ: Boynton/Cook, 1984.

Krupa, Gene H. "Perry's Model of Development and the Teaching of Freshman Writing." *Freshman English News* 11.1 (Spring 1982): 17–20.

———. *Situational Writing.* Belmont: Wadsworth, 1982.

Kuntz, Eleanor, Suzy Q. Groden, and Vivian Zamel. *The Discovery of Competence: Teaching and Learning with Diverse Student Writers.* Portsmouth, NH: Boynton, 1993.

Lloyd-Jones, Richard, and Andrea A. Lunsford. *The English Coalition Conference: Democracy Through Language.* Urbana: NCTE, 1989.

McComisky, Bruce. "Writing in Context: Postmodern Theory and Practice in the Composition Class." *Composition Forum* 8.2 (Fall 1997): 30–38.

Miller, Carolyn. "Genre as Social Action." *Quarterly Journal of Speech* 70 (1984): 151–67.

Moffett, James. *A Student-Centered Language Arts Curriculum, K–13: A Handbook for Teachers.* Boston: Houghton, 1968.

———. *Teaching the Universe of Discourse.* Boston: Houghton, 1968.

Nystrand, Martin, Stuart Greene, and Jeffrey Wiemelt. "Where Did Composition Studies Come From? An Intellectual History." *Written Communication* 10.3 (July 1993): 267–333.

Perry, William G. *Forms of Intellectual and Ethical Development in the College Years.* New York: Holt, 1970.

Petraglia, Joseph, ed. *Reconceiving Writing, Rethinking Writing Instruction.* Mahwah, NJ: Erlbaum, 1995.

———. "Writing as an Unnatural Act." Petraglia 79–100.

Russell, David. "Activity Theory and Its Implications for Writing Instruction." Petraglia 51–77.

————. "Rethinking Genre in School and Society." *Written Communication* 14.4 (October 1997): 504–54.

Ryder, Phyllis Mentzell. "Will Your Disciplinary Umbrella Cover Me?" *College Composition and Communication* 47.4 (December 1996): 599–602.

Shor, Ira. *Critical Teaching and Everyday Life*. Boston: South End, 1980.

Stewart, Donald C. *The Versatile Writer*. Lexington: Heath, 1975.

Strickland, Kathleen, and James Strickland. *Un-Covering the Curriculum: Whole Language in Secondary and Postsecondary Classrooms*. Portsmouth, NH: Heinemann, 1993.

Vygotsky, Lev. *Mind in Society*. Ed. Michael Cole et al. Cambridge: Harvard UP, 1978.

————. *Thought and Language*. Ed. and Trans. Eugenia Hanfmann and Gertrude Vakar. Cambridge: MIT P, 1962.

Weese, Katherine L., Stephen L. Fox, and Stuart Greene, eds. *Teaching Academic Literacy: the Uses of Teacher-Research in Developing a Writing Program*. Mahwah, NJ: Erlbaum, 1999.

White, Edward M. *Developing Successful College Writing Programs*. San Francisco: Jossey, 1989.

A Working Methodology of Assessment for Writing Program Administrators

Brian A. Huot
University of Louisville

Ellen E. Schendel
Grand Valley State University

Although many writing program administrators (WPAs) have little interest, experience, or expertise in assessment, there is little doubt these days that assessment is an important consideration for most of us who administer writing programs. Upper administration and even legislators are mandating that both teachers and students be assessed for quality control. And as administrators, we need to ensure that first-year writing curricula and support systems are serving the needs of students as effectively as possible. We all face the dilemma of how to use assessment without letting it drive curricula in negative ways, mandating certain approaches or materials for our teachers that are in conflict with our programmatic goals and theories.

One way of viewing assessment is as an ethical obligation of WPAs. Larry Beason argues just this point:

> For composition courses to reflect individuals' changing values and needs, we have an ongoing ethical obligation to gather data and input on what we do in composition and on how these efforts are perceived by other faculty and by students. (113)

For this reason, "empirical research and assessment are required to meet a crucial ethical duty—namely, to help us be informed enough to determine what a campus community considers valuable about composition courses" (113). We think Beason's point is important to consider, because it brings to the forefront a way of thinking about writing assessment as community-based and reformatory.

Recasting writing assessment as a potential positive force within writing programs shapes the rest of this essay. While we recognize the importance of assessment for program administration and see assessment as a means to do

WPA work effectively and ethically, this essay also acknowledges the possible pitfalls hidden in certain kinds of assessment decisions. Rather than advocate for the use of particular kinds of assessment approaches or direct WPAs toward specific assessments, then, we hope to provide information about the kinds of *choices* that administrators have, as well as the theoretical principles that support those choices. In other words, we wish to raise issues for administrators to consider when deciding on a particular assessment practice, and to highlight the beliefs and assumptions inherent in various practices. What we hope to do is provide a methodology for how WPAs can learn to work with assessment as a tool for documenting the excellence of their programs and providing ways to achieve that excellence.

We begin by giving a broad overview of assessment as a positive force within writing programs, arguing that it can instigate valuable programwide discussions about curricular and programmatic issues. We show how writing assessment can become a means for proactive change within a writing program; it can be a way of opening dialogue among teachers and administrators about their programmatic contributions and allowing those teachers and administrators to act as "change agents" within their departments (Selfe) as they examine what they as individuals and as a community value in literacy and writing instruction. We next work to show WPAs the theories and values behind some of the terms and practices associated with writing assessment. Finally, we provide an articulation of the various kinds of assessments common in evaluating student writing outside the classroom. In this way, WPAs can develop assessment methodologies that help them to see connections between the assessment decisions they make and other decisions they might make about curriculum, instructional approaches, and faculty development. Our overall aim and approach is to provide a model for thinking about assessment that allows WPAs to integrate assessment into the roles and decisions for which they now assume responsibility.

DEFINING TERMS: RELIABILITY AND VALIDITY

There are a number of texts that define the terms *reliability* and *validity* (Huot, "Validity"; White; Moss "Can?"), but because these are terms with long, ideological histories, it seems important for us to explain our uses of these terms.

> *Reliability* describes the consistency of the results from a measure. A test must be reliable if any decisions of consequence are to be made on its behalf.
>
> *Instrument reliability* refers to the ability of a test to render consistent results from one use to another. If a practice is reliable, it will work the same way again and again.
>
> *Inter-rater reliability* refers to the degree to which autonomous judges agree on scores of student performance. In writing assessment, the need

and sometimes the lack of individual raters' ability to score student writing reliably has been a major concern since the beginning of the twentieth century (Starch and Elliott). Procedures such as holistic scoring with its scoring rubrics and rater training can ensure consistency among scorers. However, it may be that there are other ways to ensure reliable scoring without the use of rubrics and rater training when raters have certain experiences and training in common (Smith).

Traditionally, reliability has been viewed as a necessary but inadequate prerequisite for establishing the validity of an assessment practice. But this relationship of reliability to validity has been called into question by scholars such as Pamela Moss, who in an article titled "Can There Be Validity Without Reliability?" defends the claim that reliability is merely a measure of agreement, and that the validity of an assessment does not depend upon consistency. Rather, for scholars such as Samuel Messick, Pamela Moss, Lorrie Shepard, and Brian Huot (see this essay's Works Cited), "validity is an integrated evaluative judgment of the degree to which empirical evidence and theoretical rationales support the adequacy and appropriateness of inferences and actions based on test scores or other modes of assessment" (Messick 13). There are important differences between this definition of validity and the traditional view that a test is valid if it measures what it purports to measure. As Shepard argues, Messick's definition demands that the consequences of an assessment on stakeholders and the community in which the assessment takes place are serious considerations in establishing the validity of a procedure. As Huot argues, Messick's view of validity demands that we construct and then examine critically assessments *in context*. And Moss argues that Messick's view demands that writing professionals conduct validity inquiries of the assessments we construct. That is, we should assess assessments to ensure that they are, in fact, positive influences on teaching and learning. Schendel and O'Neill (forthcoming) have argued that validity inquiry is necessary in order for writing professionals to make ethical decisions about assessment practices.

Therefore, there is a meta-assessment level to all assessments: validity inquiries examine the consequences of assessment on the various stakeholders involved; they address how writing assessments impact teaching and learning and students' perceptions of themselves as writers; they examine the rhetoric used to talk about assessment within a program to uncover values implied by the methods used and the way results are used. Using validity inquiry as an occasion for reflection and dialectic provides us with a tangible means through which we can become reflective practitioners, designing and implementing assessments upon which we make decisions and conduct further inquiry into our programs. In this way, program assessment and validity inquiry supply a mechanism for continual reflection, change, and experimentation.

TERMINOLOGY IN PRACTICE: METHODS OF ASSESSMENT AND THE THEORIES BEHIND THEM

Whether a WPA is taking on the task of assessing a course, a full curriculum, or individual students for reasons of placement or exit, there are certain assumptions that tie together these various assessment practices and aims.

1. All assessment can be viewed as research, because every assessment practice begins with a question and includes a methodology for addressing that question, as well as follow-up on the results. Because assessment is a form of research, the question is the deciding factor in the methodology used, and the kinds of decisions WPAs make about which methodologies to use affect the kinds of results gathered and the kinds of (limited) statements that can be made about those results.

2. Assessments are context-bound. Who will be involved in the assessment and which methods will generate the best data and the theories driving the curriculum? The answers to these questions all help to define the context, and these are all factors in the kind of assessment that will be the most effective within that particular program. In the end, the shape of the program and the intentions surrounding the use of results matter the most in designing effective assessments.

In addition to the two previous assumptions, we make several others:

3. Writing assessment is a particular kind of assessment because it is an assessment of language through language; writing is both the medium for the assessment and the thing assessed. As such, writing assessment is a rhetorical enterprise (Huot, "Toward"). Therefore, it is particularly important that validity inquiry be conducted on assessments, since part of establishing the efficacy of a particular procedure is examining the assessment in context, as it exists and happens through language.

4. Assessment is a community activity and is therefore most effective when practices are informed by local theories and assumptions and designed with input from the teachers within the program (Huot, "Toward"; Darling-Hammond).

5. Because writing assessment is a community activity, it can be a way that teachers and administrators become reflective practitioners (Schon; Hillocks), as it can be a means of making visible the theories and assumptions informing individual teachers' pedagogies and the values of the program as a whole.

6. Writing assessment can be reformative, a way of changing pedagogies, curriculum, and programmatic structures in ways that benefit teaching and learning (Yancey and Huot).

There are a number of assessment models that are informed by the above precepts, and that can demonstrate for WPAs how theories and assumptions can drive the design of an assessment. These models also demonstrate how the local context—the theories driving curriculum, the theories and attitudes and experiences of teachers and students within the program—drive the design of the assessment practice. What follows is a brief overview of literature on contemporary assessment practices.

Placement and Exit Assessments:

Recent developments in placement and exit assessments rely on teachers' own expertise and experience with the course curricula in order to make valid and reliable judgements about student writing (Durst, Roemer, and Schultz, "Negotiations;" Lowe and Huot; Harrington; Smith). Current research into how readers read and holistically score students' essays focuses on the ways that readers construct meanings and interpretations for those texts. Scholarship in self-assessment demonstrates how writing assessments are sites where selves are constructed for evaluation. Both bodies of scholarship are important to an understanding of writing assessment as participatory and reformative because they show how writing assessments are sites of knowledge construction; both the evaluators and the subjects of the evaluation play active roles throughout the assessment situation.

Research demonstrates that the reading and holistic scoring of student essays is shaped by readers' membership in various communities, that the decisions raters make derive from social structures and local contexts informing the assessment situation. Judith Pula and Brian Huot extend Huot's earlier work ("Influences") to show that holistic scorers first identify to what degree they think a particular student is "teachable" based on their experiences as teachers; Mary DeReemer shows that teachers may arrive at the same rubric score for very different reasons; and Arnetha Ball illustrates how the cultural identities of readers influence how they score essays. Other scholars (Haswell and Haswell; Black et al.) demonstrate that readers' perceptions of the gender of a writer influence how they respond to or rank a particular piece of writing. These sorts of studies complicate traditional conceptions of reliability as a necessary quality for an assessment to be valid because they show how readers draw upon their own experiences to score essays—experiences that cannot be contained in a rubric for a scoring session. Alternative assessment practices are built upon this complex understanding of how teachers make meaning when they read and evaluate student writing. Importantly, as Robert Broad notes, coming to inter-rater agreement in holistic scoring sessions can hide important differences among readers: "*Differences of interpretation and evaluation are not only inescapable, they are downright wholesome elements of everyday rhetorical experience,* elements that we do harm to ourselves and our students in trying to conceal or extirpate" (266, italics in the original), for differences in interpretations are "seamlessly bound to questions of culture and politics" (273). Peter Elbow and Kathleen Yancey note that while alternative and multiple readings of literary texts are encouraged and valued, traditional means for assessing student writing assumes one true reading. Traditional writing assessment contains very real political and social consequences that readers—who are active constructors in the knowledge generated by writing assessments—play a part in determining, though the scoring of essays according to specified guidelines limits the ability of readers to act on the readings they construct. While scholarship demonstrates that readers' experiences as teachers play an important role in the assessment process, the writing assessment practices we use may not support or even tap into information about differences among readers—differences that may in fact help us to understand the impact(s) of the writing assessments on the culture in which they occur. Edward Wolfe conducted a study that shows that essay scorers who agree most readily limit the variety and engagement of their response as readers. As an alternative to the holistic scoring of essays, William L. Smith developed a method of placement at the University of Pittsburgh in which teachers with expertise in developmental first-semester or second-semester first-year writing made decisions about placement essays based upon whether they thought the writing was representative of the writing students arriving in their classrooms would produce. This method of assessment does not require a norming session with a focus on inter-rater reliability, as it is a system based on teacher expertise.

As other researchers have noted, writing assessments can draw upon teachers' expertise and also allow them to engage in critical discussion and reflection specifically about the way they read and evaluate differently (Durst, Roemer, and Schultz; Selfe). This affords them an opportunity to become "reflective practitioners," whereby they examine the ways in which their theories and practices are in dialectic with one another (Schon; Hillocks). Ideally, this sort of reflection allows teachers a means by which to share their theories and practices with the larger community, and even to change and improve their teaching. And such assessments allow teachers to continue to shape programmatic goals and curricula—a form of localized social action within the university (Selfe; White). An example of an assessment procedure that allows for this sort of critical reflection and community action is the exit assessment at the University of Cincinnati (Durst, Roemer, and Schultz), whereby small groups of teachers have ample time to discuss why portfolios are "passing" or "failing" as well as the opportunity to express concern over their own teaching and their own students' work. This model impacts the writing program in a positive, productive way: not only does the program accomplish the goal of accurately assessing student writing but it also allows for the continuing development of the teachers and the program itself.

A second body of research that has had an impact on placement and exit assessments is that dedicated to reflection and self-assessment. This is a rather large body of research, but almost all of it is premised on the assumption that students are better learners when they think meta-cognitively about their writing, and that this rhetorical understanding of writing and students' individual writing processes is part of what should be evaluated (Yancey, *Reflection*). There are several popular means through which this self-assessment takes place in placement and exit assessment designs. In portfolio assessments, students write cover letters for their portfolios that guide readers through an evaluation of their work (Sommers; Conway; Yancey, *Reflection*).

At a growing number of universities across the United States, first-year writing students even place themselves into the writing course of their choice based upon their evaluation of their writing abilities and experiences (Royer and Gilles). "Directed self-placement" does not require students to write anything for evaluation, nor does it require teachers or administrators to evaluate student writing before students take first-year writing. It is becoming more widely used in part because of its low cost and efficiency, but also because of claims that it puts the power for assessment in the hands of students.

Writing assessment practices based on reflective writing or students' self-assessments of their own writing and writing processes are attempts to bring students—stakeholders who traditionally have had very little to do with the way they are assessed—into the assessment process. These practices are theoretically informed by considering students and teachers as *agents* rather than subjects of assessment practices. These assessments recognize that students take rhetorical responsibility for their own placement into or exit from a given course, and they presumably close the gap between instruction and assessment as students are (1) presumed to learn better through meta-cognitive writing and/or (2) sophisticated enough as writers to guide readers to a decision about writing ability or to make decisions for themselves.

Program Assessments

Prior et al. write about program assessment as research "not defined by the usual dimensions—not marked by a particular methodological orientation, disciplinary affiliation, or object of study. For us, evaluation could best be understood as a category defined in terms of the contexts of research: the goals that initiate the research, its projected use, and consequences" (186). As research into the teaching and learning that happens within a writing program, it is "an ongoing activity that we engage in as reflective practitioners" (195), not simply a bureaucratic demand. As such, program assessment is a way for a community of teachers, students, and WPAs to come together to study all aspects of a writing program: student writing, teacher-generated documents, teacher education and development, administrative structures, the efficacy of existing placement and exit assessments, the history of the writing program, and the program's place in the larger university community.

Yancey ("Historicizing") writes that program assessments are an important development in assessment because, since they do not assess individuals but rather curricula and systems, they allow for (and even require) different voices to be heard and different views to become important in considering how writing programs can be improved. In the introduction to their edited volume on the assessment of WAC programs, Yancey and Huot make four "observations" about program assessment:

> As a mode of inquiry, assessment is increasingly collaborative and democratic," for program assessments rely on extensive data generation across broad groups of people with different interests and demands for writing instruction;

Program assessment is a rhetorical enterprise [because it is the examination of the many discourses surrounding writing instruction and because it is an attempt to uncover many different narratives about writing assessment within a single program];

Much of the learning produced in the name of assessment is very subtle in nature, [because program assessments bring differing values to light, telling multiple stories rather than providing consistently clear answers to problems; and]

Program assessment is linked, directly or otherwise, to reformist agendas, [for program assessment becomes a way to propose changes, rethink curricula, and consider the way an entire system behind a program can be reworked in order to better attend to the needs of students, teachers, and administrators (12, italics added).

As program assessments are attempts to see the "big picture" (8), they are a way of understanding how "learning and teaching...interact so as to chart that interaction in order to understand how to enhance it" (10–11). In short, program assessments are grounded in assumptions that change can occur and that teaching and learning can improve because of assessment and because of the various views that different groups of people bring to the table for further discussion.

The strength of program assessments, as Cynthia Selfe points out, is that they are a means for reflective practice among teachers and program administrators. While one way of conducting a program assessment is to invite outside consultants to visit the campus for several days, interview the people involved with the program (WPAs, teachers, students, university administrators), and assess the curriculum and structures already in place, Selfe advocates "contextual assessments," whereby teachers within a program conduct the assessment. When reflective practice becomes an integral part of "contextual assessments," then teachers can view themselves as "change agents" within their programs (53):

> [T]he methodologies of reflective teaching practice (Schon; Phelps) and contextual program assessment (Guba and Lincoln; Berlak et al.)—given that they involve participants in generating questions and concerns, carrying evaluation projects, and analyzing results—can make such understandings increasingly accessible at the level of consciousness and, thus, begin to take advantage of the intimate knowledge that social agents have of the situations within which they operate (59–60).

Program assessment such as the type that Selfe advocates clearly respects and draws upon the work of teachers, putting the concept of "change" and "reform" in a local context and in the hands of educators. It becomes an opportunity to answer the sorts of questions connecting assessment and curricula that Moss poses ("Response"), and it allows for greater understanding among all teachers and administrators within a program.

Program assessment seems a particularly important kind of assessment to consider in thinking about writing assessment as a community activity geared toward reform, for it is fundamentally a critique of the systems and structures that produce writing and that produce knowledge of subjects through writing and assessment. Assessing writing programs is a way to ensure that the work done by students, teachers, and administrators is directed toward a locally defined set of purposes. This concern with the local culture of a writing program is key to note: Because they are about social interactions and the way that writing is produced and valued by a large cross-section of people within a program, program assessments are tied to certain cultural values and needs. As Williamson makes clear, "evaluation research must serve the purposes of the participants in the writing program being examined" or the program assessment will not be valued (or of value). The people who make up a writing program must be invested in the research process, for "quality assessment enriches the programs it attempts to describe and evaluate by increasing our understanding of curricula, teaching, and learning" (Huot, "Beyond" 76).

PRACTICING WRITING ASSESSMENT

This next section focuses on the kinds of writing assessments for which WPAs are most often given responsibility. We will review these various forms of assessment and talk about them in practical terms, examining the sorts of technical and theoretical issues each of the assessments might entail. We focus not only on how WPAs can best design and implement such assessments but on how each of the assessments has particular demands for justifying its use and, more important, the decisions made on its behalf. So far, we have made the case that writing assessment be a necessary part of writing program administration and that in working on writing assessment details, WPAs must be reflective practitioners; they must learn to continually examine their programs while providing evidence that the program either is working effectively or that the WPAs are effecting changes to improve it. In the next few pages we provide a way in which WPAs can work as reflective practitioners not only by using assessment to make decisions about their programs but by learning to "test the test" (Moss, "Testing").

Placement

Placement testing involves the screening of first-year college students' writing for the purpose of identifying the level of instruction or, in the case of directed self-placement, the screening of students' perceptions about their own writing. Placement testing is a pervasive part of most writing programs. In a 1994 survey (Huot, "Survey"), about 40 percent (more than 1,100 departments) of the English departments on the MLA English Department List responded, and almost all of them offered multiple-tier instruction and placement testing to select students for the various tiers. Although writing placement is commonplace on most college campuses, there is no substantial body of work on writing placement procedures or programs. This lack of research provides a real opportunity for WPAs who design and administer a placement program, but it is also frustrating for those who are faced with the design or implementation of writing placement, since there is little research to depend on.

While there is a dearth of research, WPAs do have a wide range of choices for writing placement purposes. One of the first choices facing a WPA is whether to use direct measures, which involve teachers reading student writing, or indirect measures, which are often multiple-choice tests on grammar, usage, and mechanics. The advantages of indirect measures are that they are quick and cheap. Placement is often conducted under tight time constraints, since students need to know which classes to register for. This can be especially crucial when students register late or have to come to campus for placement and registration. For placement testing, time is an important factor. One of the disadvantages of indirect measures for writing assessment are that they give the message to students, teachers, administrators, and the public at large that the important part of writing is in correctness. As well, the testing companies that produce these tests claim their validity because the scores they produce correlate with scores given by essay readers in studies they conduct—but given the scoring rubric or guidelines, it would not be difficult to conduct an essay-scoring session based upon correctness. What's even more problematic is that "concurrent validity," the measurement term for the correlation of a test like COMPASS and others produced commercially with a valued measure like the scores produced in an essay reading, has never been recognized by the literature on validity as a sufficient claim for making important educational decisions. In addition, the use of such a limited notion of validity ignores the important insights in validity theory over the last two decades. There is simply no persuasive evidence that a test containing no writing at all can measure a student's level of writing ability for placement into first-year college writing courses.

In terms of research, there are very few studies that look at the comparison of direct and indirect measures for placing students into first year writing. John Garrow's dissertation is the only full-blown research study we are aware of. Conducted at the University of Pittsburgh in the 1980s, Garrow compared Pitt's holistic scoring program at the time with two indirect measures, the verbal score of the SAT and an exercise that required students to find and correct errors in a text. He used a survey of teacher perceptions of where students should have been placed and students' grades and exit-exam results to determine what he called the "adequacy" of placement. Comparing the results of indirect and direct methods, Garrow concluded that direct methods were the most adequate form of placement. Huot's survey of placement practices, while not intending to compare direct and indirect methods for placement, did ask respondents whether they were satisfied with their placement programs. The survey found that institutions that used a writing sample for placement were more satisfied with their programs than those who used multiple-choice tests. While we regret that the research evidence against multiple-choice testing for placement purposes isn't more overwhelming, we do think that linked together, the results of Garrow's study, Huot's survey, the spurious claims for validity, and the damaging overall message that using a multiple-choice test of grammar usage and mechanics sends about a writing program make a pretty persuasive argument against the use of indirect measures for writing placement.

The most common form of direct writing assessment is holistic scoring. Like analytic and primary-trait scoring, holistic scoring uses a numerical scoring guideline or rubric and rater training to ensure that readers score essays reliably. While holistic is a little less reliable than analytic (Freedman; Hudson and Veal) or primary-trait (Hudson and Veal), it is much more cost-efficient (Hudson and Veal) and therefore most often used for placement. As detailed elsewhere (Huot, "Toward"), using holistic scoring for placement involves several steps once holistic scores have been given to an essay. These scores—remember each essay is scored at least twice—are summed together to create a sum score. The program administrator needs to create a scale of cut scores that determine what class each student can be placed into. For example, if a four-point scale were used, then it would be possible for students to receive sum scores from 2 through 8 (since the two possible scores are added together). A WPA would then choose something like 8–6 as the score indicating placement into the top class and 5–2 for the bottom course. If students needed to be placed into more than two classes, a six-point scale could be used that would yield more score points and allow a wider spread of points for placing students into more course options. Using holistic scoring, however, involves an extra step in assigning scores to class placement, since readers give essays a numerical score attuned to the rubric by which they're trained. Research on the processes of scoring student writing for placement using holistic scoring indicates that many times readers determine which class a student should go into and then look for the number on a holistic scoring scale that best represents that judgment (Huot; Pula and Huot). In effect, it is possible that a third extra step is involved, since a reader starts with a class, then converts it to a number that then has to be reconverted to a class. One other small problem with holistic scoring is that it requires time for training readers and a fairly substantial pool of papers, since raters have to be calibrated for each rater session. All of this preparation takes time, and as we mentioned at the beginning of this section, placement is often something that needs to be accomplished quickly so that students can register for their courses in a timely manner. In addition, the use of holistic scoring usually requires the computing and reporting of inter-rater reliability coefficients. In defense of holistic scoring, it should be mentioned that it is an established method most writing assessment specialists recognize.

In the last decade or so, there has been a movement in placement testing away from holistic scoring and toward locally developed measures for placing students into first-year writing classes. We'll look at four of these programs in more depth below later in this essay, but they all differ from holistic scoring in some important ways. First, the methods do away with coding decisions by numbers and then recoding those scores back into classes. Instead, decisions about placement are made directly, with raters (and even students) choosing classes outright. Other differences include the number of people used to make placement decisions. In holistic scoring all papers are read by two readers, whereas in many of the locally developed systems only one reader makes the decision. As well, instead of basing the decision on a scoring guide or rubric, readers base decisions on their knowledge of the curriculum students are entering and on their own knowledge about the teaching of writing.

William L. Smith developed the first placement system we are aware of in the late 1980s and early 1990s that eschewed the trappings of holistic scoring and streamlined the process of placing students into first-year writing courses. Smith designed a system in which teachers who had recent experience with a particular course made decisions about which students would enter that course. For example, if a teacher's extensive and most recent experience was with English 101, then she would decide whether a student was placed into 101. If she thought the student's writing qualified her for the course after or before 101, then she would refer the paper to the teacher reading for that particular course. Smith conducted a number of studies on his method and found that it was more accurate and efficient than holistic scoring. Terri Lowe and Brian Huot adapted Smith's method for reading portfolios, and found that it worked quite well and was efficient, since portfolios could be read for no more than $5 each. Richard Haswell and Susan Wyche-Smith developed a placement system at Washington State in which all student papers received one initial reading. Sixty percent of these papers placed students into regular first-year writing programs. The other 40 percent received additional readings. Susanmarie Harrington at Purdue University-Indianapolis (Indiana University) has created a program in which most students write their essays online (although students are given the option to write with a pen). These essays are appended to a secure website that readers can access either on campus or with a modem. If a reader finds that a student's essay fits the regular first-year writing course, then that student is automatically placed there. The IUPUI system is designed to meet the needs of a diverse, nontraditional student body who often register at the last minute and need placement information quickly.

The newest, and for us the most interesting, development in placement involves no student writing at all. Directed self-placement (DSP), as it is called (Royer and Gilles), involves providing students with information about the course offerings and a checklist that asks them questions about how much reading they do, how many essays they wrote in high school, what kinds of grades they earned, and how knowledgeable they are about grammar and other language conventions. Students then decide what course best suits them. Grand Valley State University, where this system was first developed, reports that it works well (Royer and Gilles). At present, there are over ten other institutions using DSP to place students into first-year writing courses.

One of the greatest advantages of using DSP is that it is quick, cost-efficient, and gives students a say about what course they are being placed into.

Exit Testing

While exit testing in writing assessment is certainly less prevalent than is placement, it's hard to know just how pervasive it might be. In assessment language, an assessment is often labeled in terms of what kinds of stakes are involved. For example, placement testing is often seen as low-stakes, whereas exit testing is characterized as high-stakes because students can be required to retake a specific course or even be denied graduation (Huot, "Beyond"; White, "An Apologia"). We are a little uncomfortable with calling placement low-stakes, since requiring a student to take and pay for an extra course is a serious decision that should not be made lightly. However, decisions based on exit testing can be of an even more serious nature, since they act as a barrier between students and their educational goals. Even though students may have satisfied all other requirements for a course or a course of study, a failed exit exam denies them the ability to enter into the next course or to receive an undergraduate degree. It is our opinion that a single assessment should never be the sole basis upon which such a momentous decision is made. For this reason, we do not recommend exit testing per se; instead, we advocate that students be made aware of the requirements for passing writing courses or the writing requirements for a specific course of study and that they have the opportunity to work toward those requirements in a variety of ways.

However, we offer a couple of different models for exit exams, which seem to us particularly solid given our overall reservations about exit testing in general. The first involves exit testing from a specific course. Russel Durst, Marjorie Roemer, and Lucille Schultz have written three articles on the portfolio exit procedures at the University of Cincinnati. This system involves basing a decision about a student's appropriate movement from one course to another upon the entire contents of a portfolio. In addition, as we mentioned earlier, these portfolios are read by three-teacher teams who read and discuss the portfolios together making a decision about whether a student's portfolio meets the requirements for the course Two things, it seems to us, make this system laudable: (1) students are judged upon an entire portfolio of work that they have had a whole semester to compile; (2) the decision is made by three different instructors who discuss the portfolio and assessment decision with one another. The important decision then about whether a student can pass from one course to another is based on an entire range of work and is only arrived at after three writing instructors have had the opportunity to discuss the students' work.

The second model(Haswell and Wyche-Smith, "Shooting") is from a program at Washington State University (WSU) that requires students to demonstrate in their junior year that they possess writing skills necessary to receive an undergraduate degree. Students write an impromptu essay that is read by a group of faculty from across campus. In addition, students who do not pass this exam can submit a portfolio of writing that was drafted in various classes. Teachers from these classes have the opportunity to work with students and help them to draft revisions of the original pieces. In this system, students are given a traditional writing examination but at the same time are allowed to support this effort with work they have done throughout their undergraduate years. Their teachers are resource people for students' efforts in demonstrating their writing proficiency, and this proficiency is judged by various faculty from across the disciplines. While faculty and administrators at WSU can point out that writing skills are documented for all students, the students themselves receive multiple opportunities to exhibit that they do possess the necessary writing skills expected from a college graduate. While we think that writing skills are best fostered through thoughtful curricula and hardworking, dedicated faculty, these two examples provide programs that give students ample opportunity to show what they can do, and they involve faculty in ways that can promote the teaching and learning of writing.

Program Assessment

While placement and exit writing assessment really depend upon local conditions and needs, writing program assessment is, as Larry Beason notes, a necessary part of administration. As Paul Prior, Gail Hawisher, Sibylle Gruber, and Nicole MacLaughlin note regarding WAC assessment, program assessment is really just a way of asking and answering questions about how well a program is working. Ethically (Beason) and practically, it is necessary for those of us who design, implement, and run writing programs to know how well they function. It is important to note that while we have been talking here about writing assessment, program assessment requires that we do more than just assess student writing, since it can only be considered a part of the whole picture of how well a writing program does its job. It is difficult to talk in practical terms about program assessment without a specific program in mind, since program assessment needs to be tailored to the program to be evaluated. It might be safe to assume, though, that in assessing a writing program it is necessary to look at the curricula being used, the teaching of those curricula, and the writing of the students themselves.

To talk about the basic components of program assessment in more detail, we'll use the ongoing assessment of the composition program at the University of Louisville (Kentucky[U of L]) as an example. This program does not mandate a particular curriculum, though it does require all instructors to meet some general objectives in terms of the amount and kinds of writing experiences students receive. The first component of program assessment at U of L, then, is to make sure that all instructors meet these goals. This is done at the beginning of each semester by the program administration, who examine all course syllabi. To ensure that these curricula are taught appropriately, the classrooms of all part-time instructors and teaching assistants are visited each semester by a full-time faculty member, who files an informal report about the visit. Any instructor who does not receive a favorable observation report is visited again by a member of the composition program staff. These reports are filed in individual instructors' teaching portfolios. In addition to these reports, instructors also file their syllabi, course materials, and assignments, and each semester instructors draft a reflection about their teaching experiences, new ideas, or materials and how effective they have been in specific classrooms. These teaching portfolios, then, provide a record of an instructor's teaching that is available to the composition program staff. In addition, these portfolios are also valuable for instructors as they finish degrees and apply for teaching positions (as we write this, two of our instructors are working on revising their portfolios for potential employers).

The third part of a writing program an assessment needs to address is the writing performances of students. Because assessing student writing can be costly and time-consuming (certainly much more than the measures we use to look at teaching and curriculum), student writing is not something that needs to be assessed every year for programmatic purposes. Depending upon institutional and accreditation pressures, we would suggest a three year-interval between assessments. Large-scale writing assessment often looks at the writing of many, many students. George Englehard, Belita Gordon, and Stephen Gabrielson, for example, reported on the writing of 100,000 students in a study from the State of Georgia's writing assessment. Because we are conducting program assessment, we are not interested looking at individual student writing except as it pertains to the program. For this reason, we have chosen to look at a small sample (about 10 percent) of student writing. Large-scale assessment often involves no more than what a student can write in less than an hour and two numerical scores given by independent judges on a numerical rubric through which they have been trained to agree. By focusing on a smaller number of students, it is possible to generate a richer amount of information in ways that are more consistent with the manner in which students and teachers work together in the classroom.

The assessment of student writing at U of L will be conducted in three different tiers. The first tier consists of the teachers who teach first-year writing courses. We will choose nine instructors, since we offer about ninety sections of first-year writing during the fall and spring semesters. Instructors will be chosen to reflect the number of classes taught by the different groups of people who staff these classes (GTAs, part-time instructors, and full-time English faculty). Nine different teachers will form three different teacher teams. Each team will read one section of each others' students' writing. They will read the writing of approximately 230 students. Teachers will read portfolios (most but not all teachers in the program use portfolios) when available. The teachers in the teams will then read three classes of student writing, assigning grades as they normally do. In addition, the teams will come up with descriptions of student performance for each of the grades and will offer a short collaborative report on the writing they read and the procedures of reading student writing together. These teams will also each read the high school and college portfolios of five students. Since Kentucky requires all high school seniors to prepare portfolios, we have encouraged first-year students from Kentucky to submit their high school portfolios for placement purposes (Lowe and Huot). It makes sense to us that reading high school portfolios and portfolios or collections of writing from first-year writing classes gives us an opportunity to gauge what effect the first-year writing experience has on students. The teams will be asked to comment on the similarities and differences available from their reading of the two different portfolios for each student.

The second-tier assessment involves the writing of thirty students, more than 10 percent of the original sample, read by classroom teachers. Fifteen of the students will come from each of the teams reading portfolios or collections (five from each team). The other fifteen will consist of all of the fifteen students who are represented by high school and college writing (five from each team). The readers for the second tier will consist of the director of composition, a part-time instructor or GTA who regularly teaches first-year writing, and faculty members from across the disciplines. This committee will meet and discuss the student writing, giving grades to the individual collections or portfolios and discussing the characteristics of those grades. As well, the committee will read the high school and college writing, discussing the progress or lack thereof of each of the students.

The third tier of the assessment will focus on the same writing as the second. The readers, however, will be chosen from assessment and writing program administrators across the country. Drawing on the initial work of Michael Allen, who pioneered the use of e-mail to gather teachers together to read student writing, and following the work of Allen, Jane Frick, Jeff Sommers, and Kathleen Yancey, who conducted program assessment online, we will use the electronic communication to bring together a group of scholars from across the country to read the sample of student writing, giving grades, characterizing those grades, and comparing students' high school writing to what they produce in their first-year college writing courses.

The composition director and one of the third-tier readers will then review the results of all three tiers, looking to see similarities and differences between the ways that classroom teachers, on-campus educators, and assessment and writing program professionals from across the country view the writing going on in first-year classes at U of L. In coming to judgments about the status of student writing, they will consider the agreement on grading within the teacher teams and the other two tiers, the characteristics of the grades written by the three tiers, and the overall performances of students according to the teachers in the program, a panel of faculty from across the institution, and a panel of experts in writing assessment. The team will write a report reflecting the status of the writing that students produce in first-year writing classrooms.

Validating Writing Assessments

As we noted earlier, "validity" means more than just whether an assessment measures what it purports to measure. It pertains to the broader question of whether the judgments being made on behalf of an assessment are actually benefiting the people involved. The most recognized and quoted definition of validity comes from Samuel Messick's 1989 ninety-page definitive statement that defines validity as "an integrated evaluative judgment of the degree to which empirical evidence and theoretical rationales support the adequacy and appropriateness of inferences and actions based on test scores or other modes of assessment" (13). Because Messick focuses on the decisions, inferences, and actions based on an assessment, he and other validity theorists conclude that each use of an assessment must be validated. In fact, Messick contends that validity should provide a rationale for assessing in the first place. Just as we have contended that it is important to see assessment as research, so, too, it is best to view validity as research and inquiry into the decisions we make based on assessment. Lee Cronbach, who with Samuel Messick shares the distinction of having been the most influential validity theorist since the 1950s, sees validity inquiry as argument. To validate an assessment, then, means to build an argument for its use and for justifying the decisions based upon its use.

In placement testing, then, we need to provide an argument that the students are being placed into the appropriate classes. This involves gathering information from their teachers about how adequately students are being placed, information about how well students do in the classes into which they have been placed, and ultimately how well students who are placed into an extra noncredit-bearing course end up writing. For example, in critiquing the use of school readiness tests, Lorrie Shepard notes that "it must be shown specifically that low-scoring children who spend an extra year in preschool or developmental kindergarten are more successful when they enter regular kindergarten (are better adjusted, learn more, etc.) than they would have been without the extra year" (406). It follows, then, that to validate a placement testing program we need to be able to document that students who spend a semester in basic writing actually do better in first-year courses.

One of the most crucial questions about placement is teachers' perceptions of how well students are being placed into their classes. The rest of the necessary documentation for validating placement is probably already available for assessment and writing program administrators, since they would have access to the records of their students' success in the courses to which they have been placed and their subsequent performance in other writing courses. To construct an argument for a system's validity, then, means that administrators would have to gather this evidence and present it in a convincing fashion. Current systems for placement—like DSP which involves students' making their own placement decisions—need to provide validation research that accounts for how well these students are doing and to make sure that factors like gender (O'Neill and Schendel) do not play an overwhelming part in decisions by students.

In exit testing, it is paramount that administrators provide evidence that the test does, indeed, represent the core performance that students need to exhibit in order to exit a course or receive a diploma. If failure to exhibit a satisfactory performance means that students have to take or retake a specific course or prepare an additional performance of their writing, then there needs to be some evidence that this is a valuable experience for them. The overriding question for validating an exit measure would be whether it accurately represents the performance necessary to be successful in the course being exited. In the case of an exit or competency examination required for the reception of an undergraduate degree, it would be important to certify that a student meets the requirements the institution sets for a college-level writer. Reliability, the consistency of the judgments being made on behalf of an assessment, is also an important part of a validation program. It is necessary, then, that assessment and program administrators make sure that their writing assessments make consistent judgments from one year to another.

Program assessment is probably the most difficult of the three to talk about in terms of validation; the decisions being made are less explicit, since we're not talking about placing a student in a particular class or exiting a student into a two-course writing sequence. However, oftentimes people make important decisions based upon program assessment. Should the decision, for example at U of L, be made to change a specific component of the composition program, or should we continue on with the program as is? It seems to us that to choose either one of those decisions demands some sort of validation argument about the efficacy of such an action. As well, the program assessment scheme at U of L seems to neglect the input of the students in the classes that make up the program. Any validation of the assessment, then, would need to include input from students about their perceptions of the program.

Before moving onto the conclusion of this essay, we think it is important to address further the issue of validating writing assessments. Much of assessment work is about defining a specific question and thinking of ways to provide information to answer that question. As assessment and program administrators, we look outward toward our curricula, our teachers, our students, and their writing. Validation supplies us with a way to turn our gaze inward toward the assessments themselves, the program guidelines, and other policies and procedures that after a while just seem normal—"just they way we do things around here." Looking inward furnishes us with reflective pause that allows us the space to become reflective practitioners. Examining our assessments and their results with a critical eye to consider the possible alternatives for doing things and finding explanations for the results we think we have achieved gives us the opportunity to see our programs and our assessments in new ways. The self-reflexive, critical stance—what Lee Cronbach calls "rival hypothesis testing"—is a crucial component of honest, ethical, and productive inquiry.

LAST THOUGHTS ON A WORKING METHODOLOGY FOR WRITING ASSESSMENT

We hope we have been able to unpack many of the issues and problems associated with writing assessment. The first part of this essay provided a general outlook on what kinds of issues and problems associated with writing assessment administration while providing a rationale for why WPAs should become involved with assessment in the first place. The second section focused on more practical issues concerning the kinds of choices WPAs have in terms of why and how they might assess student writing and their own programs. We recommended that WPAs stay away from commercially prepared assessments or even from outdated procedures like holistic scoring that require extra steps and are based upon psychometric assumptions about measurement, education, and reality (Huot, "Toward"). Instead, we urge WPAs to look at the need to assess in the way they would any other research. First and foremost, we should think of what it is we want to know about our students and our programs. These questions should be formulated by representatives of the entire community of teachers and students, providing not only the questions that can drive an assessment but also an excellent opportunity to begin important conversations about teaching and learning.

In addition to bringing together the community of teachers and learners, we also recommend that WPAs consider hiring experts to help them as they design and implement their assessments. In examining the literature on writing assessment, WPAs and their colleagues should look for consultants who, at their own institutions, have already created assessments that mirror the kinds of concerns WPAs have about their programs. Experts can help an institution organize its efforts, read pertinent literature about assessment, and design not only an assessment but the procedures necessary to validate that assessment. In instances where a report or proposal is necessary the expert can assist the WPA and other faculty in writing such documents.

In closing, we hope that we have been able to furnish an examination of the theoretical issues and practical demands facing any WPA or writing teacher who looks to become involved in assessment. We believe that assessment is a necessary and important part of writing-program administration and in being a responsible writing teacher. Assessment can provide WPAs and their programs with an important opportunity to examine in detail the kinds of writing students are doing, the ways in which teachers are working, and the kinds of programmatic decisions that can improve their efforts.

WORKS CITED

Allen, Michael, Jane Frick, Jeff Sommers, and Kathleen Yancey. "Outside Review of Writing Portfolios: An On-Line Evaluation." *WPA: Writing Program Administration* 20 (1997): 66–90.

Ball, Arnetha. "Expanding the Dialogue on Culture as a Critical Component When Assessing Writing." *Assessing Writing* 4.2 (1997): 169–202.

Beason, Larry. "Composition as Service: Implications of Utilitarian, Duties, and Care Ethics." *The Ethics of Writing Instruction: Issues in Theory and Practice.* Ed. Michael A. Pemberton. Stamford: Ablex, 2000.

Black, Laurel, et al., eds. *New Directions in Portfolio Assessment.* Portsmouth, NH: Boynton, 1994.

———. "Writing Like a Woman and Being Rewarded for It: Gender, Assessment, and Reflective Letters from Miami University's Student Portfolios." Black et al. 235–247.

Broad, Robert. "'Portfolio Scoring': A Contradiction in Terms." Black et al. 263–76.

Conway, Glenda. "Portfolio Cover Letters." Black et al. 83–92.

Darling-Hammond, Linda. "Performance-Based Assessment and Educational Equity." *Harvard Educational Review* 64 (1994): 5–30.

DeRemer, Mary L. "Writing Assessment: Raters' Elaboration of the Rating Task." *Assessing Writing* 5 (1998): 7–29.

Durst, Russel K., Marjorie Roemer, and Lucille M. Schultz. "Portfolio Negotiations: Acts in Speech." Black et al. 286–300.

Elbow, Peter, and Kathleen Blake Yancey. "On the Nature of Holistic Scoring: Inquiry Composed on Email." *Assessing Writing* 1 (1994): 91–107.

Englehard, George, Jr., Belita Gordon, and Stephen Gabrielson. "The Influences of Mode of Discourse, Experiential Demand, and Gender on the Quality of Student Writing." *Research in the Teaching of English* 26 (1992): 315–36.

Freedman, Sarah. "Influences of Evaluation on Expository Essays: Beyond the Text." *Research in the Teaching of English* 15 (1981): 245–55.

Garrow, John R. "Assessing and Improving the Adequacy of College Composition Placement." Diss. University of Pittsburgh, 1989.

Harrington, Susanmarie. "New Visions of Authority in Placement Test Rating." *WPA* 22.1/2 (1998): 53–84.

Haswell, Richard, and Janis Tedesco Haswell. "Gendership and the Miswriting of Students." *College Composition and Communication* 46 (1995): 223–54.

Haswell, Richard, Linda Schull Johnson, and Susan Wyche-Smith. "Shooting Niagara: Making Portfolio Assessment Serve Instruction at a State University." *WPA: Writing Program Administration* 18 (1994): 44–53.

Hillocks, George, Jr. *Teaching Writing as Reflective Practice.* New York: Teachers College P, 1995.

Huot, Brian. "A Survey of College and University Writing Placement Practices." *WPA* 17.3 (1994): 49–65.

———. "Beyond Accountability: Reading with Faculty as Partners Across the Disciplines." Yancey and Huot 69–78.

———. "The Influences of Holistic Scoring Procedures on Reading and Rating Student Essays." *Validating Holistic Scoring for Writing Assessment: Theoretical and Empirical Foundations.* Ed. Williamson and Huot. Cresskill: Hampton, 1993.

———. "Reliability, Validity, and Holistic Scoring: What We Know and What We Need to Know." *College Composition and Communication* 41 (1990): 201–13.

———. "Toward a New Theory of Writing Assessment." *College Composition and Communication* 47.4 (1996): 549–66.

Lowe, Teri, and Brian Huot. "Using KIRIS Writing Portfolios to Place Students in First-Year Composition at the University of Louisville." *Kentucky English Bulletin* 46.2 (1997): 46–64.

Messick, Samuel. "Validity." *Educational Measurement,* Third Edition Ed. Robert L. Linn. Washington: American Council on Education and National Council on Measurement in Education, 13–103.

Moss, Pamela A. "Can There be Validity Without Reliability?" *Educational Researcher* 23.2 (1994) 5–12.

———. "'Testing the Test of the Test': A Response to Multiple Inquiry in the Validation of Writing Tests." *Assessing Writing* 5.1 (1998): 111–22.

Prior, Paul, Gail E. Hawisher, Sibylle Gruber, and Nicole MacLaughlin. "Research and WAC Evaluation: An In-Progress Reflection." Yancey and Huot 185–216.

Pula, Judith J., and Brian Huot. "A Model of Background Influences on Holistic Raters." *Validating Holistic Scoring for Writing Assessment: Theoretic and Empirical Foundations.* Ed, Williamson and Huot. Cresskill: Hampton, 1993.

Royer, Daniel J., and Roger Gilles. "Directed Self-Placement: An Attitude of Orientation." *College Composition and Communication* 50 (1998): 54–70.

Schendel, Ellen, and Peggy O'Neill. "Exploring the Theories and Consequences of Self-Assessment through Ethical Inquiry." Forthcoming.

Schon, Donald. *The Reflective Practitioner: How Professionals Think in Action.* London: Temple Smith, 1983.

Selfe, Cynthia. "Contextual Evaluation in WAC Programs: Theories, Issues, and Strategies for Teachers." Yancey and Huot 51–68.

Shepard, Lorrie. "The Centrality of Test Use and Consequences for Test Validity." *Educational Measurement: Issues and Practice* 16.2 (1997): 5–24.

Sommers, Jeffrey. "The Writer's Memo: Collaboration, Response, and Development." *Writing Response: Theory, Practice, and Research.* Ed. Chris Anson. Urbana: NCTE, 1989. 174–86.

Smith, William L. "Assessing Reliability and Adequacy of Using Holistic Scoring of Essays as a College Composition Placement Program Technique." *Validating Holistic Scoring for Writing Assessment: Theoretic and Empirical Foundations.* Ed. Williamson and Huot. Cresskill: Hampton, 1993.

Starch, Daniel, and Edward Elliott. "Reliability of the Grading of High-School Work in English." *School Review* 20 (1912): 442–57.

Veal, Ramon, and Sally Hudson. "Direct and Indirect Measures for the Large-Scale Evaluation of Writing." *Research in the Teaching of English* 17 (1983): 285–96.

White, Edward. "An Apologia for the Timed Impromptu Essay Test." *College Composition and Communication* 46.1 (1995): 30–45.

———. *Teaching and Assessing Writing,* Second Edition. San Francisco: Jossey, 1994.

Williamson, Michael M. "Pragmatism, Positivism, and Program Evaluation." Yancey and Huot 237–58.

Wolfe, Edward M. "The Relationship Between Essay Reading Style and Scoring Proficiency in a Psychometric Scoring System." *Assessing Writing* 4 (1997): 83–106.

Yancey, Kathleen. "Looking Back as We Look Forward: Historicizing Writing Assessment." *College Composition and Communication* 50.3 (1999): 483–503.

———. *Reflection in the Writing Classroom.* Logan: Utah State UP, 1998.

Yancey, Kathleen Blake, and Brian Huot. *Assessing Writing Across the Curriculum: Diverse Approaches and Practices.* Greenwich: Ablex, 1997.

———. "Introduction—Assumptions about Assessing WAC Programs: Some Axioms, Some Observations, Some Context." Yancey and Huot 7–14.

Ten Commandments for Computers and Composition

Todd Taylor
University of North Carolina—Chapel Hill

I was probably asked to write this essay because of a 1997 article published in *WPA: Writing Program Administrator* titled "Computers in the Composition Curriculum: An Update." The title borrows directly from "Computers in the Composition Curriculum: Looking Ahead," by Jeanette Harris, Diana George, Christine Hult, and M. Jimmie Killingsworth. Even though the Harris et al. article was published in the 1989 Fall/Winter issue of *WPA*, it remains, even today, at the top of my recommended reading list for those who are trying to negotiate the increasing impact of computers on writing programs. Although the subtitle "Looking Ahead" suggests that the focus of the original article was the future, I value this article so highly because it continues to serve in the present as a concise and powerful position statement on computers and writing program administration. The authors write,

> Many writing program administrators fight so long to get a computer lab or classroom for their program that they think the battle is over once the machines are in place. We would argue, however, that a strong computerized writing program focuses on writing, not computer technology. Computers are only machines; their effectiveness depends on using them to reinforce theories that inform our pedagogy. As writing program administrators, it is our responsibility to determine the role computers play in the teaching of writing. (35)

Harris and her colleagues also note that the "one constant factor in dealing with computers is change. As writing program administrators, we must try to keep informed of the changes and to react appropriately to them" (41). It was therefore somewhat remarkable that between 1989 and 1997 *WPA* did not publish a single article about changes taking place in computers and writing. The lack of updates was probably due to the fact that writing program administrators are often asked to wear too many hats. The additional responsibility of being an expert on instructional technology is not something easily added to an often already overburdened workload. However, all indications suggest that WPAs can no longer afford to lack expertise in this area. As Cynthia Selfe noted passionately in her chair's address, "The Perils of Not Paying Attention," at the 1998 Conference on College Composition and Communication (CCCC) the genie is out of the bottle, and more:

> Allowing ourselves the luxury of ignoring technology, however, is not only misguided at the end of the 20th century, it is dangerously shortsighted. And I do not mean, simply, that we are all, each of us, now teaching students who must know how to communicate as informed thinkers and citizens in an increasingly technological world, although this is surely so. This recognition has led composition faculty only to the point of using computers, or having students do so, but not to the point of thinking about what we are doing and understanding at least some of the important implications of our actions.... An honest examination of this situation, I believe, will lead composition studies professionals to recognize that these two complex cultural formations, technology and literacy, have become linked in ways that exacerbate current educational and social inequities in the United States rather than addressing them productively. The story will lead us to admit, I believe, that we are, in part, already responsible for a bad, even a shameful, situation.... *As composition teachers, deciding whether or not to use technology in our classes is simply not the point; we have to pay attention to technology.* When we fail to do so, we share in the responsibility for sustaining and reproducing an unfair system that, scholars such as Elspeth Stuckey and Mike Rose have noted in other contexts, enacts social violence and ensures continuing illiteracy under the aegis of education. (414–15)

The mind-boggling expansion of the Internet and the advent of the personal computer thus place us in the midst of very significant technology-driven cultural changes. Mainstream commercial and political forces have for some time been exerting tremendous pressure on educational institutions to technologize. And maybe most significantly, the Internet's ability to support virtual writing classes, often referred to as "distance learning," amounts to a very tangible revolution in the way we teach, a revolution whose early manifestations are more threatening than encouraging for writing programs, teachers, and students.

In short, in order to make the kind of informed decisions that Harris and colleagues and the former chair of CCCC call for, WPAs need quality information, and they need it updated frequently. At the Eleventh Annual Computers and Writing Conference in 1995, one of the plenary speakers, Diana Natalicio, president of the University of Texas-El Paso, suggested that the biggest challenge we all face in terms of education and computers is to think creatively to find ways to use technology to bring people together. And an important dimension toward achieving that goal is keeping ourselves as informed as possible about technological change.

Unfortunately, because technology changes so rapidly there is almost no way for an essay like this one to address many of the most pressing, current issues that WPAs face regarding technology daily:

What kinds of computers should/will students use?

How can I fund regular maintenance of campus equipment?

What software applications should the writing program provide, promote, offer, endorse (this semester)?

How can I fund and enhance instructor development for teaching with computers?

Who's going to fix the machines and supervise the labs (assuming that the university/department/program provides the equipment)?

How can I locate cheap toner?

For instance, until the mid–1980s, writing with "computers" most typically involved large mainframe computers operated by campus authorities at great ideological (and often physical) distances from compositionists. From that point until the early 1990s, approaches to teaching writing with computers focused on nonnetworked, desktop, personal computers which, unfortunately, offered little or no software designed specifically for writing students. In the early 1990s local area networks (LANs) gave rise to a first generation of widely used, customized instructional software such as Daedalus and Common Space. By the end of the 1990s, the ubiquity of the Internet and of personal computers made LAN-based applications like the original Daedalus obsolete. Soon after, writing programs that relied on university-provided equipment had to adjust their strategies again as increasing numbers of campuses adopted computer-purchase policies for all of their students. We can be sure that the paradigms for teaching writing with computers will continue to change as the paradigms for computing change. At every stage in the evolution of personal computing, the nature of the computer design (mainframe, LAN, desktop, Internet-connected, or laptop), available software, and maintenance costs and requirements have dramatically shaped our approaches. Thus, we must assume that paradigms will continue to evolve. As I write this chapter at the very beginning of the twenty-first century, it seems likely that soon "personal" computers will operate more like the "dumb" terminals of the 1970s–80s in which software applications, data file—in fact, almost *everything*—resides on centralized computers, not on individual ones; most of your documents and the applications you will use to author and revise them will reside on the ubiquitous Internet. Imagine every paper ever written by your students—or, for that matter, by anyone's students—residing on the Internet; this will no doubt dramatically reshape how we teach writing.

Even though a sourcebook essay can not give you advice on which software to use today, it can provide a set of principles that can help guide the decisions you make, even when confronted with constant change. Thus, think of the ten points I present here as a philosophical compass, a way to orient yourself and your colleagues as you face the continually shifting landscape of computers and composition. There are, of course, basic management strategies that apply here as they do in every aspect of being a WPA. WPAs must effectively locate and manage funds to sustain various features of their programs. They must be effective communicators and negotiators when working with others inside and outside their programs. Such basic strategies are not worth reviewing here. On the other hand, instructional technology programs do often give rise to a set of typical problems that are worth noting. For example, planning for and attempting to calculate the costs of constant reinvestment, upgrading, and obsolescence of computer technologies are persistent problems. Historically, universities in general—not just writing programs in particular—have failed to provide adequate instructor development, training, and support. Many WPAs have experienced dramatic communication gaps between themselves and the technical support staff on which they must rely. And computer composition specialists are sometimes professionally alienated from and marginalized by their colleagues.

For years WPAs stumbled across such obstacles on the way to using computers in their programs. Very often they reinvented the wheels with which others had already struggled because they operated too often in isolation, especially when working on the cutting edge. Fortunately, the profession now has a generation of well-traveled, and perhaps well-worn, pioneers who can now help make such excursions less awkward. Based on informal conversations I've had with these pioneers as well as on my experience, which began early in graduate school, I've produced a list of ten principles (dare, "commandments") to help guide veterans and novices alike as they negotiate instructional technology. The balance of this essay will examine each of these principles in turn. They are:

1. Keep people first.
2. Identify and build from program principles.
3. Start simple.
4. Invest heavily in hands-on instructor training.
5. Revise strategies for instructing students.
6. Consult with others.
7. Expect the crash.
8. Consider access.
9. Be critical of technology.
10. Use technology as a lever for positive change.

To illustrate these ten principles, I would first like to set up a hypothetical scenario to use throughout my discussion to show how these theoretical points shape practice. Imagine that you now have $200,000 to spend to develop a computer classroom, but you have a limited background in teaching with computers. In fact, you've never seen a classroom—as opposed to a "lab"—designed specifically for writing with computers. You've never taught in a facility like this, and you've never sat in one as a student. In my case, this scenario is not so hypothetical; it literally happened to me in 1994 as I was working on my M.A. thesis on computers and writing. My university had received a sudden windfall from a large corporation that wanted to fund a networked classroom. Although the source of funding for such facilities is rarely as fortuitous as my in 1994 scenario, the point is the same: WPAs often find themselves suddenly and without enough preparation wearing a new hat, namely, that of a campus leader in instructional technology.

So, imagine, as difficult as it might be in the year 2001, that you have never seen a computer classroom before and it is now your responsibility to design a facility that accommodates twenty-five students. What would your floor plan look like? Take a piece of paper, place it on top of the diagram below, and trace the rectangular shape that's meant to represent a room that is 25" by 30". You do not need to trace the circle and square shapes. The circle represents a chair, and the square represents the approximate amount of desk space needed to hold a computer. These shapes allow you to gauge roughly the size and scale of a workstation in proportion to the room dimensions provided. Before reading further, stop and diagram your ideal floor plan for a computerized writing classroom. Be sure to include necessary components such as projection screens and printers. Doing this exercise individually within a group (large or small) can be thought-provoking, especially once you quit sketching and compare designs.

The issue of computer classroom architecture has for years been a source of much discussion, debate, and anguish. For many reasons, next to faculty salary lines, control of institutional space is perhaps the most important coin of the realm on many campuses. The control of campus space is typically associated with institutional power. This classroom architecture exercise aims to have you consider power relations as much as anything else.

Historically, there have been five conventional computer classroom designs: labs, theaters, pods, perimeters, and (most recently) wireless laptops.

> The *lab design* arranges computers in long banks, typically extending out from one wall into the center of the room. The lab design is most often predicated on the goal of fitting as many computers as possible into the available space. Since a computer workstation consumes more

floor space than a typical student desk, architects often use a lab design when renovating so that the room can hold the same number of students as before.

The *theater design* places students' workstations in rows, sometimes ascending from the front of the class like an amphitheater. This design compels students to face the front of the class, the instructor, and typically a projection screen, while allowing them to keep their hands on their keyboards.

The *pod plan* creates a series of islands around which small groups of four to six students sit while working on the computers at their island. This plan thus comprises clusters intended to enhance small-group interaction and collaboration.

The *perimeter design* places students at workstations around the perimeter of the room with their backs to the center of the room as they work on computers. Often, the center of the room contains empty tables for students to use. This design enables instructors to physically shift focus away from computer screens when necessary, and it allows them to evaluate with a quick glance the status of each student as he works. With mobile chairs and tables in the center of the room, students must focus on either their computers or nonhands-on activities such as a lecture or peer work.

However, in my estimation, the emergence of affordable *laptop computers with wireless network connections* has now ended the floor-plan debate, because all rooms can then be used to teach with computers.

I consider this floor-plan exercise a sort of Rorschach Test for educators because it aims to uncover deep-seated ideologies and assumptions about teaching with technology and because it can prompt useful reflection and dialogue on the subject. Which design (lab, theater, pod, perimeter, or laptop) best describes the plan you produced? What assumptions, goals, and ideas influenced your approach? When asked to design that classroom in 1994, I first wanted to pursue a pod plan, but I quickly learned that the combined problems of furniture cost, bringing conduits from the floor or ceiling, as well as cramped spacing made it infeasible for us. Once I settled on a perimeter plan, I was shocked to discover that a university architect had already produced a floor plan for the facility: a lab design with long banks of computers. My department had to argue vehemently to change these plans, and I am convinced that the only reason the perimeter design prevailed was that it was less expensive to wire than the lab design.

The point here is not to rehash the long-running debate on computer classroom architecture. In fact, the software you select is likely to have a much greater impact on your program than your floor plan. The point is to use classroom architecture (as a particularly tangible administrative issue) as a device to help you explore your position and to illustrate some principles to help guide the vast array of decisions you must make regarding hardware, software, maintenance, security, upgrading, instructor development, program policy, etc.

1   *Keep people first.*

Keeping people first is by far the most important but complicated of the ten commandments. In *Creating a Computer-Supported Writing Facility: A Blueprint for Action,* Cynthia Selfe argues that our goal should be to apply instructional technologies in ways that are "congruent with humanistic concerns" (xvi). I would argue that the primary and collective thesis of Selfe's published work on computers and composition is to promote a humanistic approach to technology that insists that people are more important than machines. We are all no doubt aware of the problem that Selfe's humanistic approach aims to counter: the cultural hyperbole associated with advanced technologies that justifies widespread computer adoption as an end in itself. Simply put, the classic mistake in instructional technology has been to focus so intently on the technology that we lose sight of students and teachers, of effective learning and teaching.

Perhaps nowhere is the importance of the "people first" principle more apparent than in classroom design. Floor plans that literally and figuratively allow computers to come between people violate this commandment. The lab design makes room for equipment at the expense of ergonomic teaching. In theater and pod designs, unless you have recessed monitors or laptop computers, the equipment comes between people. In contrast, the perimeter plan pushes the equipment to the boundaries of the space. Wireless laptop computers allow the most flexibility because, with movable desks, students can arrange themselves in a variety of ways depending on the context. And since laptops have a low profile, sight lines are never interrupted. However, this does not mean that a laptop or perimeter design is always preferable to others. Technology can still come between, hence *before*, people in other ways. For example, I have found that students are more prone to playing games on a personal laptop than on an institutional desktop computer.

Thus, despite the uninformed assumption that leaders in instructional technology, like Cynthia Selfe, must be reckless champions of computers, the reality is that most of them are eager to promote balanced, critical approaches that urge us to focus more on people than on machines. Following the "people first" principle is clearly the wisest, most important strategy for using instructional technology. However, I would like to suggest, perhaps for the first time, that Selfe's "humanist approach" might be somewhat more difficult to realize than it seems at first. Those who work with instructional technology, myself included, are likely to feel somewhat unduly inoculated by the idea of "humanistic" computing. That is, we are likely to feel secure about our work with computers, since we believe we do so in a way that champions and promotes the interests of students and instructors over machines. Despite good intentions, working with technology *does* generate a subtle inertia that inevitably colors our perspectives, regardless of our awareness of the need to remain critical. The enormous personal investment required to drive any new dimension of a computerized writing program—from creating a new classroom to funding new software—is almost certain to compel optimism and quiet criticism in significant ways. You might sense that your program needs new, wireless laptops to replace the failing, outdated desktop computers in your designated classroom—even though you've never taught in a laptop environment before. But the vigor necessary to campaign successfully for such change requires so much conviction that even the most disciplined of us will find it difficult to remain fully critical. Further, instructional technologists cannot escape the chicken-and-egg phenomenon: how can you know if new laptops will serve your program well until after you try them? How can you tell who really is coming first, especially since the ideological and political inertia that inevitably accompanies any innovation is difficult to overcome? Selfe writes, "if our current use of computers is marked by any common theme at all, it is experimentation at the most basic level" (*Creating* xix). If the experiment is ultimately negative, can you pull the plug? How can you determine if and when the machines are taking precedence over students and teachers? We need to be aware that experiments require leaps of faith that place students, teachers, and writing programs at risk. We may feel comforted by the "humanistic" parachute Selfe provides, but the fact is that we *are* leaping, and it is impossible to be certain that people, not machines, will always be our first concern.

2 *Identify and build from program principles.*

When cutting the first row in a field, some farmers set their plows opposite a fixed object like a tree or pole at the far end of the field and use it as a guide. They then stare at this guide, steering directly toward it as they establish the first row. This practice helps shape a straight initial row, which is important, since wavers in the first row will be multiplied throughout the field, decreasing the potential yield of the crop. Likewise, WPAs must focus intently on guiding principles as they work to integrate computers into their writing programs. Many instructors and administrators decry the attention given to composition theory in our scholarship and graduate programs, arguing that it has little to do with the daily practice of teaching writing. But, just like the farmer's guiding object, the perhaps distant, abstract principles (the theories) we hold in focus will substantially shape our practice.

Thus, any new computer venture calls for an examination and articulation of program principles and goals. Instructors ask students to base the choices they make when writing on persistent (re)evaluations of purpose and audience. Likewise, WPAs should base the choices they make regarding computers on the purpose of their program. If a program lacks a clear mission and purpose, it seems unlikely that a WPA will be able to establish complementary approaches to teaching with computers. Consequently, there can be no single, correct answer to the Rorschach floor plan exercise because each writing program needs to make local decisions based upon guiding, local principles. If your goal is to offer maximum possible access to hands-on computing, a lab design might be right for you. If you wish to promote computer literacy as an important part of your courses, a heads-up-and-hands-down theater arrangement might provide your students with abundant, step-by-step software instruction. A pod plan would work well in a program that emphasizes small-group collaboration and eschews teacher-centered learning. A perimeter design might complement a research-oriented program because instructors can easily move from student to student while helping each navigate networked information sources. Because it's so flexible, the laptop approach might work well in a seminar-type program that encourages each instructor to shape courses in individualistic ways within the program's broad, general rubric. In order to follow these first two commandments, WPAs must know what kind of teaching and learning they wish to promote so that they can in turn ask whether a particular technology is likely to complement their program. The first principle, "keep people first," quickly leads to the second, which can be restated thus: "apply technology only when it serves your pedagogy."

3   Start simple.

Our colleagues are too often divided into two polarized camps when it comes to instructional technology: those who have inhaled and those who have not. As intellectuals, compositionists who are high on technology look to get carried away with the new discoveries, possibilities, and innovation it promises. Almost universally, colleagues grow very excited, almost euphoric, when they begin to appreciate the potential of teaching in new ways. The problem is that personal and institutional limitations cannot keep pace with the imagination of an intellectual who has suddenly tapped a new source of thought and energy, and the initial euphoria typically subsides in response to these limitations. In contrast, those who reject instructional technology often do so without ever trying it.

Both groups have much to gain by starting simple. The best approach is to add one technological component at a time to your repertoire. By starting simple, the technological protagonists can avoid getting in over their heads and the antagonists can be enticed to wade in slowly. It is entirely possible for individual instructors of writing programs as a whole to have a very effective, robust computerized pedagogy using just basic e-mail. But until you have gathered some teaching experience with a particular application, like e-mail, it is difficult to tailor it to suit the needs of your pedagogy. If your reach exceeds your grasp too greatly, you are likely to either burn out or crash and burn.

For instance, your instinct might be to squeeze every last penny out of that $200,000 grant to build a classroom so that you can offer every option imaginable: the most advanced software, expensive projection and sound equipment, motorized blinds, video capture, and remote control lighting. However, buying less initial equipment and setting aside money for future upgrades and purchases is probably a better long-term plan. Buying advanced instead of top-of-the-line hardware is wise if it frees up enough money to fund teacher training workshops. If the basic aspects of instructional technology are not first well- established, you will never successfully implement more advanced applications. As a rule of thumb, instructors and programs should attempt to add no more than one application to their teaching per term.

4   *Invest heavily in hands-on instructor training.*

I have been told that the standard corporate practice is to budget $1 on technology training for every $3 spent on hardware. Colleges and universities do not follow this practice. In most cases they budget no money for training. Ironically, the most important aspect to the design you just sketched might be that which is visibly missing: space for instructor development. The first thing you should do with your technology allowance is to designate about 20 percent of it for training. WPAs who follow this practice are likely to need to defend their position. If so, this is a good opportunity to make the point that your responsibility is not so much the short-term creation of a computer *facility* as much as it is the long-term development of a *program* whose most obvious physical asset happens to be a room full of computers. And, in the same way that software is less tangible but more important than hardware, so, too, is instructor preparation less tangible but more important than the equipment. People are more important than the machines they use, and in order to design a program that will enhance teaching and learning, instructors need constant, hands-on training led by people who speak their language, which typically means that workshop leaders should be classroom teachers in a similar discipline.

5   *Revise strategies for instructing students.*

In kindergarten most of us learned how to raise our hands to speak, how to wait our turn in line, how to color within the lines, and how to interact with others. As of the year 2001 almost none of us attended computerized kindergarten; thus, instructors and students alike tend to lack the tacit understanding and socialization necessary to operate successfully in the new computer environments. In a way, we are all feral children in the new classroom because we do not yet know how to behave.

Instructors often become frustrated and perplexed when students seem unable to follow instructions as expediently as in traditional classroom settings. Consider, though, that students have had their entire lives to learn how to "get out a sheet of paper and number it from one to ten." When we ask them to do the same on a word processor, there are dozens of ways this simple imperative can go wrong or be disrupted. The student might first need to remember a personalized password to start the computer. Then she might not know where to look for the word processing application. She might get confused by a word processor that forces her to select a particular template before opening a new file. The word processor's automatic numbering function might perplex her as it takes control. She might fail to save the file properly; perhaps she saves it somewhere on the computer but doesn't know where.

The level of detail and piloting necessary to get a group of students to perform even the simplest computer task is startling to most instructors new to such teaching. Teachers do not need a set of explicit, step-by-step instructions to get their students to open their books to page 203 successfully. And there is usually no reason for teachers in traditional settings to test their instructions on a handful of live subjects before asking twenty or more students to follow them. However, Murphy's law is especially prevalent in computer classrooms: if there's a wrong button to push, someone in a group of twenty students will find it.

In fact, we are all so feral in computer environments that even once you *do* refine your instruction sets, one or two students will still encounter problems that the instructor must sort out on the fly. As a result, the amount of dead air and the tempo that accompanies teaching with computers can be very awkward at first. Instructors and students alike find it frustrating to sit idly, waiting for an entire class to arrive at the proper screen—this kind of dead air is also inevitable. Such miscues are especially troublesome considering that they represent a violation of the first commandment. While waiting for the technology to work, the computers are, at least momentarily, more important then the people using them. Instructors must make their instructions in computer environments highly explicit to minimize the amount of time and effort spent focusing on the technology itself rather than learning. Clearly, instructors need extensive training to develop the skills required to lead a class in these new ways. I prefer a perimeter floor plan for this very reason because, compared to the other designs, this plan makes it easy to see where students go wrong. Watching these miscues can improve your ability to deliver better instructions next time. The perimeter design also enables instructors to locate and help the student who is momentarily lost. Most of the time when I ask, "Who is not on the appropriate screen?" those who are lost are concentrating on their predicament and never hear my question. Floor plans that do not allow instructors to glance at all of the student monitors can make it difficult to get everyone on the same screen simultaneously.

6   *Consult with others.*

From the early days of computer writing instruction until the mid–1990s and the explosion of the Internet, instructors who worked in this area most frequently did so on their own. The sensation for such early adopters was often that of being alone in the woods with no established trails to follow. In fact, a vast majority of the early development of the field was shouldered by an originally invisible group who later gained power: graduate students. For example, graduate students at the University of Texas-Austin who developed the Daedalus Integrated Writing Environment soon after became important leaders in the field of computers and composition, making an indelible mark on its history. As of the year 2001 graduate students are still largely responsible for much of the innovation in this area, but the climate has obviously changed. Cynthia Selfe, for example, has risen to the top of the profession because of her work with technology. In other words, WPAs now have a growing number of people with whom they can consult; such people are no longer lost in the woods and can help others find their way.

Teaching is too often like sex in that it is something everyone is supposed to be able to do naturally without talking to others about it. Fortunately, compositionists tend to resist this tradition. Still, writing instructors and program administrators operate too often in isolation, and, when it comes to teaching with computers, the need to overcome the tradition of silence is especially pressing. Ideally, you can hire someone to help direct the technological aspects of your writing program. Nevertheless, external colleagues and consultants, computer faculty, architects, technicians, administrators, and students should work collaboratively instead of unilaterally when making decisions. Published scholarship such as this sourcebook as well as the growing numbers of books and journals dedicated to teaching with technology offer a great resource for reflection and planning. Material in this area tends to seem outdated more quickly than other scholarship; yet one can still mine work like Selfe's 1989 *Creating a Computer-Supported Writing Facility* for useful, important guidance. In order for instructors to refine their strategies for teaching with technology, they will need to attend workshops led by consultants both inside and outside of their writing programs.

Did your sketch for the computer classroom include a space for an on-site consultant and for a studio in which instructors can develop their teaching while others are using the classroom? You will probably find daily internal consultants as necessary as special outside help. I recommend locating computer teaching facilities in close proximity to a smaller studio for instructional development. Teachers trying to orchestrate class sessions often need someone who has experience with their particular facility to help them solve a problem that emerges suddenly. Daily on-site consultants log and address problems that can distract from learning if not resolved expediently. In addition, a dedicated development studio is almost certain to generate a sense of community among the instructors working together in this space; such community building is essential to changing the culture of your program in positive ways. Without such consultation(s), WPAs will find it difficult to keep the technological aspects of their writing programs in line with their pedagogical goals.

7 Expect the crash.

Equip your instructors with a sensibility about technology that leads them to always have a backup plan. Novice computer and writing instructors have told me repeatedly that the best advice I ever gave them was to assume that the technology can and will stop working at any moment. Remaining flexible is thus an important corollary to each of these ten commandments, particularly this one.

On the one hand, such skepticism about the reliability of technology is well-deserved—we have all experienced or witnessed some version of a computer catastrophe. On the other hand, the rate of such failures decreases as instructors and WPAs gain experience with computers and create well-designed, well-informed programs that start simple, invest heavily in teacher training, use consultants wisely, and keep program goals in focus. The systems I used in 2000 were much more reliable and instructor-friendly than those I had in 1994.

Would the classroom you designed still function well as a classroom if the computers ceased to work in the middle of a particular meeting?

8   *Consider access.*

Who will have access to the classroom you just designed? Which instructors will work in the new facility? How will they be selected? Which students will occupy these classes? Will students and instructors have access to the facility outside of class sessions? What kind of security and supervision will the classroom need to maximize access while protecting the computers from theft and negligence? If you establish a distance education component to your writing program, how can you ensure appropriate levels of access not only to computers and computer networks but also to other important entities such as libraries and student advisors?

Few WPAs are unlikely to overlook such apparent concerns. However, they also need to think about the ideological and political aspects of computer access. Increasingly, writing programs that embrace technology require students to access computers and the Internet outside of classroom space. How might courses that require computer access outside of class enable certain students but harm others?

Imagine the classroom you designed has now been in place for four years. Imagine that you followed all of the principles I've outlined so far and that the instructors in your program have made a careful but successful transition to teaching with computers. However, the computers you purchased with that $200,000 grant are now broken and obsolete. You have worked hard to maintain your focus on program goals and on people rather than machines, but now your program has a certain inertia that makes it seem impossible to return to the days before computer-assisted instruction. Everyone seems to believe that computers are now an educational fixture; thus, campuses must find a way to continue funding technology. But colleges and universities can simply no longer afford to provide students with adequate computer access using traditional approaches to generating revenue. Consequently, I am convinced that the unfortunate but only long-term approach to funding student access to technology is to pass the costs directly on to students. Campuses will increase student fees, raise tuition, or adopt policies that require students to own a computer or carry a laptop. In other words, the cost of education has simply increased as the perception that computers are essential to learning has taken hold. Tragically, when the cost of education increases even just slightly, those who can least afford the increase are the first to drop out. Richard Ohmann describes the problem aptly: "I see every reason to believe that the computer revolution, like other revolutions from the top down, will indeed expand the minds of the elite, meanwhile facilitating the degradation of labor and the stratification of the workforce" ("Literacy" 683). Nine and eleven years later respectively, Lester Faigley's and Cynthia Selfe's chair addresses to the CCCC verify that Ohmann's unfortunate vision has come to be. Further, all three of these scholars describe, in chilling terms, the unintentional complicity of writing instructors in furthering such growing inequality.

When you sketched your floor plan, did you imagine creating seats for socioeconomically privileged students while pulling seats out from under others? When a senior instructor accepted that generous grant to develop an online distance education course, did the WPA anticipate that the course might be widely replicated by the university and staffed by part-time writing instructors paid much less than a reasonable wage? As slowly, critically, or carefully as WPAs might embrace computer instruction, they still run the very real risk of ultimately contributing to the digital divide between the have and have-nots, further distancing the rich from the poor.

9 Be critical of technology.

As hopeless as the politics of technology might at first seem, maintaining a critical perspective toward computers remains our best weapon. And despite the potentially dangerous inertia of working with instructional technology, we run a much greater risk if, as Selfe warns, we fail to pay attention to it.

Being critical of technology requires a focus on the first eight commandments I have presented. WPAs must first critically examine their choices, asking on each occasion if students and teachers are being well-served by computers, not vice versa. They should consult with experienced professionals as well as acquaint themselves with the scholarship in computers and composition to reflect on and assess the evolution of their writing programs. They must be eager to resist ideological inertia when priorities and expectations grow unbalanced.

In the most practical sense, this means asking students, teachers, and consultants to generate regular evaluations that examine in equal parts the strengths and weaknesses of each development. If WPAs follow the principle of starting simple and growing one step at a time, it should be easy to identify and assess the merits of the latest experiment.

List, in equal parts, the advantages and drawbacks of your classroom floor plan. Ask someone else to do the same for your plan. Compare notes.

10 Use technology as a lever for positive change.

Technology can be a source of extreme anxiety, especially for humanist educators. At the same time, the cultural upheaval that accompanies the changing material conditions of life in the emerging global information economy also presents remarkable opportunities. Compositionists are well-positioned, in many ways, to ride the technological wave to the advantage of their students, writing programs, and personal careers. Our discipline is generally far ahead of others in its use and command of instructional technology. At first, such innovation impeded our advancement because traditional reward structures did not appreciate work with technology. This situation has begun to change, however, as high-level campus administrators increasingly feel the pressure to technologize their campuses and are thus beginning not only to recognize but to privilege such work.

Furthermore, colleges and universities are under increasing pressure to demonstrate that they are dedicated to undergraduate teaching. This pressure most directly translates into looking for ways to document "a serious commitment to teaching." The trick has always been to find ways to provide such evidence. Investing your efforts in innovative approaches to instructional technology is something instructors and program administrators can point to on a vita or in an annual program report. Others can claim that they care a great deal about and are invested in their teaching, and their student evaluations may or may not reflect these efforts. But technological innovators can always demonstrate tangible growth.

If your work with instructional technology grabs the attention of administrative leaders on your campus, you can use it to gain power for your writing program. Furthermore, a so-called paradigm shift like the move to teaching with computers creates opportunities to challenge or upset traditional practices that do not serve us well. A pod plan, for example, might (by design) reduce lecturing and increase student collaboration. The effort that you put into sketching and refining that classroom floor plan might one day help you and your writing program effect positive change. It certainly helped me.

WORKS CITED

Faigley, Lester. "Literacy After the Revolution." *College Composition and Communication* 48 (1997): 30–43.

Harris, Jeanette, et al. "Computers in the Composition Curriculum: Looking Ahead." *WPA: Writing Program Administration* 13.1–2 (1989): 35–43.

Ohmann, Richard. "Literacy, Technology, and Monopoly Capital." *College English* 47 (1995): 675–89.

Selfe, Cynthia L. *Creating a Computer-Supported Writing Facility: A Blueprint for Action.* Houghton: Computers and Composition, 1989.

———. "Technology and Literacy: A Story about the Perils of Not Paying Attention." *College Composition and Communication* 50 (1999): 411–36.

Taylor, Todd. "Computers in the Composition Curriculum: An Update." *WPA: Writing Program Administration.* 20.1–2 (1996): 7–18.

Redefining Composition, Managing Change, and the Role of the WPA

Geoffrey Chase
Northern Arizona University

WPAs have the unenviable task of serving many constituents, all of whom have different perceptions, and often contradictory expectations, about the aims and goals of composition. Meeting the expectations and demands of faculty and instructors within the writing program, colleagues in the department, colleagues from other departments, department chairs, other university administrators, students, and parents, and serving as a mediator between these many stakeholders are both critical and stressful. More so perhaps than any other program "a writing program is itself part of its institutional context, constantly shaping other features of the institution and constantly being shaped by those features" (Witte and Faigley 45).

Because of the unusual, even unique, niche which composition holds within the larger system, it is not surprising that composition has often sought to redefine itself in relationship to the university, or that the university has often sought to redefine composition. What is different about recent calls for reform or for the abolition of the composition requirement all together, as Connors notes (24), is that these calls are now coming from inside the field. WPAs have become proactive voices in this debate and are in the position to redefine their own roles as well as help alter the terrain of higher education. No longer content to tolerate programs which have grown organically, and which exploit part-timers, adjuncts, and graduate students, or to oversee writing programs that are "not so much planned or organized as inherited and casually coordinated" (White 136), some WPAs have begun to call for the end to the composition requirement while others seek dramatic reforms.

The question of whether to abolish the freshman composition requirement, or whether to pursue reform within composition programs, is a question about systems and the complicated interrelationships that define both composition and the academy at large. Thus, as WPAs, we need to think on both theoretical and practical levels about this relationship. Currently, composition courses still represent a major site of writing instruction in the academy (Bazerman 258), and it is unlikely, and perhaps undesirable, that the requirement for composition will be dropped quickly at institutions that are unable to provide alternative comprehensive sites for writing instruction. If, however, we perceive that the relationship between composition and the larger institution is problematic, we must look closely at ways in which this relationship may be redefined. We must find and create other sites for writing instruction in the academy—something WAC programs across the country already do—and we must be open to fundamental changes in composition programs themselves at the same time we address the pressing and legitimate issues raised by the New Abolitionists. It is unrealistic to assume that the relationship between composition and the academy can change if composition does not change. Moreover, it is also unrealistic to assume that the academy will remain static and that pressure to change coming from outside and inside composition will cease.

My goal in this article will not be to argue for or against the first year composition requirement. The answer to that question, as I hope to show, is, "it depends." The question that seems most cogent to me is, "How do we know how far and in what directions we should move to address the problematic position of composition in the academy?" Composition programs are complex, dynamic systems; when we tinker with one facet of a program, that tinkering will impact the entire program. Consequently, whether we engage in reform efforts or move to abolish the composition requirement, we need to take a comprehensive, holistic approach that acknowledges how the various levels of any composition program are interconnected, and the way those levels interact with the larger institution. What I propose is a model for examining the complex relationships that determine the day-to-day practices in our composition programs and in other sites for writing throughout our colleges and universities. Specifically, we need to think about the *local conditions* at our institutions, evaluate the *internal coherence* of our programs, and consider the degree to which our programs are *externally relevant*. By examining local conditions, focusing on internal coherence, and asking ourselves about external relevance, we can assess the effectiveness of our composition programs in relation to a host of complex factors which speak to the comprehensive nature of higher education. Finally, I will move to describe how considering the interlay of these features at our institution led us to make dramatic, and in some cases controversial, changes in our composition program. Thus, finally, I propose to place composition, not just writing, in a "broader view," and in that way "remain responsible to a larger social need" (Bazerman 258).

LOCAL CONDITIONS

Local conditions are those features of our colleges and universities that make our institutions distinct from each other. Budgets, teaching loads, requirements, building design, pay scales, computer availability, and the students themselves all point to differences among our campuses. These, in turn, shape attitude and morale, which also translate into powerful differences. At times, it may seem that because there are general statements we can make about higher education, all our campuses are essentially the same. This is, obviously, not the case and we would be wise as we pursue changes in our programs to focus on these differences and how local conditions shape the programs and opportunities at our schools.

Perhaps the most overt feature of local conditions is the budget. Generally, we are in a time of fiscal constraints when budgets are not likely increase dramatically. Thus, we are often in the position of finding "creative solutions" to bridge the gap between resources and needs. Unfortunately, higher education has in recent years, particularly in state-funded institutions, turned to stopgap solutions. Raised caps, part-time and adjunct instructors, and technological short cuts all stand as prime examples of these stopgap measures. The problem is that these solutions become permanent and, thus, over time, change the nature of higher education through ad hoc means. Stopgap methods sometimes take on the aura of "temporary" army barracks built during WWII: decades later they are still standing, and they have changed the landscape.

Fortunately, most local conditions, though determining features of our programs, are themselves dynamic and open to change. It is imperative that we consider dynamic conditions as we entertain openings for change within them. One way to begin this process is to examine the coherence of our programs in relation to these conditions.

INTERNAL COHERENCE

A good deal has been written about the importance of coherent programs (see, for example, White, Witte and Faigley, and Hilgers and Marsella) and so there is no need to go over this ground in detail. Nevertheless, it is important to note that a composition program must be constructed so that individual sections work together to provide a coherent educational experience at the same time that the program remains conscious of its place in the larger institution. Internal coherence rests on a programmatic footing comprised of four components: (1) common goals specific and detailed enough to be meaningful and useful, (2) common assignments, (3) standard methods for evaluation and assessment across multiple sections, and (4) a commitment to examining and discussing these shared features openly. In one way, planning for internal coherence is the easiest part of what we do. It is the area over which we have the most control, and it is the facet of administration most directly linked to the training we receive as graduate students and junior faculty.

When internal coherence is sacrificed, or abandoned, to the wishes, beliefs, and predilections of individual instructors (faculty, graduate assistants, or part-time instructors) who may have no training in teaching composition, or who may be completely unaware of the developments in this field in the last thirty years, or who may argue that they have academic freedom and thus the right to teach whatever they want, it becomes impossible to talk about a program at all and thus impossible to talk about what the relationship should be between what we do in our programs and the larger institution. Moreover, when a program lacks internal coherence, the opportunity for collaboration and cooperation among instructors is limited. Everyone is on their own. It becomes nearly impossible to talk about the overall effectiveness of the program and, finally, it becomes nearly impossible to talk about composition as it relates to the larger educational experiences of students within the program. Internal coherence, then, is essential.

EXTERNAL RELEVANCE

We need also to examine the extent to which the internal coherence of our writing programs contributes to the larger educational experience of our students. That is, we must also gauge our effectiveness on the basis of the extent to which our programs are externally relevant. We must ask ourselves how the writing that students do in our programs contributes to the overall mission of the college or university, how it contributes to what they do in the major, and how it contributes to their liberal or general education.

I am not suggesting, however, that we need only to make our programs conform to the needs and expectations of others in the university. Clearly the training, background, and experience that we have as writing instructors and as WPAs enables and compels us to help the university community think about the links between composition programs and the rest of the university. We must become spokespersons for writing who are able both to listen carefully to external expectations and to articulate clearly how these expectations might better line up with internal program goals. On this two-way street WPAs need to be adept outside their programs as well as within, able to discuss how their program contributes directly to the experience of students within it.

Before discussing how a consideration of local conditions, internal coherence and external relevance prompted us to make significant changes at my institution, let me make one other critical point. Because we are dealing with dynamic systems, and because the components of those systems—local conditions, internal coherence, and external relevance—differ, our composition and writing programs must necessarily differ also. Consequently, it is essential that we recognize that composition programs will differ widely too. In some writing intensive programs, for example, students may never take courses in composition. Instead, the writing they do may be integrated into course work. At other institutions, students might be required to take twelve hours of composition, or six, or four, but we should understand that, as Carol Hartzog notes, "no single model, no single prescription will work in all cases" (Hartzog 12). Thus, I present the following illustration as one example, *not* as the model, of how composition programs may be defined.

LOCAL CONDITIONS, INTERNAL COHERENCE, EXTERNAL RELEVANCE: OUR SITUATION

For several years in the 1980s and on into the 1990s, enrollment demand and static budgets levied a heavy toll on the composition program at Northern Arizona University. Thus, like many comp programs, the one at our university became in part something of an unfunded mandate. To meet demand, more part-time instructors were pressed into service, and the teaching load for GAs remained consistently high: two sections a semester with 24 students in each section while they were also enrolled in nine hours of graduate course work. Whereas at one time GAs might have received a slightly reduced load, at least in terms of preparation time, by working in the Writing Center, they were by the early 1990s committed every semester to cover additional sections, and the number of graduate assistants actually staffing the writing center dwindled to three or four per term. In addition, most of the graduate assistants in this program were working toward master's degrees and thus represented a population with a high rate of turnover. Finally, as a result of these conditions and constraints, the perception throughout the university community was that English composition GAs were overworked, that the writing center was not providing enough support, and that the level of instruction being offered by part-time instructors was very mixed at best. At the same time, the program was perceived by administrators as expensive and, as a result, was not likely to receive additional resources.

Thus, by the early 1990s many recognized that, in the words of external reviewers, although there were strengths, there were also significant weaknesses. And, the primary suggestion made by external reviewers was to increase budgets. When it became clear, however, that the administration could not follow these recommendations—additional resources were not going to be pumped into the program to alleviate pressures caused by increasing enrollment—we realized that we had two options. The first was to continue with business as usual and to tweak the program where possible to try to alleviate some of the pressures it faced. The second option was to overhaul the program completely. We decided to pursue this second option.

As I suggested in the opening section,... reforming or reformulating a composition program is a complex, systematic process in which different elements must be considered in relation to each other. Thus, although I will write about this process as though it happened in a linear fashion, it really did not; it was recursive and layered.

The most obvious changes we proposed were to shift from a two semester, six-hour composition requirement for all students to a one semester, four-hour requirement, and to impose a twelve-hour prerequisite for that four-hour course. These changes were both highly controversial and initially seen as a cutting back on our commitment to teach undergraduate writing. But these changes also provided us with several advantages.

As Figure 4.1 shows, the change from a six-hour to a four-hour program requirement was a strategic move to help reduce graduate assistant workloads.

	Semester I	**Semester II**
Old program structure	Enroll in 9 graduate hrs. *and* 2 sections of ENG 101 (24 students/section, total 48)	Enroll in 9 graduate hrs. *and* 2 sections of ENG 102 (24 students/section, total 48)

	Semesters I and II
New program structure	Enroll in 9 graduate hrs. *and* 1 section of ENG 105 (24 students/section), *and* 1 section of ENG 205 (2 credit electives open to all students having met composition requirement, 16 students/section), *or* Tutor for 6 hrs./week in Writing Lab, *or* Mentor beginning GA's, *or* Work with faculty teaching writing intensive courses across campus.

Figure 4.1 GA Responsibilities Under Old and New Programs

Because at our institution (local conditions) it is impossible for graduate students to teach more than six hours a semester, we knew that by shifting to a four-hour course we were creating a program in which a GA's teaching load could not easily be doubled should enrollment increase. Second, by imposing a twelve-hour prerequisite we were reducing the number of incoming students we would need to accommodate in composition classes. Because we have about a 25% attrition rate at the end of the fall semester for entering students, and a total rate of 33% by the end of the spring semester (these attrition rates did not change when we implemented our new program), a twelve-hour prerequisite would significantly reduce our student enrollment pressure. These changes enabled us to move away from using part-time instructors altogether and to lower class size. Thus, we moved to a program with no part-time instructors and one where GAs could teach smaller numbers of students in four-credit-hour classes, with other assigned duties for two other credit hours.

These changes allowed us to use GAs in more varied ways. In addition to teaching a required four-hour course, they could undertake such other responsibilities as working in the writing center, working with faculty and students across campus to help writing efforts in courses outside of English, mentoring new graduate assistants coming into the program, or finally, teaching a two-credit elective writing class for students who had completed the required writing class. Thus, with these shifts we were able to address issues of external relevance (the writing center and using GAs to work with other departments), and internal coherence (providing mentors for all new GAs). At the same time we reduced GAs' overall workload.

As I have already suggested, however, internal coherence is a key component of any program, and the mentoring we provided using experienced GAs was only one way to build that coherence. To move further toward greater coherence within the program, we made several other key changes. First, we rewrote the curriculum and asked GAs to teach from standard syllabi. Second, we implemented an assessment program that worked vertically through the program. Let me elaborate on each of these changes in turn.

Because most of the instructors teaching in our composition program were students working toward their master's degrees, most of them had no experience as teachers and no substantive awareness of how to teach writing effectively. We realized that if we were going to use these inexperienced students as the primary instructors in a required course, we had an obligation to provide as much guidance and support as we could. The standard syllabi helped do so by giving these graduate students a scaffolding. The standard syllabi also provided a common experience for instructors and students in the program. That is, the composition program became a core experience that students could share outside the classroom. Further, it provided a common experience for GAs so that they could work together as a community to address the challenges of teaching a required composition course to a diverse range of students. The standard syllabi thus went a long way toward creating possibilities for focus and coherence.

At the same time, the standard syllabi were written with the university mission, and thus external relevance, in mind. First, the course was designed to help students become more effective readers and writers by providing them with a range of texts (poetry, fiction, essay, letters, autobiography, encyclopedia entries, academic journal articles, etc.). Learning to analyze these texts rhetorically, students could develop broad-based strategies for reading that would help them work more effectively in any other courses that they might take in liberal studies or in their major. More specifically, we sought to design a curriculum which would help students "evaluate new discourses as they became visible and relevant"; at the same time we provided them with "the tools of rhetorical analysis that [would] allow them to explicitly recognize, analyze, and respond to the particularities of the discourse systems and situations that they may move into" (Bazerman 257–58). Second, the course was thematically focused on issues of environmental sustainability. Our university sees as part of its overall mission the need to help students address environmental issues as well as the more specific problems facing the Colorado Plateau on which we are located. The course, then, was designed to dovetail with the larger curriculum in terms of both the skills it helped students achieve and its larger philosophical and pedagogical orientation.

Another key component of the program which helped us move toward internal coherence revolved around issues of assessment. On one hand, we wanted to do a good job of assessing the work that students in the program did; we wanted measures that were valid and reliable. Thus, once again, in part because we would be working with so many inexperienced teachers, we wanted to provide a strong framework for assessment that would work not just in individual sections but across the program. Accordingly, we implemented a portfolio assessment program that would work program-wide. All students would submit portfolios at the middle and the end of every semester, and their portfolios would be read and evaluated by at least two or three other instructors. The instructors would, in addition, take part in norming sessions at least three times during a semester: at the very beginning, just before the midterm portfolios were to be evaluated, and just before the final evaluation process at the end of the semester. As a result of what was for us a new approach to assessment, we could spend more time training instructors in assessment and, once again, provide opportunities for them to discuss a common practice.

Finally, in terms of assessment, we rewrote the course evaluation forms instructors give to their students. The new forms reflect more specifically the common goals of the course and provide opportunities for students to assess their own progress and commitment. We abandoned the generic evaluation instrument that was used across our college in favor of one which asked questions such as, "How often did your instructor make connections between what you were reading and your writing?" and "How well did your instructor describe the portfolio approach to evaluation to you?"

I suggested that budgetary realities and constraints must be a part of our thinking as we contemplate the ways in which we might reform composition programs. One key is to consider the relationship between what we can do with what we have, what we would need in order to make our program stronger, and what are reasonable financial requests. In our case, for example, to stay with the old program, to put people back into our writing center, to stop using part-time instructors, and to lower class size would have required that we increase our budget by about 30%. While we might argue that such an increase is desirable, we also recognized that it was not likely given current budget constraints. At the same time, as I have already suggested, to continue with the program as it had evolved would have meant continuing with a program that was problematic. We were, in essence, promising to deliver more than our budget limits allowed us to offer.

As it turns out, our new program costs about the same as the old program; we haven't saved a lot of money. What we have been able to do is use our resources in different ways. The result is a series of trade-offs, the biggest two of which involve dropping the number of required hours from six to four, and the imposing of a twelve-hour prerequisite. On the other side of the scale, however, we now have GAs who teach in an effective and coherent program, who are gaining a range of teaching experiences, and who, because they are not pushed so hard, are more effective. We have returned to a fully staffed writing center, and we are able to provide more support for writing-intensive courses across campus.

In all, we have achieved a balance which is workable here. The university community supports the new program which has been running full tilt for four years, and students in our courses are positive about the instruction they receive. Most importantly, students and faculty across campus agree that the program is making a difference in the way that students write. And, finally, faculty across campus are grateful for the support and direction they now receive from the composition program.

Still, I would want to reiterate the key point—because local conditions differ, composition and writing programs will differ. It is unrealistic and unwise to assume that what works effectively on one campus is well suited to another campus without local adaptation. If local configurations and their relationship to each other remain in the foreground as WPAs undertake composition reform, we are more likely to develop effective writing programs anywhere.

Composition programs need to change and develop over time. Ours certainly does as we continue to find ways to integrate what we do more effectively with the larger institution. Thus, I fully expect that in coming years, our program will develop in new directions, respond to new demands and, thus, will not be the same program it is today. This is as it should be. What will remain constant, I hope, is that these changes will continue to reflect judgments that are locally responsive, internally coherent, and externally relevant. In this way, effective programs will be able to address complex, dynamic forces and all the facets inevitable in a university setting.

WORKS CITED

Bazerman, Charles. "Response: Curricular Responsibilities and Professional Definition." *Reconceiving Writing, Rethinking Writing Instruction.* Ed. Joseph Petraglia. Mahwah, NJ: Erlbaum, 1995. 249–60.

Connors, Robert J. "The New Abolitionism: Toward a Historical Background." *Reconceiving Writing, Rethinking Writing Instruction.* Ed. Joseph Petraglia. Mahwah, NJ: Erlbaum, 1995. 3–26.

Hartzog, Carol P. *Composition and the Academy: A Study of Writing Program Administration.* New York: MLA, 1986.

Hilgers, Thomas L., and Joy Marsella. *Making Your Writing Program Work: A Guide to Good Practices.* Newbury Park, CA: Sage, 1992.

White, Edward. *Developing Successful Writing Programs.* San Francisco: Jossey, 1989.

Witte, Stephen P., and Lester Faigley. *Evaluating College Writing Programs.* Carbondale: Southern Illinois UP, 1983.

Copyright WPA: *Writing Program Administration.* 21 (Fall 1997): 46-54.

The Role of AP and the Composition Program

Daniel Mahala
University of Missouri—Kansas City

Michael Vivion
F. Hoffman-La Roche

A few years ago, our department was prompted by a note from the university's admission office to review our policy of granting six hours of credit for a grade of 3 or better on the Advanced Placement (AP) English exam. Our review of the AP program and of the history of the department's acceptance of AP credit led us to a few surprises. The note asked that the department consider the review in light of the change in the AP's English exam from one test to two: the Language and Composition test and the Literature and Composition test. The admissions officer recommended that the department consider awarding up to twelve hours to students who had taken both exams and had received a 3 or better. His expressed concern was not that the department would fail to review this recommendation favorably but rather exactly how the department would choose to award the twelve hours.

The major surprise was how little members of the English Department knew about the AP test and the credit we granted for it. No one, for example, had known about the separation of the AP English exam into two distinct parts. It follows that no one knew either the content recommended by the College Board (CB) or tested by the Educational Testing Service (ETS) for the two AP courses.[1] In fact, for some time even the admissions office had been granting six credits in composition, no matter which test was reported. We also discovered that there was no university policy for a regular review of any of the tests that the university accepts for credit. In other words, the departments that accept credit-by-examination had virtually conceded the responsibility to grant certain university credit to various national testing agencies.

This realization led to some major questions that arose in our discussion and that are pertinent to writing program administrators and department chairs across the country. Do the exams that lead to the granting of credit reflect mastery of the same knowledge, the same critical thinking abilities, and the same academic competencies as the courses for which they substitute? In accepting credit for these tests, what conceptions of the discipline of English— that is, of composition, language, and literature—are we implicitly endorsing? What constitutes acceptable evaluation of the knowledge and competencies for which we would wish to grant six or even twelve hours of college credit?

The authors believe that acceptance of AP credit should be based on principled answers to such questions. Clearly, WPAs have an important role to inform colleagues about AP programs in arriving at such answers, since the tests frequently provide the basis for exemption or credit for writing courses. If our experience is any guide, however, most departments have not based their acceptance of AP credit on reasoned endorsement of the views of language, literature, and rhetoric that, as we will show, AP exams represent. By sharply criticizing the views implicit in the AP program and by showing how they conflict with the goals of our own program, we do not primarily wish to argue on behalf of our own curricula or theory of "English" but to enable departments to base their AP policies on the same sorts of deliberations about language, literature, and rhetoric that attend other decisions about programs, teaching, and research. Unfortunately, the economic and political forces we describe in this paper are likely to continue to shape the development of AP programs and policy more than departmental debate unless WPAs and other well-positioned educators do more to inform colleagues about AP.

We have found, for instance, that many WPAs are startled to learn that *more than 67%* of the 134,000 students taking the 1991 Language and Composition or Literature and Composition exams received the CB/ETS's rating of "qualified" or better. These students, who have received a grade of 3, 4, or 5 on either exam, are led to expect college credit for their scores. Of the remaining third of test-takers, 29% were "possibly qualified" (with a score of 2), and less than 4% received "No recommendation" (*1991 AP English: Free Response Scoring Guide* 40–1). Moreover, as James Vopat has reported, these grade distributions are determined *in advance* of the actual essay grading. Thus, as Vopat comments, the success rate of 96% remains consistent from year to year and marks "a decided shift of emphasis from the original intent of the AP program and test. What began in the late 1950s as a 'concern for the academic progress of the gifted student' (Jameson 1) has become a reward system that validates mediocrity" (Vopat 58–9). Vopat, following David Owen, goes on to note that colleges are content to validate this arrangement because "it enables them to give the equivalent of scholarships without spending any money" (Owen, qtd. in Vopat 62). The economics are clear. As long as AP can make good on its claim that "[n]early all the 2,200 colleges that most AP students attend give credit or advanced placement or both" (Student Guide 2), exams should be easy to sell. For $65, students shoot for 3–6 college credits with two to one odds in their favor; and for $130, the prize is 6–12 credits.

If these figures are surprising, educators should consider pressures favoring expansion of the AP and other standardized exams. For instance, this year the Coordinating Board for Higher Education in our own state (CBHE) began lobbying for AP courses in all Missouri high schools. Already, the CB claims that 1,200 institutions award a full year's credit to students with "satisfactory grades" on the AP exams, and if competition for student enrollments heats up, we can expect the number to grow. Finally, a host of pressures have been building nationwide that favor long-term expansion of AP testing: mandates for standardized assessment, escalating college costs, and growing student anxiety about incurring debt in an economy where college degrees don't necessarily translate into jobs.

The most obvious objection to accepting these tests as substitutes for coursework is that they emphasize multiple-choice questions far more than most college teachers do in their own classrooms. For many teachers, the nature of these multiple-choice questions, whether challenging or not, is not the issue; they are simply an inappropriate way to assign college credit. Moreover, the multiple-choice section in both exams is weighted more heavily than the essay section. Thus, even though students ordinarily spend two of three hours on the essay section (67% of total exam time), the essays count for only 55% of the score. Forty-five percent of the score is ordinarily based on the one-hour, multiple-choice section (*Advanced Placement Course Description* 9; *Student Guide* 16, 52). For those who believe that the measure of education should be the ability to deal with complex ideas in speech and writing, this extra weighting of the multiple-choice section delivers a harmful message to students; in the overall scheme of things, writing is not worth the time it takes.

Nevertheless, 55% of each test is essay. Typically (as on the 1991 exams), students write three essays, with an average time of forty minutes for each. On such short essays, however, it is questionable whether the test measures the writing competencies most emphasized in modern composition classes. In our English I and English II composition courses, for example, students write multiple essays in which they learn through practice the importance of rethinking, revising, and editing. These courses stress an epistemic rhetoric in which students learn not only the ways in which writing communicates the known, but also how writing can discover new connections and new knowledge. Students taking these courses receive credit for each class based on our evaluation of an entire semester's work.

The AP students who receive three hours of college credit for either the Language and Composition exam or the Literature and Composition exam are typically evaluated on three in-class essays; yet in the past, students receiving at least a 3 on either of these tests received credit for six hours, three credits each for our required English I and English II classes. In the exam setting, they might be expected to do surface editing but not substantive revision. As many composition scholars have noted, in fact, the kind of writing such an exam calls for is inimical to the emphasis of modern literature and composition pedagogy on the epistemic functions of language and the development of complex ideas. As Bartholomae and Petrosky put it, "highly complicated ideas, which frequently call for highly complex and therefore easily mistaken syntax, are perhaps too risky for this [exam] situation. A writer's thoughtfulness might be valued as much, but probably not more than his ability to control error" (100–01). Plainly, in our case, the AP essays did not validly represent the kinds of writing emphasized in our curriculum.

So what view of English as a discipline does the AP English program represent? The most salient fact about the AP English programs is that more exams are given in English than in any other subject. Although 29 AP exams are now offered in 16 disciplines, more than 37% of the 360,000 students who took the 1991 AP exams took one of the English exams. Clearly, students are understanding undergraduate "English" as one of the easiest subjects to "test out of" in the university. The *Student Guide* acknowledges that "compared with your regular high school English courses, the AP courses will *probably* be more demanding" [emphasis ours], but it also dangles the bait of tuition savings and the 67% success rate before the students' eyes (*Student Guide* 2, 5, 7).

This understanding, of course, dovetails nicely with the popular understanding that English inculcates "basic skills" preliminary to the intellectual work of the university. This argument was also given by our registrar for accepting AP credit. "Superior" students (his designation) should not be required to take something as basic as freshman composition if they have already mastered the skill. Moreover, this trivialized view of writing is encouraged by the structure of the AP English program and its promotional literature. The *Student Guide,* for instance, tells students that they "might expect" *six* credits for the Literature and Composition exam, but only *three* credits for the Language and Composition exam (83). Clearly, this is one reason students are taking the Literature and Composition exam by a margin of more than 3 to 1. This exam structure reproduces the split between rhetoric and literature so often lamented in English departments. Significantly, both exam titles feature the word "composition" in the secondary position, implying that one studies "literature," or (with less profit) "language," but "composition" only as a means to those higher ends. Indeed, the *Student Guide* represents writing as an activity that requires no practice or scrutiny but merely as a passive by-product of literary consumption: "It is probably true that if you sat down and read the complete three-volume edition of Edward Gibbon's *Decline and Fall of the Roman Empire* and then wrote a paper about it, you would find that your writing style would reflect Gibbon's great classical style with long periodic and balanced sentences, great series of elegant phrases and clauses, and an elevated, lofty tone. Therefore, read omnivorously and you won't even have to be taught how to write" (10). Such arguments may have seemed credible when universities served an elite who sought a veneer of gentlemanly culture. As most literary and composition scholars agree, though, such romantic aestheticism hardly serves the interests of students struggling to gain a critical foothold amid the myriad textual manipulations with which mass media surround them (Scholes 15).

Moreover, educators who might take comfort in the thought that students receiving AP credit will have assuredly studied and written about some challenging texts may be surprised to learn that *students need not take any AP course at all to receive credit through the exams.* Grades received in AP courses are generally not considered in the granting of credit; indeed, students can expect that little or nothing of the material studied in their AP courses will actually appear on the exam. To be sure, the wide range of sample syllabi that the CB distributes as examples of the AP Literature and Composition curriculum represent much of the challenge and diversity of "English."[2] These syllabi show the possibility of studying texts as divergent as the *Iliad*, *The Assistant*, or *Their Eyes Were Watching God*, as well as the possibilities of organizing AP courses according to the instructor's choice of formal, thematic, or historical approaches; however, these syllabi can be very deceiving to educators who suppose that these syllabi represent a reliable picture of what "qualified" students have studied. To say the least, the optional nature of the AP course casts some doubt on AP's claim that "the examination may be the heart of the AP Program, but it is not the lifeblood or the spirit" (McQuade 3).

On the Language and Composition exam, multiple-choice questions focus on rhetorical analysis of passages presented within the exam. Students are not responsible for bringing any of the material from their AP classes to the exam; they are expected, however, to be able to apply certain things they may have learned in the class. They choose stylistic preferences, grammatically correct answers, name styles, or answers that demonstrate reading comprehension, interpret figurative language, perform rhetorical analysis. The texts presented for analysis are challenging and interesting.

The presumptions about language and rhetoric implicit in the exam are in many ways fundamentally at odds with those of our English I and II courses. Mainly, the exam tests students' ability to recast sentences or carry out analysis of passages in these terms. For instance, one type of question expects students to choose, with no discursive context whatsoever, the best "revised" sentence "in terms of conciseness, idiom, logic, and other qualities found in well-written sentences" (*1987 AP English Language and Composition Examination* 5). While such questions may test a student's facility with sentence transformations, they also further what many rhetoricians would consider an arhetorical view of language; sentences are presumed atoms of meaning about which stylistic decisions can be made in isolation from a writer's communicative intentions.[3] Similarly, another typical question demands analysis of short passages in terms of "rhetorical devices," "elements" and "modes" that are presumed to be universal ingredients of arrangement or style: "The first and second paragraphs of the passage both present A) elaborate metaphors B) series of parallel constructions C) extended definitions D) concessions to opposing viewpoints E) cause and effect relationships" (*1987 AP English Language and Composition Examination* 8). By sharply focusing on the form of passages in isolation from content, questions like these reduce rhetoric to a repository of preconceived formal patterns that are mechanically analyzed by readers and, presumably, applied by writers. In fact, assumptions of questions like these can be placed within contemporary rhetorical traditions. They derive from positivist rhetorics, described by

Berlin and others, that see language mainly as a passive medium secondary to the generation of ideas, a mechanical tool for transmission of messages (see, for instance, Berlin, *Rhetoric and Reality* 7–11; *Writing Instruction* 62–76; Fish 474–78; Knoblauch and Brannon 58–61).

On the essay questions, the exam gives credence to the assumption frequently made in such rhetorics: that "the writing process" is a universal set of cognitive operations that does not change significantly even in radically different rhetorical contexts. Learning "the process" of writing simply creates improvement in all circumstances. Of course, the AP *Teacher's Guide* does acknowledge that writing processes vary among writers and even for any single writer. It also notes objections of teachers who "have pointed out that the AP examination is oriented to product" (McQuade 19). In the end, however, differences between timed writing on surprise topics and writing to probe, develop, and revise formulations of a self-generated idea don't amount to much: "Should AP students learn the process of writing? Absolutely....Conditions during the examination may not favor the production of a student's best writing, but that is no reason to withhold instruction that might help the student to produce better writing when conditions *are* favorable.... If the class has established a routine of peer coaching and editing in small groups, students can use all they know about the process of writing to help one another improve the first drafts they write in the classroom" (McQuade 20; see also Gadda et al. 6). How can the student "use" peer feedback, discussion, brainstorming, revision, and other composing strategies when the timed writing situation doesn't permit it? The CB doesn't say, but it does keep grades high by ensuring that readers "take all these [exam] circumstances into account when judging the merits of each essay" (*The 1991 AP Examination in English Literature and Composition* 24; see also Jensen 18). Because AP exams are scored holistically, revision and editing are not a part of the evaluation. Indeed, the CB advises students (with good reason) to avoid "the need to revise your thinking in mid-paper" (*Student Guide* 13).[4]

A popular format for the essay sections is to provide a reading, then ask the students to write an essay analyzing rhetorical devices (ETS, *1991 English Language and Composition Exam*, question 1) or authorial tone and attitude (question 2). In these types of questions, students are expected to have a ready catalogue of "elements," "components," and "devices" of expression that they can apply to analysis. Other questions might ask students to support an opinion with personal experience or references to some unspecified reading; to choose a piece of writing, film, or television and write an essay about a given topic; or simply to agree or disagree with ideas presented in a selection (usually excerpted). Typically, these questions provide more latitude for students. Still, in this context it is understandable that the "average essays" that the CB lists as samples for the 1991 exam are rough, undeveloped, and only 200–400 words long (*1991 AP English: Free Response* 6–7, 12, 16–17). One of the three "average" samples for the 1991 exam (keep in mind average in this context means "qualified") is only a paragraph long.

The assumptions about writing underlying such questions are at odds with our writing program's curriculum. In our English I and II courses, emphasis is not on formal analysis of completed passages, mechanical manipulation of isolated sentences, or timed writing but on the student's struggle to discover and articulate meaning. We assume that writing processes that make the search for meaning possible are not necessarily available on demand and are not always even available to conscious control. To resist premature closure of thought and to cultivate a tolerance for generative ambiguity and uncertainty, we often deliberately subvert student attempts to circumvent thought through imposition of formulas, the "elements," "modes," and "devices" tested by the exam.[5] Of course, we expect students to work toward formal coherence in their writing, and we expect them to master a variety of conventions of discourse; however, the fullest sense of form that we wish students to master—that is, form as an organic outgrowth of a real communicative intention in a real rhetorical situation—derives more from epistemic rhetorics described by Berlin ("Rhetoric and Ideology" 488–493) than from positivist rhetorics assumed by the exam.

Questions used on the Literature and Composition exam, too, can readily be placed in contemporary debates about literary theory. The types of questions are, in fact, very similar to the ones described above (excluding the "revisions" of atomic sentences). More emphasis is placed on "close reading" of selected passages. Generally, a mechanical, arhetorical view of language prevails, typically associated in literary contexts with long-outmoded "scientific" versions of New Criticism. As on the Language and Composition Exam, meaning is presumed to exist in the "text itself," not in terms of the text's relationship with its contexts of production or reception. For instance, the *Teacher's Guide* acknowledges that "[t]he territory occupied by facts seems to be shrinking in current critical theory as theorists recognize the power, even the right, of each reader to determine the meaning of the text.... [However], the AP Examination assumes the distinction between objective and subjective.... [T]he unstable boundary between objective and subjective is conceded in the direction to choose the 'best' answer to the multiple choice questions, not the 'right' answer" (McQuade 11), even though only the right answer receives credit. Clearly, the very format of the exam demands that meaning must be located in snippets of texts and that experts are authorized to determine without argument the "best" meanings. The format demands that meaning have a reality *in the text as pure object*. Hence, the *Teacher's Guide* emphasizes teaching "close reading" and annotating texts to identify formal devices: "Something has to *be* there in order to circle it [in annotation]; some pattern has to be *seen* before one can draw a series of boxes around words or phrases and connect them with arrows" (McQuade 12).

No doubt many teachers of writing and literature would ascribe to the theories we have been criticizing. In programs where such a theory holds programmatic sway, using this exam to grant credit might be appropriate; however, we suspect that in most programs, decisions to accept AP credit are not consciously intended to endorse such an approach to literary texts. Yet universities have widely ceded the right to construct such a vision of English to the CB/ETS.

Putting aside for a moment these objections, what would the appropriate credit be for this exam in our program, again assuming that the decision had been made to grant credit at all. Our English I class is an introduction to critical inquiry, to the symbolic processes through which men and women probe the nature and relationship of humanity and its world. We have no freshman or sophomore class in stylistics, reading comprehension, or grammar. Granted that the description of the recommended readings in the AP brochure is impressive—Addison, Eiseley, Morrison, Carlyle, Mencken, et al. On the other hand, knowledge of and familiarity with these writers don't find their way into the test; therefore, humanities credit for a class on the expository essay would be inappropriate. Our English II class focuses on cultural studies. This course requires extended documented essays from students, thus making it outside the range of the AP exam. Consequently, the exam does not measure knowledge and experience equivalent to that offered in our courses.

The primary issue is one which, from the size of the list of universities that accept AP credit, most universities are ignoring. Simply stated, should America's colleges and universities grant college credit through tests given by agencies outside education? Should we instead waive lower-level requirements while maintaining the same number of hours for graduation?

We welcome the opportunity to make advanced courses that support our curriculum available to high school students for credit. Our university has accepted the premise stated in the AP *Teacher's Guide:* "that college-level material can be taught successfully to able and well-prepared secondary school students" (McQuade 1). Indeed, our college runs an extensive high school/college credit collaborative program. In this program, however, the university takes its own class to the high school campus. We collaborate with able high school teachers and invite them to discussions that affect the evolution of our curriculum. As part of the AP program, the CB sends "practical descriptions of college-level courses" to the schools. Who should be offering such practical descriptions?

As we have argued, the AP exam's assumptions about rhetoric, language, and literature are contrary to our program's assumptions; however, programs founded on different assumptions may discover a compromise in the name under the initials. AP stands for "Advanced Placement," not Credit by Examination. In this sense the name is clever because it implies that the exam is a placement exam, not an exam that measures work completed or knowledge acquired. Obviously it is to the CB/ETS's financial benefit to encourage universities to offer credit; many fewer students would pay to take the exam if it were only a placement exam.

Finally, our department resisted the registrar's request that the department grant twelve credits for the two AP exams. Most of the composition faculty resisted granting composition credit for either test, but not everyone in the department agreed. In the end, we compromised; we raised the score necessary to receive credit from 3 to 4. Students who scored 4 or better on the Language and Composition exam would receive 3 credits for our English I composition course, and students who scored 4 or better on the Literature and Composition exam would receive 3 general humanities credits plus credit for a one-credit course called "Writing About Literature." The registrar responded to these changes with dire warnings about the potential damage that raising the acceptable AP score from 3 would have on potential scholarship students from high schools with active AP programs. He didn't want the university to lose potential scholarship students because they might not receive credit for their AP work. Such is the power of the College Board and Educational Testing Service.

It is not necessary to accept our curriculum or our vision of English to be disturbed by the growing power of the CB/ETS. Whatever philosophical commitments we as WPAs and teachers hold, we neither control the content of AP courses nor supervise the teachers. If we grant credit for these tests, it is our responsibility to *choose* to do so and to inform our colleagues about the tests accordingly. We must reconcile our beliefs about what our programs are *for* with what is tested by the CB/ETS. We must know what's on the tests. Judging by our own experience, it is a responsibility we have been too often failing.

NOTES

1. We often refer to the College Board and ETS together by the acronym CB/ETS because it is often difficult to distinguish where power and responsibility resides between the two organizations. Relationships between the two organizations are thoroughly interdependent, although somewhat obscure. The College Board was one of the founders of ETS in 1947. Today, ETS is quick to emphasize its continued servitude and accountability to the College Board, which it describes as a "non-profit membership organization" of "more than 2,700 colleges, schools, school systems, and education associations" (*Information for Coordinators* 3). A number of critical studies in the last fifteen years, however, have documented how ETS has, since 1947, "dwarfed its parent" both in revenues and power (Owen 6). Nairn quotes an anonymous interview with a College Board professional that the CB/ETS relationship is "like the Greek myth of the parent consumed by the child" (310). According to Owen, the "confidential contract" between ETS and the Board gives ETS "'authority and primary responsibility' not only for 'design, prototype development, and operation of programs and services' but also for 'the monitoring of ETS performance in the field'" (Owen 6). In other words, ETS writes, administers, and retains legal ownership of the tests, as well as supervises its own fulfillment of contractual obligations with the Board. Owen reports that the Board could, if it gave ETS a contractually specified three and a half years notice, "take its business elsewhere," but he quotes a former Board president that this possibility is "so hypothetical and improbable that it's not worth discussing" (6). These contractual arrangements became public only after ETS failed to win a protective order covering the court record of a lawsuit (*Denburg v. ETS*, Superior Court of

New Jersey), which forms, according to Owen, "a treasure trove of information about ETS that is available nowhere else" (296).

      In addition, the two organizations are economically interdependent to an extraordinary degree; for instance, almost half of ETS's $133 million in revenues in fiscal 1983 were from College Board programs (Owen 7). In 1980, Nairn reported the Board received 90% of its income from ETS programs and less than 1% from dues from member institutions (310). For further accounts of the historical interdependence of the CB and ETS, see Crouse and Trusheim 25–39, Nairn 306–31, Owen 6–17, Vopat 52–54, 62–64. For the CB's account of its role in founding ETS and the early inter-organizational relationship, see Fuess 176–207.

2. Obviously, the issue of "diversity" of works represented in the AP exam and curriculum would receive lively debate in many English departments. While writers like Tillie Olsen, Zora Neal Hurston, and Toni Morrison have found their way into the AP canon, some secondary teachers report strong reservations about teaching novels not well known or established in the canon, since the Literature and Composition exam's open question requires students to cite only works "of acknowledged literary merit." For examples, see McGee, and Spender.

3. For a full critique of this presumption, see Dillon, *Constructing Texts* 6–20. Dillon refutes what he calls, following James Moffett, the "particle view of language." In Dillon's terms, this view mistakenly supposes that reading proceeds from "bottom to top," that is, from words to sentences to paragraphs to discourses: "Normally, the discourse context gives top-down guidance in the perception of sentences: it enables readers to project expectations about where the sentence is going and to look for words and phrases that refer to things under discussion and are likely to be coming next. This point is widely recognized today, though its consequences have not been fully digested." Using multiple examples, Dillon shows that stylistic improvements of decontextualized snippets of discourse often turn out not to be improvements at all when a "motivating context" for the original construction is provided (8). Such motivating contexts can easily be constructed for the AP test sentences that complicate the test-makers' choice of a "best" (i.e., stylistically superior) sentence.

4. David Foster sums up an abundance of research (Flower, Sommers, Faigley, and Witte) demonstrating that "the major difference between skilled and unskilled writers is the latter's tendency to limit revision to changing words and sentences and editing mechanical errors" (6–7). Foster shows in detail how the AP essay questions "subvert the importance of [the revision] process" and how the multiple-choice sentence-revising questions on the Language and Composition exam "encourage exactly that kind of revising behavior identified with inexperienced freshman writers" (10–11).

5. In addition to the formulaic view of writing, several researchers have observed a disturbing degree of self-closure towards writing and learning among former AP students. In a small-sample developmental study of former AP students, for instance, Karen Spear and Gretchen Flesher report that AP students they studied who did not take freshman writing "manifest a sense of closure toward writing— that what is to be known about writing is limited to mastery of skills, and they have mastered them." Spear and Flesher's interviews with these students lead them to conclude that the attitudes and writing practices they learned in AP were harmful to their development. "[These students] make…intellectual gains only by overcoming much of what they have learned, at least about writing, in AP. All

needed to overcome the message of the AP course that they were finished developing as writers—a message that the decisiveness of the AP exam and subsequent waivers for college writing requirements unfortunately reinforce" (Spear and Flesher 40, 47; for a similar account of self-closure among AP students in first-year composition, see Henderson).

WORKS CITED

Bartholomae, David, Anthony Petrosky. *Facts, Artifacts and Counterfacts: Theory and Method for a Reading and Writing Course.* Upper Montclair: Boynton, 1986.

Berlin, James. "Rhetoric and Ideology in the Writing Class." *College English* 50 (1988): 477–94.

———. *Rhetoric and Reality: Writing Instruction in American Colleges, 1900–1985.* Carbondale: Southern Illinois UP, 1987.

———. *Writing Instruction in Nineteenth-Century American Colleges.* Carbondale: Southern Illinois UP, 1984.

Brannon, Lil, C. H. Knoblauch. *Rhetorical Traditions and the Teaching of Writing.* Upper Montclair: Boynton/Cook, 1984.

College Entrance Examination Board. *1991 AP English: Free Response Scoring Guide and Sample Student Answers.* N.p.: College Entrance Examination Board, 1991.

———. *The 1991 Advanced Placement Examination in English Literature and Composition and Its Grading.* N.p.: College Entrance Examination Board, 1992.

———. *A Student Guide to the AP English Courses and Examinations 1992.* N.p.: College Entrance Examination Board, 1991.

———. *Advanced Placement Course Description: English (May 1993).* N.p.: College Entrance Examination Board, 1992.

———. *The Entire 1987 AP English Language and Composition Examination and Key.* N.p.: College Entrance Examination Board, 1988.

———. *Information for Coordinators: Advanced Placement Examinations (May 68, 11–15, and 18–19, 1992.* N.p.: College Entrance Examination Board, 1991.

Crouse, James, and Dale Trusheim. *The Case Against the SAT.* Chicago: U of Chicago P, 1988.

Dillon, George L. *Constructing Texts: Elements of a Theory of Composition and Style.* Bloomington: Indiana UP, 1981.

Educational Testing Service. "Set of free-response questions used in recent years" (Item number 255053). Princeton: Educational Testing Service, n.d.

Faigley, Lester, and Stephen Witte. "Analyzing Revision." *College Composition and Communication* 32 (1981): 400–14.

Fish, Stanley. *Doing What Comes Naturally: Change, Rhetoric, and the Practice of Theory in Literary and Legal Studies.* Durham and London: Duke UP, 1989.

Foster, David. "The Theory of AP English: A Critique." *Advanced Placement English: Theory, Politics, and Pedagogy.* Eds. Olson, Metzger, and Ashton-Jones. Portsmouth, NH: Boynton, 1989. 3–24.

Fuess, Claude M. *The College Board: Its First Fifty Years.* New York: College Entrance Examination Board, 1950.

Gadda, George, Ejner Jensen, Finlay McQuade, and Harriet Wilson. *Teacher's Guide to Advanced Placement Courses in English Language and Composition.* N.p.: College Entrance Examination Board, 1985.

Henderson, Sarah. "Why Do I Have To Be Here? The Advanced Placement Student in First-Year Composition: Problems and Issues in Cognitive Development." *Conference on College Composition and Communication Covention.* Cincinnati (19–21 Mar. 1992).

Jameson, Robert. *An Informal History of the AP Readings 1956–76.* N.p.: College Entrance Examination Board, 1980.

Jensen, Ejner. *Grading the Advanced Placement Examination in English Language and Composition.* N.p.: College Entrance Examination Board, 1987.

McGee, Tim. "The Adolescent Novel in AP English: A Response to Patricia Spencer." *English Journal* (Apr. 1992): 57–58.

McQuade, Finlay. *Teacher's Guide to Advanced Placement Courses in English Literature and Composition.* N.p.: College Entrance Examination Board, 1992.

Nairn, Allan. *The Reign of ETS: The Corporation that Makes Up Minds. The Ralph Nader Report on the Educational Testing Service.* Washington: Nairn, 1980.

Olson, Gary, Elizabeth Metzger, and Evelyn Ashton-Jones, eds. *Advanced Placement English: Theory, Politics, and Pedagogy.* Portsmouth: Boynton, 1989.

Owen, David. *None of the Above: Behind the Myth of Scholastic Aptitude.* Boston: Houghton, 1985.

Scholes, Robert. *Textual Power: Literary Theory and the Teaching of English.* New Haven: Yale UP, 1985.

Sommers, Nancy. "Revision Strategies of Student Writers and Experienced Adult Writers." *College Composition and Communication* 31 (1980): 378–88.

Spear, Karen, and Gretchen Flesher. "Continuities in Cognitive Development: AP Students and College Writing." *Advanced Placement English: Theory, Politics, and Pedagogy.* Eds. Olson, Metzger, and Ashton-Jones. Portsmouth: Boynton, 1989. 25–51.

Spencer, Patricia. "YA Novels in the AP Classroom: Crutcher Meets Camus." *English Journal* (Nov. 1989): 44–46.

Vopat, James B. "The Politics of Advanced Placement English." *Advanced Placement English: Theory, Politics, and Pedagogy.* Eds. Olson, Metzger, and Ashton-Jones. Portsmouth, NH: Boynton, 1989. 52–64.

Writing Across the Curriculum

Martha Townsend
University of Missouri—Columbia

WAC'S HISTORY, THEORY, AND INFLUENCES

Writing across the curriculum (WAC) is an educational movement that developed more or less simultaneously in the United States and the United Kingdom in the late 1960s and early 1970s. In its most general sense, WAC refers to the notion that writing should be an integral part of the learning process throughout a student's education, not merely in English courses but across the entire curriculum. In the United Kingdom, where the movement is more widely known as "language across the curriculum," the activity occurs principally in secondary education. In the United States, WAC is largely, though not entirely, a postsecondary phenomenon. Some estimates suggest that approximately one-half of American higher education institutions—from two-year community colleges, four-year liberal arts colleges, professional schools, to large research universities—have some form of WAC. Programming ranges from merely informal encouragement for faculty to assign "more writing" to well-supported, highly structured curricular requirements (e.g., writing-enhanced or writing-intensive classes) backed up by WAC-trained specialists who consult with faculty on assignment design, integration of writing into course goals, and assessment.

The phrase "writing across the curriculum" originated with a mid–1960s research project at the University of London Institute of Education conducted by James Britton et al. to determine the kinds of writing young students were being asked to produce. Their study of more than 2,000 student writing samples, in all subjects, from eighty-five classes at sixty-five schools showed that children were not being exposed to the range of options available. The 1975 report of this work, *The Development of Writing Abilities (11–18)*, is one of WAC's founding documents. Britton and his colleagues centered their examination of student writing on function and audience, taking their theory of function from linguist Roman Jakobson and their theory of audience from James Moffett's *Teaching the Universe of Discourse*.

The degree of cross-fertilization in work on WAC between the United States and the United Kingdom is seen in the cross-referencing of each other's work and the use by both sides of the same theorists. Britton et. al., for example, cite Janet Emig's *The Composing Process of Twelfth Graders* (1971), while Emig's seminal WAC essay, "Writing as a Mode of Learning" in *College Composition and Communication* (1977), cites Britton's *Language and Learning* (1977). Both draw on views from philosophy and psychology in the figures of Jerome Bruner, A. R. Luria, Jean Piaget, Michael Polanyi, and Lev Vygotsky. Notable contributors from composition/rhetoric to theorizing about or practicing WAC pedagogies (described below) include Charles Bazerman, John Bean, Kenneth Bruffee, Toby Fulwiler, Anne Herrington, James Kinneavy, Elaine Maimon, Susan McLeod, Barbara Walvoord, and Art Young. David Russell's *Writing in the Academic Disciplines 1870–1990: A Curricular History* provides the historical framework for writing in American higher-education writing, that is, beyond the traditional composition classroom.

WAC's relatively rapid growth in U.S. higher education can be attributed to numerous social and educational factors. Changing educational demographics, increased demand for higher education, declining test scores, open admissions policies, increased expectations on the part of employers and educators, and media attention (e.g., "Why Johnny Can't Write," *Newsweek*, Dec. 9, 1975) have contributed to a perceived literacy crisis. "Students can't write anymore" is a frequent (but uncritically examined) complaint heard from faculty and the general public alike. WAC is, arguably, one response to ameliorating this "problem." Kinneavy, for example, concluded his essay on WAC in *Teaching Composition: 12 Bibliographic Essays* by saying that its "promise seems most favorable—writing across the curriculum may be the best academic response to the literacy crisis in English-speaking countries, though it cannot be a total social response" (377). At the same time, however, some administrators have unfortunately seen WAC as a cost-saving method of increasing writing instruction without adding more teachers to their faculty ranks or without providing the faculty development necessary to ensure programmatic success.

CHARACTERISTICS OF WAC PROGRAMS

WAC programs are highly individualized, one might even say that they are highly idiosyncratic. No single method characterizes the movement. Wide variations occur in its practice. Unifying these variations, though, is an understanding that learning to write is a vastly more complex process than is usually acknowledged and that WAC is not a movement to cure error, eliminate misspellings, or ensure correct punctuation and grammar use. As Russell points out, "The WAC movement, unlike most of its predecessors, attempts to reform pedagogy more than curriculum....It asks for a fundamental commitment to a radically different way of teaching, a way that requires personal sacrifices, given the structure of American education, and offers personal rather than institutional rewards" (295).

Pedagogies associated with WAC are consistent with current research in composition. They include multiple short writing assignments; revision, often based on both teacher and peer review; problem- or genre-based assignments; and evaluation criteria specific to and distributed with the assignment. Pedagogies adopted from arenas beyond composition include "active" rather than "passive" teaching and learning techniques; critical, or higher-order, thinking emphases; collaboration and group work; less teacher lecturing and more student discussion. As faculty in the disciplines become more aware that "poor writing" can be the result of students' lack of discipline-specific knowledge and conventions (and of faculty's own unawareness of how to create meaningful assignments tied directly to course goals), writing assignments often become more specific and better explained. Typically, WAC programs incorporate some combination of both "learning to write" and "writing to learn" in their goal statements. Writing centers often anchor WAC programs, or writing center tutorial services are provided, so that composition specialists can pick up where discipline-based faculty may not feel comfortable. (See Mullin, "The Varied Roles of Writing Centers in WAC" in *WAC for the New Millennium* in McLeod, et. al.)

Administrative structures for WAC programs can be faculty-, student-, or curriculum-centered.

> *Faculty-centered* programs emphasize improving teaching and learning via faculty workshops, seminars, and informal teaching colloquies; newsletters featuring "best practices"; grants for course development; travel reimbursement for professional conferences when faculty's papers report on teaching with writing; and the like.

> *Student-centered* programs emphasize improvement in writing per se; peer review of fellow students' writing; preparation for writing in one's career; access to a writing center for additional tutorial help; and the advantages of using writing to strengthen learning and, perhaps, prepare for graduate study.

> *Curriculum-centered* programs emphasize a requirement that must be satisfied for general education purposes, for advancing to upper-division status, for admission to professional study, or for graduation.

In actuality, of course, these boundaries overlap in varying degrees, and probably no WAC program fits into one category exclusively. But institutions can and do vary with regard to the programmatic emphases they choose and the resources devoted to each component. Any of these administrative structures can occur in WAC programs housed either within or outside of English departments, with WAC courses being taught by faculty across the disciplines.

Some institutions offer *WAC-based composition courses* taught by English department instructors: sections of composition for students majoring in the social sciences; sections for students majoring in the humanities and arts; and so on. Another variant is English department–based composition courses that focus on writing in any of a collection of academic disciplines. Numerous textbooks have been created for these purposes, e.g., Maimon et al., *Readings in the Arts and Sciences* (Little, Brown, 1984); Behrens and Rosen, *Writing and Reading Across the Curriculum* (HarperCollins, 1982); Feldman, *Writing and Learning in the Disciplines* (HarperCollins, 1996); Hansen, *A Rhetoric for the Social Sciences* (Prentice-Hall, 1998); and Hult, *Researching and Writing Across the Curriculum* (Allyn and Bacon, 1996).

More common, though, are *WAC programs in which courses are offered in the disciplines* by faculty in those disciplines: history professors offering writing-enhanced or writing-intensive courses in history, math professors doing the same in math, and so on. (See Townsend, "Writing Intensive Courses and WAC" in *WAC for the New Millennium* in McLeod, et. al.) Typically, a cross-disciplinary faculty committee, with some guidance by a WAC specialist, will determine the criteria for establishing such courses. Maintaining and ensuring course integrity once established, though, is another matter, one that numerous institutions have struggled with. (See White's section on writing-intensive courses in Chapter 8 in *Teaching and Assessing Writing.*) The degree to which WAC programs of this kind are successful depends on numerous complex factors: informed leadership, coupled with authority; administrative support, both philosophical and fiscal; and faculty support, which often ties to reward structures (or, more commonly, the lack thereof).

Less prevalent are *WAC programs at institutions that have decided against designating courses with some version of the "writing-intensive" label,* but which endeavor to infuse writing throughout all courses, with all faculty sharing responsibility for student writing instead of a marked few. Campuses undertaking any type of new WAC program should realize that what's usually needed to "improve student writing" is, in reality, a campuswide change in attitude toward student writing, a substantive change in campus culture that involves everyone—faculty, administrators, students, and staff. The process of effecting this change is slow and needs to be continuously moved along. WAC advocates should be prepared for the long haul.

NATIONAL TRENDS IN WAC TODAY

Despite the somewhat onerous-sounding caution above, WAC appears at present to be a strong, vital, growing enterprise in American higher education. (See McLeod and Miraglia, "WAC in a Time of Change" in *WAC for the New Millennium* in McLeod, et. al.) The biennial National WAC Conferences—1993, 1995, 1997 in South Carolina; 1999 at Cornell; 2001 in Indiana—have generated burgeoning interest over the years, to the extent that the conference will become an annual event starting in 2002. The *National Network of WAC Programs,* a directory of programs and directors maintained by Chris Thaiss at George Mason University, has grown from its initial listing of some 30 programs in 1981 to more than 650 in 2000. The network, under Thaiss's leadership, has convened a WAC Special Interest Group at CCCC (Conference on College Composition and Communication) annually since 1981; compositionists newly interested in WAC continue to attend each year. *Language and*

Learning Across the Disciplines, edited by Sharon Quiroz and Michael Pemberton, published since 1994, continues to receive increasing numbers of submissions and subscribers. The Writing Program Administration listserv ⟨wpa-l@asu.edu⟩, initiated by David Schwalm at Arizona State University, hosts frequent lively conversations about WAC, including inquiries about administering existing programs, developing new ones, and seeking qualified compositionists to lead WAC workshops at points around the entire country. Professional publications on WAC—articles, dissertations, book chapters, whole books—appear with increasing frequency (Anson et al.). Not least, MLA job lists over the last several years have announced numerous openings for WAC directors and faculty with WAC backgrounds. No doubt additional positive indicators could be found as well.

Writing instruction plays a significant role in U.S. general education programs; not surprisingly, WAC programs are a distinct subset of that activity (Bean). Inasmuch as one of the hallmarks of general education is continual reform, WAC plays an ongoing role as colleges and universities continually rethink how writing instruction should be delivered (Townsend). One aspect of this shifting curriculum is seen in the proliferation of both lower- and upper-division writing-intensive courses, not to mention the concomitant issues that attend transferring such courses among and between institutions. Many public institutions are under pressure from legislatures and policymakers to facilitate simpler transfer policies for students. The process of articulating often disparate requirements will no doubt challenge WPAs in the next years.

Given its overarching aim of influencing pedagogical practices in the college classroom, WAC often takes on new "partners" as other new initiatives related to teaching appear (Walvoord). Technology is a prime example as more teachers rely on e-mail, hypermedia, and the Internet to construct their classes. (See Reiss and Young's "WAC Wired: Electronic Communication Across the Curriculum" in *WAC for the New Millennium* in McLeod, et. al.) Service learning is another example; many campuses have embraced this concept in recent years, and faculty are realizing that writing about service-learning activities can deepen students' involvement and understanding of their projects. (See Joliffe, "Working Documents: Writing and Service Learning Across the Curriculum" in *WAC for the New Millennium* in McLeod, et. al.) Yet another is a growing affiliation between WAC and centers for teaching excellence and faculty development. These affiliations represent an extraordinarily logical coming together of two different kinds of academic programs that nonetheless have a central overlapping interest. (See Walvoord, "Teaching and Learning Centers and WAC" in *WAC for the New Millennium* in McLeod, et. al.) Of several more "partnerships" that could be mentioned, learning communities have offered WAC a warm welcome. The national trend toward creating undergraduate learning communities has provided opportunities for linked courses and team-taught interdisciplinary courses. (See Zawacki and Williams, "Is It Still WAC?: Writing Within Interdisciplinary Learning Communities" in *WAC for the New Millennium* in McLeod, et. al.)

IMPLICATION OF WAC TRENDS FOR WPAs

WPAs of non-WAC composition programs should be aware of and attuned to the developments in higher education described above. Even though WPAs' responsibilities do not include oversight of WAC-based activities, nonetheless WAC is pervasive enough that all composition professionals need to have an informed opinion when administrators, colleagues, or students seek information.

In times of fiscal retrenchment, a not unlikely administrative inquiry might be, "What do you think of our university implementing a new writing across the curriculum program? I understand from the provost at 'XYZ' that they've been able to move considerable writing instruction into the disciplines, thus eliminating a whole course in the English department." The unspoken line is "and it didn't cost them anything, since the faculty teaching the new courses were already there to begin with; XYZ has thus reclaimed thousands of dollars." Under these conditions, the new WAC program at XYZ is certain to be foundering, to put it politely. Non-WAC WPAs should be prepared to speak to the advantages of WAC programs and pedagogies, but also to counter the ill-conceived notion that WAC is a cost- saving method of improving writing instruction and student writing. Most WAC practitioners believe WAC to be an excellent faculty-development initiative, but administrators often need to be apprised of costs for conducting workshops and supporting ongoing WAC efforts.

On a more positive note, non-WAC WPAs should be conversant with the pedagogical implications for students transferring to and from other institutions that have WAC requirements. They may find incoming transfers, who were academically acculturated at an institution with WAC, asking where the writing-intensive courses are or how to receive tutoring on an upper-division science paper. Students transferring out, with no WAC background, may find themselves at a disadvantage at a new institution where a writing "culture" exists. Likewise, faculty in the disciplines, arriving from an institution where WAC was well supported, could become wonderful allies and help to educate faculty and students about the benefits of using writing-across-the-curriculum pedagogies.

WAC WPAs should be mindful of their roles as change agents on campus. Given the much wider array of academic constituencies with whom they work, WAC WPAs must be prepared to maintain relationships and interact comfortably with key administrators and faculty leaders, students in all disciplines, and myriad staff who perform essential functions such as flagging courses in schedules, certifying that students have satisfied graduation requirements, and reminding faculty to submit documentation for course approval. Sometimes WAC WPAs can be one step closer than composition directors to the employers who hire the institution's graduates and to state policy makers who lobby for tighter controls over assessment.

Like all WPAs, WAC WPAs should be prepared to argue for continued and improved institutional support. Some initiatives that require ongoing lobbying include faculty development workshops and follow-up consultation, state-of-the-art writing centers, and reasonable time for program staff to conduct WAC-related research (essential to ensuring a credible presence on campus). They should be especially prepared to address the various forms of resistance that WAC faces, particularly the lack of solid reward structures for faculty in the disciplines who assume the extra teaching-with-writing burden (Fulwiler and Young). WAC WPAs should be alert to finding new "partners" and be willing to work with new, perhaps unexpected, curricular developments.

Not least, WAC WPAs should be mindful of their own particular professional development issues. Accepting a WAC directorship as an untenured faculty member or in a nonfaculty line is a judgment call best deliberated upon at length. Some have been successful under these conditions; many have not. Program reporting lines can be tricky. Because most WAC directors' responsibilities are campuswide, they need access to institutional authorities who will be effective advocates. And they need authority of their own, vested in the best manner the institution can provide. More than one WAC WPA has noted the "black hole" aspect of their work, due to the diverse and amorphous nature of their responsibilities. New WPAs, WAC and non-WAC, might consider attending the National Council of Writing Program Administrators' annual summer workshop, a venue attested to by many for introducing them to essential information.

ASSESSMENT ISSUES/WAC RESEARCH

WAC WPAs face the same complex array of assessment issues that non-WAC WPAs do, with the addition of working with faculty assessing student writing in all disciplines. The WAC WPA must be prepared to speak knowledgeably about writing assessment as it pertains to individual students and whole programs to all of the constituencies mentioned in this essay. Complicating that responsibility is the lack of WAC programmatic standardization, the highly individualized nature of WAC programs from one institution to another referred to at the start of this essay. Also complicating the task is that typically, WAC programs "belong" to the whole faculty, while WAC courses "belong" to subsets of the faculty; each group has a stake in the other's success but also an involvement in the other's context and constraints. (See Condon, "Power, Hegemony, and WAC Assessment: Whose Value? Whose Evaluation?" in *WAC for the New Millennium* in McLeod, et. al.)Numerous authors have called for caution in assessing WAC programs, with the preponderance favoring constructivist over positivistic paradigms. Fourteen chapters in the first book-length study of WAC program assessment demonstrate the range of thinking on WAC program assessment, from portfolios to formal program review to theoretical bases to the role of faculty in the process (Yancey and Huot). The National Council of Writing Program Administrators' *Guidelines for Self-Study to Precede a Writing Program Evaluation* can be easily adapted for WAC programs. (See White, "Resource C" in *Teaching and Assessing Writing*.) The council also sponsors a consultant/evaluator service that conducts writing program reviews, from which several WAC programs have benefited. (See Townsend, "Integrating WAC Into General Education: An Assessment Case Study" in Yancey and Huot)

Any new educational movement needs some time to establish a place in the literature of its field. WAC, with its fairly short history of only thirty some years, is no exception. One place to begin is by examining the extant research, and probably the best place to do that is with David Russell's "Research on Writing in the Disciplines: A Review of the Qualitative Studies" in *WAC for the New Millennium* in McLeod, et. al. Russell reports on some eighty naturalistic studies of college-level writing in the disciplines. He suggests that one of WAC's most significant achievements is the development of expertise of real value to others. He also notes that this systematic review, not previously done, is necessary to determine what further avenues of inquiry should be opened.

Perhaps the most frequent, and vexing, questions posed by administrators when asked to support new WAC initiatives are, How do you know this works? How can you justify doing this instead of, or in addition to, what we're already doing? Even though rightly asked, these questions beg a larger issue, still largely unresolved: how do educators know that any of the currently used methods of instruction are effective? Often we don't. Often pedagogies are in place because of tradition or because teachers use the methods by which they were taught. Assessing teaching and learning are among the most challenging tasks facing educators. Nonetheless, research that seeks to address these questions is needed. Given WAC's propensity for multiple objectives (student writing improvement, faculty development) and multiple forms (depending on the institutional milieu), problems in undertaking WAC research are not small. Gail Hughes lays out the territory well in "The Need for Clear Purposes and New Approaches to the Evaluation of WAC Programs."

Daunting problems and challenging tasks notwithstanding, for many compositionists working in WAC, this subfield of the profession is enormously rewarding and immensely satisfying. It is quite possible to feel that one is making a specific, practical, and significant contribution to higher education, both for students and for faculty in the disciplines.

WORKS CITED AND OTHER RESOURCES ON WAC FOR WPAs

Anson, Chris M., John F. Schwiebert, and Michael M. Williamson, comps. *Writing Across the Curriculum: An Annotated Bibliography*. Westport: Greenwood, 1993. More than one thousand entries, divided into two categories: scholarship and pedagogy. The literature on WAC has grown appreciably since 1993, but this volume provides good introductory remarks and many standard books and articles are listed.

Bazerman, Charles, and David Russell, eds. *Landmark Essays on Writing Across the Curriculum.* Davis, CA: Hermagoras, 1994. Whereas Anson offers brief annotations of the seminal articles in WAC, this book offers reprints of twelve entire essays divided into four sections: Twentieth Century Beginnings, Recent Programmatic and Institutional Projects, What Happens in the Disciplinary Classroom?, and Writing in the Disciplines.

Bean, John C. *Engaging Ideas: The Professor's Guide to Integrating Writing, Critical Thinking, and Active Learning in the Classroom.* San Francisco: Jossey, 1996. Simply put, the best WAC book for any amount of money. Theoretically well-informed, but very practically oriented, this book offers easily accessible ideas for using writing to enhance learning across the disciplines. Works nicely as a text for WAC workshops.

———. "The Role of Writing-Across-the-Curriculum in General Education: A Guide for Administrators and Curriculum Planners." *Perspectives: Journal of the Association of General and Liberal Studies* 22 (Fall 1992): 138–59. WAC and general education go hand in hand. This article is useful for the many institutions undertaking the always ongoing reform of general education.

Britton, James. *Language and Learning.* Baltimore: Penguin, 1971. Predecessor to Britton's seminal volume.

Britton, James, Tony Burgess, Nancy Martin, Alex McLeod, and Harold Rosen. *The Development of Writing Abilities (11–18).* Hong Kong: Macmillan Education, 1975. Reports the authors' 1966–71 study of more than two thousand scripts, in all subjects, from eighty-five classes at sixty-four schools in the United Kingdom. The authors looked at function and audience in students' writing. One of the seminal WAC texts, this book provides much of the theory that undergirds WAC.

Emig, Janet. *The Composing Processes of Twelfth Graders.* Urbana: NCTE, 1971. Also one of the studies that informed early thinking about WAC, this volume is a revision of Emig's doctoral dissertation completed in 1969 at Harvard University. It is interesting to examine the work being conducted in the United States at roughly the same time that Britton and his colleagues were doing theirs in England.

———. "Writing as a Mode of Learning." *College Composition and Communication* 28 (1977), 122–128. Perhaps *the* article that established the role of writing in learning, in addition to its role in communicating what has already been learned.

Fulwiler, Toby, and Art Young, eds. "The Enemies of Writing Across the Curriculum." *Programs That Work: Models and Methods for Writing Across the Curriculum.* Portsmouth: Boynton, 1990. Descriptions of fourteen successful WAC programs across the United States, written by the people who direct and teach in them. Looks at the nature and history of each program; successful practices and strategies; problems and solutions; funding sources; and predictions for the future.

Gebhardt, Richard C., and Barbara Genelle Smith-Gebhardt, eds. *Academic Advancement in Composition Studies: Scholarship, Publication, Promotion, Tenure.* Mahwah, NJ: Erlbaum, 1997. This book will be useful to those programs that have WAC professionals who are assistant professors working toward promotion. While the book focuses on composition more broadly construed than WAC, the fourteen chapters nonetheless offer a variety of ways of thinking about professional advancement that WAC specialists should be familiar with too.

Herrington, Anne, and Charles Moran, eds. *Writing, Teaching, and Learning in the Disciplines.* Research and Scholarship in Composition 1. New York: MLA, 1992.

This book contains fourteen essays divided into five parts: Historical Perspectives; Disciplinary and Predisciplinary Theory; Teachers' Voices: Reflections on Practice; Studies in the Classroom; and Disciplinary Values, Discourse Practices, and Teaching.

Hughes, Gail F. "The Need for Clear Purposes and New Approaches to the Evaluation of Writing-across-the-Curriculum Programs." *Assessment of Writing: Politics, Policies, Practices.* 158–173. Ed., Edward M. White, William D. Lutz, and Sandra Kamusikiri. New York: MLA, 1996. A useful chapter on evaluating WAC programs that appeared before the publication of Yancey and Huot collection.

Jakobson, Roman. "Linguistics and Poetics." Ed. Thomas A. Sebeok. *Style in Language.* Cambridge: MIT P, 1960. Jakobson's notion of a hierarchy of speech functions significantly influenced the work of Britton et al.

Kinneavy, James L. "Writing Across the Curriculum." Ed. Gary Tate. *Teaching Composition: Twelve Bibliographical Essays.* Fort Worth: Texas Christian U P, 1987. 353–77. One measure of WAC's growth is that Tate's first edition of *Ten Bibliographic Essays* did not include a chapter on WAC at all. Kinneavy's essay in the second edition says that WAC "may be the best academic response to the literacy crisis in English-speaking countries" (377).

Langer, Judith A., and Arthur N. Applebee. *How Writing Shapes Thinking: A Study of Teaching and Learning.* Urbana: NCTE, 1987. Contains research that helps establish WAC's claim of enhancing learning in secondary education: "...there is clear evidence that activities involving writing (*any* of the many forms of writing we studied) lead to better learning than activities involving reading and studying only" (135).

McLeod, Susan H., and Margot Soven, eds. *Writing Across the Curriculum: A Guide to Developing Programs.* Newbury Park, CA: Sage, 1992. This book contains twelve chapters covering virtually every aspect of starting a new program.

McLeod, Susan H., Eric Miraglia, Margot Soven, and Christopher Thaiss, eds. *WAC for the New Millennium: Strategies for/of Continuing Writing Across the Curriculum Programs.* Urbana: NCTE, forthcoming 2001. Twelve chapters by WAC specialists describe how WAC has adapted to meet new challenges and suggest strategies for continuing WAC in an atmosphere of change. Sample chapter topics include assessment, technology, writing centers, learning communities, peer tutoring, writing-intensive courses, ESL, service learning, and teaching and learning centers.

Moffett, James. *Teaching the Universe of Discourse.* Boston: Houghton, 1968. Provides essential background and theory for the WAC movement.

Russell, David R. *Writing in the Academic Disciplines, 1870–1990: A Curricular History.* Carbondale and Edwardsville: Southern Illinois UP, 1991. The history of the WAC movement in the United States, divided into three sections: The Triumph of Specialization; The Search for Community: Writing and General Education; and The Postwar Era. Extensively researched and packed with fascinating historical data.

Townsend, Martha A. *Instituting Changes in Curriculum and Teaching Style in Liberal Arts Programs: A Study of Nineteen Ford Foundation Projects.* Dissertation Abstracts International, 52, 06A, 1991. (University Microfilms No. 91–34898). Describes a five-year philanthropic program designed to encourage writing instruction as a central component of general education reform. Most of the nineteen colleges and universities selected to participate integrated writing into discipline-based courses.

Describes the projects and outcomes and includes recommendations for institutional administrators overseeing writing-enhanced general education programs.

———. "Writing Across the Curriculum." *Encyclopedia of Language Arts.* 1299–1302. Ed. Alan C. Purves. New York: NCTE, 1994. Written in lay terms for policy makers and other professionals interested in education, this short essay introduces the concept of WAC and is followed by sections on Theory/Influences/History; Characteristics of WAC Programs; and Current Controversies/Issues. A concise introduction for anyone.

Walvoord, Barbara E. "The Future of WAC." *College English.* 58.1 (1996): 58–79. Views WAC within a "movement" framework and indicates the challenges WAC must meet to survive: setting goals, addressing "macro" issues, rethinking old answers to "micro" issues, and dealing with assessment.

Walvoord, Barbara E., Linda Lawrence Hunt, H. Fil Dowling, Jr., and Joan D. McMahon. *In the Long Run: A Study of Faculty in Three Writing-Across-the-Curriculum Programs.* Urbana: NCTE, 1997. Reports on the long-term impact on faculty who have participated in WAC programs, through interviews, questionnaires, classroom observations, student evaluations, and course documents from more than seven hundred faculty. The authors report that the most meaningful changes faculty found were changes not in teaching strategy but in teaching *philosophy.*

Walvoord, Barbara E., and Lucille P. McCarthy. *Thinking and Writing in College: A Naturalistic Study of Students in Four Disciplines.* Urbana: NCTE, 1990. Examines teachers and students in business, history, human sexuality, and biology classes.

Walvoord, Barbara E., and Virginia Johnson Anderson. *Effective Grading.* San Francisco: Jossey, 1998. Similar in format, style, and usability to Bean's *Engaging Ideas.*

White, Edward M. *Teaching and Assessing Writing.* San Francisco: Jossey, 1994. Contains essential information, cautions, and warnings that WAC programs and teachers should be aware of. "Resource D" illustrates how one higher education system developed an evaluation system for its WAC program.

Yancey, Kathleen Blake, and Brian Huot, eds. *Assessing Writing Across the Curriculum: Diverse Approaches and Practices.* Greenwich: Ablex, 1997. Contains fourteen chapters by experienced WAC professionals, offering a range of possibilities for evaluating programmatic effectiveness.

The Future of WAC

Barbara E. Walvoord
Notre Dame University

As Writing Across the Curriculum marked its twenty-fifth anniversary in 1995,[1] a number of assessments, predictions, and proposals for the future appeared. What I notice first when chain-reading them is the pervasive sense of uncertainty. Writers identify "troubling trends" (Thaiss, "Future"), "roadblocks to WAC" (Soven, "Conclusion"), "threats" (Cornell and Klooster), or "enemies of WAC" (Young and Fulwiler). Dangers include lack of full institutional support, the high cost of some WAC programs, the compartmentalized structure of academia, counterproductive attitudes and assumptions about writing and learning in the university, research and service demands on faculty, faculty workload, the faculty reward system, current emphasis on quantification and testing in the academy, lack of an appropriate theoretical and research base for WAC, and leader retirement or burnout. WAC may lose sight of its radical educational critique (Mahala). Or WAC programs may become instruments of those who would try to "fix" student writing, to shift responsibility for writing away from themselves, or to use language to restrict access to education (Russell, "Lessons"). Having led WAC programs for twenty-five years, I've seen all these threats and enemies at work. But the "enemies" frame may limit WAC's responses to the complexities of its next quarter century.

A FRAME FOR LONG-RANGE PLANNING: WAC AS A SOCIAL MOVEMENT ORGANIZATION

One helpful frame for long-range planning is the literature on what sociologists call "social movement organizations." "Movements" are "collective attempts to promote or resist change in a society or group" (Benford 1880). Movements spawn "social movement organizations," which "acquire and deploy resources, mobilize adherents, and plot movement strategy" (Benford 1883). For example, the feminist movement, which began in

275

informal consciousness-raising groups, spawned organizations like NOW, the National Women's Political Caucus with its state and local chapters, and so on. WAC is different from the women's or civil rights movements, but it fits the movement frame because of its change agenda and its collective nature—faculty talking to one another, moving to effect reform (Walvoord, "Getting").

For the "movement" scholarship, I have relied heavily on two sources: a forty-two-page essay on "Social Movements" by Doug McAdam, John D. McCarthy, and Mayer N. Zald, in the 1988 *Handbook of Sociology*, and a shorter essay on "Social Movements" by Robert Benford in the 1992 *Encyclopedia of Sociology*. The authors are themselves contributors to the research about movements, and their literature reviews are similar. Where a point is particularly crucial for WAC, or where their summaries diverge, I have gone back into the sources they cite.

Social scientists have progressed from seeing movements as aberrations to seeing them as "simply politics by other means," and therefore always part of the ongoing scene (McAdam 127–28). A particular movement is influenced by social and political conditions. A movement depends on a shift in public perception: something that has always seemed tolerable must now seem intolerable. This shift occurs for individuals in what Parker J. Palmer calls the "Rosa Parks moment"—a moment in which the individual chooses no longer to live a divided life, chooses to be whole. Populations also shift. For example, public tolerance for drinkers shifted to intolerance for the "killer drunk," enabling, without much political controversy, the raising of legal drinking ages (Gusfield).

Social movement organizations have complex roles, and their choices influence the fate of the movement. The literature's distinction between macro-level and micro-level choices is important to this essay. At the *macro* level, the organization must define its relationship to other movement organizations: Will it cooperate? Compete? Where will the organization place itself along the radical-moderate continuum defined by existent groups? The organization must also define its relationship to the "state" (that is, the university administration). Will the organization collaborate with the "state" or confront it? What use can it make of "friends" within the bureaucracy? Also, how will enemies and countermovements influence strategy? Finally, how will the organization use the media and technology?

At the *micro* level, movement organizations must decide, first, who is a member and what membership will require. How will members be recruited, sustained, motivated, and rewarded? Second, what will be the organizational form? John Lofland defines six forms, two of which are relevant to WAC: the association sustained by volunteers and the bureau employing staffers.

Third, will the organization's strategies aim primarily at changing personal behavior or at changing structures and organizations? What tactics will be most successful—boycotts? legislative campaigns? Or, in WAC's case, workshops? curricular requirements?

Resources are a fourth micro-level concern. One question is whether to become reliant on resources outside one's membership—for example, the "state," or sympathetic non-members.

Movements and their organizations may flourish and die down cyclically over time, as has, for example, the U.S. women's movement—and the interdisciplinary writing movement (Russell, *Writing*). Across these cycles, the nature, structure, and rhetoric of a movement may change (Benford 1888).

After its initial flourish, a movement or organization may follow any trajectory, or a combination of several (Zald and Ash). One trajectory is routinization and oligarchization as the organization develops patterns of action and an entrenched leadership group. This trajectory may sound negative, but it is not necessarily inimical to the organization's achievement of its objectives. Co-optation is another trajectory. One of the most common fates of U.S. movements, argues Murray Edelman, is for the state to create an agency that addresses the movement's concerns through symbols rather than substance (*Symbolic, Political*).

Other trajectories include demise, radicalization, schism, and stagnation. A movement may become an "interest group" (also called a pressure group), losing its ideological quality and focusing on protecting its own interests (Roberts and Edwards 83–84; Browne 122–28). However, McAdam, McCarthy, and Zald emphasize that no such list can fully represent the variety of trajectories that a movement or any of its organizations may have as it constructs its own complex web of relationships and choices at both the micro and macro levels (718).

Though the success of movements has been difficult to establish, it appears that movements have more often succeeded in changing cultures and attitudes than in changing structures or dislodging elites (Benford 1885). Movements may effect widespread changes in personal behavior, as for example the women's movement is credited with changing the behavior of many women not directly involved with the movement (Mueller).

Movements may have outcomes not directly related to achieving their goals, but important nonetheless. One is the *diffusion of tactics*—tactics pioneered in one movement will be adopted by others (Marx and Wood; Tilly). Another outcome is the *diffusion of personnel*—adherents continue their activities in other movements or in systems, as, for example, white former civil rights activists have been active in the women's movement and have penetrated businesses, government, and education (McAdam). A movement or organization may *serve as a network within which another movement or organization arises*. This is important because most new members of movements are recruited along already established lines of interaction—friends, relatives, fellow workers, and so on (McAdam). Finally, a possible outcome of movements is *countermovements or general resistance*.

INTERPRETING WAC'S PAST WITHIN
THE "MOVEMENT" FRAME

To interpret WAC within the "movement" frame reveals its characteristics, strengths, and problems in ways that may help us think creatively about them. WAC, like any movement, was influenced by societal factors. It may be seen in part as a move by writing faculty to extend their power and influence, helped by widespread perception that student writing was inadequate ("Why Johnny Can't Write"). Like past interdisciplinary writing movements (Russell, *Writing*), WAC was born in a time of increasing pressure for access by previously underserved populations. Faculty faced hard questions about the meaning of education, equality, literacy, democracy, diversity, knowledge, power, and liberation.

Would WAC avoid becoming an interest group or being co-opted? Would it shape worthy goals and realize them? Would it last? The answers to these questions began to emerge through WAC's early choices. One significant choice was WAC's early attention to micro, rather than macro, concerns. This happened for several reasons.

First, there was no highly publicized Rosa Parks in WAC, no flare of rebellion against a defined oppressor, but instead a quiet and local flowering. WAC did not enlarge itself by becoming a national organization with a nationally articulated agenda and a media image, but by the springing up of campus WAC programs. Though the National Writing Project and the National Network of WAC Programs served in some ways loosely as national centers, WAC in higher education was spread primarily through conferences and through traveling workshop leaders such as Toby Fulwiler, Elaine Maimon, and me. WAC resembled independent congregations linked by itinerant preachers rather than a strongly organized central church with a central orthodoxy.

WAC was "local" in another way. Whereas Women's Studies, for example, formed a whole new interdisciplinary organization (the National Women's Studies Organization) with its own conferences and journals, WAC's theory and research were folded within the journals and conventions that served writing faculty. Literature specifically for faculty across disciplines, in those early days, was largely limited to "how-to" literature (Thaiss, *Writing*; Walvoord, *Helping*).

WAC goals at the local level were variously influenced by faculty frustration over students' lack of writing skills; by impulses to assess students; by the reform vision of James Britton's British group, who urged the use of expressive writing and more broadly the integration of the child's language into the classroom; by "process" pedagogy; by theories which emphasized how novices learn discourse conventions; and by liberation pedagogy embodied, for example, in the writings of Paulo Freire. Goals on local campuses ranged from helping Johnny and Janie (and Juan and Juwanda) write to helping liberate them in various senses of that term, from emphasizing expressive writing to emphasizing students' command of the conventions of discourse communities. A sense of the variety of goals can be gained from skimming Fulwiler and Young's *Programs That Work*.

The decentralization of the movement onto individual campuses and the plethora of goals and philosophies that arose meant that each campus organization had strong local ownership and the flexibility to work for local change in its own setting. Some changed their campuses in significant ways (see Kipling and Murphy for an example). To visit scores of them each year, as I do, is to see how uniquely they have adapted themselves to the different cultures and needs of their institutions. However, local WAC programs were vulnerable to co-optation, becoming special interest groups, settling for narrow goals and limited visions, or simply being wiped out in the next budget crunch or the next change of deans.

Early WAC programs often provided the only significant faculty workshops on a campus. WAC was generally not directly opposed by administrators; in fact, it was often supported—at least verbally. Faculty colleagues, while sometimes skeptical or resistant, did not organize formal countermovements. The technological reformation with its radical impact on teaching and learning was not yet clearly foreseen by most faculty.

All this meant that early WAC tended to ignore the macro-level concerns mentioned in the movement literature—how to relate to other movement organizations, the administration, enemies, countermovements, and the media/technology. Instead, WAC focused on micro-level concerns—strategies, organizational form, membership, and resources.

For its strategies, WAC was not one of those movements that chose boycotts or sit-ins or marches aimed at systems and bureaucracies. WAC chose to change individual teacher behavior by persuasion, and, in some programs, to provide supplementary teacher figures who had special expertise (such as writing center tutors, writing teachers in "linked" or team-taught courses, or student "fellows" attached to courses in the disciplines). To change teaching, WAC worked with teachers directly, usually through workshops, but sometimes through linked courses or team-teaching. Persuasion was an obvious strategy because, given faculty autonomy, it is hard to change teaching by external directives.

WAC's choice to focus on faculty development rested upon an assumption that Hargreaves calls "psychologistic"—that is, the assumption that teachers are ineffective because they lack knowledge or training, and thus the way to reform education is to train teachers more effectively. Hargreaves contrasts that view to the "sociologic" view, which emphasizes the structural forces that determine teachers' choices and actions in the classroom. The psychologistic assumption makes sense, since faculty are often unfamiliar with the interactive pedagogies that WAC and others encourage and that research suggests are productive (see Chickering and Gamson). A problem is that classroom changes eventually bump against structural issues—reward systems, departmental cultures, the atomization of education, and the use of language skills as gateway barriers for students, to name a few.

WAC chose to focus on writing, and WAC programs were usually led by a writing or English faculty member. That placed WAC leaders in the role of teachers or experts vis-à-vis their colleagues. Fulwiler's title "Showing Not Telling in a WAC Workshop" eschews telling, but it does not eschew the role of the WAC leader as the possessor of something to show. That something was often the power of writing—the leader's field of expertise. Second, the emphasis on writing as the answer allowed the *question* to be left vague: What sort of student learning did WAC aim for? What were WAC's central goals, beyond getting more teachers to use writing?

Workshops were the backbone of the WAC movement, and they tended to generate high energy and enthusiasm. They offered new, often liberating ideas to faculty who often had had little exposure to theory and research on pedagogy. Writing provided a way to make the classroom interactive. Workshops appealed to faculty's need for community, collegiality, and cross-disciplinary interaction. The power of WAC to change faculty lives and practice, even five, ten, or fifteen years later, is documented in my and my colleagues' forthcoming study (Walvoord et al., *WAC*).

In the workshops, leaders would emphasize the power of "writing to learn" and discuss how to help students master the discourse of the discipline. Topics varied from philosophical explorations of the nature of literacy and the learning goals of classrooms to demonstration of practical strategies such as informal writing, peer collaboration, and draft response (Fulwiler, "Showing"; Herrington). Consonant with WAC's emphasis on individual over structural change, leaders worked hard to present strategies that were feasible within present structural constraints—for example, how to use journals in large classes.

The phrase "writing to learn" was in part an attempt by WAC leaders to give a more accurate picture of the workshops' focus on learning, not just on grammar. It was in part an attempt to woo those faculty who were more interested in their students' learning than in writing as they perceived it. It reflected Britton's theories, which were, however, as John M. Ackerman and Daniel Mahala point out, variously interpreted in campus workshops. I would note that WAC leaders might have seemed to focus on "learning," but in fact they tended to be proponents, above all, of writing, and of the power of writing in virtually every classroom and discipline.

WAC recruited faculty into the workshops primarily through word of mouth and gentle arm-twisting by leaders. Its form of organization locally, then, was the loosest of Lofland's types—a volunteer association.

Research on how innovations are disseminated suggests that workshop attendees in the first years were "early adopters"—people who are willing to take risks and to adopt new ideas and who are horizontally well integrated into the community of their peers (Rogers). In contrast, "middle" and "late" adopters tend to be vertically integrated within their disciplines and sensitive to what supervisors want from them. They adopt innovations only when those innovations have become common currency. After "early adopters" are recruited, how does WAC bring in the middle and late adopters whose patterns and needs are different?

WAC's definition of membership tended to be event-based. It defined members as those who had attended workshops or participated in one of the linked programs. WAC's reports to administrators typically focused on how many had participated; WAC usually did not define membership by faculty's beliefs and strategies in the classroom—again, a mode that left wide latitude for varying interpretations and theories of WAC.

Rewards and motivations for members were largely intrinsic: collegiality and the satisfaction of improving one's teaching. (In "teaching fellow" or "linked" programs, WAC provided the assistance of writing faculty and student fellows as a motivation and a reward.) Research suggests that intrinsic rewards are powerful motivators for faculty (see McKeachie). Like any workforce that has high autonomy, faculty are controlled largely by colleague esteem and by socialization rather than by direct supervision or extrinsic rewards. But despite some workshop claims ("journals don't need to take a lot of time"), WAC urges careful and thoughtful attention to teaching. How are those to be sustained when the extrinsic reward system fails to support teaching excellence, or even discourages it?

The lack of extrinsic reward meant that WAC did not have to define who had performed reward-worthy acts and what those acts might be. Again, the goals and outcomes of WAC could remain vague.

WAC programs often focused on the workshop as the event that would create the central change, and then on "follow-up" activities—a concept ill-designed to capture the imagination of early adopters who are experimenters, movers, risk-takers. Mary Jane Dickerson and her colleagues admit that it has been hard to get University of Vermont faculty into workshops after the initial one (60). In my experience, UV is not alone.

WAC was usually funded through the discretionary budgets of supportive administrators or through grants. Both placed a high value on innovating, not sustaining. Grants did so because that is their express mission. Administrators often work for what they view as the long-range good of the institution, but it's only natural that each new administrator tends to look for new programs that bear his or her special stamp. Further, as finances tightened, funding from the provost's discretionary funds became more tenuous. In movement terms, WAC remained fully dependent upon funding from the "state" and from sympathetic supporters outside the primary membership: WAC did not pass the hat at workshops or collect membership fees from individual faculty.

Workshop participants formed a potential power bloc on a campus. They often worked together locally, or in local consortia, to instigate second-stage WAC activities—curricular reform, university collaboration with schools, changes in assessment, revision of composition programs, student support programs such as writing centers, even sometimes faculty reward systems

(Soven, "Beyond"; Walvoord, "Getting" 17; Walvoord and Dowling). But they did not form a strongly centralized national organization with a national reform agenda for higher education.

WAC initially tested the efficacy of its workshops by end-of-workshop participant evaluations. As funders, critics, or new deans began saying, "show me that these strategies enhance learning," WAC developed a further literature of outcomes. Student learning, WAC researchers discovered, was dreadfully hard to measure and even harder to link to the workshop in any significant way. If they didn't have it already, leaders developed a strong appreciation for the difficulty of student outcomes assessment (Fulwiler, "Evaluating"; Klaus). Faculty behavior was an alternative indicator. Much of WAC outcomes research has measured teachers' adoption of specific WAC-named strategies such as freewriting, draft response, and journals (see Walvoord et al., *WAC*). However, WAC never developed a standard test of WAC outcomes; again, decentralization was the norm. As researchers began to discover that faculty often changed or abandoned WAC strategies, there arose a literature about faculty "resistance" (see Swanson-Owens; Swilkey).

In *WAC in the Long Run* I and my colleagues critique WAC research and argue that WAC measured faculty behaviors in limited ways and did not develop robust theories to explain teacher development before and after WAC or teacher "resistance" to WAC. The problem was how to measure outcomes in ways that increasingly sophisticated and learning-centered publics demanded. What *do* faculty do after workshops? What *do* students learn, and what should they learn? How *does* writing help to achieve learning goals?

WAC programs—local, voluntary, and vulnerable—naturally tried to find a more secure seat within their institutions. The dominant strategy has been the curricular requirement. One form is "linked" or "paired" courses, where students take a writing course along with a course in another discipline, and the faculty or graduate students teaching those courses collaborate tightly or loosely or not at all. Another is the "Writing-Intensive" course (any course, including General Education, "Second Writing," and "Freshman Seminars," that is required to have a strong writing component). "W-I" courses are not new (Towson State University's dates to 1976), but they have become very common in the past decade.

Like any strategies, curricular requirements have addressed some of the problems that arose from WAC's earlier choices but neglected others or created new ones. Curricular requirements addressed WAC's membership problem by drawing into WAC's net all faculty or graduate students assigned to teach W-I or linked courses. Some programs offered extrinsic rewards such as limited class sizes, stipends, or course load reductions. Curricular requirements provided ongoing activity—the teaching of the course—across which continuous follow-up meetings and colleague support could take place. Requirements addressed WAC's measurement problem by providing demonstrable indicators—number of W-I or linked sections, students who had the requisite numbers of W-I marks on their transcripts, teachers who were now obligated to report what they were doing. These measures still did not address student learning outcomes, but they provided numbers to fill up WAC reports; they could be taken for measures of success. Further, WAC, like a department, now offered curricular requirements, and it controlled faculty work; thus it had a stronger claim to an office, a staff, a director with released time, and an ongoing, line-item budget. Thus secured, it might be better able to work from within to address structural issues.

One way of viewing the spread of W-I and linked courses is that it represents the achievement of what WAC has worked for—a more secure place within the institution and a mechanism for ensuring that writing is used in many courses.

But the curricular requirement strategy created new problems of its own. First, curricular requirements tend to change the roles of both WAC leaders and WAC "members." The leaders may change, in Patricia Dunn's apt phrase, from a "we" to a "they" in faculty eyes ("*They* are making us teach these W-I courses"). WAC leaders become not helpers but enforcers.

The definition of "member" changes from a committed volunteer to a dutiful citizen fulfilling a departmental assignment—or, in Lofland's terms, a staffer in a bureaucracy. This may draw middle and late adopters into WAC's net, but it may also diffuse the energy, commitment, and community that were so striking at the beginning. The goal of the WAC program and its workshops may narrow to merely ensuring that the requirements of W-I or linked courses are being met. Edward M. White has detailed additional difficulties. For example, department heads may assign required W-I courses to the inept instructors who can't otherwise attract students, or to the least powerful teachers, or to adjuncts or T.A.s. W-I or linked courses may be stripped of faculty development support. Both students and faculty may come to believe that no writing need be done in non-W-I or non-linked courses, so the institution ends up with less writing than it had before. Faculty who are teaching linked courses may treat writing faculty or graduate students as mere paper-graders or grammar checkers.

In short, then, widespread curricular requirements addressed some of WAC's problems but left or created others.

THE FUTURE OF WAC

So now what? What does viewing WAC as a movement and telling its past within that frame imply for its future? This section will outline challenges facing WAC.

Movements rise and fall. Their goals, strategies, and rhetoric change over time. WAC in twenty-five years will be gone or radically different. But that might be the best evidence of its success, because it will have changed, as every movement organization must change.

But co-optation, schism, becoming a special interest group, or dying without moving toward one's goals are trajectories to avoid. I believe one thing that will help is constant clarification of goals at both the national and local levels. Ackerman, Mahala, Russell ("Social," "Communications"), and others have questioned whether WAC has been true to the radical reform agenda implicit in Britton's theories. One might also ask, Why Britton's? What *is* the original or founding vision? Is it still vital? That is a crucial debate. WAC must find ways to enlarge that debate beyond writing specialists. Further, WAC must be more active in other national debates about the goals of educational reform.

Informed by such national debates, each local WAC program must wrestle with its goals and means. I suggest that a campus goal statement begin "we seek student learning that is…" and then state how it believes such learning can be achieved in its own setting. Stated in terms of student learning, the goal will help WAC adherents distinguish between the implementation of the goal and the entrenchment of their own organization, between the impact they hope to have and the organizational structures that have facilitated that impact in the past, between enemies and potential allies. Individual campus programs' decisions will differ and must be respected. Nationally, WAC needs to provide support for wise and well-informed local decisions. Possible vehicles are itinerant leaders functioning now as consultants about goals and strategies (Writing Program Administrators runs an organized consulting service) and national conferences (the twenty-seventh anniversary WAC conference in Charleston, SC, February 6–8, 1997, will emphasize such issues. Write Angela Williams at The Citadel for information).

The debate should rage hotly, both nationally and locally, but one form it should *not* take is for factions to name themselves separately ("Writing in the Disciplines" or "Language Across the Curriculum") and name "WAC" as a discredited faction (Gere; Parker and Goodkin). When the debate takes that form, two dangers emerge: one is schism, as proponents identify themselves with one or the other faction. The other is that people who don't understand the full conversation may hear that all of "WAC" has been discredited (I've heard people say this), and they won't make fine distinctions between WAC and WID or LAC. That may be what led news reporter Anne Matthews, covering the MLA meeting in 1991, to conclude (and to print in the New York Times Magazine!) that WAC was one of the things that was "out" at MLA that year. The whole movement suffers when this happens.

Macro Challenge: To Work with Other Movement Organizations

WAC programs, which have traditionally focused on micro issues, must now devote significant attention to macro issues. The first macro challenge is the need to work with other organizations.

Since WAC was born, four national forces have sprung up to pursue national reform agendas, and WAC is neither *one of them* nor *visible within them*. One force is the national education associations, primarily the American Association for Higher Education, which has drawn significant grant funding as WAC programs have lost it. AAHE has two strong national journals (*Change* and *AAHE Bulletin*) and a sheaf of monographs. It runs numbers of national and regional conferences annually. It pushes various reforms including active learning, peer review, assessment, total quality management, the use of cases for teacher training, teaching portfolios, and others. But except for an occasional piece on WAC by Edward M. White, WAC is almost totally absent from the reforms discussed by AAHE.

A second force is the university-based institutes and centers for higher education, such as those at Northwestern University, Princeton, Syracuse, and others. Attracting grant money, they blend research with programmatic leadership. WAC research is largely absent from their, and the larger, higher education research conversation.

A third force that has adopted a national reform agenda is funding agencies themselves. For example, the PEW Charitable Trust has launched a costly national campaign for "restructuring" higher education. Could WAC have captured their interest and shaped their efforts? It didn't.

The fourth force is governing bodies—for example accrediting agencies, boards, and legislatures. Only occasionally has the spread of WAC become a major part of those bodies' agendas. In Florida, an administrative rule adopted by the State Board of Education requires that students have to write a certain number of words, but without accompanying regulations about faculty development or other WAC-related reforms—which suggests some dangers inherent in having a national force take over one's agenda!

I'm not arguing that WAC should have joined these forces; I'm noting that it has not. WAC is uniquely local; even its mandates—curricular requirements—are almost always local. Where WAC conferences are sometimes notable for their lack of administrators, the conferences of these other forces are often notable for their lack of rank and file faculty. WAC has a tradition of bottom-up faculty talk, of transformational workshops, as its wellspring. Many of the other forces are products of a new era—the era not of access but of accountability.

These forces radically change WAC's environment. On my campus this year, faculty could have attended workshops not only on WAC, but on assessment, the math pedagogy reform known as "Harvard Calculus," improving teaching in engineering or economics, achieving a "teaching culture" in departments, oral communication, visual communication, critical thinking, diversity, instructional technology, teaching portfolios, student portfolios, student evaluations, or General Education reform. While department heads on my campus are being asked to pony up newly instituted W-I courses (which must also feature critical thinking and be interactive), departments are also being required to assess student learning, to have faculty spend 10 percent more time on teaching (Ohio law), to hold annual reviews for tenured faculty, and to increase retention. All these efforts have a reform agenda of improving student learning. Some are driven by powerful engines—state mandates, accrediting agency requirements, national organizations.

I believe that the most likely scenario over the coming decade is for a multitude of education reform programs to coexist in a shifting kaleidoscope, with some programs disappearing as they can no longer draw funds or faculty, and new programs arising. The fluctuations will be encouraged by the funding sources for such groups—grants and administrators—which still favor innovation over sustenance.

That Darwinian scenario, however, will be moderated by the rise on some campuses of what Palmer calls institutional "spaces where movement-style work can be done" (17). One of these may be the offices that manage various mandates—assessment, the freshman year experience, General Education, and W-I courses. WAC's choice to push curriculum reform through W-I and linked courses was an early stake-out of such an institutional space. Other spaces are English departments and writing centers, where WAC on some campuses is already well established. Another space will be the increasingly popular "teaching/learning" centers. These centers may become relatively permanent, endowed or line-item offices that encourage and fund initiatives for student learning. Centers may be able to get grants because they are not tied to any particular program but can ride the newest innovations. But alternatively, these centers may tie up existing funding for faculty development, allow the university to claim it values student learning, be ignored by most faculty (Austin), and prevent more effective faculty development from arising. The danger in all institutional spaces is that they may become merely symbolic—a common fate for U.S. movements, the literature suggests.

In the presence of the four national forces and within the Darwinian struggle marked by certain privileged spaces, WAC must decide how to relate to other movement organizations. It cannot ignore them, and on most campuses, I believe, WAC cannot survive as Switzerland; it simply does not have the funding base, the powerful national engines, the "new" look that will attract funding, or the ability to retain followers to itself alone, after the workshop. Those followers themselves often want to, and must, combine WAC with assessment, critical thinking, and other movements. WAC, I believe, must dive in or die.

One path is for WAC to become, or fold into, a teaching/learning center of the type becoming ever more popular on campuses today. I've mentioned the dangers of such centers, but they could be powerful levers for change, could mean increased stability and resources, and could facilitate collaboration with other movements.

Another path is to collaborate with others outside such a center. The University of Cincinnati has so far eschewed a center for fear it will be resisted or ignored by faculty as an administrative bastion. Instead, the leaders of all teaching/learning initiatives, including WAC, meet regularly with faculty, student, and administrative representatives as a coordinating council.

Another possible collaborative role for WAC is what the movement literature calls dissemination of tactics or personnel, or becoming a network through which other movements form. I've seen WAC members move into ethical thinking, critical thinking, assessment, oral communication, and other areas. Their nature as risk takers and early adopters, which brought them to WAC, now carries them into new innovations. Self-confidence they gained in WAC makes them effective change agents. Such growth is a common outcome of WAC, my and my colleagues' research suggests (*WAC*). WAC can deliberately foster this growth. For example, on my own campus, the WAC program helped initiate a new program in which departments work to understand their cultures and effect changes. We in WAC contributed staff time, snuck their stuff into our duplication and mailing systems, and generated their labels from our mailing lists. The former chair of the WAC Committee now directs that WAC child. WAC views this program as essential to its goals, since, as Russell points out (*Writing*), the departmental reward systems and ways of carrying out daily business are such powerful forces in academe that real reform must affect them. We cannot send workshop attendees, all fired up, back into departments that don't support their new ideas. Christopher Thaiss predicts that WAC in the future will merge into more broadly conceived interdisciplinary ventures and that "One way to measure the success of your WAC workshops is to see, over the years, how many other cross-curricular initiatives sprout up" ("Future" 99).

In such collaborations and disseminations, WAC may survive strongly as a discrete unit, known for its strength in garnering bottom-up faculty commitment, for its research about language and learning, and for the new strengths it will build. But it is also possible that on some campuses, WAC, which has always depended for its power upon the force of individual change and individual commitment, will survive not in name nor in organizational form, but in the actions of the changing, committed faculty who were nurtured in WAC and who now move out into broader aspects of reform, using what they learned in WAC.

Macro Challenge: To Define WAC's Relationship to Institutional Administration

A significant macro-level concern for all reform efforts today is to define relations with administrations. In higher education, the current battle by faculty to defend their autonomy is likely to heat up, as administrations, boards, legislatures, and accrediting agencies become more "managerial" (Bergquist) and increasingly regulate workload, assessment, and so on. Dwindling resources may exacerbate tensions (El-Khawas 32).

A WAC program that has used W-I courses may be caught on the "they" side of the faculty backlash. Even without W-I programs, a WAC program that pushes for changes in the reward system, for better assessment of teaching as the basis for improving and rewarding it, or for other structural changes that boards and legislatures are also demanding, risks becoming a "they." Even WAC's old agenda—showing faculty how to teach better within present constraints—may backfire if faculty see it as a way of making them do more work for the same money within the same constraints. Faculty unions have in some cases demanded faculty development as a right and in other cases fought it as an administrative ploy (Bergquist 137).

In the face of this conflict, WAC may take two courses. One is to work on what may be perceived as the administrative side, serving the people who come into its net and looking for productive grounds on which to encourage faculty-administrative cooperation. It's possible to do quite a lot of good in such a position. Movements, says the literature, often benefit greatly from sympathetic supporters within the "state." Movement-style work may be done, or supported, from the administrative side.

All this "side" stuff, of course, is actually silly. The "faculty side" and the "administrative side" are what Mary Louise Pratt calls "utopias"—idealized unities where in fact there exist many currents, many discourses. Raymond Williams identifies, within an organization, the dominant, residual, and emergent forces (121–26), and Bergquist names the four "cultures" that coexist in academe.

However, my own bias is that, in general, WAC should try to stay on what faculty will perceive as the faculty side, especially where faculty-administration tension is high. Considerable faculty autonomy is likely to remain despite erosions. Intrinsic motivations have always been powerful for faculty (Clark and Corcoran; McKeachie). Colleagues' influence has been a strong factor in faculty productivity (Blackburn et al.; Boice; Creswell; Finkelstein, "Faculty," *American*). Being a "we" is one of WAC's traditional strengths, differentiating it from other reform movements such as assessment, Total Quality Management, and so forth. WAC might use its faculty strength in the broader effort for educational reform.

But staying on the faculty side does not mean abandoning efforts to address the structures of higher education. At the University of Cincinnati, the WAC office recently surveyed faculty and students about what *they* thought the university should do to enhance undergraduate learning (note that the question was broader than writing). The most frequent response was "change the reward system." WAC is working now with a university-wide committee to bring about that and other structural changes. To play its central role in this process, WAC built on its reputation as a "we," it moved away from its focus on writing toward a broader concern for education reform, and it seized an opportunity to fill a genuine institutional need.

Macro Challenge: To Define
WAC's Relationship to Technology

WAC may transcend writing in the ways I have suggested, but its traditional strength has been to explore the role of writing, and more generally language, in learning. There's an increasing need for that exploration. But WAC can no longer just introduce the idea of handwritten journals; it must deal with network bulletin boards, distance learning, and multimedia presentations by both students and teachers, as lines blur between writing and other forms of communication and between classrooms and other learning spaces.

On my own campus, WAC is moving into closer relationship with the instructional technology center leaders. They have the technical expertise but need help developing faculty training that goes beyond "here's this nifty software." They need avenues to recruit faculty who are not "early adopters" of technology (Geoghegan; Short). They welcome dialogue to explore the political and social implications of new technologies.

Micro-Level Challenges: To Reexamine the Meaning
of "Member," "Workshop," and "Follow-Up"

So far, I have said that WAC must pay more attention to macro-level concerns than it did earlier. But I think WAC also must fundamentally reexamine its old answers to micro-level concerns, particularly its traditional workshop-plus-follow-up model, its leadership, its theories of faculty development, and its delivery of services to faculty. And it must deal with assessment.

The word "follow-up" reveals an underlying assumption that the centrally located workshop led by a writing specialist is the key transforming event, which needs only "follow-up" to maintain the conversion. That thought pattern spells demise or stagnation once the recruitable faculty have been through a workshop. WAC must see itself not as a transforming workshop plus "follow-up" but as part of a sustaining set of services, a network, a culture, within the university, that supports ongoing, career-long, self-directed growth for faculty. The theoretical and research base for this view of the faculty is beginning to be established (Baldwin; Baldwin and Blackburn; Blackburn; Blackburn, Chapman, and Cameron; Hargreaves and Fullan. See also my and my colleagues' fuller discussion in *WAC*).

Transcending current leadership ranks means creating leadership roles that do not privilege traditional credentials in English. At UC, the WAC office is sponsoring one-hour brown-bag lunch discussions led by varied faculty on varied topics and planned by a committee that includes some folks who have not attended a WAC workshop. Other forms that allow broad faculty leadership are "cases" that faculty groups discuss (Anson et al.; Hutchings); "teaching circles," where faculty meet regularly as equals to help one another with teaching; "coaching," where pairs visit each other's classrooms; mentoring of new faculty by teaching-award winners; or computer bulletin board discussions.

Transcending the workshop model also means offering services to faculty at their desks and in their classrooms. In 1994, 79 percent of faculty who responded to a questionnaire at UC indicated they had, in the past two years, read something about teaching. (The respondents were 112 members of eight departments that had, as departments, volunteered to work to improve and reward teaching. The questionnaire was returned by 85–100 percent of the full- and part-time faculty in those departments.) How can WAC best feed this individual quest for inspiration and information? Robert Morris College is experimenting not only with the national public television programs familiar to many of us but also with other ways of getting ideas and information into faculty hands through print material, videos, and computerized resources. Some campuses, including UC, offer individualized consultations with faculty, including taping or observation of their classrooms.

To do these things, WAC may well collaborate with other movements, and that may blur the definition of "member" and even of "WAC." But I firmly believe that in this redefinition lies WAC's most important survival— not necessarily the survival of WAC programs as currently formed and named, but the survival of WAC's goals for faculty career-long growth and for student learning.

Challenge: To Deal with Assessment

Assessment will be a powerful part of the context in which WAC and its allies must work. Accrediting agencies are demanding that each institution implement it. Legislatures and boards are going to base funding upon it. As faculty development initiatives vie for funding, each will be asked to show outcomes. Further, assessment, rightly understood and properly controlled, asks useful questions: "What sorts of learning are happening in our classrooms? What factors help produce the learning we want?"

On one hand, WAC has much to offer to assessment. WAC leaders often bring a humanistic sensibility and a keen eye for the relations between assessment, language, culture, access, power, and politics. They appreciate the complexity of assessment and the dangers inherent in simplistic measures. WAC must not characterize assessment as the enemy but must help to shape this powerful force that will not go away. Further, WAC must assess its own work in new ways. I and my colleagues (*WAC*) have argued that WAC so far has assessed outcomes too narrowly, looking to see whether faculty have continued to use WAC-defined classroom strategies such as journals and draft response, and labeling as "resistors" those who have not. WAC must develop robust theories of faculty lifelong development and of how workshops and other kinds of stimulation contribute to faculty vitality and effectiveness.

CONCLUSION

I have argued here that viewing ourselves within the "movement" framework helps WAC to understand its past and its future in a world of change. I have cited the research about movements and the choices they must make at the macro and the micro levels. I have indicated the challenges I think WAC faces in the future: to change, to set goals, to address macro issues, to rethink old answers to micro issues, to deal with assessment.

But it is the *power* of a movement that, finally, I covet for WAC, for its allied movements, and for each faculty member. That power, as Palmer notes, has its source not merely in counting "enemies" or in trying to achieve a secure spot in the organizational structure of the university. That power is the power of the Rosa Parks moment—a personal decision not to live the divided life—to be whole, to care about students and about learning. It is the power of community that was so strong in those early WAC workshops. It is the power in local WAC groups that sit down together to shape a reform agenda for their own situations. It is the power of the communities we will form in the future as we widen our scope, disperse our tactics and followers, serve as networks for new movements, collaborate with colleagues, and dance in intricate patterns with the administration. It is the power that movements sometimes have to change individuals, to change a culture. And the end of that change is its beginning—we want for our students and for ourselves the power of language, of learning, of community, to liberate, to empower, to make us whole. As WAC is uniquely local, the working out of these goals will be local. And in their working, "enemies" is not the point. WAC must act now as a mature reform organization, bound in some ways by its quarter century of choices, needing to reinterpret, to dive in, to take its place in what history may call the era of teaching, the era of education reform; must work to refine and reshape its goals and to move skillfully, powerfully, visibly or invisibly, among the complex forces and discourses of the academy.

NOTE

1. The first WAC workshops appear to have taken place at Central College in Pella, Iowa, in 1970; see David Russell's *Writing in the Academic Disciplines* and Mildred Steele's account.

WORKS CITED

Ackerman, John M. "The Promise of Writing to Learn." *Written Communication* 10 (1993): 334–70.

Anson, Christopher, Joan Graham, David Joliffe, Nancy Shapiro, and Carolyn H. Smith. *Scenarios for Teaching Writing.* Urbana: NCTE, 1993.

Austin, Ann E. "Faculty Cultures, Faculty Values." *Assessing Academic Climates and Cultures.* Ed. William G. Tierney. *New Directions for Institutional Research No. 68.* San Francisco: Jossey, 1990. 61–74.

Baldwin, R. G. "Adult and Career Development: What are the Implications for Faculty?" *Current Issues in Higher Education* 2 (1979): 13–20.

Baldwin, R. G., and Robert T. Blackburn. "The Academic Career as a Developmental Process: Implications for Higher Education." *Journal of Higher Education* 52 (1981): 598–614.

Benford, Robert. "Social Movements." *Encyclopedia of Sociology,* 1992, vol. 4.

Bergquist, William H. *The Four Cultures of the Academy: Insights and Strategies for Improving Leadership in Collegiate Organizations.* San Francisco: Jossey, 1992.

Blackburn, Robert T. "Career Phases and Their Influence on Faculty Motivation." *Motivating Professors to Teach Effectively.* Ed. James Bess. San Francisco: Jossey, 1982. 95–98.

Blackburn, R. T., D. Chapman, and S. Cameron. "Cloning in Academe: Mentorship and Academic Careers." *Research in Higher Education* 15 (1981): 315–27.

Boice, Robert. *The New Faculty Member: Supporting and Fostering Professional Development.* San Francisco: Jossey, 1992.

Britton, James. *Language and Learning.* London: Penguin, 1970.

Britton, James, Tony Burgess, Nancy Martin, Alex McLeod, and Harold Rosen. *The Development of Writing Abilities (11–18).* London: Macmillan, 1975.

Browne, Ken. *An Introduction to Sociology.* Cambridge, Eng.: Polity, 1992.

Chickering, Arthur, and Zelda Gamson. "Seven Principles for Good Practice in Undergraduate Education." *The Wingspread Journal,* 1987. Available from American Assoc. for Higher Education.

Clark, Shirley M., and Mary Corcoran. "Individual and Organizational Contributions to Faculty Vitality: An Institutional Case Study." *Faculty Vitality and Institutional Productivity: Critical Perspectives for Higher Education.* Ed. Shirley M. Clark and Darrell R. Lewis. New York: Teachers College P, 1985. 112–38.

Cornell, Cynthia, and David J. Klooster. "Writing Across the Curriculum: Transforming the Academy?" *WPA: Writing Program Administration* 14 (1990): 7–16.

Creswell, John. *Faculty Research Performance.* ASHE-ERIC Higher Education Report No. 4. Washington, DC: Assn. for the Study of Higher Education, 1985.

Dickerson, Mary Jane, Toby Fulwiler, and Henry Steffens. "The University of Vermont." *Programs That Work: Models and Methods for Writing Across the Curriculum.* Ed. Toby Fulwiler and Art Young. Portsmouth: Boynton, 1990. 45–63.

Dunn, Patricia. "Comment on 'Writing Utopias.'" *College English* 54 (1992): 729–33.

Edelman, Murray. *The Symbolic Uses of Politics.* Urbana: U of Illinois P, 1964.

———. *Political Language: Words that Succeed and Policies that Fail.* New York: Academic, 1977.

El-Khawas, Elaine. *Campus Trends 1994.* Washington: American Council on Education, 1994.

Finkelstein, Martin J. "Faculty vitality in higher education." Working paper prepared for the National Center for Educational Statistics Forum on "Integrating Research on Faculty," Jan. 10–11, 1993, Washington D.C.

———. *The American Academic Profession: A Synthesis of Social Inquiry Since World War II.* Columbus: Ohio State UP, 1984.

Freire, Paulo. *Pedagogy of the Oppressed.* New York: Seabury P, 1970.

Fulwiler, Toby. "Evaluating Writing Across the Curriculum Programs." McLeod 61–76.

———. "Showing Not Telling in a Writing Across the Curriculum Workshop." *College English* 43 (1981): 55–63.

Fulwiler, Toby, and Art Young, eds. *Programs That Work: Models and Methods for Writing Across the Curriculum.* Portsmouth, NH: Boynton, 1990.

Geoghegan, William. "Stuck at the Barricades: Can Information Technology Really Enter the Mainstream of Teaching and Learning?" *AAHE Bulletin* (Sept. 1994): 13–16.

Gere, Anne, ed. *Roots in the Sawdust: Writing to Learn Across the Disciplines.* Urbana: NCTE, 1985.

Gusfield, Joseph. *The Culture of Public Problems: Drinking and Driving and the Symbolic Order:* Chicago: U of Chicago P, 1981.

Hargreaves, Andy. "Teaching Quality: A Sociological Analysis. *Curriculum Studies* 20 (1988): 211–31.

Hargreaves, Andy, and Michael G. Fullan, eds. *Understanding Teacher Development.* New York: Teachers College P, 1992.

Herrington, Anne J. "Writing to Learn: Writing Across the Disciplines." *College English* 43.4 (1981): 379–87.

Hutchings, Patricia. "Windows on Practice: Cases About Teaching and Learning." *Change* 25.6 (Nov.–Dec. 1993): 14–21.

Kipling, Kim J., and Richard J. Murphy, Jr. *Symbiosis: Writing in an Academic Culture.* Portsmouth, NH: Heinemann, Boynton, 1992.

Klaus, Carl H. "Research on Writing Courses: A Cautionary Essay." *Freshman English News* 11.1 (Spring 1982): 3–14.

Lofland, John. *Protest: Studies of Collective Behavior and Social Movements.* New Brunswick: Transaction, 1985.

Mahala, Daniel. "Writing Utopias: Writing Across the Curriculum and the Promise of Reform." *College English* 53.7 (1991): 773–89.

Maimon, Elaine. Preface. McLeod and Soven ix–xiv.

Marx, Gary, and James Wood. "Strands of Theory and Research in Collective Behavior." *Annual Review of Sociology* 1 (1975): 363–428.

Matthews, Anne, "Deciphering Victorian Underwear." *New York Times Magazine* 10 Feb. 1991: 434.

McAdam, Doug. "Micromobilization Contexts and Recruitment to Activism." *International Social Movement Research* 1 (1988): 125–54.

McAdam, Doug, John D. McCarthy, and Mayer N. Zald. "Social Movements." Ed. Neil J. Smelser, *Handbook of Sociology,* Newbury Park, CA, Sage, 1988.

McKeachie, Wilbert J. "Perspectives From Psychology: Financial Incentives Are Ineffective for Faculty." *Academic Rewards in Higher Education.* Ed. D. R. Lewis and W. E. Becker, Jr. Cambridge, MA: Ballinger, 1979. 3–20.

McLeod, Susan H., ed. *Strengthening Programs for Writing Across the Curriculum.* New Directions for Teaching and Learning No. 36. San Francisco: Jossey, 1988.

McLeod, Susan H., and Margot Soven, eds. *Writing Across the Curriculum: A Guide to Developing Programs.* Newbury Park, CA: Sage, 1992.

Mueller, Carol. "Women's Movement Success and the Success of Social Movement Theory." Presented at the annual meeting of the American Sociological Assn., San Antonio, TX, 1984.

Palmer, Parker J. "Divided No More: A Movement Approach to Educational Reform." *Change* 24.2 (March/April 1992): 10–17.

Parker, Robert P., and Vera Goodkin. *The Consequences of Writing: Enhancing Learning in the Disciplines.* Upper Montclair, NJ: Boynton, 1987.

Pratt, Mary Louise. "Linguistic Utopias." *The Linguistics of Writing: Arguments between Language and Literature.* Ed. Nigel Fabb, Derek Attridge, Alan Durant, and Colin MacCabe. New York: Methuen, 1987. 48–66.

Roberts, Geoffrey, and Alistair Edwards. *A New Dictionary of Political Analysis.* New York: Arnold, 1991.

Rogers, E. M. *Diffusion of Innovations.* 3d ed. New York: Free, 1982.

Russell, David. "Writing across the Curriculum and the Communications Movement: Some Lessons from the Past." *College Composition and Communication* 38 (1987): 184–94.

———. "Writing Across the Curriculum in Historical Perspective: Toward a Social Interpretation." *College English* 52 (1990): 52–73.

———. *Writing in the Academic Disciplines, 1870–1990: A Curricular History.* Carbondale: Southern Illinois UP, 1991.

Short, Douglas. "Enhancing Instructional Effectiveness: A Strategic Approach." Unpublished paper from Institute for Academic Technology, IBM Corporation, 2525 Meridian Parkway, Suite 400, Durham, NC 27713.

Soven, Margot. "Beyond the First Workshop: What Else Can You Do to Help Faculty?" McLeod 13–20.

———. "Conclusion: Sustaining Writing Across the Curriculum Programs." McLeod and Soven 189–97.

Steele, Mildred. *The Development of the Communication Skills Program at Central College, Pella, Iowa.* Unpublished document produced at Central College for the Conference on Learning through Communication Skills, Nov. 8, 1985. Available from Barbara Walvoord, Dept. English, M.L. 0069, Univ. Cincinnati, Cincinnati, OH 45221–0069.

Swanson-Owens, Deborah. "Identifying Natural Sources of Resistance: A Case Study of Implementing Writing Across the Curriculum." *Research in the Teaching of English* 20 (1986): 69–97.

Swilky, Jody. "Reconsidering Faculty Resistance to Writing Reform." *WPA: Writing Program Administration* 16.1–2 (Fall/Winter 1992): 50–60.

Thaiss, Christopher. "The Future of Writing Across the Curriculum Programs." McLeod 91–102.

Thaiss, Christopher, ed. *Writing to Learn: Essays and Reflections on Writing Across the Curriculum.* Dubuque: Kendall, 1983.

Tilly, Charles. "Repertories of Contention in America and Britain, 1750–1830." *The Dynamics of Social Movements.* Ed. Mayer N. Zald and John D. McCarthy. Cambridge, MA: Winthrop, 1979. 126–55.

Walvoord, Barbara E. "Getting Started." McLeod and Soven 13–21.

Walvoord, Barbara E., and H. Fil Dowling, Jr., with John R. Breihan, Virginia Johnson Gazzam, Carl E. Henderson, Gertrude B. Hopkins, Barbara Mallonee, and Sally McNelis. "The Baltimore Consortium." Fulwiler and Young 273–86.

Walvoord, Barbara E., Linda Hunt, H. Fil Dowling, Jr., and Joan McMahon. *WAC in the Long Run: A Study of Faculty in Three Writing Across the Curriculum Programs.* NCTE, under contract.

Walvoord, Barbara E., Tami Phenix, Virginia Slachman, and Lisa Udel. "Not Resistance, Not Conversion, But Self-Directed Development: A Longitudinal Study of University Faculty After a WAC Workshop." Paper presented at the annual Conference on College Composition and Communication, Nashville, March, 1994.

Walvoord, Barbara Fassler. *Helping Students Write Well: Strategies for All Disciplines.* 2d ed. New York: MLA, 1986.

White, Edward M. "The Damage of Innovations Set Adrift. *AAHE Bulletin* 44 (Nov. 1990): 3–5.

Williams, Raymond. *Marxism and Literature.* New York: Oxford UP, 1977.

Young, Art, and Toby Fulwiler. "The Enemies of Writing Across the Curriculum." Fulwiler and Young 287–94.

Zald, Mayer N., and Roberta Ash. "Social Movement Organizations: Growth, Decay and Change." *Social Forces* 44 (1966): 327–41.

PART V

PROMOTION AND PROFESSIONAL ISSUES FOR WPAs

Understanding Larger Discourses in Higher Education: Practical Advice for WPAs

Douglas D. Hesse
Miami University—Oxford, OH

Thanks mainly to Bertholt Brecht, most readers know that Galileo survived the Roman Catholic Inquisition by recanting his claim that the earth was not the center of the universe. For this he was rewarded with house arrest during the last years of his life. Probably fewer of us know the fate of Giordano Bruno, a Dominican monk and philosopher who in the late 1500s, immediately before Galileo, also advocated the Copernican position, extending it to assert that the universe is eternal and infinite. Finding Bruno unwilling to recant, the Inquisitors burned him at the stake on February 17, 1600.

Both men possessed specialized knowledge and beliefs at odds with a large and powerful social institution, the Roman Catholic Church. While it may have been relatively safe to hold these positions within the narrower disciplines of astronomy and philosophy, such as they were at the time, expressing them more publicly, against entrenched social formations, proved disastrous.

Four hundred years later there is something of a lesson here for WPAs, whose disciplinary knowledge and values sometimes collide with larger institutional and systemic ones. However, I don't want to press the analogy too hard; as tragic and destructive as they may be, being denied tenure or promotion or losing a curricular battle is something less than being burned at the stake, although some central administrators may seem to wear the cloak of inquisitor too easily. Neither do I want to draw fast lessons from the choices that Galileo and Bruno made. Both tried to expand professional knowledge into public spheres, and there is power in both martyrdom and self-preservation.

My message in this essay is simpler and less dramatic. WPAs cannot afford to act like composition studies centers in the academic galaxy, let alone the social, political, and economic universe in which that galaxy exists. They should not be surprised when matters of curriculum, policy, or assessment that strike them as self-evident do not strike others the same way. In saying

299

this, I do not mean to advocate a career of recanting or, worse, of never assert-ing professional positions that may clash with existing dogmas. Rather, WPAs should analyze the broader contexts in which they and writing programs exist. To his credit, if not to his avail, Galileo understood his hostile audience and took extraordinary rhetorical measures to soften the blow of his message. Similarly—and with more success than Galileo because of the solidification of the rationalist university—WPAs will benefit from analyzing their circum-stances. Furthermore, I'll argue that doing so is not merely defensive postur-ing; it creates opportunities.

Of course, it's important to understand how departmental, college, faculty senate, and central administration cultures may view as heretical the gospels of writing process, the constructed nature of discourse conventions, the neces-sarily shifting definitions of "good writing," the existence of writing as a disci-pline in its own right, and so on. However, my present focus is less on internal contexts than external ones. I explore professional organizations devoted to aspects of higher education that WPAs may only perceive askance, organiza-tions whose agendas and activities seek to represent the interests of higher administrators, boards of trustees, and so on. Writing administrators should not be surprised to learn that just as professional groups such as the Conference on College Composition and Communication (CCCC) or the Council of Writing Program Administrators (WPA) exist to forward the interests of composition-ists, so do groups like the American Association of Higher Education (AAHE) and the Association of American Colleges and Universities (AAC&U) function for administrators and institutions. Further, such groups sometimes have activist agendas supported through initiatives and grants and disseminated through conferences, workshops, and publication series.

At some times, even, one can say that association agendas create specific educational policies or activities. For example, Earnest Boyer's work for the Carnegie Foundation for the Advancement of Teaching in the late 1980s had powerful effects on raising the identity of professors as teachers, not simply researchers who happened to teach. Magnified (largely unintentionally) through conservative critiques of universities and faculty members, Boyer's work occasioned discussions of faculty activities and rewards, even leading to the formation of "centers for teaching excellence" and similar enterprises on many campuses. More frequently, however, the effects of these professional agendas are diffuse, helping more subtly to influence educational climates. Even in such conditions, WPAs can benefit from even a passing familiarity with these groups.

One other prefatory remark: Ph.D. education is almost exclusively disci-plinary enculturation. Because disciplinary knowledge and conventions are so extensive and subtle, students spend their time reading and writing mainly to audiences who broadly share their interests and perspectives. Disciplines and their members reproduce themselves. This surely includes English departments, which beget the largest percentage of WPAs, and even includes rhetoric and composition programs, despite their historical embrace of interdisciplinary orientations. Owing to the very nature of the work, emerging graduate courses in writing administration promise to shift students' gazes slightly outside English studies, and it is possible for scholars such as Richard Miller to be taken seriously in calls for WPAs to become intellectual bureaucrats. Still, faculty members, especially those involved in graduate programs, take professional identities primarily from the academic discipline or subdiscipline, not the institution or broader educational systems. As a result, it is perfectly understandable why WPAs have tended to withhold attention from the educational organizations discussed below, have tended, even, to regard them with skepticism or contempt as the precious domains of administrators. Yet many administrators, boards, and pundits view loyalty to disciplines or departments rather than to institutions or publics as a continuing source of trouble, as described below.

The work that follows is divided into three parts. The first and most substantial section characterizes several educational associations and organizations, giving special emphasis to their current agendas and initiatives. The second briefly characterizes themes within the broad literature on higher education with which most WPAs historically have been fairly unfamiliar. The third suggests practical things WPAs might do to acquire useful knowledge about educational discourses beyond composition studies.

PART I: ASSOCIATIONS AND ORGANIZATIONS

There are well over a dozen significant national organizations devoted to higher education and its administration, by which I refer to entities whose concerns transcend or ignore disciplinary boundaries, focusing instead on student, faculty, public, and curricular agendas and the management of institutional resources. Beyond these organizations are numerous regional groups, institutes, and centers. Instead of comprehensively analyzing all of them, I'll focus on four whose efforts most directly affect WPAs, most important among them being the AAHE and the AAC&U. The Appendix to this chapter offers a more inclusive list and contact information.

The American Council on Education

The eighty-year-old American Council on Education (ACE), whose 1,800 institutional members include a range of colleges, universities, and other education-related groups, is devoted to coordinating higher education efforts. ACE aspires to function as a combination clearinghouse and partner to efforts by other organizations whose own web pages, for example, are linked via ACE's site and whose journals and publishing series are referenced there too. (The interconnections among these various associations are perhaps best exemplified by the physical proximity of so many at Dupont Circle in Washington, D.C.). Recent initiatives illustrate ACE's emphasis on "educational opportunity and a strong higher education system [as] essential cornerstones of a democratic society" (American). Those activities range from exploring how colleges might promote civic responsibility to raising public awareness about affording and financing college education.

Efforts toward creating a "strong" system include programs to change and transform institutions, and while change for ACE has much to do with curricular efforts, it also has to do with money. The organization convened a group, for example, to "address the high cost of tenure appeals and look at strategies to reduce incidents and costs" ("Initiatives"), and it sponsors the Academic Excellence and Cost Management National Awards Program to promote innovations that contain costs and communicate fiscal accountability. WPAs should understand that there are organized political efforts within higher education, not just without, giving impetus to enterprises such as distance education and two-tiered faculty arrangements. One organization is most striking in these pursuits.

Association of Governing Boards of Universities and Colleges

Perhaps the most resonant faculty-rallying cries are for academic freedom and self-governance—or, more modestly, shared governance. In recent years, faculty have deployed the rhetorical position that "the university is its faculty and its students" to argue limits to administrative authority, favoring, of course, the faculty portion of that identity, citing students' transitory and apprenticeship roles. By claiming their centrality, especially as organized around disciplinary knowledge, faculty have attempted to position administrators rather as clerical staff charged with keeping the institution running and in accordance with professors' desires.

Quite obviously not everyone shares this view. The Association of Governing Boards of Universities and Colleges (AGB) provides resources and guidance to college and university trustees, regents, presidents, chancellors, and "senior administrators," some 34,000 of them in all, in affiliation with 1,800 college and university campuses (Association, "About"). Much of the recent activity of the organization has been devoted to articulating the rights and responsibilities of governing boards and college presidents, and faculty perceptions that higher education is moving toward a top-down management structure are substantiated, at least in theory, by positions such as the 1998 "AGB Statement on Institutional Governance."

This statement forcefully asserts that governing boards are the ultimate authority in a range of institutional decisions. Strictly speaking, this has always been true, but the AGB seeks to extend this authority to levels that typically have been the province of faculty. Faculty members, after all, are "divided in their loyalties" between their academic disciplines and their institution's welfare, and internal governance arrangements have become "cumbersome" (Association, "AGB Statement"). In response, boards must exert ultimate responsibility for determining institutional missions, in consultation with "the chief executive"—though not, explicitly, academic senates or similar bodies. The statement, moreover, asserts that "governing boards have the sole responsibility to appoint and assess the performance of the chief executive"; this has long been true in an ultimate sense, but faculty roles in these processes receive no mention in the AGB statement. Boards must attend to colleges as "business enterprises," albeit ones that differ markedly from those in the for-profit sector. And boards must be wary of institutional policies and practices prescribed by higher education associations or disciplinary organizations; WPAs should not be surprised, then, that policies such as the NCTE recommendation on class size for writing courses or the WPA Outcomes Statement do not have force simply because groups of disciplinary experts have agreed on them.

I cite the AGB less because its workings directly affect WPAs than because it is important to be reminded that broad contexts for higher education are not always shaped with assumptions that faculty regard as foundational. AGB regularly releases reports, conducts surveys, and proposes policy issues. Browsing them, faculty might understand how beliefs that programs and practices should best emanate, naturally, from professors may meet structural resistance from provosts and presidents who are increasingly asked to represent constituents beyond the campus.

American Association of Higher Education

Considerably more familiar to WPAs—and more directly useful—is the AAHE. AAHE pursues a broad range of issues but has developed certain programmatic areas for long-term commitment, including assessment, faculty roles and rewards, service learning, and teaching. Each of these areas is coordinated by professional staff directors within AAHE, and as of this writing Barbara Cambridge, a former WPA and president of the Council of Writing Program Administrators, directs the AAHE Teaching Initiatives Project and previously led the Assessment Forum.

Whereas some associations are organized through institutional membership, AAHE's 9,500 members are individuals, a combination of faculty and administrators across disciplines as well as people outside of higher education. The organization sponsors several conferences each year, with an annual National Conference on Higher Education and other meetings devoted to assessment and faculty roles and rewards. The membership of the organization and the foci of its meetings and projects promote interactions across disciplines and faculty/administrator divides. For WPAs, an association such as AAHE provides not only a sense of how matters of concern are framed nationally by constituents beyond writing programs but also a means for work on local concerns. Administrators are frequently responsive to faculty participating in efforts they perceive to be not just a discipline but for the greater good of the institution, sometimes sending to meetings small teams that include deans or other campus leaders. For example, each year AAHE invites campus teams of six to eight people "in a position to influence their institution's next steps in undergraduate academic reform" to attend its Summer Academy (cosponsored by ACE and others). A WPA interested in transforming writing instruction on campus may find a vehicle such as the Summer Academy more effective than purely local efforts that lack a broader national imprimatur.

As I noted earlier, AAHE's ongoing projects will appear familiar to WPAs. The Assessment Forum provides extensive materials defining the topic, advocating principles, and outlining practices. Although we sometimes seem to forget it, writing and writing programs are hardly the only entities to be assessed on campuses. For the success of their own efforts, WPAs would do well to understand discourses of assessment broader than those within composition studies. The same can be said for service learning, another in-depth focus within AAHE, which has published a volume on composition and service learning, the first in a series, coedited by Linda Adler-Kassner, herself a WPA. Given composition's emphases on process, collaboration, peer work, and teacher intervention, writing programs have long been centrally concerned with pedagogy, at a time when other disciplines have not. However, WPAs' commitment and knowledge often are ignored due to the complex ways that writing instruction has been marginalized in the academy (Trimbur; Miller). WPAs would do well, then, to ascertain the possible involvement of their campus in activities such as the Teaching Initiatives Project, which may provide a vehicle for asserting their expertise in teaching.

Finally, WPA lore is replete with tales of tenure and promotion gone astray when institutions have failed to understand the intellectual value of administrative work. The Council of Writing Program Administrators has adopted a statement on these practices, which has been endorsed by the CCCC Executive Committee. The Modern Language Association's statement on "Making Faculty Work Visible" is also helpful. The AAHE Forum on Faculty Roles and Rewards complements these disciplinary efforts by raising wider issues about evaluating faculty efforts through numerous monographs and a series of working papers.

Association of American Colleges and Universities

Founded over ninety years ago by presidents of liberal arts colleges, the AAC&U now offers membership to more than 700 institutions, distributed almost equally across research universities, masters institutions, and liberal arts colleges; some community colleges are also included. Each member campus is officially represented by its president, chief academic officer, and three faculty members, although other faculty and administrators may became associate members. WPAs would find it useful to learn whether their campus belongs to AAC&U (a good occasion for a professional contact with the provost or dean, although the information is more plainly available via the Internet), who their official faculty representatives are (and if there are any openings or turnovers), and whether the campus maintains a list of associate members.

AAC&U differs from the organizations previously described by focusing more exclusively on curricular and educational issues, often from a progressive viewpoint. A sample of current initiatives, for instance, includes programs on diversity, racial legacies and learning, the status and education of women, science education and civic responsibilities, women and scientific literacy, and boundaries and borderlands. A substantial series of monographs and reports includes works in those areas as well as in assessment, general education, service learning, and others. Among these resources, one in particular stands out: a comprehensive set of electronic resources titled "The Knowledge Network" and available online at ⟨http://www.aacu-edu.org/KnowNet/index.html⟩.

Like other associations, AAC&U sponsors workshops and conferences, many of them organized around campus teams. For WPAs, the annual Asheville (North Carolina) Institute on General Education might be of particular value. Institutional teams gather to work on projects by themselves, with other groups, or with consultants, and presentations and workshops take up common issues. A series of ten-day institutes entitled "Boundaries and Borderlands: The Search for Recognition and Community in America" grew out of AAC&U's project entitled "American Commitments: Diversity, Democracy, and Liberal Education." Members of campus teams receive hefty packets of books and articles in advance of the institutes, whose long duration enable extensive cross-disciplinary exchanges and work on campus projects. Participation in the institutes is competitive (the 2000 meeting was restricted to forty schools) because they are subsidized by grants from the William and Flora Hewlett Foundation, the NEH, the Ford Foundation, and so on.

In fact, AAU&C, like most of these associations, operates significantly through grants in support of specific projects. Its "Preparing Future Faculty" program, sponsored with the Council of Graduate Schools, has been supported by grants from the Pew Charitable Trusts and the National Science Foundation, for example, and the Carnegie Foundation for the Advancement of Teaching has collaborated on other enterprises. The world of academic grant making is an intricate web of competitions and agreements among foundations and government sources, higher education and disciplinary associations, institutions or consortia of institutions, and programs or individual faculty. A "Preparing Future Faculty" effort channeled through NCTE by the Council on Graduate Schools and AAC&U, for example, relied on a large private grant. WPAs interested in external support for local efforts would do well to understand initiatives funded through these associations and should not be surprised that they may have to adjust their wishes to match others' agendas.

Other Associations and Organizations

I trust the four examples I've described will sketch the kinds of professional associations that exist. Brief characterizations of others add more lines to the picture. EDUCAUSE, for example, is devoted to transforming education through information technologies. Its membership includes some 1,600 colleges and universities and more than 150 corporations. The organization is interesting, then, for understanding how business efforts, especially those involving computing and networking, drive educational agendas and, perhaps, vice versa. EDUCAUSE sponsors professional development activities, pursues strategic/policy initiatives, and maintains extensive online and print resources. The Society for College and University Planning (SCUP) is more abstract in its focus, concentrating on the "promotion, advancement, and application of effective planning in higher education," leaving the ends of those efforts unspecified, although there is a slant toward the physical plant and institutional resources (Society). It aspires to serve primarily upper-level administrators, including presidents, provosts, deans, financial officers, and project managers, as well as architectural and engineering consultants.

WPAs can benefit from knowing the work of groups other than membership associations. The Carnegie Foundation for the Advancement of Teaching focuses on the scholarship of teaching. Perhaps contrary to expectations, the foundation does not award grants but rather uses its endowment to support its own research and publications. These activities have had considerable effect on higher education in the last decade, as reports authored by Ernest Boyer in particular have become part of the conventional lore about teaching reform, especially at research universities. The Carnegie Foundation is also source of the most widely used taxonomy of institutional types in American higher education ("Carnegie"), which familiarly categorizes schools as Doctoral/Research Universities-Extensive or Intensive; Intensive; Master's Colleges and Universities-I or II; Baccalaureate College-Liberal Arts, General, or Bacalaureate/Associates; Associates Colleges; Specialized Colleges; and Tribal Colleges and Universities. The Center for the Freshman Year Experience at the University of South Carolina, to cite a more restricted example, assembles information and sponsors conferences about, obviously, the nature of the first year of college, including freshman seminars, learning communities, and advising. Given the centrality of freshman courses to writing programs and the ways that schools increasingly look to first-year composition to carry goals beyond writing instruction, WPAs will find useful research and perspectives through this center.

Finally, although I have purposefully been ranging far from English and composition studies, I want to emphasize that WPAs shouldn't miss resources closer to their disciplinary homes. Most obvious, of course, is the Council of Writing Program Administrators, whose 700 members come from a range of institutionals and program types, from research university to two-year college freshman composition programs to writing majors to writing centers to writing across the curriculum (WAC). WPA sponsors a summer workshop and conference, a meeting in conjunction with CCCC, a research grants program, a journal (*WPA: Writing Program Administration*), a newsletter, a web site, policy statements, and a lively listserv. All WPAs should be familiar with a key position statement, "The Intellectual Work of Writing Administration," which provides guidelines for tenure and promotion.

Faculty in composition studies are well-acquainted with CCCC, the journal it sponsors, and its annual conference, but they may be less familiar with various position statements adopted by CCCC and its parent organization, the National Council of Teachers of English (NCTE). These include policies on class size and teacher workload, assessment, censorship, principles and standards for teaching writing, national language policies, tenure and promotion guidelines for work with technology, and many others. As WPAs try to change or justify campus practices, they are frequently asked to describe their efforts in relation to national standards. Familiarity with existing position statements, then, can save a good deal of time and lend weight to local arguments.

Historically, composition teachers have perceived less direct interest in the Modern Language Association (MLA). But this perception has scarcely been warranted in recent years. Not only has MLA increased its publishing list in writing studies, it has entered into an agreement with CCCC to publish a regular bibliography in rhetoric and composition. Both MLA and its suborganization devoted to departmental governance, the Association of Departments of English (ADE), have developed position statements valuable to WPAs, including guidelines for class size and workloads, guidelines on the use of part-time and adjunct faculty, and a statement on relationships between teaching and scholarship in tenure and promotion.

PART II: BOOKS AND PERIODICALS

As a consequence of job searching, most WPAs are at least passingly familiar with *The Chronicle of Higher Education*, a thick weekly in tabloid format that functions as a sort of *New York Times* or *Wall Street Journal* of higher education. (And if The *Chronicle* is the *New York Times*, then something like *Lingua Franca* is higher education's *USA Today*, albeit with considerably more intellectual weight.) As a source of job postings, from adjunct instructorships to system presidents, the *Chronicle* is perhaps the richest common in the higher education village. But WPAs should recognize the reportage here, from news at individual campuses to trends within individual disciplines, notes on scholarly books, notices of conferences, and extensive reports of national survey data on everything from faculty salaries by institution to student attitudes and values. Curricular innovations reported in the *Chronicle* will catch the attention of administrators more readily than will the same ideas presented in composition journals. For example, Dan Royer and Roger Gilles' *CCC* article on directed self-placement in freshman composition was summarized in a *Chronicle* e-mail sent daily to all registered subscribers. This caused more than a few WPAs' phones to ring around the country in the fall of 1998, as deans wondered if this apparent cost-saving practice might be adopted at their institutions ("A Glance"). Even the advertisements, centered increasingly of late on hardware and software approaches to administrative and pedagogical problems, help faculty understand some of the environment of academic administration.

But of course there are higher education periodicals beyond the *Chronicle*, including several published by the associations described above and, not surprisingly, sometimes representing organizational views. So, for example, an article in *The Presidency*, published by the ACE, may argue for the place of "remediation" in the higher educational system (Moses). At the same time an article in *Trusteeship*, published by the AGB, may argue of remediation that, "it's time to stop this practice, and if two-year and four-year institutions can cooperate, every college or university can meet its enrollment targets" (Koplick 22). I don't mean to imply that such periodicals have party lines but rather that they reflect as much diversity of viewpoints as, say, *College English*—and as little.

AAHE publishes *The AAHE Bulletin* and *Change*; AAC&U publishes *Liberal Education* and *Peer Review*; SCUP publishes *Planning for Higher Education*. Some of these periodicals have rather the flavor of professional trade magazines, while others are more scholarly, containing research reports, for example. Among these latter are the *American Journal of Education*, *Education Policy Analysis Archives*, *Higher Education Policy*, *Journal of Higher Education Policy and Management*, and the *Review of Higher Education*. It would hardly be worthwhile for WPAs to read many of these periodicals regularly. However, browsing tables of contents now and then can pinpoint academic terrains beyond the writing program, and may sometimes provide broader support for a particular program initiative. (I stop short of advocating using these journals as sources of conversation openers at academic parties.)

The national associations also sponsor extensive report, monograph, and book series, sometimes alone, as with the ACE/Oryx Press series on higher education, sometimes in collaboration with commercial or academic publishers. In respect to publishing, then, they function just the way NCTE or MLA does. As a result, the higher education literature in print is vast (though I will say that a fair proportion of it consists of revised conference talks and opinion pieces rather than thorough research). AAC&U, for example, catalogs dozens upon dozens of publications, a list that under only one topic of central interest to WPAs, General Education, includes the following titles:

Assessing General Education

Current Issues in Liberal Education: Meaning of the Degree

Integrity in the College Curriculum

A New Vitality in General Education

Strong Foundations: Twelve Principles for Effective General Education Programs

Handbook of the Undergraduate Curriculum: A Comprehensive Guide to Purposes, Structure, Practices, and Change

The *Handbook*, published in cooperation with Jossey-Bass, is a 700–plus-page overview of institutional issues and structures that can function as an academic map to WPAs.

Compositionists most familiar with presses such as Southern Illinois, Pittsburgh, and SUNY will need to look elsewhere for general higher education books—to university presses active in this area, such as Duke, Johns Hopkins, and Chicago, and to commercial publishers such as Erlbaum. The Heinemann Boynton/Cook of higher education publishing is Jossey-Bass, with which WPAs may be familiar as the publisher of Ed White's books on program administration, *Developing Successful Writing Programs* and *Teaching and Assessing Writing*. They may also be familiar with volumes in one of its

New Directions series, which the company bills as journals but which will strike many as freestanding volumes, each with a thematic title and table of contents, each with a different editor. Jossey-Bass sponsors eleven New Directions series, including ones for Adult and Continuing Education, Community Colleges, Higher Education, Institutional Research, Student Services, and Teaching and Learning. This last series regularly has volumes directly related to writing, such as Mary Deane Sorcinelli and Peter Elbow's *Strategies for Assigning and Responding to Writing Across the Disciplines*. The New Directions volumes are particularly useful for WPAs leading WAC or other campus writing workshops, since they generally contain a good proportion of practical advice to theory, in a form appealing to more general academic audiences, and at a cost within the materials budgets of many programs. Another important monograph series published by Jossey-Bass is the ASHE-ERIC Higher Education Report Series, produced in association with the American Society for the Study of Higher Education and the ERIC Clearinghouse.

Some titles map landscapes more exotic (and perhaps more frightening) to WPAs, especially those carrying traces of Jossey-Bass's interest in educational sites such as corporate training. Consider just one example, *The "E" Is for Everything: E-Commerce, E-Business, and E-Learning in the Future of Higher Education*, a book in which distance learning meets dot-com and the union is celebrated. Many writing traditionalists, even progressive ones, will be put off by the ethos of this and other books, which they may see as embracing the globalizing of the academy. Still, I recommend at least knowing the terms in which some would construct the future of education.

Space limitations prevent me from characterizing the literature of higher education in even the most cursory detail. To suggest some of its outlines, I've included a few recent titles in the Appendix to this essay, but they are less of a reading list or study itinerary than the equivalent of a smattering of travel brochures designed to encourage WPAs to imagine new intellectual destinations.

PART III: SPECIFIC RECOMMENDATIONS FOR WPAS

My purpose in this essay has been to illustrate the kinds of higher education conversations occurring outside English and composition studies and to suggest some approaches to those professional parlors. Along the way I've characterized current initiatives and programmatic foci. But these change as politicians, publics, and academics identify new issues. While concerns about assessment, the nature of general education, cost and access, and instructional technology are not likely to diminish soon, my explanations have been intended to explain how WPAs might understand broad academic discussions rather than to argue for their involvement in specific projects that, by the time of this publication, may no longer exist. Toward those ends, WPAs might follow two practices.

1. Discern which higher education movements and agendas are most important on their own campuses. Just because all these national associations, periodicals, and books exist doesn't mean that they are equally important from institution to institution. WPAs would do well to schedule meetings with deans, provosts, and other institutional leaders to find out which associations the school belongs to, which professional meetings these leaders themselves attend. They might ask simple questions like "What kinds of things in the higher education literature do you read if you have the time?" "What issues are most important in higher education these days" "Who or what group is saying the most useful things about that issue?" or "What professional meetings do you attend?" Busy administrators often have even less time to contend with the professional literature than do faculty members, so one has to be diplomatic when raising these questions. But as a way of building professional contacts with potential administrative mentors, the process of learning how the institution is aligned within various academic discourses is a useful one. Some higher education conferences and institutes are built around institutional teams, and in the course of learning about the state of things on campus, WPAs can identify themselves as potential team members. Particularly when assessment or curricular matters are prominent in a meeting agenda, WPAs and their programs can benefit substantially by being involved. Faculty members react, cynically on occasion, to a new program or initiative with, "Well, the dean must have just returned from a conference." Perhaps she did. Isn't it better to understand the broader context in which a new program is being constructed?

2. Identify what initiatives are being supported by professional organizations. This is the reverse side of my first piece of advice. Associations may be pursuing enterprises that aren't as yet issues on the local campus: faculty roles and rewards, for example, diversity in the curriculum, teaching portfolios, and so on. A WPA interested in making certain changes may do so more readily if he or she can tie them to broader national initiatives. When these initiatives carry grant possibilities (as, for example, AAC&U's Preparing Future Faculty program did), all the better. Beyond that, extracompositional meetings and publication venues open new discourse communities for WPAs looking to publish their work on program administration. However, a small cautionary note is in order, since English department-based colleagues are probably less likely to weigh heavily a presentation at an AAHE forum, for instance, than they should: building a tenure/promotion case that is too dependent on work "outside" English studies might not be rewarded. My suggestion, then, really has more to do with how local arguments are bolstered by their connection to broader initiatives than with how WPA careers are advanced through wider professional involvement. How might your interests as a WPA be forwarded by those initiatives?

At the beginning of this essay I suggested a self-preservation rationale for WPAs paying attention to wider discourses within higher education. Better, at least marginally, I implied, to end up like Galileo, alive and unburned by encounters with powerful institutions, than like Bruno, "right" but most emphatically silenced. I hope the preceding pages have provided something beyond cautions, however. WPAs ought to perceive more opportunities than pitfalls when trying to think like academicians other than English or composition faculty. And they ought to know why ideas for their programs may need fitting to worlds in which those ideas may actually find life.

WORKS CITED

Adler-Kassner, Linda, Robert Crooks, and Ann Watters, eds. *Writing the Community: Concepts and Models for Service Learning in Composition*. Washington: AAHE, 2000.

Association of Governing Boards of Universities and Colleges. "About AGB." 26 February 2000. ⟨http://www.agb.org/about.cfm⟩.

———. "AGB Statement on Institutional Governance." 26 February 2000. ⟨http://www.agb.org/governance.cfm⟩.

Boyer, Ernest. *Scholarship Reconsidered: Priorities of the Professoriate*. Menlo Park: Carnegie, 1997.

"Carnegie Classification of Colleges and Universities." ⟨http://www.carnegiefoundation.org/Classification/index.htm⟩26 February 2001.

Council of Writing Program Administrators. "Evaluating the Work of Writing Administration." *WPA: Writing Program Administration: Writing Program Administration* 22.1–2 (fall–winter 1998): 85–104. "Initiatives of the American Council on Education." 8 February 2001. ⟨http://www.acenet.edu/initiatives.html⟩ 26 February 2001.

"A glance at the September issue of *College Composition and Communication:* Student self-placement in remedial writing courses." *The Chronicle of Higher Education: Magazine and Journal Reader*. 29 September 1998. E-mail archived on-line to subscribers at ⟨http://chronicle.com⟩.

Katz, Richard N., and Diana G. Oblinger, eds. *The "E" Is for Everything: E-Commerce, E-Business, and E-Learning in the Future of Higher Education*. EDUCAUSE Leadership Strategies, vol. 2. San Francisco: Jossey, 2000.

Koplik, Stanley. "The Consequences of Remedial Education." *Trusteeship* 7.5 (September–October 1999): 18–22.

MLA Commission on Professional Service. "Making Faculty Work Visible: Reinterpreting Professional Service, Teaching, and Research in the Fields of Language and Literature." *Profession 1996*. New York: MLA, 1996. 161–216.

Miller, Richard E. *As If Learning Mattered: Reforming Higher Education*. Ithaca: Cornell UP, 1998.

Moses, Yolanda. "Taking a Stand on Remediation." *The Presidency* 2.3 (fall 1999): 20–25.

American Council on Education. "Mission Statement." 26 February 2000. ⟨http://www.acenet.edu/About/mission.html⟩.

Royer, Daniel J., and Roger Gilles. "Directed Self-Placement: An Attitude of Orientation." *College Composition and Communication* 50.1 (September 1998): 54–70.

Society for College and University Planning. "Frequently Asked Questions." ⟨http://www.scup.org/questions.htm⟩.

Sorcinelli, Mary Deane, and Peter Elbow, eds. *Strategies for Assigning and Responding to Writing Across the Curriculum*. New Directions for Teaching and Learning #69. San Francisco: Jossey, 1997.

Trimbur, John. "Literacy and the Discourse of Crisis." *The Politics of Writing Instruction: Postsecondary*. Ed. Richard Bullock and John Trimbur. Portsmouth: Boynton, 1991. 277–96.

White, Edward. *Developing Successful Writing Programs*. San Francisco: Jossey, 1989.

———. *Teaching and Assessing Writing*, Second Edition. San Francisco: Jossey, 1994.

APPENDICES

Selected Higher Education Associations and Organizations

American Council on Education (ACE)
One Dupont Circle NW
Washington, DC 20036
202 939-9300
http://www.acenet.edu

American Association for Higher Education (AAHE)
One Dupont Circle, Suite 360
Washington, DC 20036-1110
202 293-0073
http://www.aahe.org

American Association of Community Colleges
One Dupont Circle NW, Suite 410
Washington, DC 20036
http://www.aacc.nche.edu

Association for Institutional Research (AIR)
114 Stone Building
Florida State University
Tallahassee, Florida 32306-4462
http://www.airweb.org

Association for the Study of Higher Education (ASHE)
211 Hill Hall
Columbia, MO 65211-2190
573 882-9645
http://www.ashe.missouri.edu

Association of American Colleges and Universities (AAC&U)
1818 R Street NW
Washington, DC 20009
http://www.aacu-edu.org

Association of Departments of English (ADE)
New York
[Offices moving at time of this writing]
http://www.ade.org

Association of Governing Boards of Universities and Colleges (AGB)
One Dupont Circle
Suite 400
Washington, DC 20036
202 296-8400
http://www.agb.org

Carnegie Foundation for the Advancement of Teaching
555 Middlefield Road
Menlo Park, CA 94025
http://www.carnegiefoundation.org

Council of Writing Program Administrators (WPA)
Department of English
Miami University
Oxford, OH 45046
513 529-1393
http://www.cas.ilstu.edu/english/hesse/wpawelcome.htm

EDUCAUSE
1112 16th Street NW, Suite 600
Washington, DC 20036-4822
202 872-4200
http://www.educause.edu/

Modern Language Association (MLA)
New York
[Offices moving at time of this writing]
http://www.mla.org/

National Council of Teachers of English
1111 Kenyon Road
Urbana, IL 61801-1096
http://www.ncte.org

Society for College and University Planning
311 Maynard Street
Ann Arbor, MI 48104-2211
734 998-7832
http://www.scup.org

A Sampling of Periodicals in Higher Education

American Journal of Education: http://www.journals.uchicago.edu/AJE/
Change (AAHE)
Chronicle of Higher Education: http://chronicle.com/
Education Policy Analysis Archives: http://olam.ed.asu.edu/epaa/
Higher Education Policy: http://www.elsevier.com/inca/publications/store/3/0/
    9/1/0/
Journal of Higher Education Policy and Management: http://www.tandf.co.uk/
    journals/ listings/soc.html
Lingua Franca: http://www.linguafranca.com
Peer Review (AAC&U)

Planning for Higher Education (SCUP)
The Presidency (ACE)
Review of Higher Education: http://www.bc.edu/bc org/avp/soe/cihe/direct1/
    Review.html
Trusteeship (AGB)

A Sampling of Recent Books in Higher Education

Bates, A. W. *Managing Technological Change: Strategies for College and University Leaders.* San Francisco: Jossey, 1999.

Bok, Derek. *Universities and the Future of America.* North Carolina: Duke UP, 1990.

Brookhart, Susan M. *The Art and Science of Classroom Assessment: The Missing Part of Pedagogy.* ASHE-ERIC Higher Education Report Series 27:1. San Francisco: Jossey, 2000.

Cohen, A. M. *The Shaping of American Higher Education: Emergence and Growth of the Contemporary System.* San Francisco: Jossey, 1998.

Messick, Samuel J., ed. *Assessment in Higher Education: Issues of Access, Quality, Student Development, and Public Policy.* Mahwah, NJ: Erlbaum, 1999.

Mestenhauser, Josef A., and Brenda J. Ellingboe, eds. *Reforming the Higher Education Curriculum: Internationalizing the Campus.* Phoenix: ACE/Oryx P, 1998.

Murphy, Stanley D., and John P. Eddy, eds. *Current Issues in Higher Education: Research and Reforms.* Lanham: UP of America, 1998.

O'Brien, George Dennis. *All the Essential Half-Truths about Higher Education.* Chicago: U Chicago P, 1998.

Palloff, R. M., and K. Pratt. *Building Learning Communities in Cyberspace: Effective Strategies for the Online Classroom.* San Francisco: Jossey, 1999.

Palomba, C. A., and T. W. Banta. *Assessment Essentials: Planning, Implementing, and Improving Assessment in Higher Education.* San Francisco: Jossey-Bass, 1999.

Schmitz, B. *Core Curriculum and Cultural Pluralism: A Guide for Campus Planners.* Washington: Association for American Colleges and Universities, 1996.

Shapiro, N. S., and J.H. Levine. *Creating Learning Communities: A Practical Guide to Winning Support, Organizing for Change, and Implementing Programs.* San Francisco: Jossey-Bass, 1999.

Tierney, William G., ed. *The Responsive University: Restructuring for High Performance.* Baltimore: Johns Hopkins UP, 1998.

Toma, J. Douglas and Richard L. Palm, eds. *The Academic Administrator and the Law: What Every Dean and Department Chair Should Know.* ASHE-ERIC Higher Education Report Series 26:5. San Francisco: Jossey-Bass, 1998.

Professional Advancement of the WPA: Rhetoric and Politics in Tenure and Promotion

Jeanne Gunner
Santa Clara University

The professional issues surrounding tenure and the WPA have a long history. Looking at the articles and documents that have over time addressed the WPA's professional advancement, we get an archaeological view of the field of writing program administration, from its inception, professional formation, imbrication in the larger English Studies field (despite the still-lingering literature-composition divide) and, today, the claiming of professional respect as WPAs successfully move through tenure and promotion—a mark of systemic professional attainment, even if ironically reached at a time when tenure is a contested, perhaps fading professional condition. Still, the WPA in the majority of English departments nationwide is not likely to be working among disciplinary colleagues; that is, the WPA is still, in most cases, the lone expert in rhetoric-composition in the department. That makes for an extra challenge in preparing for tenure and promotion reviews, for evaluation in whatever shape of administrative position one holds. Because the familiar categories of literary specialization do not apply, the WPA needs to do a significant amount of educating and winning over en route to professional advancement. Helping colleagues to understand WPA as an academic and scholarly endeavor has been and is a difficult task, and it's likely to continue for some time to be the pivotal issue in WPA tenure cases. Finding time to do research and publish as we direct a writing program is a major challenge, but the level of productivity will not be a factor if the nature of our work is not first valued as scholarly, as in and of itself a foundation for tenure consideration.

When it comes to matters of professional advancement, WPAs, like other experts in rhetoric and composition, have as their greatest benefit their expertise in rhetoric and composition. For without question, such matters are deeply rhetorical, and success is intimately related to our ability to use our disciplinary knowledge to inform our professional self-representation. Professional advancement—the path that we follow as we accrue credentials and seek the rewards they make available to us—can be seen as a rhetorical and political matter involving multiple, often conflicting communities and requiring strategic mobilization of disciplinary and institutional power. Even though we typically think of advancement as a matter of individual achievement, career progress might better be defined as a process of forming memberships and alliances. Thus, professional advancement—in the form of tenure and promotion especially—is ultimately a radically collaborative activity, and success along the way means being able to communicate, negotiate, and convince.

It's difficult to generalize about WPA professional advancement. Our working conditions vary greatly from institution to institution; few norms exist for the position beyond heavy workloads and institutional politics. Our own backgrounds are also diverse: we may come out of literary studies, education, rhetoric-composition; we may have come into WPA positions after having received tenure, or it may be our first postgraduate position; we may meet with great institutional support or be completely embattled, in disciplinary and financial terms. We may find such situations can change rapidly, for example, with the exit of a "good" dean or pressure from a state legislature. Our motives for taking on the position might vary as well: for some, WPA work is itself a professional goal; for others, the only available route to an academic appointment is in an English department. Despite the array of institutional contexts and personal situations in the field, a few common professional issues nevertheless emerge from the work we do and the academic culture in which it takes place. And a few observations seem to apply in most cases. They boil down to these: educate yourself; do the groundwork; get involved.

For the WPA in particular, the need to recognize interconnectedness, or rhetorical positioning, along with means of agency, or political power, is especially acute. The faculty guide to the tenure process that each institution provides is undoubtedly essential reading, but equally undoubtedly reading that requires detailed and repeated contextualizing. No one road to tenure exists, even at a given institution, even among the multiple cases that come up at one time, and so the ability to read institutional contexts and to form professional liaisons is an essential skill in successful WPA career planning. And the ideal time to begin this work is at the point of defining it, when the job description and terms of advancement are still negotiable items.

Before this discussion can go any further, one essential piece of information must be highlighted, since it provides an immediate means of following the above advice. The first and best thing a WPA who is hoping to advance professionally can do is to join the WPA organization, the Council of Writing Program Administrators. The WPA is an academic professional organization dating back to 1976. It is the most important site of professional community, information, and support that any WPA can have, and joining the WPA is probably the best professional step anyone involved in this field can take. Its journal, *WPA: Writing Program Administration: Writing Program Administration*, is an outlet for WPA scholarship and a source of historical, theoretical, and practical knowledge for all who direct or participate in writing programs. The organization sponsors an annual workshop for new WPAs, an annual conference on writing program administration (the agenda for which is unrestricted, with topics covering a full range of theoretical and practical professional concerns), a research grant program, and a consultant-evaluator service (discussed below). Its members come from the full range of institutional types (community college, college, university) and positions (WPAs, WAC and writing center directors, writing program faculty). References to the organization and its functions will appear repeatedly in the following pages, for its work over the last twenty-five years has made its name synonymous with professional advancement. The following discussion attempts to identify the crucial stages on the way to tenure consideration. Individual WPAs will need to adapt the points according to their actual situations, but historical experience suggests that we can be active agents in enhancing the likelihood that program administration will be valued as the scholarship-informed work that, at its best, it clearly is.

PRETENURE PLANNING

The tenure process really begins at the point of hire. So much is established and decided with the initial appointment; the first contract forms the terms of the later tenure petition. That means that the WPA to be has a good deal of groundwork to cover before signing a contract. A truism for almost all academic careers is that the best time for negotiating special working conditions is before any contract is written; it's the time a pre-junior faculty member, as the object of institutional wooing, has the most negotiating power. It's an opportune time to show oneself to be professionally informed and politically savvy as well as to ensure that the conditions are in fact likely to allow one to compete for tenure later. Attaining balance in the demands of administration, teaching, scholarship, and service—not to mention private life—is going to be easier (easier—not easy) if plans have been made to allow for it, rather than if the need emerges out of a high-pressure, high-tension work situation several years into the position.

1. *Start with the job description.* In negotiating the terms of a WPA position, you can draw on the available external tools, such as the Portland Resolution (see Appendix B, this volume) and use them in relation to the institutional context you're entering. The first is the lesser challenge. The Portland Resolution, a document sponsored by the Council of Writing Program Administrators, provides a guideline for defining the WPA position and working conditions. It lists the array of responsibilities that might reasonably be associated with a WPA position, even as it clarifies that no one person ought to be expected to take on all such tasks and as it details the necessary support systems for WPA effectiveness. The Portland Resolution is a valuable document

to share with administrators as the terms of a contract are being discussed. As with any contract negotiation, the critical move is getting what is informally agreed on put into written form; having the Portland Resolution available provides convenient language for this step. A second document sponsored by the WPA organization, "Evaluating the Intellectual Work of Writing Administration," argues for WPA work as scholarly production, and having this document to share with administrators can again be a very effective tool in negotiating terms, especially expectations for tenure. It would be ideal to have a written agreement from the start that the scholarship of program administration will be weighted equally with traditional scholarly forms.

The contract you agree to shapes the work you will do and creates the program, department, and campus profile you will be expected to develop. The terms of the appointment should be explicit, detailed, and as comprehensive as possible. Start with a job description that is designed to allow for professional success. Ask for an official job description. If one does not exist, offer to collaborate on writing it so that it can be used as part of the employment agreement. Find out who will need to assent to it for it to have real, binding validity; this might include the department faculty and administrators beyond the department level. Study any description that is already in place. Compare it to the Portland Resolution categories. Consider the job title and ask about its origins, since title is often the site of conflicting values; a department that agrees to hire a director of freshman composition might have a different set of assumptions than one in which an equivalent position is called writing coordinator.

2. *Define Terms.* Carefully consider the job requirements as they have been presented to you and as you have observed are likely to exist. Articulate these for yourself, ask the department chair and other administrators who are negotiating with you to review them and make any changes, and use these "talking points" for contract terms. Is the course release for administrative duties equivalent to those duties? Is there course release for research? Is the WPA expected to work all or part of the summer? Will the contract and its salary terms reflect any such expectation? What staff assistance is in place? What is the WPA's line of reporting (chair, dean, some other administrator)? What is the length of time until tenure consideration? What are the publication expectations? Will a pretenure review take place? What travel support and research assistance are available?

3. *Negotiate the teaching load.* Measure the administrative duties in relation to the teaching load, and again in relation to the regular faculty load. Consider the relative amount of work involved in graduate and lower-division writing courses. Consider the scheduling of courses: might a lighter fall term help with the heaviest administrative work period? Consider the politically sensitive matter of directing a program but not teaching its primary courses—a complaint often lodged against those whom James Sledd has called the "boss compositionists" who direct freshman programs but teach only at the graduate level. The range of courses taught often correlates with a department's sense

of a faculty member's usefulness. And teaching freshman composition is a strong statement about the intellectual engagement offered by such work, a statement that might be especially meaningful in a research university context, where bias against composition's disciplinary status is often acute.

In any negotiation, you need to be as informed as possible about local values and institutional conditions if you're to be effective and avoid errors in judgment and expression. Rhetorical ability again enters into it, and any freshman guide to rhetoric gives us the relevant questions. What are your goals/purposes in the situation? Where are the points of common interest between you and the department and institution? Can you identify and articulate mutually beneficial terms? What means of persuasion are available to help the involved parties reach consensus? On which points are you able to compromise—what can you live with, and what is simply unacceptable? Are you ethically able to enter into a contract that does not meet your minimum expectations, knowing that you'll be back on the job market in a few years?

Defining terms is always a good place to start with any project, and in the case of signing on to serve as a WPA it's an extremely wise first step. But terms can be renegotiated, so it's not too late to review all the above issues even if you've been in the position for a year or more. The only bad plan is to use your tenure review as the opening point in a dialogue on institutional expectations.

The WPA who has worked out a detailed job description and terms of employment should have a head start on tenure case planning. If these two items are in place, then the WPA can focus on developing a specific tenure plan. This is a long-term strategy outlining the steps you'll need to take in order to arrive at the tenure review with the record of professional accomplishments and network of associates that will supply the strongest professional argument for tenure.

4. *Study the institutional guidelines.* It's obviously important that you do what any faculty member coming up for tenure should attend to. Be sure, for instance, to read the institution's official tenure protocols, usually available in a faculty handbook or other publication from the academic administration. Review these with the departmental chair, with a colleague who has recently gone through the tenure process, with a faculty governance leader. A systematic investigation into local tenure practices—think of it as a kind of ethnographic research project—can help you as you position your own case and can also serve as an antidote to local legends and horror stories, both of which abound on this topic. But a WPA's case has an additional feature that takes special handling, and that's the split nature of the position, the administrative aspect of the WPA's scholarly profile. Tenure has historically been associated primarily with research and publication, secondarily with teaching excellence, and almost never with administrative expertise. WPAs represent a new academic cultural form, and since tenure reviews are universitywide, few faculty members in disciplines other than English will have much exposure to or way of thinking about the professional and scholarly issues raised by WPA work.

Understanding the protocols helps you take active responsibility for your case. Clarify the order of events: the deadlines for submitting material, the policy on submitting materials after the file has left the department, the file's committee routes and dates of review, the point(s) at which you will receive feedback, the site of the final decision. Knowing the appeal policy in case of a negative tenure decision is also empowering; there is life after such an event, and you should be prepared to negotiate again if you feel your case is strong. The time frame for appeals is typically brief; once again, educating yourself and doing the groundwork is essential.

5. *Seek out mentors.* Seeking out a reliable cultural informant, an experienced faculty member who supports your work and can advise on your career progress, is another effective means of preparing early for the later tenure case. The ideal situation is to find mentors in and out of the department—a colleague who understands the department's values and procedures, and another from a different discipline and department who has experience with campus politics and committee practices. Mentors can help interpret WPA work to other colleagues and help the WPA see where the fault lines are— where perceptions of WPA work might be problematic, where some direct contact might help in educating colleagues—as well as where the minefields are likely to be and contact is to be avoided. The WPA has to take responsibility for making decisions about self-presentation, but mentors can provide perspectives not otherwise available. The mentor-protegé relationship has an interesting synergy, since the mentee's professional success becomes entwined with the mentor's. Mentors form a kind of investment group you can draw on: they can advise, support, and defend your work.

6. *Establish a prototype tenure file.* Spend the summer before you file the petition for tenure by beginning the file assembly process or revising the file—thus strengthening, not just collecting, the tenure documents. Begin early—during the first year is not too soon—to collect evidence of your work. The faculty handbook will detail the required contents of the tenure file. Develop a filing system that matches its categories (typically: scholarship, teaching, and service). Even if you don't have time to write a detailed report on a project you've taken on, you can drop a brief memo into a file folder so that that particular task can be described in full later. You might want to subdivide the scholarship file to include traditional and scholarly administrative work: curricular or assessment projects you design and oversee in the program, faculty development seminars you've designed, academic policy documents informed by research you've done, and so on, thus distinguishing such scholarship-informed work from the kind that is more usually considered administrative. Administrative work, too, should be documented: procedures you develop for scheduling, handling grade disputes, staff oversight, and hiring issues.

In the teaching file, especially if your institution places equal emphasis on teaching and scholarship, collect syllabi, assignments, and a broad range of sample student work. The student work should illustrate pedagogic methods and emphases: include portfolios that show student portfolio letters and multiple revisions with instructor comments, for example. It should also show the range of courses you've taught. Have colleagues observe your class (multiple times, if possible) and write a letter for this file. Since your courses are likely to be seen as models for the writing program, use the teaching file as an advertisement for your program's best features, and identify which parts result directly from your work.

Be especially careful in defining which aspects of your work will be placed in the service category, since much of what we know to be intellectual work for a WPA might appear to be service to those unfamiliar with the field. While a WPA's service work is apt to be more extensive and specialized than that of a regular faculty member, you might not want your service profile to look radically different from a typical faculty member's; you do not want to tilt the sense of the whole away from scholarship by creating a service-heavy impression.

7. *Arrange a pretenure review.* Many institutions require a midprobationary review, though the review's formality varies greatly from place to place. In most cases the goal is to help candidate and department measure the candidate's progress toward tenure. In some instances the results of the review have real bearing on the later tenure review outcome, since the initial review will outline in fairly explicit terms what the department expects the candidate to complete before coming up for tenure consideration (for example, finish a book, publish two refereed articles, teach a graduate course), and these recommendations become tenure decision criteria later. A pretenure review gives you valuable input, and if your department does not routinely review its tenure-track members, ask the chair to do so, or to adapt whatever evaluation procedure is in place to function as a "mini tenure" review, for your case.

To sound the theme again: WPAs have often been blindsided in the actual review process when they discover, too late, that much of their scholarly administrative work has been discounted. The risks are especially high in traditional literature departments, where not only scholarly administrative work but any work in rhetoric-composition may be seen as second-class, as not true scholarship. And such biases can prevail even in the most collegial environments; as with any unexamined bias, such views can be invisible to those who hold them and then surface at what, for the candidate, is a critically decisive moment. A pretenure review is an essential litmus test for the institutional values that will apply at the tenure review itself.

8. *Consider requesting an external writing program review.* The Council of Writing Program Administrators offers a consultant-evaluator service. For a fee, the council sends two senior members of the field, experienced WPAs, to campus to evaluate the writing program, its conditions, curricula, administrative structure—as many facets of the program as the reviewee wishes. This review can be extremely useful on multiple strategic levels. It can document via outside observers the internal strengths and problems of a program, help determine causes, and recommend means of amelioration. It can provide convincing support for a WPA's efforts to make structural changes in a program

or help convince administrators that certain institutional conditions interfere with important program goals—that more funding, for example, is needed for basic program work. Having two national-level colleagues who know you and your program is another benefit of the review; when the time comes either or both might be logical choices to serve as outside reviewers for your tenure file.

The review also entails preparing an extensive self-study of the program. While writing this report is time-consuming, it's a document that will be useful on multiple occasions. It serves as a prototype program description, gathering together essential information on courses, curriculum and pedagogy, goals, faculty, institutional setting, and WPA working conditions. It would be an excellent study to include in a tenure file.

9. *Get involved at the national level.* Professional development necessarily involves not only the WPA's work at his or her own institution but his or her involvement with a national network of area specialists—the larger WPA community. Being involved at the national level provides a WPA significant means of agency, in the field and at the home institution. Professional membership is a way of establishing professional identity. The benefits can't be overestimated: once you make national contact, a wealth of professional opportunities open up. There is really a network out there, and at whatever point you enter it, you gain access to professional projects and sites that provide opportunities for your own professional development. And when you come up for tenure, you'll need a community of scholars who can be called on to evaluate your work.

The Council of Writing Program Administrators is the primary site for national connection. Through it, you'll learn of and have a chance to participate in research and publication projects. Attending the annual WPA conference is a great way to enter into the conversation and activities the organization sponsors. Its journal is a valuable source of professional knowledge; it's also a possible publication site for your own work. Its articles form a comprehensive bibliography on the WPA field, and each issue carries announcements about grants, new publications, and other professional opportunities.

A related network is the WPA listserv (see the Introduction to this volume). With more seven hundred subscribers, it's an excellent forum for WPA issues, practical questions, and collegial support; it's also a very effective way into the professional community, since it allows you to form virtual relationships with WPAs across the country, many of whom you'll meet at the WPA conference, CCCC, and other national forums. On the list you'll see the formation of conference panel sessions, development of book projects, posting of job openings, answers to bibliographic queries, and even a discussion of tenure cases.. For new WPAs, it's a convivial and convenient way to become acculturated.

10. *Take charge of representing your work.* A WPA position is a political position, for many complex reasons. First, academic literacy is a contested site; traditionally defined as primarily a matter of adhering to standards, it ends up being (mistakenly) aligned with students' intellectual ability, even their moral worth, so defining and implementing standards of written competence (a job in the WPA's purview) can embroil the WPA in conflicts over academic

and social values. Second, the literature-composition divide enmeshes WPAs in disciplinary politics. A subset of this division is the roiling debate over labor, as in the exploitation of part-time writing faculty. The WPA thus is inevitably involved in complex issues related to status and economic practices. WPAs, especially those involved in WAC programs, are expected to be ambassadors for writing instruction and student interests. Because WPAs are identified with a low-status field, associated with teaching rather than research, the WPA, not surprisingly, may meet with resistance at worst or misunderstanding at best from colleagues across the institution. This means that the WPA has extra work to do in terms of professional self-representation.

When it comes to applying for tenure, self-representation is a critical part of the documents that go forward to department, university committee, and senior academic officers. The introduction to the file is likely to be a personal statement you prepare. Rhetoric and politics, once again, need to be the guides.

The two versions of an excerpt from a personal statement below came out of an actual tenure case: mine. I wrote the first version for the midprobationary review, the second for my actual tenure review. The first reflects a naïve and idealized sense of my position as WPA in an English department made up primarily of literary scholars. The italicized sentence is, in the first version, the only reference I made to the split nature of my appointment; I did not attempt to explain how my program administration work formed part of my scholarly project.

Personal Statement (I)

I came to my position as Director of Core Composition last year with the goal of synthesizing my interests in teaching, research, and administration, enabled by the departmental and campus commitment to integrated studies. This effort to unite the strands of my professional endeavors remains the cornerstone of my work, and is one which has been much assisted by the department's collegial environment and the generous professional encouragement I have received, in the department and University as a whole. I would like to begin by acknowledging this support and expressing my deep appreciation for it.

Directing Core Composition: The Integrated Nature of the Position

My position may be considered as split into two types of responsibilities, teaching/research and administration, but I have instead approached my work here as multiple expressions of a single mission. The teaching of writing is at the center of what I do, a concern that is expressed in as well as beyond the classroom, as it is enacted at the course, program, department, Core, and national levels. Through the curricula I have designed, my teaching is a point of fusion for my scholarly interests, for it enables me to draw together the study of writing, literature, and critical theory, fostering at the same time the department's commitment to a unified notion of English studies....

I did not interpret my areas of specialization for the audience, nor did I attempt to educate my readers about the scholarship of administration. The result was a positive review, accompanied by a recommendation that I delay coming up for tenure for a year longer than initially planned so that I would have the chance to publish more and to publish on "composition theory." The publishing I had done in writing program administration and basic writing theory was not visible to my readers as "real" scholarly work. My colleagues, all of them very supportive and well-intentioned, had a vague notion of what constitutes "composition theory," and clearly it did not include program administration or basic writing. Although I had been advised by a senior colleague—a would-be mentor—to explain my position and work in the opening section of the statement, and although I knew the local context—two individuals in rhetoric-composition had already been denied tenure, despite departmental support in both cases— I wrote without giving sufficient thought to audience and context. I was lucky to have the preliminary review teach me a lesson that was hard, but hardly comparable to the pain and chagrin of learning it at the point of the actual tenure review. I rejected the department's suggestion to defer my petition for another year, but only after I was fairly sure I had gotten a more realistic sense of the context and the strategies I could employ to counter a department's nervousness and lack of essential information about my work. I revised the personal statement in the following way. (Again the lines related to my position and work are italicized.)

Personal Statement (II)

The Department of English, which I joined as Director of Core Composition in fall, 1996, has been a congenial and supportive site for my teaching, scholarship, and administrative work, and the campus commitment to integrated studies has enabled me to pursue my interests in composition-rhetoric, literature, and writing program administration as a unified academic project. The collegial environment and the generous professional encouragement offered by the Department and University as a whole have enabled my recent professional achievements. I would like to begin by acknowledging this support and expressing my appreciation for it.

Terms of Appointment and Academic Specialization

Because my position differs from the usual tenure-track model, it may be helpful to review here the terms of my appointment. I came to Santa Clara as an Associate Professor with an agreement to petition for tenure in my third year. My position consists of 50% time spent in teaching, research, and service (with the weighting of 40–40–20 applied to this portion of my work), and 50% time spent in administration, directing Core Composition. In my file, I include evidence of my achievements in teaching, scholarship, and service, as well as my administrative work....

My areas of specialization within the larger field of Rhetoric-Composition (itself an area of specialization within English Studies) are Writing Program Administration theory and Basic Writing. In Rhetoric-Composition, the administration of writing programs is considered a scholarly field. A national organization devoted to this field (The Council of Writing Program Administrators, or "WPA: Writing Program Administration") sponsors a refereed journal (WPA: Writing Program Administration) as well as an annual conference. Many universities whose English departments offer doctoral degrees or specializations in Rhetoric-Composition offer graduate courses in Writing Program Administration theory (among these are the Universities of Illinois, Wisconsin, and Kansas, SUNY Buffalo, Purdue, and St. Louis University). The annual MLA convention program includes several sessions devoted to writing program administration theory, as does NCTE's annual Conference on College Composition and Communication. The WPA: Writing Program Administration organization works closely with the MLA, NCTE, ADE (Association of Departments of English), and other national groups on such issues as curricular standards, faculty development, and shared research agendas.

Included in my file is the WPA: Writing Program Administration-sponsored document, "Evaluating the Intellectual Work of Writing Administration," which helps explain the scholarly nature of the Writing Program Administrator position. It is not "administrative" in the usual sense of the term. At Santa Clara, in fact, the WPA: Writing Program Administration does not have responsibility for such tasks as scheduling and course assignment. Administrative duties of this sort differ from program administration, which entails the synthesis of research findings from such areas as composing theory, pedagogy, cognitive studies, assessment, Writing Across the Curriculum, and other fields of inquiry, to create an institution-specific writing program, support faculty development in teaching writing, and, through these activities, encourage students' continuing growth as thinkers and writers.

"Basic Writing," my secondary area of specialization, encompasses composing theory, applied linguistics, curricular studies, and pedagogy, with a focus on what was once considered "remediation," though current thought has reformulated this notion in more complex and theoretically informed ways. My particular interests lie in the politics of Basic Writing and historical study of Basic Writing theory.

My appointment thus reflects two types of responsibilities, teaching/research and administration. In practice, though, I have approached my work as multiple expressions of a single mission....

This section formed a preamble. After discussing my teaching (SCU is a liberal arts, teaching-centered institution), I then introduced my scholarly work with the following explanation/argument:

The Scholarship of Writing Program Administration

Influencing institutional practice has been a major motivation behind the scholarly work I have done in the area of Writing Program Administration theory. As WPA at Santa Clara, I have undertaken programmatic curricular revisions, initiated a major assessment program, made hiring decisions for composition classes, consulted with colleagues new or returning to teaching writing, advised administrators and faculty on campus writing policy, helped begin planning a Writing Center: these are activities that depend on scholarly expertise in the field of composition-rhetoric. No administrative policy discussion or decision of a truly professional caliber can take place without recourse to knowledge of the theory of the field and familiarity with national thought and practice—the kind of knowledge I bring to our departmental and campus considerations of writing.

In addition to reconceiving the purpose and audience for the personal statement, I did the same for the entire tenure file format, customizing the institutional rubric to meet the needs of my individual case and position. With the help of local mentors, national mentors, and generous colleagues in the WPA who knew my work from our shared professional community and served as outside reviewers, my petition for tenure was successful. Rhetoric and politics: use them as revision heuristics.

A NOTE ON POST-TENURE PROMOTION

Earning tenure is less an endpoint than a shift of relations. Like tenure, advancement after tenure is the product of path construction: of consciously choosing to seek out professional experience in areas that open up later choices. As with pretenure planning, it's not too soon to begin laying the groundwork for promotion as soon as one is tenured. For WPAs, the two most common paths in post-tenure career advancement are the traditional scholarly mode of publication and national involvement, and the administrative track of chair and deanship or other administrative posts. It's at this point that the split nature of the WPA appointment—its scholarly and administrative aspects—changes from being problematic because atypical in the academy to being a competitive edge on the higher administration track. With tenure comes increased opportunity for local and national involvement, in service positions, governance, and higher administration, and expanding one's work into these broader professional contexts is a substantial part of the case for full professorship.

The administrative track can involve administrative positions within one's institution, but one can also target administrative leadership positions in professional and government organizations. At the home institution, the WPA is in an excellent position to work with a broad collegial base, to demonstrate strategic administrative ability, and to learn about the various offices and interactions that make up the campus sphere of administrative power. Working on assessment is one way into extradepartmental administrative roles, as is curricular development work. WPAs who handle large budgets have a stronger background for dean positions than do those faculty members whose work is purely academic. If academic administration appeals to you as a career track, then put in the time on projects that let you develop knowledge of budget, policy, general education curriculum, and other related administrative activities.

At the national level, there are administrative positions in professional organizations and governmental agencies. Joining professional groups not only is an essential part of professional development but also opens up opportunities for committee membership, task forces, and elected positions. Such volunteer labor has extremely valuable training benefits. You can gain knowledge and skills in organizational leadership and budgetary matters in addition to the academic content of the work. This expertise then qualifies you to compete for professional appointment in the organizations. NCTE is one example of a professional organization whose leaders are drawn from its ranks.

WPA work is stimulating, challenging, and frustrating; it demands innovative thinking and patience with repetitive routines; it consumes one's time and opens up a multitude of professional opportunities. As with any career, the WPA position must be managed: we must both enact the role and theorize it in relation to contexts and values so that we come to the tenure process with the defined tasks completed and with the rhetorical and political expertise to represent our work effectively. WPAs can be tenured and promoted based on their administrative and other forms of scholarship, and each successful petition helps strengthen the claim for professional parity within English departments. May your case be the next to add to this trend.

WORKS CITED

Acculturation and Politics

Bishop, Wendy, and Gay Lynn Crossley. "How to Tell a Story of Stopping: the Complexities of Narrating a WPA's Experience." *WPA: Writing Program Administration* 19.3 (1996): 70–79. Derived from a near-ethnographic study of one WPA's daily working life, this article very effectively illustrates the political and economic pressures most WPAs are likely to confront. The authors ultimately question the possibility of truly professional status for WPAs. It is valuable as a portrait of the landscape in which a WPA must produce administrative results and also as an illustration of creative scholarship deriving from that troubled site.

Council of Writing Program Administrators. "Evaluating the Intellectual Work of Writing Administration." *WPA: Writing Program Administration* 22.1 (1998): 85–104. This WPA-sponsored statement provides a means of defining WPA work as scholarship, with the goal of helping WPAs present their work for tenure and promotion. The statement profiles the tenure cases of a literary scholar, a writing teacher, and a WPA. In the first two cases, we see the likelihood of a successful tenure petition enhanced by the cases having "clear exchange value" in the academic market; in the third case, the unconventional nature of WPA work makes evaluation difficult because it deviates from conventional academic careers. The authors argue that WPAs must help their evaluators define WPA work as intellectual—to see its "exchange value" in terms of the familiar academic professional paradigm. The statement offers explicit criteria for defining WPA work in this way (using categories such as program creation, curricular design, faculty development, and others), and it includes specific guidelines for developing WPA evaluation criteria. An essential resource for all WPAs.

Hult, Christine. "The Scholarship of Administration." *Resituating Writing: Constructing and Administering Writing Programs*. Portsmouth, NH: Boynton, 1995. 119–31. Counters the troubling question, "Is the position of WPA a career death sentence for its occupants?" with another, one that suggests a solution: "What is the scholarship of administration?" Defines this term as the "systematic, theory-based production and oversight of a dynamic program," comparing WPA scholarship to performance. Discusses sites and forms of scholarship, suggests evaluation measures for tenure cases, and describes an "administrative portfolio" for this purpose—a helpfully detailed discussion.

Janangelo, Joseph. "Somewhere Between Disparity and Despair: Writing Program Administrators, Image Problems, and the MLA Job Information List." *WPA: Writing Program Administration* 15.1–2 (1991): 60–66. A critique of English literature departments' views of the WPA position, with a focus on the career problems inherent in badly conceived appointments. Highlights the political challenges a WPA encounters, especially of tenure track; the dangers of a hybridized literature/composition administrative position; and the way exploitation of a WPA's labor is often presented as a "career opportunity."

Olson, Gary A., and Joseph M. Moxley. "Directing Freshman Composition: The Limits of Authority." *College Composition and Communication* 40.1 (February 1989): 51–59. A foundational article on WPA authority, much of the later discussion of the WPA position derives from this piece. Reports on research into chairs' perceptions of the WPA position and shows that these values have little or nothing to do with real administrative authority. The authors advocate putting exact limits of the position's authority in writing before accepting it and, in what has been the most influential part of the piece, argue that the WPA should always be a tenured member of the faculty.

Acculturation and Politics

Anson, Chris M., and Robert L. Brown, Jr. "Subject to Interpretation: The Role of Research in Writing Programs and Its Relationship to the Politics of Administration in Higher Education." *The Writing Program Administrator as Researcher*. Ed. Shirley K. Rose and Irwin Weiser. Portsmouth: Boynton, 1999. 141–52. Emphasizes the need to be able to "read" one's institution. Profiles a WPA at a Research I institution, where her program work ultimately did not translate into the necessary tenure "credit" but, despite her unsuccessful bid, where she gained enough expertise to compete for tenure at a smaller university that valued her program knowledge. The overall focus is on the split nature of WPA research—its local and national importance.

Barr-Ebest, Sally. "Gender Differences in Writing Program Administration." *WPA: Writing Program Administration* 18.3 (1995): 53–73. Funded by a WPA research grant, Barr-Ebest conducted a study of women WPAs and found their career situation, measured in terms of scholarly production, rank, release time, and salary, to be significantly different from—that is, inferior to—that of men WPAs, despite equivalent preparation. Provides a profile of active professional lives, details the stages of WPA career advancement, gives a table of common WPA tasks, and looks at the nature of published work in relation to tenure expectations and outcomes. It also shows the difficulty of balancing professional and personal life and suggests that WPA work has a negative effect on women's professional advancement, since such work, when performed by a woman, is more likely to be seen as service. Includes the story of Barr-Ebest's own tenure battle—ultimately a successful one, but complicated by the view that WPA work is not scholarly. Includes specific advice for WPAs, especially women, who are trying to advance and/or secure their careers.

Green, Geoffrey. "Welcome to Paradise!" *The Future of Doctoral Studies in English*. Ed. Andrea Lunsford, Helene Moglen, and James F. Slevin. New York: MLA, 1989. 47–51. Though this piece invokes a newly hired assistant professor of literature as its hero and is aimed at graduate students about to move into the job market, it satirically but accurately represents the acculturation process, showing how, from the start, new faculty are being evaluated, "sized up" for long-term promise—often by criteria that go beyond the academic and which may be affected by past department history.

Maid, Barry M. "How WPAs Can Learn to Use Power to Their Own Advantage." *Administrative Problem-Solving for Writing Programs and Writing Centers: Scenarios in Effective Program Management*. Ed. Linda Myers-Breslin. Urbana: NCTE, 1999. 199–211. Outlines a decision-making process for a tenure-track WPA faced with a politically sensitive administrative problem—in this case, an exit exam. Discusses how the author handled a real-life scenario of the same sort. The goal is for the WPA to take active control without creating tenure-threatening results.

Miller, Susan. *Textual Carnivals: The Politics of Composition*. Carbondale: Southern Illinois UP, 1991. Miller's book is the premier ideological critique of the WPA position and institutional purpose. It provides a systematic analysis of the WPA's problematic position in academic institutional relations—a theorizing of the WPA as the mediator of high and low social groups.

Peters, Bradley. "Enculturation, Not Alchemy: Professionalizing Novice Writing Program Administrators." *WPA: Writing Program Administration* 21.2–3 (1998): 121–36. Valuable for novice WPAs, the article describes the author's experience as a non-tenured "visiting" WPA. Having been immersed in the center of an English department's culture and political life, he reflects on a mapping process: a WPA should learn to "critically read" the program he or she enters, begin changes at the infrastructural level to attain a collaborative model, and then begin a "dialogue with the superstructural level" to plan for the program's future. He advocates a holistic enculturation of program and setting, with the WPA an active agent in this process. A careful, helpful agenda for a program administrator, whether tenure-track or not.

Recchio, Thomas, and Lynn Z. Bloom. "Initiation Rites, Initiation Rights." *WPA: Writing Program Administration* 14.3 (1991): 21–26. The authors describe their acculturation process in their then-new positions, one as a tenure-track WPA, and illustrate the critical importance of reading the local context—of "engagement in a dynamic process," as they call it. Their ironic tone as they cover the realities of contract violation, shifts in tenure values, and other horror stories of the newly hired does not diminish the accuracy of the picture they paint of common WPA culture-shock situations. They argue for making such situations the sites of productive change.

Schell, Eileen. "Who's the Boss?: The Possibilities and Pitfalls of Collaborative Administration for Untenured WPAs." *WPA: Writing Program Administration* 21.2–3 (1998): 65–80. In a discussion of WPA leadership styles, Schell analyzes the benefits and problems of a codirector position, with attention given to gendering/gendered professional issues. Ends with a set of questions that embody the challenges a tenure-track WPA faces.

Schuster, Charles I. "The Politics of Promotion." *The Politics of Writing Instruction: Postsecondary*. Ed. Richard Bullock and John Trimbur. Portsmouth, NH: Boynton, 1991. 85–95. [Reprinted in this part.] Addresses the "perception" problem—the literature faculty's view of rhetoric-composition specialists, especially those willing to take an administrative position. In an unforgettable analogy, Schuster suggests that WPAs are seen as versions of Boxer, the horse in George Orwell's *Animal Farm* "who works tirelessly and selflessly for the farm" and, inevitably, "collapses between the shafts of a cart while hauling a load of stone to the mill" (86). Like Boxer, "writing specialists follow their career track to its inevitable end" (87). In concluding, he notes changing trends and improved outlooks for professional advancement, even as he gives a historical overview of bias against rhetoric-composition as a scholarly endeavor.

Slevin, James F. "The Politics of the Profession." *An Introduction to Composition Studies*. Ed. Erika Lindemann and Gary Tate. New York: Oxford UP, 1991. 135–59. Takes us through the hiring of a fictionalized rhetoric-composition Ph.D. into a WPA position, in which she faces the kind of exploitative work "opportunity" Janangelo warns against. Details the job description problems, the institutional values that conflict with the job and therefore attainment of tenure, and the curricular beliefs that will make program changes difficult. A thorough and perceptive analysis of the political challenges of the WPA position.

Evaluation

Beidler, Peter G. "The WPA Evaluation: A Recent Case History." *WPA: Writing Program Administration* 14.3 (1991): 69–73. The author recounts his experience as a new WPA with a WPA consultant-evaluator review. He includes six of the specific recommendations that resulted and shows how the process helped him establish the professional, scholarly role of rhetoric-composition in his department. Beidler gives valuable advice for those who are thinking about requesting a visit from the WPA evaluation team—and he emphasizes throughout how helpful completing the required self-study turned out to be.

Council of Writing Program Administrators. "Guidelines for Self-Study to Precede a Writing Program Evaluation." *WPA: Writing Program Administration* 17.1–2 (1993): 88–95. An exhaustive guide to preparing a report on one's program, useful for an actual consultant-evaluator visit (an external program review) or for one's own local purposes. Provides detailed questions within the following areas: program background, including institutional values; curriculum; instructional methods; evaluation of and response to student writing; assessment; faculty status, working conditions, and development; program structure and context; the WPA position; and related instructional units (WAC, ESL, writing center).

Gebhardt, Richard C., and Barbara Genelle Smith Gebhardt. *Academic Advancement in Composition Studies: Scholarship, Publication, Promotion, Tenure*. Mahwah: Erlbaum, 1997. A gold mine of detailed discussions on professional advancement. Includes a WPA-focused essay by Duane Roen, "Writing Administration as Scholarship and Teaching"; also has pieces relevant to career advancement for writing center directors and community college, ESL, and basic skills faculty/administrators. Includes essays on gender and promotion, mentoring and external reviews, the chair's role in promotion/tenure issues, and a dean's view of the process. All of the essays are written by experienced current and former WPAs.

Jones, Jesse. "Evaluating College Teaching: An Overview." *Evaluating Teachers of Writing*. Ed. Christine Hult. Urbana: NCTE, 1994. 30–45. An overview of teaching-evaluation methods, the Works Cited entries provide valuable sources for learning about evaluation of one's own teaching as a tenure review factor and conducting evaluation of others' pedagogical work, a central WPA task.

"Responses to 'Evaluating the Intellectual Work of WPAs: A Draft.'" *WPA: Writing Program Administration* 20.3 (1997): 17–22. Three WPAs respond to the Intellectual Work document draft. Interesting depictions of different WPA situations and commentary on problems of evaluating a WPA's work, including the question of ownership of administrative/intellectual property—a question complicated by one's tenure status.

The Politics of Writing Promotion

Charles I. Schuster
University of Wisconsin—Milwaukee

Composition is a dangerous business, dangerous for reasons that I hope to make clearer in this essay. I don't intend by this statement that specialists in the area of rhetoric and composition are "dangerous" in any romantic sense. Those who profess writing and the teaching of writing are not swashbucklers or highwaymen; they are not the top guns of the academy. Quite the contrary, most rhetoricians, reflective of the discipline of English, believe in institutional values. They are conservatives—and conservators—in the tradition of Fred Newton Scott and John Dewey. Most love to teach and are profoundly committed to the pedagogical rewards that emerge from undergraduate and graduate writing classrooms. Many are schooled even as graduate students in the intricacies of administration and naturally are selected to administer programs in their own departments. Many of them are messianic about what they do, who they are, their talk laced with phrases about "empowerment" and "discourse communities," "enfranchisement" and "literacy." If they are revolutionary at all, it is in their zeal to promote writing as a fundamental activity of thinking and learning and to integrate it into all disciplines, *including* the study of literature. That such talk is "revolutionary" at all is part of the problem writing specialists face in their own institutions and their own departments.

English department faculty often view the writing program as the dark sister, the Maggie Tulliver of academe. The plight of such programs is that their faculty pervert the values of the establishment. Whereas most faculty in English find themselves awash in horror at the thought of teaching freshman composition, most members of the writing faculty choose to do so. Whereas most English faculty worship that critical entity known as "the book," with faculty prestige and salary depending entirely on publishing between hard covers, the discipline of rhetoric is driven like its sister, linguistics, by the article, the journal essay, the academic conference. Whereas most English faculty are at best disinterested administrators, most writing specialists are schooled in administration, quite literally, and take advantage of their expertise to develop curriculum and community support for their endeavors. Whereas many literature faculty define the classroom as an authoritarian field of inquiry in which professors maintain a privileged speaking role while students learn primarily through listening and imitating, composition faculty create collaborative classrooms and writing workshops, thereby undercutting the traditional professorial power structure. As a result of these differences, English department literary faculty often look upon their compositional brothers and sisters as incompetent, idiosyncratic, confused, valueless, untenurable. Thus the problem—a problem of perception, of value, of institutional pressures, of ideological difference.

READINGS

This problem of writing within the academy, within its own home department, is strikingly reminiscent of a well-known parable that has much to say about social aspirations and class hegemony. I am thinking of George Orwell's *Animal Farm*, with its analysis of authoritarian and democratic class structures, its condemnation of communistic inequities. Most of the "characters" in *Animal Farm* are venal, weak, cynical, or cowardly, but one character in particular possesses considerable virtues: Boxer the horse. Boxer is a proletarian hero, like Stephen Blackpool in *Hard Times*, and he meets an equally unkind fate. Orwell describes Boxer as "an enormous beast, nearly eighteen hands high, and as strong as any two ordinary horses put together. A white stripe down his nose gave him a somewhat stupid appearance, and in fact he was not of first-rate intelligence but he was universally respected for his steadiness of character and tremendous powers of work" (4). It is Boxer, along with Snowball, who preserves the rule of the animals during the Battle of the Cowshed. It is Boxer who works tirelessly, selflessly for the farm. While all the animals (except the pigs, of course) work long days, Boxer also works part of each night as well, hauling stone for the mill, bringing grain into the barn. Ultimately, Boxer decides to work harder: "'From now onwards I shall get up a full hour earlier in the mornings'" (72). Inevitably, of course, his strength gives out, and Boxer collapses between the shafts of a cart while hauling a load of stone to the mill. Squealer, that most unctuous of pigs, claims that the workhorse is being sent to a fine hospital, but we know better. It is the knacker who comes and takes Boxer to the glue factory; the pigs spend the money earned from the sale on another case of whiskey for their nightly revels.

In the polities of English departments, composition specialists are like Boxer—not always, not inevitably, but often enough to give this analogy genuine force. This is not because they are forced into the role by pernicious chairpersons or scheming deans, although they are generally required to do more than their fair share of minding the farm. This is not because there is a national conspiracy against the discipline of rhetoric. Rather, one finds a complex ratio of motivations, circumstances, and historic inevitability. In characterizing Boxer, Orwell notes that the horse has two slogans: "'I will work harder' and 'Napoleon is always right,'" and that these two homilies were for the horse "a sufficient answer to all problems" (53). So it often is for specialists in writing. The Puritans of English departments, they generally believe both in the ethos of work and, less fortunately, in the beneficence of authority. Their zeal to teach and serve smothers that other extremely useful instinct: self-survival through the salvation of publishing. Too often they lack the pragmatic, hard-edged, usefully complicated, ironic intellectual footing of their colleagues who know that the system rewards a belief in self, not community. Too often they believe that hard work, and hard work alone, will be their salvation.

Composition specialists thus find the role of Boxer an easy one to play: it fits their psychology, their sense of mission, their tendency toward professional martyrdom, their work ethic. Like Boxer, they believe in "working harder." Like Boxer, they are committed to improving the condition of their farm and know that it is they—and no one else—who can accomplish this goal. They are quite often the responsibility bearers in an English department, the ones who care about undergraduate education, curricular reform, high school–college articulation. Moreover, English department faculty find it easy to let them assume this role of Boxer: Who else would choose to do all the work of teaching writing and administering freshman composition? (That is, after all, part of their "stupidity.") Who else is better equipped to administer composition programs, serve on college and university committees, direct the writing center? Isn't that their training? After all, that's why a composition specialist was hired in the first place—to haul the stone and get up an hour earlier every morning even if it means career death at the age of seven. And, secure in their knowledge that Napoleon is always right, that rewards follow responsibilities as surely as government always rules wisely, writing specialists follow their career track to its inevitable end.

Most of us know stories of composition colleagues denied promotion and tenure. Brought in to teach writing, they taught writing. Asked to administer freshman composition, they administered. Required to publish in their discipline, they placed essays in *College Composition and Communication, College English, Rhetoric Review, Freshman English News*—journals often scorned by departmental review committees. Numbers of them founded journals, initiated writing-across-the-curriculum programs, developed campuswide writing centers. Even so—even though they met their professional obligations and were liked and respected by their colleagues, chairpersons, and deans—they were still denied tenure and/or promotion. Many of the most famous faculty in rhetoric and composition have, at one time or another in their careers, received some such professional setback. To list them here would be to write a veritable *Who's Who* of composition.

The genius of Orwell's *Animal Farm* is its applicability to a wide array of governmental and bureaucratic operations. Given the hierarchies that inevitably exist within a department, a university, it is equally inevitable that some individual, some class of individuals will assume the role of Boxer. For the past several academic generations, rhetoric/composition has hauled the stone. For many years, this work was literally done by women: spouses, part-timers, faculty adjuncts. In many ways, it is indeed "women's work," for the teaching of writing demands that an instructor be nurturing as well as demanding. It demands a collaborative, collegial, interactive relationship between teacher and student that is currently identified with a "feminist" model of teaching as opposed to a "masculinist" model. The masculinist model privileges lecturing, competition, a Darwinian view of the classroom in which students must prove themselves capable or be eliminated; such an individualistic ideology is utterly inappropriate to teaching writing and, I would add, to most teaching altogether. Unfortunately, it is the masculinist model that predominates and carries prestige; the feminist model bespeaks a "service" role that most English faculty find abhorrent. [See Miller.]

If we extend this psychoanalytic, gender-based model further, we derive another useful "reading" of rhetoric within traditional English departments. If the specialty of writing represents the female principle, then literary criticism (New Criticism, Critical Theory, even Feminist Theory) is the father, the husband, the phallocentric principle. After all, most English departments are defined by literature and literary critical interests. In large part, these interests establish curricular programs; they hire and fire; they constitute executive committees, graduate policy committees, chairpersons. They wield the wand of power; they constitute the maypole around which most of us parade our obeisance. Married to these figures (and an uneasy marriage it is) are the writing faculty, dutiful wives who do much of the dirty work: teaching writing, reading myriad student essays, training TAs and lecturers, administering testing programs. That is the primary function of the composition wives: to maintain the house and raise the children, in this case the thousands of undergraduates who enroll in composition classes. Thus do they conspire in their own oppression.

In *The Daughter's Seduction,* Jane Gallop applies Freud's and Ernest Jones's insights on male/female relations to describe a model of desire. For Gallop, male/female relations are always a step apart because the male desires the woman, but the locus of the woman's desire is the children. Says Gallop: "The man wants to be with his woman; the woman stays 'for the sake of the children.' This is not a balanced, symmetrical dual relation, but one of three parties. The child is to the woman what the woman is to the man" (24). The lack of reciprocity creates unequal relations, hegemony, resentments, resistance.

To disrupt this power relation, the "woman," I believe, has several choices. She can forswear her love of the child, abandon the nurturant role of "mother," and enter into a love relation with the man. She can become the man, adopt a phallocentric mode of being, and in the process either shed the need for the male or subject him, make him "female." She can attempt androgyny, for herself and others—both male and female—and thus inscribe a sexless world or one that is polymorphically perverse. She can expunge the male presence from her society, through ideological or even physical means, and adopt a life of homosexuality. She can redefine sexuality and sexual power relations, move from "desire" to "sexuality," from active/passive relations to one of mutuality and contiguity (Gallop 28–32). No matter which choice she takes, she (and her male lover) will likely need long-term counseling, made all the harder because he possesses no understanding of her dilemma, no innate sympathy to serve as a spur to reform, and every reason to maintain the status quo. From his perspective the status quo is all he knows and all he needs to know: her role in life is after all a biologic imperative, as inevitable as hiring and firing composition faculty.

Part of the problem results from the inevitable hierarchic relations that obtain within the academy. University life is class life, almost feudal in its stipulation of working class and ruling class. Not only are professors at the top and students at the bottom, but such positioning also exists in relation to what we study, what we write and analyze. According to Nancy Comley and Robert Scholes, the discipline of English is characterized by binary oppositions based on "value": literature and nonliterature, imaginative expression and expository writing, consumption (the reading of approved texts) and production (the writing of student essays). In such a pairing, it is the second of each of these terms that is subordinate, less valued, less rewarded. Within the college English classroom, Comley and Scholes describe a hierarchy of four levels of writing with literature at the top and "student compositions" at the bottom (Emig 173). Thus those of us whose world is permeated with student writing are by definition among the expendable lower class; we are laborers, factory workers, piece workers. Such work may be necessary, but it is not important enough to reward with salary, benefits, and tenure. Often it is only in administration that one finds salvation; comp directors are sometimes seen as valuable—at least as long as they agree to run the writing program. As the dean of my previous university asked in 1984: "If we granted Charles Schuster tenure, what would he do in the English department once he no longer directed the composition program? What in the world *could* he do?" Like Boxer, I would have to be sent to the knacker as soon as I no longer hauled the stone.

As James Berlin has made clear, this kind of thinking has been characteristic of American university life for the past 75 to 100 years and is only just now beginning to change. It is a philosophy of education that has presumed that students must "learn" composition before graduating from high school, that "poetic" expression is privileged and "rhetorical" forms impoverished, that the teaching of writing is essentially a skills-based, form-based, error-based, handbook-based activity which assumes that writing is a mere transcription of thought, a basic activity like riding a bicycle that once learned is never forgotten (Berlin chs. 2 and 3 in particular). Nor is this "philosophy of English" accidental; as Berlin states:

> In tacitly supporting the impoverished notion of rhetoric found in the freshman writing course, academic literary critics have provided a constant reminder of their own claim to superiority and privilege, setting the range and versatility of their discipline against the barrenness of current-traditional rhetoric, the staple of the freshman course. (28)

The value of teaching literature is more self-evident: it extends the reach of culture and creates a shared sympathy and understanding of aesthetic objects. It develops multicultural awareness, unpacks the mind, makes us more sensitive to the imaginative powers of language. The value of teaching writing is inevitably suspect, as Trimbur, Miller make clear, and thus must be contained within a basic-skills ideology. Such a view, of course, runs counter both to the two thousand year tradition of rhetoric within Western culture and to the view of most rhetoric and composition specialists that writing is constitutive to thinking and being (see Neel's excellent analysis, especially ch. 6). The wonder is not that the discipline of writing is in such a sorry condition but that it is in any condition at all.

WRITINGS

Only five years ago, this essay might have continued as an almost endless keening. But recent developments suggest a turning point in the relations between writing specialists and their departmental and university colleagues. The past 25 years have seen a resurgence of interest in composition, a dramatic revaluation of the fundamental importance of writing, a revitalized understanding of the institutional and disciplinary importance of rhetoric as a discipline. The Modern Language Association has created the Division of Teaching Writing and is beginning to attract specialists who are promoting interest in subjects rhetorical such as literacy, the essay, and discourse theory. Jobs for assistant professors specializing in writing and rhetoric abound; indeed, there are many more positions than qualified candidates to fill them. Although some rhetoricians have still been denied tenure and promotion, more of them have achieved those career goals and a small number have also been appointed to distinguished chairs (at the Universities of Mississippi and Connecticut and Texas Christian University to name just three). The number of registrants for the Conference on College Composition and Communication continues to climb, as does the number of scholarly journals and private and university presses demonstrating a significant commitment to publishing work in rhetoric and composition. Although work in "writing" is still difficult to publish, especially book-length projects, the situation is improved. More and more English departments are agreeing to allow writing specialists to publish work in their own refereed journals rather than requiring them to work by day in comp and then moonlight by publishing in lit. In large part, these positive developments reflect a general understanding that individuals specializing in that baggy discipline known variously as rhetoric, composition, and writing instruction can claim the right to work for promotion within their chosen field—even if evaluating that work remains a difficult problem for many departments and divisional committees.

Improvement notwithstanding, there are certain actions that I would recommend to produce a healthier climate for both specialists in rhetoric and the English departments they serve. Significant reforms are needed, all the harder to obtain because they must come about through a change of mind, a shift in the value structure. Unfortunately there is no reason for established and powerful faculty to foster reforms that will inevitably disrupt the pedagogy and politics of English departments, even if those changes have a positive effect on the discipline as a whole. Departments, like the institutions they serve, respond to new developments slowly and cautiously; fortunately, both history and what is being called "the literacy crisis" are creating an urgency toward reform. Without continued, positive change, English departments may well find themselves losing their composition programs and their student-credit-hour power base as writing specialists heed the advice of Maxine Hairston and form their own departments. Such a move, I think, would be unfortunate but it will also become inevitable unless the literature faculty achieve a genuine, productive relationship with their colleagues in rhetoric and writing. To forestall such a consequence—or others equally unfortunate—I think the discipline of English needs to transform itself in light of recent historical and disciplinary developments.

For example, English departments should strongly consider becoming departments of rhetoric—or departments of textual studies or departments of discourse. Jasper Neel, for example, celebrates the sophistic tradition of rhetoric and concludes that "for Isocrates, as well as for his teacher Gorgias and his predecessor Protagoras, rhetoric and writing belong at the center of the curriculum because rhetoric and writing are the ways to make choices in a world of probability" (211). Jonathan Culler believes that the essential focus of our attention should be "on two correlated networks of convention: writing as an institution and reading as an activity" (131). Although Culler is mainly interested in proposing structuralist poetics as "the theory of the practice of reading" (259), his emphasis on rhetoric and the constitutive importance of reading and writing echoes a similar argument that John Gerber made twenty years ago. Gerber, one of the original founders of the Conference on College Composition and Communication and one of the handful of great English department chairs during the 1960s and 1970s, argued that English departments had one goal: to train "our contemporaries to read and write" (20). Although modestly stated, this formulation describes the essential mission of English: how to read literary and rhetorical texts—and how to produce them. Such a reorientation does not require a name change; rather, it requires a sea change, a change of view. It requires that faculty concern themselves with how writers make meaning, with notions of textual production and interpretation, with the ways that culture shapes understanding by and through written discourses.

Graduate training in English departments should assume a leadership position in promoting this point of view. Of course, faculty create graduate programs and must believe in their own curriculum. I would hope that all faculty could subscribe to the description I have just offered. Whatever their differences, English faculty must conceive of our discipline broadly so as to include the analysis and production of poetry, novels, essays, film, business writing. Our responsibility as an English department faculty is to engage a whole variety of written discourses—from a freshman student essay to *King Lear*—in order to promote better reading and writing. Our graduate students must learn how to teach, conduct research, write, and reflect. They must become theoreticians of their own methodologies, self-reflective word processors, philosophers of language. Graduate training that reflects this definition will collapse the distinctions between "literature" and "writing instruction" and rehabilitate the discipline of English. In many cases, graduate training drives the department, and inevitably those graduate students become the future of our discipline.

Departments should sponsor faculty colloquia on the issues confronting our discipline. Department-specific, these colloquia might consider "the focus of our introductory literature course" or "improving the writing of our undergraduate English majors." I would urge departments to establish a "long-range planning committee" to think through such issues and promote productive debate among the various interests represented within the department. Such discussion is in the interests of all parties. As Stephen North has made clear, English departments have become "literary studies" departments in part by eliminating speech, theater, linguistics—that is, by so narrowing themselves as to become intolerant, fragile, irritable, and querulous. North argues that "in view of this stultifying homogeneity, composition, with its vital methodological diversity, constitutes new blood that English departments need very badly" (19). Clearly faculty in literary studies have at least as much to gain by such conversation and reform as those in writing.

Departments need to reevaluate teaching loads in regard to teaching composition. A typical literature class requires a faculty member to prepare lectures or discussions after reading (or rereading) a text; it usually requires little or no writing from the students. A typical composition class requires that a professor create a curriculum, assign writing (preferably two to three times a week), and respond to that writing thoughtfully. Rewarding as that work is, it is also constant and often overwhelming. Citing Richard Lloyd-Jones, Charles Altieri states that

> when the emphasis is on reading papers, the teacher approaches each composition as a human attempt at self-expression, looks for the writer's purpose, sees how well it is realized, and tries to help the person gain a richer understanding of the issue and find better rhetorical strategies. Consider now the plight of someone teaching thirty or thirty-five students in a class, with three such sections in a quarter. This is more students than one would have in classes on simple skills like tennis. We know that fifteen can be taught well, but even forty-five in three classes for a quarter, to say nothing of every quarter, become a severe drain on the attention and sympathy a teacher can offer individual writers. (Literature teachers, in contrast, can attend to only a few chosen students who support their self-image.) (27)

As Altieri implies, composition faculty consider teaching literature like going on a paid vacation, the work load being so much lighter. If faculty trained in writing instruction are to teach composition—and most of them both need and want to do just that—then departments must provide them compensatory release time so they can pursue their own research and publication. In my view, a writing class should count at least as a double teaching load: If a typical load for a literature professor is six courses a year, then a professor of composition should teach only three.

Departments need to reevaluate the importance of teaching, particularly the importance of teaching undergraduate composition. To quote Charles Altieri once again:

> The average regular faculty member (or, worse, the temporary staff member) who teaches composition faces a potentially rewarding task but must continually bear witness to the waste of human potential. Guilt and frustration vie with each other to suppress rage, until despair seems a state of relief and comfort. No wonder the self-delight of teaching literature becomes an alternative so enviable that the composition instructor only waits for the day when he or she can join the elite. Then the teacher can share the blind righteousness of colleagues in other disciplines as they glibly complain to classes of ten or fifteen that the students cannot express themselves. (27)

For Altieri, writing in *The ADE Bulletin,* the answer is for the ADE to "prepare and circulate to deans [I would add departmental chairs as well] a statement on qualifications for promotion and tenure in English departments. The statement must make clear what is distinctive about the teaching of writing and reading, and it must suggest, following the model of the class-size statement, that different kinds of institutions need different standards" (26). Such a statement is long overdue, and it should be reinforced by genuine departmental commitment to tenuring and promoting faculty who have demonstrated excellence in the teaching of reading and writing. Additionally, departments must recognize the contributions made by many writing faculty to the community; these faculty develop specialized courses for K–12 English teachers and create in-service programs, writing workshops, word-processing facilities, and other programs that strengthen that essential bond between public school and college English teachers. Except perhaps in the two percent of graduate English departments in America that place an exclusive premium on scholarly publication, such a valuation of teaching writing is essential.

Departments need to hire assistant professors in rhetoric and composition as colleagues and specialists, not as administrators and not as temporary staff members. No departments I know of would hire a beginning assistant professor of literature to chair the department or direct the graduate program. Yet these same departments choose freshly minted PhDs to direct writing centers and composition programs. Such a strategy undermines both the candidates and the programs they are asked to develop. Tenure and promotion confer equality, authority, power, influence. An untenured assistant professor who directs composition makes every decision with one eye glancing toward her senior colleagues and the other toward the dean. Moreover, administering a program drains away time best devoted to teaching, research, and

publication. And it often makes enemies of certain colleagues, since the interests of a composition program inevitably conflict at certain points with those
of the graduate or undergraduate literature programs. Departments should
hire colleagues, not administrators. Writing specialists must define themselves—and be defined by their departmental peers—as colleagues in order
to survive the tenure wars in their departments.

Departments should hire, whenever possible, at least one senior professor in the area of rhetoric and composition. Whenever I advise job candidates
in rhetoric, my first suggestion is "go where a senior colleague will protect
you." Departments need to hire at a senior level so that a representative of the
writing interest will be free to speak, to serve, to vote, to support the growth
and development of writing within the department and the university, and
to protect assistant professors.

Finally, the most essential reform is to remind ourselves that reading and
writing, literature and composition comprise a necessary and dialogic relation within every English department. I mean this in the most Bakhtinian of
senses. A dialogic relation maintains the power of both terms; indeed, each
constitutes the other even in their oppositeness. This sustained but delicate
relation is akin to the Bakhtinian concept of *vzhivanie*, which Gary Morson
and Caryl Emerson translate as "'live entering' or 'living into'" (10). "In
vzhivanie," Morson and Emerson explain, "one enters another's place *while
still maintaining one's own place*, one's own 'outsideness,' with respect to the
other" (11). Disciplines live on one another's borders; this is particularly true
of textual production and textual analysis, two complementary views of
the same event.

Literature and composition are complements of each other; rather than
oppositional they are appositional, each educating students to the reach and
grasp of language. I have no doubt that future historians who assess the
diminished power and influence of literary studies in America during the past
twenty-five years will locate this failure at the disjuncture between the study
of literary texts and the study of written production. This artificial distinction
must be erased if the discipline of English Studies is to be healthy, and only a
healthy discipline can incorporate difference by rewarding specialists in both
reading and writing with tenure and promotion.

WORKS CITED

Altieri, Charles. "The ADE and Institutional Polities: The Examples of Tenure and
    Composition." *ADE Bulletin* 74 (Spring 1983): 24–27.
Berlin, James. *Rhetoric and Reality: Writing Instruction in American Colleges,
    1900–1985.*Studies in Writing and Rhetoric. Carbondale: Southern Illinois
    UP, 1987.
Culler, Jonathan. *Structuralist Poetics: Structuralism, Linguistics, and the Study of Litera-
    ture.* London: Routledge, 1975.
Emig, Janet. *The Web of Meaning.* Portsmouth, NH: Boynton, 1983.

Gallop, Jane. *The Daughter's Seduction: Feminism and Psychoanalysis.* Ithaca: Cornell UP, 1982.

Gerber, John C. "Suggestions for a Commonsense Reform of the English Curriculum." *The Writing Teacher's Sourcebook.* Ed. Gary Tate and Edward Corbett, New York: Oxford UP, 1981. 20–26.

Hairston, Maxine. "Breaking Our Bonds and Reaffirming Our Connections." *College Composition and Communication* 36 (1985): 272–82.

Miller, Susan. "The Feminization of Composition." *The Politics of Writing Instruction: Postsecondary.* Ed. Richard Bullock and John Trimbur. Portsmouth, NH: Boynton, 1991. 39-53.

Morson, Gary Saul, and Caryl Emerson, eds. *Rethinking Bakhtin: Extensions and Challenges.* Evanston: Northwestern UP, 1989.

Neel, Jasper, *Plato, Derrida, and Writing.* Carbondale: Southern Illinois UP, 1988.

North, Stephen M. "Research in Writing, Departments of English, and the Problem of Method." *ADE Bulletin* 88 (Winter 1987): 13–20.

Orwell, George. *Animal Farm.* New York: Harcourt, 1946.

Trimbur, John. "Literacy and the Discourse of Crisis." *The Politics of Writing Instruction: Postsecondary.* Ed. Richard Bullock and John Trimbur. Portsmouth, NH: Boynton, 1991. 277-95.

PART VI

APPENDICES

Appendix A
Statement of Principles and Standards for the Postsecondary Teaching of Writing

INTRODUCTION: WRITING INSTRUCTION IN AMERICAN COLLEGES—THE COMMITMENT TO EDUCATIONAL QUALITY

A democracy demands citizens who can read critically and write clearly and cogently. Developing students' powers as critical readers and writers demands in turn the highest quality of instruction. This quality is the goal to which the Conference on College Composition and Communication (CCCC), the learned society founded in 1949 to serve as the professional association for college teachers of writing, is committed. And yet the achievement of this goal is at risk, for the quality of writing instruction is today seriously compromised. The purpose of this document is to examine the conditions that undermine the quality of postsecondary writing instruction and to recommend alternatives to those conditions.

Quality in education is intimately linked to the quality of teachers. Higher education traditionally ensures this quality by providing reasonable teaching loads, research support, and eventual tenure for those who meet rigorous professional standards. Such standards are applied and such support extended to virtually all faculty in higher education—but rarely to those who teach writing. At all levels of the academic hierarchy current institutional practices endanger the quality of education that writing teachers can offer their students. The teaching, research, and service contributions of tenure-track composition faculty are often misunderstood or undervalued. At some postsecondary institutions such faculty members are given administrative duties without the authority needed to discharge them; at others they are asked to meet publication standards without support for the kind of research that their discipline requires. The English graduate students who staff many writing programs are regularly assigned teaching duties that they cannot responsibly discharge without neglecting their own course work.

More disturbing still is the situation of those college teachers of writing who now constitute an enormous academic underclass. More than half the English faculty in two-year colleges, and nearly one-third of the English faculty at four-year colleges and universities, work on part-time and/or temporary appointments. Almost universally, they are teachers of writing, a fact that many consider the worst scandal in higher education today. These teachers work without job security, often without benefits, and for wages far below what their full-time colleagues are paid per course. Increasingly, many are forced to accept an itinerant existence, racing from class to car to drive to another institution to teach. The CCCC recognizes, with respect and gratitude, the extraordinary contributions that so many of these teachers have made to their students and schools. But it is evident that their working conditions undermine the capacities of teachers to teach and of students to learn. These conditions constitute a crisis in higher education, one that dramatically affects the public interest.

"The responsibility for the academy's most serious mission... should be vested in tenure-track faculty."

This crisis must concern all faculty and administrators at postsecondary institutions. As the American Association of University Professors (AAUP) has affirmed, when institutions depend increasingly on faculty whose positions are tenuous and whose rights and privileges are unclear or nonexistent, those freedoms established as the right of full-time tenurable and tenured faculty are endangered. Moreover, the excessive reliance on marginalized faculty damages the quality of education. Even when, as is often the case, these faculty bring to their academic appointments the appropriate credentials and commitments to good teaching, their low salaries, poor working conditions, and uncertain futures mar their effectiveness and reduce the possibilities for loyalty to the institution's educational goals. All lose: teachers, students, schools, and ultimately a democratic society that cannot be without citizens whose education empowers them to read and write with critical sophistication.

With these considerations in mind, and in response to the many educators who have requested our help in developing standards for effective writing programs, we provide the following guidelines. These guidelines are based on the assumption that the responsibility for the academy's most serious mission, helping students to develop their critical powers as readers and writers, should be vested in tenure-track faculty. That is the standard to which every institution should aspire. Because assumptions to the contrary have become well-entrenched in institutions of higher learning during the past fifteen years, however, we offer guidelines as well for the professional recognition and treatment of part-time and temporary full-time faculty during the period when these positions are being transformed to the tenure track. It is our hope and expectation that this period of transition will be brief. Ultimately, every institution should extend to teachers of writing the same opportunities for professional advancement (e.g., tenure and promotion) and the same encouragement of intellectual achievement (e.g., support for research and reasonable teaching responsibilities) that they extend to all other faculty. As colleges have the right to expect of writing specialists the highest level of performance, so they have the obligation to extend the greatest possible support. To do less is to compromise writing instruction for future generations of American students.

I: PROFESSIONAL STANDARDS THAT PROMOTE QUALITY EDUCATION

Tenure-track Faculty

To provide the highest quality of instruction, departments offering composition and writing courses should rely on full-time tenured or tenure-track faculty members who are both prepared for and committed to the teaching of writing. The teaching of writing courses need not be limited, however, to those faculty members whose primary area of scholarship is rhetoric and composition. Because of the significant intellectual and practical connections between writing and reading, composition and literature, it is desirable that faculty from both areas of specialization teach in the composition program. Ideally, faculty from each area should have the training and experience necessary to teach in both the literature and composition programs.

Whenever possible, faculty professionally committed to rhetoric and composition should coordinate and supervise composition programs. Evidence of this commitment can be found in research and publication, participation in professional conferences, and active involvement in curriculum development and design. Those who supervise writing programs should also be involved in determining policy and budget for their programs.

Research in rhetoric and composition is a legitimate field of scholarship, with standards comparable to other academic fields. In salary, tenure, and promotion considerations, research and publication in rhetoric and composition should be treated on a par with all other areas of research in English departments. As recommended in the "Report of the Modern Language Association's Commission on Writing and Literature" (MLA/Profession 88, 1988: 70—76), postsecondary institutions should count seriously certain kinds of professional activity, sometimes undervalued within current measures of scholarly achievement, that are particularly important to this field. These activities include: (1) the publication of composition textbooks as a primary form of original research; (2) collaborative research on articles and books that draw on diverse scholarly backgrounds and research orientations; (3) professional activities such as workshops and seminars for faculty at all levels; and (4) the particularly demanding administrative service that is often a regular part of a composition specialist's responsibilities. These are "measures of evaluation and standards of practice that do justice to the professional achievements of teachers of rhetoric and composition" (MLA/Profession 88, 73).

Because it is fundamentally necessary to the quality of education at all levels, research in rhetoric and composition should be supported not only at research institutions but also at those institutions primarily dedicated to teaching.

While insisting on the importance of research in rhetoric and composition, we join with those professional associations and learned societies that have affirmed that postsecondary institutions should develop flexible standards governing tenure, standards that accurately reflect the mission of the institution. At the vast majority of colleges and universities, and even at research institutions, distinguished teaching and service should warrant serious consideration for tenure and promotion.

Graduate Students

Graduate students' teaching experience should be understood as an essential part of their training for future professional responsibilities. They are primarily students and should never, for mere economic expediency, be used to replace tenure-track faculty in the staffing of composition programs. Graduate students' teaching loads should not interfere with their progress toward their degrees: an average of one course per term is ideal; more than two courses per term is unreasonable.

"Teaching loads should not interfere with progress toward degrees."

Graduate teaching assistantships for writing courses should be awarded only to students who (1) demonstrate superior writing ability and (2) present evidence of successful experience in the teaching of composition or who have had training in the teaching of composition. The standards for admitting graduate students and for awarding teaching assistantships should not be compromised by the need to staff the composition program.

Each institution should provide adequate training and supervision of graduate writing instructors, and this training should be conducted by someone with appropriate preparation or experience in rhetoric and composition.

Nearly all graduate students teaching writing in English departments are fully in charge of their classes. Because the university entrusts to them such serious responsibility, their special status among graduate students should be recognized and their compensation, benefits, class size, and course load should be adjusted accordingly. In this adjustment, attention should be given to hours spent inside and outside of class and to the increased responsibility for grading, classroom management, and preparation.

Part-Time Faculty

CCCC and other professional associations generally recognize two legitimate reasons for hiring part-time faculty: (1) to teach specialized courses for which no regular faculty are available and that require special practical knowledge (e.g., hiring a distinguished reporter to teach one class in journalism) and (2) to meet unexpected increases in enrollment. Abuses in this second category are cause for the most serious concern. Assuring and sustaining quality in education is incompatible with relying, purely for fiscal expediency, on part-time faculty appointments in rhetoric and composition.

The commitment to quality education requires that the number of part-time writing teachers in the second category be kept to a minimum. We recognize, however, that at the present time many administrators and department chairs have become dependent on part-time faculty lines. In the process of transforming these lines to the tenure track, administrators should impose severe limits on the ratio of part-time to full-time faculty. The percentage of part-time instructors in writing programs should not exceed what is necessary to meet unexpected increases in enrollment. When more than 10 percent of a department's course sections are taught by part-time faculty, the department should reconsider its hiring practices.

> "Assuring and sustaining quality in education is incompatible with relying, purely for fiscal expediency, on part-time faculty appointments."

To ensure that students receive the instructional excellence to which they have the right, the educational qualifications and experience of all part-time faculty should meet the highest professional standards. Part-time teachers of writing should demonstrate (1) superior writing ability, (2) professional involvement with composition theory and pedagogy, and (3) evidence of successful experience in the teaching of composition.

Recommendations for part-time faculty. Administrators and department chairs should recognize the professional status of part-time teachers. Recommendations 1–5 below apply to all part-time faculty, even those hired only occasionally to meet truly unexpected increases in enrollment. Recommendations 6–10 apply especially to part-time faculty who are regularly employed, even when departments abide by the 10 percent guideline recommended above. These faculty members, described by AAUP guidelines as those "whose contribution to the academic program of the institution and to its academic life is equal to that of a full-timer except for the proportion of time given to the position," deserve special consideration in matters of governance, job security, and incentives for professional development. That we recommend the following guidelines for the just treatment of part-time faculty should in no way be construed as condoning the practice of relying on part-time positions instead of full-time, tenure-track positions.

1. Expectations for part-time instructors' teaching, service, and research should be made clear, in writing and at the time of hiring, and these instructors should be evaluated according to those written expectations.

2. Whenever possible, part-time instructors should be hired as much in advance of their teaching assignments as possible. We recommend the preceding term.

3. They should receive an adequate introduction to their teaching assignments, departments, and institutions.

4. They should receive a salary that accurately reflects their teaching duties and any duties they are asked to assume outside the classroom. Compensation, per course, for part-time faculty should never be lower than the per-course compensation for full-time faculty with comparable experience, duties, and credentials. Part-timers should be eligible for the same fringe benefits and for the same cost-of-living, seniority, and merit salary increases available to full-time faculty.

5. Part-time faculty should be given mailboxes, office space, telephones, and clerical support.

6. They should be given a voice in the formulation of department policy regarding courses and programs in which they teach (e.g., by voting at department meetings and by serving on curriculum and hiring committees).

7. They should have the same right as full-time faculty to participate in the design of evaluation procedures.

8. They should have access to research support and travel funds to attend professional conferences.

9. During the period when departments are converting part-time positions to full-time tenured lines, departments should offer long-term contracts to part-time faculty who have demonstrated excellence in teaching.

10. Part-time faculty who have been employed for six or more terms or consecutively for three or more terms should not be terminated without a full term's notice.

Taking into account recommendations made by the AAUP ("The Status of Part-Time Faculty," 1980), we recognize that some institutions have responded innovatively to requests for tenure-track part-time positions. Where such positions are entirely the equal of full-time positions in terms of eligibility for tenure, prorated salary, fringe benefits, merit raises, support for research, participation in governance, and so on we find this practice acceptable. But such positions are and should be exceptions. The quality, integrity, and continuity of instruction and the principle of academic freedom are best ensured by a full-time tenured or tenure-track faculty.

Full-Time Temporary Faculty

The permanent use of temporary faculty is a contradiction in terms and should be avoided. As the AAUP repeatedly insists, the regular employment of full-time temporary faculty is "unjust and inequitable" and represents "a threat to academic freedom" ("On Full-Time, Non-Tenure-track Appointments," 1978). Two guidelines should be followed.

Full-time temporary appointments should be used only to fill nonrecurring instructional needs (e.g., short-term visiting professorships or replacements for tenure-track faculty on leave). The use of these positions to provide instruction that is a regular part of the institution's curriculum is exploitative.

The rights and privileges afforded to individuals with full-time temporary appointments ought to be congruent with the policies of the AAUP, and their working conditions and salaries ought to be in compliance with those outlined in this document for teachers of writing.

"The permanent use of temporary faculty is a contradiction in terms."

We recognize that where an institution has relied heavily on part-time positions, their transformation to full-time tenure-track lines may have to proceed in stages. Except in the cases noted above (visiting professorships and leave replacements), full-time temporary positions are tolerable only as a stage in converting part-time to full-time tenure-track positions.

II: TEACHING CONDITIONS NECESSARY FOR QUALITY EDUCATION

The improvement of an individual student's writing requires persistent and frequent contact between teacher and student both inside and outside the classroom. It requires assigning far more papers than are usually assigned in other college classrooms; it requires reading them and commenting on them not simply to justify a grade but to offer guidance and suggestions for improvement; and it requires spending a great deal of time with individual students, helping them not just to improve particular papers but to understand fundamental principles of effective writing that will enable them to continue learning throughout their lives. The teaching of writing, perhaps more than any other discipline, therefore requires special attention to class size, teaching loads, the availability of teaching materials, and the development of additional resources that enhance classroom instruction. For these reasons, we offer the following guidelines, widely supported by professional associations in English.

"The teaching of writing...requires special attention to class size, teaching loads, the availability of teaching materials, and the development of additional resources that enhance classroom instruction."

No more than twenty students should be permitted in any writing class. Ideally, classes should be limited to fifteen.

Remedial or developmental sections should be limited to a maximum of fifteen students.

No English faculty members should teach more than sixty writing students a term. In developmental writing classes, the maximum should be forty-five.

The effectiveness of classroom writing instruction is significantly improved by the assistance students receive in writing centers. Centers provide students with individual attention to their writing and often provide faculty and graduate students with opportunities to learn more about effective writing instruction. Because these centers enhance the conditions of teaching and learning, their development and support should be an important departmental and institutional priority.

Because rhetoric and composition is a rapidly developing field, all writing instructors should have access to scholarly literature and be given opportunities for continuing professional development.

Because writing instruction requires so much individual attention to student writing, it is important that all instructors have adequate and reasonably private office space for regular conferences.

The institution should provide all necessary support services for the teaching of writing, including supplies, duplication services, and secretarial assistance.

For more information, contact:

College Composition and Communication
National Council of Teachers of English
1111 Kenyon Road
Urbana, IL 61801

217 328-3870

This statement has been accepted and approved for publication by the CCCC Executive Committee.

Appendix B
"The Portland Resolution"

BACKGROUND

The theme of the 1990 Council of Writing Program Administrators Conference was "Status, Standards, and Quality: The Challenge of Wyoming." Christine Hult, editor of WPA: Writing Program Administration, presented a paper at the conference that essentially called for extending the challenge of the Wyoming Resolution—and the subsequent Conference of College Composition and Communication's (CCCC's) "Statement of Principles and Standards for the Postsecondary Teaching of Writing"—to WPAs. In "On Being a Writing Program Administrator," she invited WPAs to begin a dialogue toward the formulation of a statement of professional standards by the WPA organization. Such a statement would outline prerequisites for effective administration of writing programs as well as equitable treatment of WPAs. At the pre-conference workshop, participants were working on a similar document, which they dubbed the "Portland Resolution." A representative committee was commissioned by the WPA Executive Committee to draft a document; their combined work was presented at the 1991 summer conference and also sent to WPA members in *WPA News* to solicit comments toward revision of the document. This final version of the Portland Resolution, accepted by the Executive Committee at its 1992 CCCC meeting, is intended to help both WPAs and those with whom they work and to whom they report develop quality writing programs at their institutions.

GUIDELINES FOR WRITING PROGRAM ADMINISTRATOR POSITIONS

I. Working Conditions Necessary for Quality Writing Program Administration

Many WPAs at colleges and universities, and department or division chairs at community colleges, find themselves in untenable job situations, being asked to complete unrealistic expectations with little tangible recognition or remuneration, and with few resources. The CCCC statement points out the exploitation of writing teachers at all levels, including program administrators: "The teaching, research,

Guidelines for Writing Program Administrator Positions Adopted by the Council of Writing Program Administrators, 1992. Published in *WPA: Writing Program Administration* 16.1/2 (Fall/Winter 1992): 88-94. Christine Hult and the Portland Resolution Committee: David Joliffe, Kathleen Kelly, Dana Mead, Charles Schuster.

and service contributions of tenure-track composition faculty are often misunderstood or undervalued. At some postsecondary institutions, such faculty members are given administrative duties without the authority needed to discharge them; at others, they are asked to meet publication standards without support for the kind of research that their discipline requires." The following guidelines are intended to improve working conditions for more effective administration of writing programs.

1. *Writing job descriptions for WPAs.* Each institution is responsible for providing clear job descriptions or role statements for its WPAs (see Part II below). Such descriptions should be flexible enough for WPAs and the institution—and open to negotiation, especially when hiring a new WPA or starting a new writing program. The institution is responsible for providing a clear formula for determining "equivalence" for a WPA. What responsibilities are equivalent to teaching a full load (as determined by that institution)? What release time will be given for administration and staff development? What administrative work will be counted as "scholarship" in tenure and promotion decisions?

In addition, WPA positions should be situated within a clearly defined administrative structure so that WPAs know to whom they are responsible and whom they supervise. WPAs should not be assigned to direct a program against their will or without appropriate training in rhetoric and composition and commensurate workplace experience. If a WPA needs specialized training in any area outside the usual purview of rhetoric and composition studies, the institution must be prepared to provide for and fund that training.

2. *Evaluating WPAs.* The institution is responsible for setting forth informed guidelines for assessing the work of a WPA fairly and for determining how administrative work is to be compared to traditional definitions of teaching, research, and service in decisions involving salary increases, retention, promotion, and tenure.

Assessment of a WPA should consider the important scholarly contribution each WPA makes by virtue of designing, developing, and implementing a writing program.

3. *Job security.* WPA positions should carry sufficient stability and continuity to allow for the development of sound educational programs and planning. The WPA should be a regular, full-time, tenured faculty member or a full-time administrator with a recognizable title that delineates the scope of the position (e.g., director of writing, coordinator of composition, division or department chair). WPAs should have travel funds equivalent to those provided for other faculty and administrators and should receive a salary commensurate with their considerable responsibilities and workload (including summer stipends).

Requirements for retention, promotion, and tenure should be clearly defined and should consider the unique administrative demands of the position.

4. *Access.* WPAs should have access to those individuals and units that influence their programs—English department chairs or heads, deans, the faculty senate, humanities directors, budget officers, people in admissions and in the registrar's office, and those who have anything to do with hiring, class sizes, placement. WPAs should have ample opportunities and release time to work in close consultation with colleagues in related fields and departments—writing center directors, freshman advisers and freshman affairs officers, basic skills or developmental writing faculty, English-as-a-second-language specialists, student counseling services, and committees on student issues such as retention or admissions standards.

5. *Resources and budget*. WPAs should have the power to request, receive, and allocate funds sufficient for the running of the program. Resources include, but should not be limited to, adequate work space, supplies, clerical support, research support, travel funds, and release time. WPAs should be provided with administrative support—e.g., clerical help, computer time, duplicating services—equal in quality to that available to other program directors and administrators.

II. GUIDELINES FOR DEVELOPING WPA JOB DESCRIPTIONS

Each institution should carefully consider the role statements or job descriptions for its WPAs. Depending upon the size and scope of the writing program, the amount of administrative work expected of each WPA will vary considerably. Typically, however, WPAs have been exploited in these positions—given unrealistic workload expectations with little credit for administrative work.

At large institutions with diverse programs staffed by numerous faculty or graduate assistants, several WPAs may be needed (e.g., director and associate director of writing, writing center director, basic writing director, computer writing lab director, director for writing across the curriculum, and so on). At smaller institutions with fewer faculty and less diverse programs, fewer WPAs may be needed. It is also desirable to provide advanced graduate students with administrative experience in the form of internships or assistantships to the WPAs.

The following outline suggests both the scope of preparation needed to be an effective WPA and the diverse duties that WPAs at various institutions may perform. This list is illustrative of the kinds of duties WPAs typically are engaged in: it is not descriptive of an "ideal" WPA. Nor should it be inferred that each WPA should be assigned all of these duties. On the contrary, the workload of each WPA should be carefully negotiated with the administration annually in the form of a role statement or job description to which all parties can agree.

1. Preparation for a WPA should include knowledge of or experience with the following:
   - Teaching composition and rhetoric
   - Theories of writing and learning
   - Research methods, evaluation methods, and teaching methods
   - Language and literacy development
   - Various MLA, NCTE, and CCCC guidelines and position statements
   - Local and national developments in writing instruction
   - Writing, publishing, and presenting at conferences
2. Desirable supplemental preparation may include knowledge of or experience with the following areas:

   Business
   - Accounting
   - Business administration
   - Grant writing
   - Information systems and computers

- Personnel management
- Records management
- Public relations

Education
- Curriculum design
- English as a second language
- Testing and evaluation
- Psychology of learning
- Developmental or basic writing

3. As a particular institution negotiates job descriptions with each WPA, the responsibilities of the WPAs may be selected from among the following comprehensive list:

Scholarship of Administration
- Remain cognizant of current developments in teaching, research, and scholarship in rhetoric, composition, and program administration.
- Pursue scholarship of teaching and curriculum design as part of the essential work of the WPA.

Faculty Development and Other Teaching
- Teaching a for-credit graduate course in the teaching of writing
- Designing or teaching faculty development seminars
- Training tutors
- Supervising teaching assistants and writing staff
- Evaluating teaching performance: observing and evaluating teaching assistants and adjunct faculty in class; reviewing syllabi and course policy statements; reviewing comments on student essays and grading practices
- Preparing workshops and materials, conducting workshops, and conducting follow-up meetings
  Undergraduate writing, reading, language, teaching, courses, etc.

Writing Program Development
- Designing curricula and course syllabi
- Standardizing and monitoring course content
- Serving on or chairing departmental committees on writing
- Initiating or overseeing WAC programs
- Developing teaching resource materials/library
- Interviewing and hiring new faculty and staff
- Selecting and evaluating textbooks (which may include establishing and supervising a textbook committee, maintaining a liaison with the bookstore, and ensuring that orders are properly placed)

Writing Assessment, Writing Program Assessment, and Accountability
- Coordinating assessment and placement of students in appropriate writing courses

- Administering writing-placement exams and diagnostics (including creating and testing an appropriate instrument, acting as second reader for instructors, and notifying the registrar and instructors of any change in placements)
- Administering competency, equivalency, or challenge exams
- Creating, or having access to, a database of information on enrollments and faculty and student performance
- Administering student evaluations of teachers
- Evaluating data on student retention, grade distribution, grade inflation, enrollment trends
- Reporting to supervisors, chairs, deans, etc.
- Conducting program reviews and self-studies

Registration and Scheduling
- Determining numbers of sections to be offered
- Evaluating enrollment trends
- Staffing courses
- Monitoring registration

Office Management
- Supervising writing program office, secretary, and staff
- Supervising maintenance of office equipment and supplies
- (Managing computer lab and staff)*
- (Managing writing center staff)*
- *May be separate positions.

Counseling and Advising
- Arbitrating grade disputes and resolving teacher and student complaints such as placement, plagiarism, grade appeals, scheduling problems (which may include acting as liaison with the appropriate office)
- Writing letters of recommendation for graduate students, adjuncts, and tutors

Articulation
- Coordinating writing courses and instruction with other academic support services (e.g., study skills center)
- Coordinating with English-as-a-second-language programs
- Coordinating with remedial/developmental programs
- Coordinating with high school (AP, CLEP, concurrent enrollment) programs
- Coordinating with the department of English education programs
- Revising and updating any publications of the writing program
- Discussing the writing program with administrators, publishers' representatives, parents, prospective students

Appendix C
WPA Outcomes Statement for First-Year Composition

Revised for Publication in WPA Journal

INTRODUCTION

This statement describes the common knowledge, skills, and attitudes sought by first-year composition programs in American postsecondary education. To some extent, we seek to regularize what can be expected to be taught in first-year composition; to this end the document is not merely a compilation or summary of what currently takes place. Rather, the following statement articulates what composition teachers nationwide have learned from practice, research, and theory. This document intentionally defines only "outcomes," or types of results, and not "standards," or precise levels of achievement. The setting of standards should be left to specific institutions or specific groups of institutions.

Learning to write is a complex process, both individual and social, that takes place over time with continued practice and informed guidance. Therefore, it is important that teachers, administrators, and a concerned public do not imagine that these outcomes can be taught in reduced or simple ways. Helping students demonstrate these outcomes requires expert understanding of how students actually learn to write. For this reason we expect the primary audience for this document to be well-prepared college writing teachers and college writing program administrators. In some places, we have chosen to write in their professional language. Among such readers, terms such as "rhetorical" and "genre" convey a rich meaning that is not easily simplified. While we have also aimed at writing a document that the general public can understand, in limited cases we have aimed first at communicating effectively with expert writing teachers and writing program administrators.

These statements describe only what we expect to find at the end of first-year composition, at most schools a required general education course or sequence of courses. As writers move beyond first-year composition, their writing abilities do not merely improve. Rather, students' abilities not only diversify along disciplinary and professional lines but also move into whole new levels where expected outcomes expand, multiply, and diverge. For this reason, each statement of outcomes for first-year composition is followed by suggestions for further work that builds on these outcomes.

RHETORICAL KNOWLEDGE

By the end of first year composition, students should

- Focus on a purpose
- Respond to the needs of different audiences
- Respond appropriately to different kinds of rhetorical situations
- Use conventions of format and structure appropriate to the rhetorical situation
- Adopt appropriate voice, tone, and level of formality
- Understand how genres shape reading and writing
- Write in several genres

Faculty in all programs and departments can build on this preparation by helping students learn

- The main features of writing in their fields
- The main uses of writing in their fields
- The expectations of readers in their fields

CRITICAL THINKING, READING, AND WRITING

By the end of first-year composition, students should

- Use writing and reading for inquiry, learning, thinking, and communicating
- Understand a writing assignment as a series of tasks, including finding, evaluating, analyzing, and synthesizing appropriate primary and secondary sources
- Integrate their own ideas with those of others
- Understand the relationships among language, knowledge, and power

Faculty in all programs and departments can build on this preparation by helping students learn

- The uses of writing as a critical thinking method
- The interactions among critical thinking, critical reading, and writing
- The relationships among language, knowledge, and power in their fields

PROCESSES

By the end of first-year composition, students should

- Be aware that it usually takes multiple drafts to create and complete a successful text
- Develop flexible strategies for generating, revising, editing, and proof-reading
- Understand writing as an open process that permits writers to use later invention and re-thinking to revise their work
- Understand the collaborative and social aspects of writing processes
- Learn to critique their own and others' works

- Learn to balance the advantages of relying on others with the responsibility of doing their part
- Use a variety of technologies to address a range of audiences

Faculty in all programs and departments can build on this preparation by helping students learn

- To build final results in stages
- To review work-in-progress in collaborative peer groups for purposes other than editing
- To save extensive editing for later parts of the writing process
- To apply the technologies commonly used to research and communicate within their fields

KNOWLEDGE OF CONVENTIONS

By the end of first-year composition, students should

- Learn common formats for different kinds of texts
- Develop knowledge of genre conventions ranging from structure and paragraphing to tone and mechanics
- Practice appropriate means of documenting their work
- Control such surface features as syntax, grammar, punctuation, and spelling

Faculty in all programs and departments can build on this preparation by helping students learn

- The conventions of usage, specialized vocabulary, format, and documentation in their fields
- Strategies through which better control of conventions can be achieved

---

Appendix D
Guidelines for the Workload
of the College English Teacher

NCTE COLLEGE SECTION
STEERING COMMITTEE

In an era of increasing public concern over the writing and reading ability of college students, it is especially important that the workload of English faculty members be reasonable enough to guarantee that every student receive the time and attention needed for genuine improvement. Faculty members must be given adequate time to fulfill their responsibility to their students, their departments, their institutions, their profession, the larger community, and to themselves. Without that time, they cannot teach effectively. Unless English teachers are given reasonable loads, students cannot make the progress the public demands.

Economic pressures and budgetary restrictions may tempt administrations to increase teaching loads. With this conflict in mind, the College Section of the National Council of Teachers of English endorses the following standards:

1. English faculty members should never be assigned more than 12 hours a week of classroom teaching. In fact, the teaching load should be less, to provide adequate time for reading and responding to students' writing; for holding individual conferences; for preparing to teach classes; and for research and professional growth.

2. No more than 20 students should be permitted in any writing class. Ideally, classes should be limited to 15. Students cannot learn to write without writing. In sections larger than 20, teachers cannot possibly give student writing the immediate and individual response necessary for growth and improvement.

3. Remedial or developmental sections should be limited to a maximum of 15 students. It is essential to provide these students extra teaching if they are to acquire the reading and writing skills they need in college.

4. No English faculty member should teach more than 60 writing students a term: if the students are developmental, the maximum should be 45.

5. No more than 25 students should be permitted in discussion courses in literature or language. Classes larger than 25 do not give students and teachers the opportunity to engage literary texts through questions, discussion, and writing. If lecture classes must be offered, teachers should be given adjusted time or assistance to hold conferences and respond to students' writing.

6. Any faculty members assigned to reading or writing laboratories or to skills centers should have that assignment counted as part of the teaching load.

Identifying and addressing the individual needs of students is a demanding form of teaching.

7. No full-time faculty member's load should be composed exclusively of sections of a single course. (An exception might occur when a specific teacher, for professional reasons such as research or intensive experimentation, specifically requests such an assignment.) Even in colleges where the English program consists mainly of composition, course assignments should be varied. Repeating identical material for the third or fourth time the same day or semester after semester is unlikely to be either creative or responsive.

8. No English faculty member should be required to prepare more than three different courses during a single term. Even if the faculty member has taught the same course in previous years, the material must be reexamined in the context of current scholarship and the presentation adapted to the needs of each class.

9. The time and responsibility required for administrative, professional, scholarly, and institutional activities should be considered in determining teaching loads and schedules for English faculty members. These responsibilities cover a broad range, such as directing independent study, theses, and dissertations; advising students on academic programs; supervising student publications; developing new courses and materials; serving on college or departmental committees; publishing scholarly and creative work; refereeing and editing professional manuscripts and journals; or holding office in professional organizations.

From NCTE's WWW page: "Guidelines for the Workload of the College English Teacher." Reprinted with permission.

Appendix E
Position Statement on the Preparation and Professional Development of Teachers of Writing

CCCC TASK FORCE ON THE PREPARATION OF TEACHERS OF WRITING

To provide effective instruction in writing for learners at any age and at all academic levels, teachers need, first of all, experience in writing, and also some theoretical knowledge to guide classroom practice. To help meet this need, the Conference on College Composition and Communication presents this position statement. We hope it will be discussed and followed, in the preparation of teachers of writing at all levels, by college and university English departments, faculty of teacher preparation programs, faculty and administrators in elementary and secondary schools, and staffs of state departments of public instruction.

The recommendations offered here are consistent with those offered in earlier publications of NCTE and CCCC that deal with the preparation of teachers of writing, with findings of research on the composing process, and with studies on the teaching and learning of writing.

I

Programs for the preparation and continuing education of teachers of English and language arts, at all levels, should include opportunities for prospective and active teachers:

    1. *to write,*

        (a) as a means of

            (1) developing, shaping, representing, and communicating our perceptions of our world, our experiences, our beliefs, and our identity,

            (2) finding sensory and aesthetic pleasure in working with and playing with language,

The members of the CCCC Task Force on the Preparation of Teachers of Writing were Lou Kelly, University of Iowa, Chair; Forrest Burt, Texas A&M University; Wallace Douglas, Northwestern University; Richard Gebbardt, Findlay College (Ohio); Roseann Gonzalez, University of Arizona; James Lee Hill, Albany State College (Georgia); and Sam Watson, Jr., University of North Carolina at Charlotte.

(3)   developing our various intellectual skills;

(b)   in a variety of forms, e.g.,

    (1)   prose that attempts to express what we think, feel, and imagine,

    (2)   poems representing experience and the fruits of imagination,

    (3)   narratives: autobiographical, fictional, historical,

    (4)   scripts for performance in class, on television, in film and radio,

    (5)   informative records and reports;

(c)   in response to a variety of authentic rhetorical situations in which our work will be read and responded to by others, including teachers, classmates, family, and friends; readers of school and community publications; audiences at public readings of our work.

2.   *to read and respond to the writings of students, classmates, and colleagues,*

(a)   making supportive comments that express respect for others' ideas and feelings and encourage writers to use writing as a means of personal, academic, and professional growth,

(b)   asking probing questions that help writers see what they have not expressed clearly and convincingly and what they have not presented effectively (perhaps because their knowledge is limited, or their point of view is narrow, or they do not recognize the implications of what they say).

3.   *to become perceptive readers of our own writing,* so that we can ask questions about, clarify, and reshape what we are trying to express.

4.   *to study and teach writing as a process,*

(a)   by reflecting on how our own writing grows from initial idea to final draft;

(b)   by studying authors' journals and notebooks for indications of their composing processes, and by comparing successive drafts of their work;

(c)   by working with learners while they are composing:

    (1)   exploring interests and experiences, and discovering subjects for writing,

    (2)   composing first drafts,

    (3)   rereading and reacting to their own writing, evaluating the clarity and effectiveness of their ideas,

    (4)   responding to their own questions and reactions and those of other readers,

    (5)   revising, throughout the steps above,

    (6)   editing final drafts for punctuation, spelling, usage, and other conventions.

5.   *to experience writing as a way of learning* which engages us in intellectual operations that enable or require us

(a)   to interpret what we experience and discover in light of what we already know, making connections, seeing relationships;

(b)   to re-shape impersonal data into knowledge that is meaningful to us personally;

    (c)   to perform essential activities of mind such as analyzing, synthesizing, evaluating, testing, asserting;

    (d)   to use what we already know in searching for what we don't know, making hypotheses, imagining new patterns.

6. *to learn to assess the progress of individual writers by responding to complete pieces of their writing and studying changes in their writing.*

7. *to study research and other scholarly work in the humanistic discipline of the teaching of writing, including research on*

    (a)   the development of writing abilities and styles

    (b)   the ways in which language "means"

    (c)   the theory of discourse

    (d)   how the English language works

    (e)   the composing processes of individual writers

    (f)   the rhetorical effects of different pieces of writing.

8. *to study writing in relation to other disciplines,*

    (a)   to learn the insights offered by

        (1)   applied linguistics (including language acquisition and development and second language learning; sociolinguistics, including study of dialects; psycholinguistics—i.e., the study of the way human beings process language),

        (2)   psychology: cognitive and interpersonal,

        (3)   history and anthropology;

    (b)   to learn what is asked of writers by professionals in other disciplines, including

        (1)   the arts of language

        (2)   the fine and performing arts

        (3)   history

        (4)   the social sciences

        (5)   the natural sciences.

II

To enable teachers of English and language arts to develop the practical and theoretical knowledge recommended here, CCCC urges

1. college and university English departments

    (a)   to provide opportunities for the faculty to develop knowledge of theory and skill in the teaching of writing,

    (b)   to develop undergraduate and graduate courses that offer the experiences enumerated in I,

    (c)   to require that courses in literature ask students to write, give them guidance in writing, give them supportive and probing responses to their writ-

ing, and encourage them to view writing as a way of reacting to and learning about literature;

2. faculty of teacher education programs

   (a) to provide prospective and active teachers the opportunities listed
   under I,

   (b) to assure that prospective and active teachers have the opportunities to
   work with individual learners and groups of learners, so that these teachers can apply what they are learning from the theories and practice of
   writing discussed in I,

   (c) to work with state departments of education in assuring that the
   emphases in I are incorporated into the criteria for

      (1) approving teacher education programs

      (2) certifying teachers of English;

3. teachers and administrators in elementary and secondary schools

   (a) to provide opportunities for all teachers of English and language
   arts to develop theoretical knowledge and skill as teachers
   of writing,

   (b) to encourage teachers to give their students the experiences with
   writing listed in I, 1–5,

   (c) to assist teachers in learning to respond to students' writing and
   assess their progress as writers;

4. staffs of state department of public instruction

   (a) to work with faculties in teacher education on assuring that the emphases
   in I are incorporated into the criteria for

      (1) approving teacher education programs and

      (2) certifying teachers of English,

   (b) to give moral and financial support to in-service programs in writing for
   elementary and secondary teachers of English.

Appendix F
Evaluating the Intellectual Work of Writing Administration

Council of Writing Program Administrators

HISTORY AND BACKGROUND
OF THIS STATEMENT

Preamble

It is clear within departments of English that research and teaching are generally regarded as intellectual, professional activities worthy of tenure and promotion. But administration—including leadership of first-year writing courses, WAC programs, writing centers, and the many other manifestations of writing administration—has for the most part been treated as a management activity that does not produce new knowledge and that neither requires nor demonstrates scholarly expertise and disciplinary knowledge. While there are certainly arguments to be made for academic administration, in general, as intellectual work, that is not our aim here. Instead, our concern in this document is to present a framework by which writing administration can be seen as scholarly work and therefore subject to the same kinds of evaluation as other forms of disciplinary production, such as books, articles, and reviews. More significantly, by refiguring writing administration as scholarly and intellectual work, we argue that it is worthy of tenure and promotion when it advances and enacts disciplinary knowledge within the field of Rhetoric and Composition.

1. Introduction: Three Cases

A Literary Scholar: Rewarding the Production of Knowledge

In her fourth year as a tenure-track assistant professor at a land-grant university, Mary C. came to her current position after teaching for two years at a private university where she had established a good reputation for both her scholarship and her teaching. Her present department places considerable emphasis on teaching, at least for a research university, and her colleagues have taken special note of her pedagogical skills in their annual evaluations, recognizing that teaching quality will play some role for both the dean and the provost in decisions on tenure and promotion. Nonetheless, Mary has wisely concentrated on publishing refereed articles, poems in magazines with good literary reputations, and a book with a major university press. After all, the format for promotion and tenure at her university identifies these as "categories of effort" that weigh heavily in the awarding of tenure and in promotion to higher rank. The guidelines also emphasize the importance of quality in scholarly efforts as measured not just by the judgment of her departmental colleagues but also by outside evaluators who provide an estimate of the currency and value of her scholarship as well as the prestige and visibility of the outlets in which her work appears.

By describing Mary's achievements in this familiar manner, we may be able readily to understand why she is likely to be promoted—and why her chances for advancement differ markedly from other instructors within the broad field of English literature and composition, particularly those who work as writing administrators. To do this, we need to view her work, despite its undeniably humanistic content, as the production of specific commodities—albeit scholarly commodities—with a clear exchange value, perhaps not on the general market but certainly in academic institutions. While Mary's colleagues and others who read her work can appreciate it for its uses—for the personal value of her insights into literary works or as poetry worth sharing with friends and students—the institution assigns it positive importance because the work assumes recognizable and conventional forms to which value can be readily assigned, and the valuations are likely to be recognized and accepted by most colleagues and academic departments. Because Mary's work takes conventional forms and has a recognized exchange value, her institution uses it as a basis for justifying its decision to award her with tenure and promotion—a justification it owes to the university community, to the board of regents, and to the academic community in general.

A Composition Teacher/Scholar: Rewarding Pedagogy and Pedagogical Knowledge

Twenty years ago Doug R. might have been an uncertain candidate for tenure and promotion. An assistant professor at a regional state university with a large composition program, Doug has published a number of articles in highly regarded journals in rhetoric and composition studies, though his publication record is by no means extensive.

Doug's institution, however, has a well-developed system for student and departmental teaching evaluations, and Doug scores especially high on his classroom performance in both student questionnaires and on the frequent faculty observations filed by a variety of senior colleagues within the department, including the chairperson and the writing program director. Moreover, both by contract and by informal agreement, both the department and the administration at Doug's institution are required to take into account demonstrated excellence in teaching when evaluating faculty for tenure and promotion. It helps as well that Doug's specialty is composition, an academic specialty that is viewed by the administration as central to the university's undergraduate mission.

Doug's academic achievements, especially as a classroom teacher, have made it likely that he will be tenured and promoted. His pedagogical efforts take forms recognized by his colleagues and his institution and they are assigned value by accepted procedures. In combination with his published scholarship (and typical departmental committee service), Doug's teaching—which has been evaluated and quantified and made visible—becomes a strong factor in his promotion. Doug is also an innovative teacher who has shared his contributions to curricular design and pedagogy through workshops at his own institution and through presentations at national conferences. Besides having value for his colleagues and for students, these efforts appear on his vita: they constitute an important part of his reputation as a professional.

A Writing Administrator: A Problematic Case

Cheryl W. has been working hard as an assistant professor and writing director at a medium-sized university, a position for which she was hired after taking a Ph.D. in rhetoric and composition and teaching for two years (ABD) at a college with a nationally known WAC program. Cheryl has a teaching load of only One/Two, but her responsibilities are overwhelming: supervision and curriculum design for a large first-year composition program, TA training, design and administration of an emerging WAC program (with faculty workshops and publicity), many hours in the office dealing with student issues and writing reports, and an occasional graduate course in composition theory. In addition, Cheryl has guided development of five upper-level writing courses for both English majors and students in other fields, in the process greatly expanding the writing program. Cheryl's department and her institution support the growth of her program, perhaps because she has carried it out both diplomatically and professionally.

Unfortunately, Cheryl has published only a handful of refereed articles, far below the expected level for candidates for tenure and promotion at her institution. Moreover, because she has a relatively light teaching load, she has not been able to develop as thorough and far-reaching a reputation as a teacher as have most of her colleagues, and she has to face the expectation, held by her university faculty generally, that anyone with such a light teaching load should have published much more. This expectation is not the result of any hostility towards rhetoric and composition as a field; indeed, two of her colleagues, one of whom works in rhetoric and technical communication and the other of whom specializes in composition research and teacher training, have published a good deal and are considered prime candidates for tenure and promotion. Cheryl and her supporters suspect, in fact, that the productivity of these other two writing specialists may become an argument for denying her tenure and hiring someone who will be productive in ways that the department and the institution can readily recognize and value.

While many members of Cheryl's department agree that she has been working hard, they are not sure that she has been doing "real work." Others, who think her efforts have been valuable to the department, have difficulty specifying her accomplishments other than stating that "she has done an excellent job running the writing program." The problem is particularly clear to one of Cheryl's colleagues, the former director of the writing program, who recognizes the specific tasks involved in activities like supervising teaching assistants and who also recognizes that Cheryl has accomplished these tasks with energy, vision, and expertise. This colleague sums up the problem facing Cheryl and her supporters this way: "First you have to be able to specify exactly what it is that you do as a WPA; then you have to convince people that your work is intellectual work, grounded in disciplinary knowledge, demanding expertise, and producing knowledge or other valued ends, not simply busy work or administrivia that anyone with a reasonable intelligence could do; and finally you have to demonstrate that your work has been both professional and creative—worthy of recognition and reward." Unless Cheryl can do these things, her efforts will not have value within her own institution, nor will they have exchange value when she applies for another position, unless, of course, that institution has already developed a clear definition of the intellectual work of a writing administrator and can evaluate Cheryl's work within these terms. Right now, however, Cheryl will have to list her administrative categories in the small box labeled "Service" on her institution's tenure/promotion form, a category distinguished by its lack of clear definition in contrast to the detailed subcategories under "Research" (books, articles, chapters, reviews, presentations, and grants) and "Teaching" (student evaluations, supervisory reports, curriculum development, presentations and publications). Unless there is a way to demonstrate the intellectual value of her work, Cheryl is unlikely to be rewarded for her administrative work and will be denied tenure and promotion.

2. The Production of Knowledge and the Problem of Assigning Value to Academic Work

Terms like "exchange value" and "use value" and the concepts they embody help lay bare the system of academic judgments and rewards we are all familiar with, a system that lies behind the three cases described in the previous section. Academic institutions grant tenure and promotion (and hire) because they share the same understandings and values. Although departments of English, and institutions of higher education generally, may differ substantially as to the particularities of what they value—teaching, book publication, scholarly articles, local publishing, community outreach, etc.—there is considerable congruence among them concerning the ways they quantify academic work.

We use the term "quantify" advisedly. Tenure and promotion are granted on the basis of criteria that might be said to be objective. They are too familiar to rehearse here, but they might be generally described with the phrase "professional accomplishment" as measured and indicated by books, articles, conference presentations, teaching evaluations, etc. These accomplishments are concrete and can be evaluated; they can be counted, weighed, analyzed, and held forward for public review. In most departments of English, for example, to have a book accepted by Oxford, Yale, or Harvard University Press is to be assured of tenure and promotion. In colleges that place a primary value on undergraduate instruction, a faculty member whose teaching evaluations place her in the top three percent is similarly likely to be tenured and promoted. Perhaps more important than their quantifiable nature, these accomplishments are largely familiar to faculty and administrators; they are exactly the kinds of accomplishments that have been considered by universities for years in cases of tenure and promotion. Familiarity breeds ease of use; university machinery works most smoothly and efficiently when there is little or no quarrel about the means by which decisions are made. Indeed, in the case of scholarship, many of us might agree that the all-too-prevalent tendency to prefer quantity over quality is a clear sign of intellectual work turned into a quantifiable commodity. What this tells us, however, is that academic systems of evaluation and reward have for a long time assigned clear exchange values to scholarship and are now on the way to doing so with teaching.

Activities other than research and teaching, however, have little exchange value, no matter how highly they might be valued on an individual basis by fellow faculty, by administrators, or society. Only when such activities lead to a move outside faculty ranks, to a deanship, perhaps, do they take on exchange value. Otherwise, they generally appear under the ill-defined and seldom-rewarded category of "service" in promotion and tenure evaluations, a category to which the work of writing administrators is too often relegated.

In academe, work that long has been categorized as "service" occupies a wide spectrum and has proven extremely difficult to describe and evaluate. The 1996 report of the MLA Commission on Professional Service "Making Faculty Work Visible: Reinterpreting Professional Service, Teaching, and Research in the Fields of Language and Literature" states the problem clearly:

Service has functioned in the past as a kind of grab-bag for all professional work that was not clearly classroom teaching, research, or scholarship. As a result, recent efforts to define it more precisely (as "professional service") have tended to select out one subset of these activities and fail to account for all the clearly professional work previously lumped together under this rubric…. Yet it is hard to come up with a principled definition based on common features or family resemblances among all these activities and to avoid confusions with the concept of citizenship (184).

We do not expect to resolve the problem completely in this document. The MLA report provides useful information with its distinctions between applied work and institutional service (see 184–188). It also challenges the traditional view of service as a separate category of faculty work by identifying service, teaching, and scholarship as sites of both "intellectual work" and "professional citizenship" (162–63, 173)—an approach which means that "research is no longer the exclusive site of intellectual work" (177) and that service "can also entail substantive intellectual labor" (178).

Another helpful perspective is found in Ernest Boyer's *Scholarship Reconsidered: Priorities of the Professioriate*. Boyer argues that scholarship is not one category but is rather distributed over four somewhat distinguishable categories: Discovery, Integration, Application, and Teaching. The one that concerns us here is Application. Boyer makes clear that "Colleges and universities have recently rejected service as serious scholarship, partly because its meaning is so vague and often disconnected from serious intellectual work" (22). More importantly, Boyer argues that:

a sharp distinction must be drawn between citizenship activities and projects that relate to scholarship itself. To be sure, there are meritorious social and civic functions to be performed, and faculty should be appropriately recognized for such work. But all too frequently, service means not doing scholarship but doing good. To be considered scholarship, service activities must be tied directly to one's special field of knowledge and relate to, and flow directly out of, this professional activity. Such service is serious, demanding work, requiring the rigor—and the accountability—traditionally associated with research activities (22).

Let us emphasize the main point here: "To be considered scholarship, service activities must be tied directly to one's special field of knowledge and relate to, and flow directly out of, this professional activity. Such service is serious, demanding work, requiring the rigor—and the accountability—traditionally associated with research activities." What Boyer is arguing is not that all service should count; rather, service can be considered as part of scholarship if it derives from and is reinforced by scholarly knowledge and disciplinary understanding. As Boyer makes clear, in work of this sort, "theory and practice vitally interact, and one renews the other" (23).

Clearly there are many service activities that support and enhance departmental and university structures. Service on departmental and college-level committees is one of the clearest examples. Serving as the director or coordinator of an academic program may be another. Such service is considered a form of scholarship, however, only if it flows from and contributes to the scholarship of the field. In our terms, such work is intellectual: it requires specific expertise, training, and an understanding of disciplinary knowledge.

An example may be in order. Let us presume that the director of a first-year writing course is designing an in-house placement procedure so that students new to the college can be placed into the appropriate course in the first-year composition sequence. She will need to decide whether to use direct or indirect measures of writing ability; will need to assess the implications that the placement procedure will have on high school curriculum; will want to consult research on such things as the nature of writing prompts, whether an objective test and a writing test should be used together, and the optimal amount of time for the exam. Thus what some see as a simple decision (place students according to an ACT score) is, in reality, complex intellectual work involving disciplinary knowledge, empirical research, and histories of practice.

An additional dimension of this kind of intellectual work is that it neither derives from nor produces simplistic products or services. Rather, it draws upon historical and contemporary knowledge, and it contributes to the formation of new knowledge and improved decision making. These kinds of practices lead to new knowledge and innovative educational programs, and contribute to thoughtful and invigorated teaching.

3. Evaluating the Work of Writing Administration

What this document is arguing is that a definition of writing administration as intellectual work in colleges and universities must take into account the paradigm established by research and scholarship. At its highest level, this means the production of new knowledge (what *Scholarship Reconsidered* calls the "scholarship of discovery"). But the contemporary scholarly paradigm embraces a much broader spectrum of intellectual work. For instance, "The Disciplines Speak," the report of a national working group of representatives from sixteen different professional associations (including CCCC and MLA), indicates that scholarly activity can be demonstrated in ways as diverse as "publishing the results of one's scholarly research, developing a new course, writing an innovative textbook, implementing an outreach program for the community...or assisting in a K–12 curriculum project" (Diamond and Adam 13). And the MLA's "Making Faculty Work Visible" offers this list of some of the "projects and enterprises of knowledge and learning" in English studies:

- creating new questions, problems, information, interpretations, designs, products, frameworks of understanding, etc., through inquiry (e.g., empirical, textual, historical, theoretical, technological, artistic, practical);
- clarifying, critically examining, weighing, and revising the knowledge claims, beliefs, or understanding of others and oneself;
- connecting knowledge to other knowledge;
- preserving... and reinterpreting past knowledge;
- applying aesthetic, political, and ethical values to make judgments about knowledge and its uses;
- arguing knowledge claims in order to invite criticism and revision;
- making specialized knowledge broadly accessible and usable, e.g., to young learners, to nonspecialists in other disciplines, to the public;
- helping new generations to become active knowers themselves, preparing them for lifelong learning and discovery;
- applying knowledge to practical problems in significant or innovative ways;
- creating insight and communicating forms of experience through artistic works or performance (175–76).

Within this contemporary scholarly paradigm, writing administration may be considered intellectual work when it meets two tests. First, it needs to advance knowledge—its production, clarification, connection, reinterpretation, or application. Second, it results in products or activities that can be evaluated by others— for instance, against this list of qualities which, according to *The Disciplines Speak*, "seem to characterize that work that most disciplines would consider 'scholarly' or 'professional'":

- the activity requires a high level of discipline-related expertise.
- the activity…is innovative.
- the activity can be replicated or elaborated.
- the work and its results can be documented.
- the work and its results can be peer-reviewed.
- the activity has significance or impact (14).

In order to be regarded as intellectual work, therefore, writing administration must be viewed as a form of inquiry which advances knowledge and which has formalized outcomes that are subject to peer review and disciplinary evaluation. Just as the articles, stories, poems, books, committee work, classroom performance, and other evidence of tenure and promotion can be critiqued and evaluated by internal and external reviewers, so can the accomplishments, products, innovations, and contributions of writing administrators. Indeed, such review must be central to the evaluation of writing administration as scholarly and intellectual work.

Defining and evaluating the work of writing administrators is a process that needs to be made explicit so that those who do this work—and they are often beginning faculty who are over-worked, over-stressed, and untenured—stand a real chance of succeeding professionally within departmental and institutional contexts. On a national level, this process not only can provide guidelines to help institutions and faculty understand and properly evaluate the work of writing administrators, but also produce some degree of empirical data that can create an exchange value for administrative accomplishments parallel to that already in place for research and teaching.

The remainder of this document will suggest guidelines which we hope will prove useful to individuals, committees, and departments working to develop materials and policies for evaluating writing administrators ("WPAs," as they are often called). First, Section 4 will propose five descriptive categories within which the intellectual work of a WPA can be best considered. Then, in Section 5, we will suggest several evaluative criteria by which merit pay increases as well as tenure and promotion decisions can be made fairly and thoughtfully in terms of the quality and the quantity of intellectual work achieved by a writing administrator. Finally, Section 6 will provide a framework that can be used to organize the accomplishments—and to help in the evaluation—of individuals devoted to writing administration.

4. Five Categories Of Intellectual Work

Although writing administration, like the work of any other administrative figure on campus, is subject to a variety of different interpretations, we propose that much of it can be understood as falling within one or more of these categories: Program Creation, Curricular Design, Faculty Development, Program Assessment, and Program-Related Textual Production.

Program Creation

Whatever the specific focus of administration (first-year course, WAC program, writing center, etc.), one of the primary scholarly accomplishments of writing administration is the creation of a program. By creation, we mean those specific activities that reconceive the philosophy, goals, purposes, and institutional definition of the specific writing program. Program creation is not something that every writing administrator does or should do; if a WPA inherits a well-designed program that is generally viewed positively by students, faculty, and campus administrators, then it is likely that the program will be maintained. Even in such cases, however, a person engaged in the intellectual work of writing administration can add, modify, or otherwise develop a significant new emphasis or supplementary support system. For example, a writing administrator might create a Writing Center to support and enhance undergraduate instruction; or he might revise the emphasis of second-semester composition by altering the programmatic goals from a traditional research paper to shorter essays emphasizing academic discourse or cultural studies.

Our point here is that program creation is a strong indication of intellectual work, since successful programs are grounded in significant disciplinary knowledge, a national perspective that takes into account the successes and failures of other composition programs, and a combined practical and theoretical understanding of learning theory, the composing process, the philosophy of composition, rhetorical theory, etc. An obvious corollary is that writing programs that fail, other than when attacked on the basis of budget and ideology, often do so because they lack this scholarly foundation.

Curricular Design

Although closely related to program creation, curricular design is a somewhat differentiated use of scholarly knowledge that is still strongly representative of intellectual work. Indeed, although we separate the categories for the sake of elaboration, they greatly overlap. Curricular design is the overall articulation of the administrative unit: the establishment of a programmatic architecture that structures and maintains the various components of the composition program being evaluated. Curricular design does not inevitably depend on or illustrate scholarly knowledge; in combination with program creation, however, it is strongly indicative of intellectual work.

Once a WPA has engaged in program creation, for example by developing an innovative curricular emphasis for English 101, the next step is to integrate that new emphasis within the curriculum. That is likely to mean reconfiguring course requirements, altering curricular emphases, choosing new textbooks that more fully endorse the new vision, etc. Another example can be drawn from Writing Across the Curriculum (WAC), a program that is often independent of any specific department but whose director must often be promoted and tenured within English. Program design for a WAC director might include the articulation of requirements and standards by which the program includes some courses and excludes others, the development of criteria for evaluating the success of specific courses, the creation of well-articulated expectations so that faculty across the disciplines include writing in their courses with some degree of commonality. Curricular design is not a purely technical matter; it requires an understanding of the conceptual, a grounding in composition history, theory, and pedagogy. This is inevitably the case since its chief goal is to lead the writing program toward a coherent and explicit philosophy.

Faculty Development

Whether working with faculty, teaching assistants, lecturers, adjunct faculty, or under-graduate peer tutors, it is clear that no writing program can succeed unless its staff is well trained and generally in accord with the overall programmatic goals and method-ologies. Thus one of a writing administrator's chief responsibilities is to maintain a strong staff development program. The chief responsibilities, here, are to: develop and implement training programs for new and experienced staff; communicate current ped-agogical approaches and current research in rhetoric and composition; provide logisti-cal, intellectual, and financial support for staff activities in course design, pedagogical development, and research; maintain an atmosphere of openness and support for the development and sharing of effective teaching ideas and curricular emphases; maintain open lines of communication among administrators, support staff, and faculty; etc.

Although it is often overlooked, faculty and staff development depends primar-ily on one factor: the degree to which those being administered value and respect the writing administrator. Staff development cannot be accomplished by fiat. Instructors cannot simply be ordered and coerced, no matter how subordinate their position within the university. Thus faculty development, when it truly accomplishes its pur-pose of improving teaching and maintaining the highest classroom standards, is one of the most salient examples of intellectual work carried out within an administrative sphere. To be an effective administrative leader, a WPA must be able to incorporate current research and theory into the training and must demonstrate that knowledge through both word and deed.

Program Assessment and Evaluation

Accountability is one of the over-riding concepts in higher education generally, and in writing administration specifically. No single method or paradigm exists that is appropriate for all composition programs; on the contrary, each writing administra-tor must develop site-specific measures for the assessment and evaluation of the goals, pedagogy, and overall effectiveness of the composition program. In a composition pro-gram, that assessment may take the form of portfolios; in that case, the scholarly exper-tise of the WPA takes the form of designing the portfolios, creating a rigorous and meaningful assessment procedure by which the portfolios can be evaluated, etc. In a WAC program, the writing administrator would likely need to develop assessment measures in order to demonstrate that writing-enhanced classes are indeed consoli-dating the knowledge of majors across campus and producing undergraduate stu-dents that have achieved a genuine measure of compositional ability.

In order to achieve meaningful assessment (by which we mean overall determi-nation of programmatic effectiveness) and meaningful evaluation (that is, specific determination of students and instructors), writing administrators must bring to bear scholarly knowledge concerning holistic scoring, primary trait scoring, descriptive analysis, scoring rubrics, and other information that spans various disciplines. This knowledge and its application are essential if the program is to demonstrate its value and be assured of continuing funding.

Program-Related Textual Production

By this category, we mean the production of written materials in addition to confer-ence papers, articles in refereed journals, scholarly books, textbooks, and similar prod-ucts that would be evaluated the same whether produced by a WPA or any other faculty member. (Textbooks are a special case. Clearly, not every textbook offers evidence of intellectual work; a grammar work book that asks students to fill in the blanks or a reading anthology that is highly derivative and lacking in substantive pedagogical apparatus may not meet national and departmental definitions of intellectual work. Many textbooks, however, represent significant advances in instruction, both locally and nationally, and are, therefore, important ways for compositionists to demonstrate their scholarly expertise.)

Besides such products, numerous other texts must be considered as part of the writing administrator's resume of scholarly production. These include such things as innovative course syllabi which articulate the WPA's curricular design; local, state, and national funding proposals for the enhancement of instruction; statements of teaching philosophy for the composition curriculum; original materials for instructional workshops; evaluations of teaching that explicitly articulate and promote overall programmatic goals; resource materials for the training of staff as well as for the use of students in classrooms, writing centers, and other programs. Clearly boundaries must be set; not every memo, descriptive comment, or teaching evaluation embodies the concept of intellectual work. But any responsible system of evaluation needs to acknowledge that individuals engaged in the intellectual work of administration concretize their knowledge—and build a reviewable record—through the authorship of a body of textual materials related to program creation, curricular design, faculty development, and program assessment.

5. Evaluative Criteria

Writing administrators provide leadership for many different kinds of programs—such as first-year courses, writing-across-the-disciplines programs, writing centers, and law programs—and they work in a wide variety of institutional settings—among them, two-year colleges, private four-year colleges, and large universities with an array of doctoral offerings. So it is it not possible to establish a fixed set of criteria by which to evaluate writing administrators. It is possible, however, to offer general guidelines and suggestions which WPAs, personnel committees, department chairs, and others can use as they prepare materials and develop personnel policies that fit specific institutional contexts.

Guideline One

The first guideline is based on the previous section, which describes five broad areas in which the intellectual work of writing administration occurs. We urge that materials and policies for the evaluation of WPAs focus on the following areas:

- Program Creation
- Curricular Design
- Faculty Development
- Program Assessment and Evaluation
- Program-Related Textual Production

Guideline Two

The second guideline attempts to clarify what sort of activities and products within the five categories should be considered "intellectual work." We suggest that a particular product or activity of a WPA is intellectual work when it meets one or more of these four criteria:

- It generates, clarifies, connects, reinterprets, or applies knowledge based on research, theory, and sound pedagogical practice;
- It requires disciplinary knowledge available only to an expert trained in or conversant with a particular field;
- It requires highly developed analytical or problem solving skills derived from specific expertise, training, or research derived from scholarly knowledge;
- It results in products or activities that can be evaluated by peers (e.g., publication, internal and outside evaluation, participant responses) as the contribution of the individual's insight, research, and disciplinary knowledge.

Guideline Three

The third guideline suggests more specific criteria that can be used to evaluate the quality of a product or activity reflecting a writing administrator's intellectual work:

- Innovation: The writing administrator creates one or more new programs, curricular emphases, assessment measures, etc.
- Improvement/Refinement: The WPA makes changes and alterations that distinctly and concretely lead to better teaching, sounder classroom practices, etc.
- Dissemination: The WPA, through workshops, colloquia, staff meetings, and other forums, is able to communicate curricular goals, methodologies, and overall programmatic philosophy in such a way as to lead to positive and productive results for students, instructors, and school.
- Empirical Results: The WPA is able to present concrete evidence of accomplishments; that evidence may take the form of pre- and post-evaluative measures, written testimonials from students and staff, teaching evaluations, etc.

That list, of course, is far from comprehensive. Indeed, as "Making Faculty Work Visible" puts it, "[i]ntellectual work in a postsecondary setting may excel in various ways," among them, "skill, care, rigor, and intellectual honesty; a heuristic passion for knowledge; originality; relevance and aptness; coherence, consistency, and development within a body of work; diversity and versatility of contribution; thorough knowledge and constructive use of important work by others; the habit of self-critical examination and openness to criticism and revision; sustained productivity over time; high impact and value to a local academic community like the department; relevance and significance to societal issues and problems; effective communication and dissemination" (177).

Guideline Four

The fourth guideline emphasizes the centrality of peer evaluation to describing and judging the intellectual work of writing administration. The Council of Writing Program Administrators encourages the use of peer review in evaluating the intellectual work of WPAs. This will likely require the WPA to create a portfolio that reflects her or his scholarly and intellectual accomplishments as an administrator; this portfolio would be reviewed by outside evaluators selected by the department in consultation with the person being evaluated.

6. Implementation

The Council of Writing Program Administrators is convinced that WPAs can be evaluated on the basis of their administrative work and that the four guidelines sketched above can help in the process by providing clear categories to organize the work of the writing administrator and by providing meaningful criteria by which to review that work.

Implicit in the guidelines of Section 5 is a framework that can be used to organize accomplishments—and to help in the evaluation—of faculty who are involved in writing administration:

A. The Work of Writing Administration

Description of activities and products organized by the five categories in Guideline One. (As the final paragraphs of Section 5 indicate, evaluation could include a wide range of program-related written materials "in addition to conference papers, articles in refereed journals, scholarly books, textbooks, and similar products that would be evaluated the same whether produced by a WPA or any other faculty member.")

B. Evidence of Intellectual Work

Representative activities and products with evidence relating to Guideline Two.

C. Quality of Intellectual Work

Representative activities and products with evidence relating to Guideline Three.

D. Peer Review

Reports from scholars and writing administrators qualified to evaluate the materials against broad professional standards.

That general framework could serve as an heuristic for writing administrators preparing personnel materials and as an organization for their portfolios, and it might work to guide reviews of portfolios by the institution. Given the wide range of duties possible for a given writing administrator—and the wide range of institutions within which WPAs work—that framework can also serve as a starting point for revision and refinement by writing administrators, personnel committees, department chairs, and others working so that the evaluation of writing administrators fits distinctive local conditions.

If you are engaged in such work, the Council of Writing Program Administrators hopes you find this document a useful source of ideas about the intellectual work of writing administration and how this work can be evaluated. There are, of course, many other resources that you can turn to as you develop responsible means to evaluate writing program administrators. Here is a brief list of reports, articles, and books (the first several of which were quoted in this document):

Ernest L. Boyer. *Scholarship Reconsidered: Priorities for the Professoriate.* Princeton: Carnegie Foundation for the Advancement of Teaching, 1990.

Robert M. Diamond and Bronwyn E. Adam, eds. *The Disciplines Speak: Rewarding the Scholarly, Professional, and Creative Work of Faculty.* Washington: American Association for Higher Education, 1995.

MLA Commission on Professional Service. "Making Faculty Work Visible: Reinterpreting Professional Service, Teaching, and Research in the Fields of Language and Literature." *Profession* 1996. New York: MLA, 1996. 161–216.

Offprints are available from the MLA.

WORKS CITED

"ADE Statement of Good Practice: Teaching, Evaluation, and Scholarship." *ADE Bulletin* No. 105 (Fall 1993): 43–45.

Bloom, Lynn Z. "The Importance of External Reviews in Composition Studies." *Academic Advancement in Composition Studies*. Ed. Richard C. Gebhardt and Barbara Genelle Smith Gebhardt. Mahwah: Erlbaum, 1997.

Council of Writing Program Administrators. "Guidelines for Self Study to Precede a Writing Program Evaluation." *Teaching and Assessing Writing*. Edward M. White. San Francisco: Jossey, 1994.

——. "Guidelines for Writing Program Administrator (WPA) Positions." *WPA* 16.1–2 (Fall–Winter 1992): 89–94.

Hult, Christine. "The Scholarship of Administration." *Theorizing and Enacting Difference: Resituating Writing Programs within the Academy*. Eds. Joseph Janangelo and Christine Hansen. Portsmouth: Boynton, 1997.

"Report of the Commission on Writing and Literature." *Profession* 88. New York: MLA, 1988. 70–76.

Roen, Duane H. "Writing Administration as Scholarship and Teaching." *Academic Advancement in Composition Studies*. Ed. Richard C. Gebhardt and Barbara Genelle Smith Gebhardt. Mahwah: Erlbaum, 1997.

HISTORY OF THIS DOCUMENT

"Evaluating the Intellectual Work of Writing Administration" evolved over several years since the WPA Executive Committee began developing an "intellectual work document" on the scholarly and professional activities of writing administrators. Robert Schwegler, Gail Stygall, Judy Pearce, and Charles Schuster—consulting with Executive Committee members and others—developed approaches which Charles Schuster drafted into the version published in the Fall/Winter 1996 issue of WPA as a way to solicit additional response. Following discussion of that draft and various responses at the July 1997 Executive Committee meeting, Richard Gebhardt coordinated a revision effort and drafted versions discussed, modified, and approved by the Executive Committee during its meetings in 1998. The Council of Writing Program Administrators recommends this document as a source of ideas about the intellectual work of writing administration and about how this work can be evaluated responsibly and professionally.

Appendix G
ADE Guidelines for Class Size and Workload for College and University Teachers of English: A Statement of Policy

In response to the nationwide discussion of deficiencies in reading and writing, the English profession has called attention to poor teaching conditions and excessive workloads at all levels of education. We have urged the improvement of teacher-training programs by recommending that prospective and practicing English teachers receive better instruction in the art of reading and writing. We have developed special programs for students entering higher education who come from increasingly varied backgrounds with different competencies and needs. We have established programs in rhetoric and composition in many colleges and universities to encourage research and to disseminate its results.

Despite an abundance of experienced teachers to provide sound instruction in English, we find that in many institutions the number of courses taught by each instructor and the number of students in each class, especially in writing courses, has reached unacceptable levels. This problem has become acute in independent and public institutions alike.

In the light of these circumstances, the Association of Departments of English presents the following guidelines for maximum class size and workload in English. These guidelines are a revision of ADE's 1974 and 1980 statements, and they reaffirm policy statements of the National Council of Teachers of English (1966), the National Junior College Committee (1968), and the American Association of University Professors (1969).

I. NUMBER OF STUDENTS IN WRITING COURSES

Recommendation: College English teachers should not teach more than three sections of composition per term. The number of students in each section should be fifteen or fewer, with no more than twenty students in any case. Class size should be no more than fifteen in developmental (remedial) courses. No English faculty member should teach more than sixty writing students a term; if students are developmental, the maximum should be forty-five.

The process of learning to write clearly and effectively is not a simple matter of acquiring information or memorizing rules. It requires a parallel and simultaneous process of learning to read with more sophistication. Because reading and writing are related activities, learning to write entails a complex interaction between writer and reader. Students write; teachers respond. But a teacher's response must be more than "correcting" and more than perfunctory grading. Evaluations must involve a detailed reaction, often in conference with the student, to each piece of writing.

Good teachers want to teach as many students as they can teach well. But if teachers are forced to respond to the writing of more than sixty students weekly, they will necessarily oversimplify their responses. Their students will not learn that the basic ingredient of good writing and good reading is the ready and vigorous ability to understand, to formulate, and to express ideas. Students will regard their own writing as a mere exercise, unworthy of careful attention or serious thought.

Students in developmental (remedial) composition need considerable individual help and more detailed responses. Students in advanced composition, business and technical writing, or creative writing are likely to produce a greater volume of more complex writing; thus a greater proportion of a teacher's time is required to respond to what they have written.

II. NUMBER OF STUDENTS
IN LITERATURE COURSES

Recommendation: College English teachers should teach no more than thirty-five students in a literature course and no more than twenty-five in a writing-intensive course. For each additional thirty-five students, a teacher should have a qualified assistant to help with the evaluations of written assignments.

One essential objective is to transmit the sense of discovery and pleasure associated with reading imaginative literature. The acquisition of corollary skills in analysis and expression should accompany the emphasis on reading. Classroom discussions and substantial written assignments are essential features of such courses, but they are feasible only with classes of fewer than thirty-five students.

Certain general and advanced literature courses that include historical and biographical background and critical surveys may be conducted by lecture for larger classes. For example, departments may schedule these courses in order to give students access to distinguished scholars and lecturers. In such courses, examinations rather than frequent essays provide an adequate, though not ideal, measure of student performance.

Honors courses and seminars that require students to conduct research and to produce sustained critical essays should be restricted to fifteen students because close individual guidance is essential.

III. HOURS OF INSTRUCTION

Recommendation: College English teachers should spend no more than twelve hours per week per semester in the classroom if they are involved in undergraduate instruction exclusively and no more than nine hours per week if they are involved in graduate instruction. Although this document stipulates the maximum teaching loads commensurate with quality teaching, it should not preclude a department's varying workloads among teachers. Institutions that require faculty members to publish for tenure and promotion should lower teaching loads, especially for junior faculty members.

Limitations on the number of courses assigned to teachers are essential to guarantee quality instruction. The hours spent with students in the classroom constitute only a fraction of an English teacher's responsibility. That responsibility includes time spent in organizing and preparing material to be used in the classroom and in responding to work students have done inside and outside the classroom, whether in literature or in composition courses. It also includes hours spent in the office working with students individually and hours spent in the professional study that is necessary for keeping up with current scholarship.

The proportion of time a teacher spends on out-of-class activities varies, depending on the kind and level of courses offered. Whatever the assignment and the type of college, sufficient allowance must be made for preparation, responses, conferences, and professional improvement. Without these allowances, teaching can become mechanical and learning can be diminished. The responsibility for assigning and adjusting workloads of individual faculty members should rest with the department.

IV. VARIETY OF COURSES

Recommendation: College English teachers should be neither restricted to teaching several sections of the same course nor assigned to prepare more than three different courses in a given semester.

In general, the proper number of different courses likely to ensure excellent teaching is two or three; that is, there should be enough variety to promote freshness but not so much as to prevent thorough preparation.

V. VARIABLE WORKLOADS

Recommendation: College English departments, in order to make the best use of their teachers' interests and abilities, should be allowed to adopt variable workload policies.

Flexibility should be exercised in assigning individual teaching loads. A flexible policy will take into account the scope of a teacher's interests and the range of a department's responsibilities.

VI. ADMINISTRATIVE DUTIES

Recommendation: College English teachers should have a reduced teaching load if they have been assigned major administrative duties.

With the increased need to comply with internal and external regulations (e.g., those of academic governance, collective bargaining, equal opportunity employment, affirmative action assessment, and accountability), additional duties have accrued to department members, especially to chairs. To ignore the burden of such responsibilities by requiring chairs to teach a full load is inequitable. The same principle applies to directors of composition, writing laboratory, or graduate study programs and to other faculty members who are required to contribute substantially to departmental and college governance.

VII. PART-TIME
AND TEMPORARY APPOINTMENTS

Recommendation: Part-time and temporary teaching appointments should be avoided as a rule.

Temporary appointments are often abused, particularly when these teachers work under trying conditions for inequitable remuneration. Since integrity of commitment and continuity of effort are essential to ensure quality teaching, every effort should be made to fill continuing departmental needs with full-time appointments.

Revised March 1992

Association of Departments of English

10 Astor Place

New York, NY 10003-6981

Reading 8

Appendix H
The Buckley Amendment
"Protection of the Rights and Privacy of Parents and Students"

PROTECTION OF THE RIGHTS AND PRIVACY OF PARENTS AND STUDENTS

Sec. 513. (a) Part C of the General Education Provisions Act is further amended by adding at the end thereof the following new section.

Family Educational Rights and Privacy Act of 1974.

"PROTECTION OF THE RIGHTS AND PRIVACY OF PARENTS AND STUDENTS

"Sec. 438. (a)(1) No funds shall be made available under any applicable program to any State or local educational agency, any institution of higher education, any community college, any school, agency offering a preschool program, or any other educational institution which has a policy of denying, or which effectively prevents, the parents of students attending any school of such agency, or attending such institution of higher education, community college, school, preschool, or other educational institution, the right to inspect and review any and all official records, files, and data directly related to their children, including all material that is incorporated into each student's cumulative record folder, and intended for school use or to be available to parties outside the school or school system, and specifically including, but not necessarily limited to, identifying data, academic work completed, level of achievement (grades, standardized achievement test scores), attendance data, scores on standardized intelligence, aptitude, and psychological tests, interest inventory results, health data, family background information, teacher or counselor ratings and observations, and verified reports of serious or recurrent behavior patterns. Where such records or data include information on more than one student, the parents of any student shall be entitled to receive, or be informed of, that part of such record or data as pertains to their child. Each recipient shall establish appropriate procedures for the granting of a request by parents for access to their child's school records within a reasonable period of time, but in no case more than forty-five days after the request has been made.

20 USC 1232g.

Hearing.

"(2) Parents shall have an opportunity for a hearing to challenge the content of their child's school records, to insure that the records are not inaccurate, misleading, or otherwise in violation of the privacy or other rights of students, and to provide an opportunity for the correction or deletion of any such inaccurate, misleading, or otherwise inappropriate data contained therein.

Release of records, parental consent requirement.

"(b)(1) No funds shall be made available under any applicable program to any State or local educational agency, any institution of higher education, any community college, any school, agency offering a preschool program, or any other educational institution which has a policy of permitting the release of personally identifiable records or files (or personal information contained therein) of students without the written consent of their parents to any individual, agency, or organization, other than to the following—

"(A) other school officials, including teachers within the educational institution or local educational agency who have legitimate educational interests;

"(B) officials of other schools or school systems in which the student intends to enroll, upon condition that the student's parents be notified of the transfer, receive a copy of the record if desired, and have an opportunity for a hearing to challenge the content of the record;

"(C) authorized representatives of (i) the Comptroller General of the United States, (ii) the Secretary, (iii) an administrative head of an education agency (as defined in section 409 of this Act), or (iv) State educational authorities, under the conditions set forth in paragraph (3) of this subsection: and

"(D) in connection with a student's application for, or receipt of, financial aid.

"(2) No funds shall be made available under any applicable program to any State or local educational agency, any institution of higher education, any community college, any school, agency offering a preschool program, or any other educational institution which has a policy or practice of furnishing, in any form, any personally identifiable information contained in personal school records, to any persons other than those listed in subsection (b)(1) unless—

"(A) there is written consent from the student's parents specifying records to be released, the reasons for such release, and to whom, and with a copy of the records to be released to the student's parents and the student if desired by the parents, or

"(B) such information is furnished in compliance with judicial order, or pursuant to any lawfully issued subpoena, upon condition that parents and the students are notified of all such orders or subpoenas in advance of the compliance therewith by the educational institution or agency.

Records, accessibility for audit.

"(3) Nothing contained in this section shall preclude authorized representatives of (A) the Comptroller General of the United States, (B) the Secretary, (C) an administrative head of an education agency or (D) State educational authorities from having access to student or other records which may be necessary in connection with the audit and evaluation of Federally-supported education program, or in connection with the enforcement of the Federal legal requirements which relate to such programs: *Provided.* That, except when collection of personally identifiable data is specifically authorized by Federal law, any data collected by such officials with respect to individual students shall not include information (including social security numbers) which would permit the personal identification of such students or their parents after the data so obtained has been collected.

"(4)(A) With respect to subsections (c)(1) and (c)(2) and (c)(3), all persons, agencies, or organizations desiring access to the records of a student shall be required to sign a written form which shall be kept permanently with the file of the student, but only for inspection by the parents or student, indicating specifically the legitimate educational or other interest that each person, agency, or organization has in seeking this information. Such form shall be available to parents and to the school official responsible for record maintenance as a means of auditing the operation of the system. Written request.

"(B) With respect to this subsection, personal information shall only be transferred to a third party on the condition that such party will not permit any other party to have access to such information without the written consent of the parents of the student.

"(c) The Secretary shall adopt appropriate regulations to protect the rights of privacy of students and their families in connection with any surveys or data-gathering activities conducted, assisted, or authorized by the Secretary or an administrative head of an education agency. Regulations established under this subsection shall include provisions controlling the use, dissemination, and protection of such data. No survey or data-gathering activities shall be conducted by the Secretary, or an administrative head of an education agency under an applicable program, unless such activities are authorized by law. Surveys.

"(d) For the purposes of this section, whenever a student has attained eighteen years of age, or is attending an institution of postsecondary education the permission or consent required of and the rights accorded to the parents of the student shall thereafter only be required of and accorded to the student.

"(e) No funds shall be made available under any applicable program unless the recipient of such funds informs the parents of students, or the students, if they are eighteen years of age or older, or are attending an institution of postsecondary education, of the rights accorded them by this section.

"(f) The Secretary, or an administrative head of an education agency, shall take appropriate actions to enforce provisions of this section and to deal with violations of this section, according to the provisions of this Act, except that action to terminate assistance may be taken only if the Secretary finds there has been a failure to comply with the provisions of this section, and he has determined that compliance cannot be secured by voluntary means.

Ante, pp. 568–71
Effective date.
20 USC 1232g
note.
20 USC 1232g
note.

"(g) The Secretary shall establish or designate an office and review board within the Department of Health, Education, and Welfare for the purpose of investigating, processing, reviewing, and adjudicating violations of the provisions of this section and complaints which may be filed concerning alleged violations of this section, according to the procedures contained in sections 434 and 437 of this Act."

Effective date.
20 USC 1232g
note.
20 USC 1232g
note.

(b)(1)(i) The provisions of this section shall become effective ninety days after the date of enactment of section 438 of the General Education Provisions Act.

(2)(i) This section may be cited as the "Family Educational Rights and Privacy Act of 1974."

PROTECTION OF PUPIL RIGHTS

Ante, p. 571.

Sec. 514. (a) Part C of the General Education Provisions Act is further amended by adding after section 438 the following new section:

"PROTECTION OF PUPIL RIGHTS

20 USC 1232h.

"Sec. 439. All instructional material, including teacher's manuals, films, tapes, or other supplementary instructional material which will be used in connection with any research or experimentation program or project shall be available for inspection by the parents or guardians of the children engaged in such program or project. For the purpose of this section 'research or experimentation program or project' means any program or project in any applicable program designed to explore or develop new or unproven teaching methods or techniques."

Definition.

Effective date.
20 USC 1232h
note.

(b) The amendment made by subsection (a) shall be effective upon enactment of this Act.

LIMITATION ON WITHHOLDING OF FEDERAL FUNDS

Supra.

Sec. 515. (a) Part C of the General Education Provisions Act is further amended by adding after section 439 the following new section:

"LIMITATION ON WITHHOLDING OF FEDERAL FUNDS

20 USC 1232i.
Ante, p. 572.

"Sec. 440. Except as provided in section 438(b)(1)(D) of this Act, the refusal of a State or local educational agency or institution of higher education, community college, school, agency offering a preschool program, or other educational institution to provide personally identifiable data on students or their families as a part of any applicable program, to any Federal office, agency, department, or other third party, on the grounds that it constitutes a violation of the right to privacy and confidentiality of students or their parents, shall not constitute sufficient grounds for the suspension or termination of Federal assistance. Such a refusal shall also not constitute sufficient grounds for a denial of, a refusal to consider, or a delay in the consideration

of, funding for such a recipient in succeeding fiscal years. In the case
of any dispute arising under this section, reasonable notice and
opportunity for a hearing shall be afforded the applicant."   Effective date.
(b) The amendment made by subsection (a) shall be effective upon   20 USC 1232i
enactment of this Act.   note.

Public Law 93–380—Aug. 21, 1974 Section 513.

Appendix I
Guidelines for Self-Study to Precede WPA Visit

At their March 1993 workshop, a committee of WPA Consultant-Evaluators reviewed the "Guidelines" which have directed campus self-studies for over a decade. What began as editing turned into massive revision, as the committee began incorporating recent conceptual and organizational changes in writing programs into the document. Since this document represents a WPA vision of what is important about a writing program, the following draft appears here for all interested members to make comments and propose changes. The document will be revised in light of comments received and presented to the WPA Executive Committee at their CCCC meeting in March. Send all suggestions by January 1, 1994, to Professor Edward White, English Department, California State University, San Bernardino, San Bernardino, CA, 92407.

DRAFT DOCUMENT

One month before the WPA consultant-evaluators are scheduled to visit your campus, you should send them a self-study. The purposes of this self-study are, through the process of writing it, to help you understand more clearly the reasons for the visit and to acquaint the consultants with your institution.

Ideally, this self-study will be prepared by a team, including the writing program administrator at your institution and others who arc directly involved in your writing program, not by one individual.

The self-study should be largely a narrative report that focuses on the main concerns you have about your writing program. The questions below are intended to help you think of all the possible facets of your program you might want to describe in your self-study. You need not answer all these questions, and they are not intended as an outline for your report.

The final self-study should be about 10 pages in length, not including any supporting documents.

I. General Background

    A. Focus of the Visit

        1. What are the program's current concerns?

        2. What changes in the program are being contemplated?

        3. What issues would you like the consultant-evaluators to address?

B. Current Institutional Conditions

1. What specific institutional changes are affecting your writing program?

2. What specific characteristics of your student body affect your program?

C. Missions

1. What is the mission of your institution?

2. What is the mission of your writing program?

3. How does the mission of your program support the mission of your institution?

D. Philosophy and Goals

1. What are the principles or philosophy of the writing program(s) at your institution?

2. What are the goals of your program?

3. How do these goals reflect the program's philosophy?

4. How do your program's practices enact the philosophy and goals?

II. Curriculum

A. Philosophy and Goals

1. What are the philosophy and goals of the writing program(s) at your institution?

2. Do the goals of the writing program(s) accord with the goals of the institution as a whole?

3. How are the philosophy and goals communicated to the teachers, the students, and the appropriate administrators?

B. Courses and Syllabi

1. What writing courses are currently taught in your institution? By what departments are they taught?

2. How are these courses sequenced or otherwise related? Which courses are required, and of whom are they required?

3. If your institution identifies some students as "basic writers," how are their needs addressed?

4. Are the syllabi for the courses uniform or different for each teacher? (Or do some teachers follow a uniform syllabus, while other teachers follow their individual syllabi?) If the syllabus is uniform within each course or for several sections within each course, who is responsible for developing it?

5. If the syllabus is uniform within each course, what opportunities do individual teachers have for experimentation with the syllabus? If the syllabi are individual, what ties or links make the course cohere across the sections?

6. What is the logical basis for the sequence of assignments within each course? How does that sequence relate to the goals and philosophy of the program?

7. How much writing, and what kinds of writing, must students do for each course?

8. What kinds of reading are assigned in the writing courses? What instruction is given to students in the reading of these texts? In the reading of their own drafts?

C. Instructional Methods and Materials

1. What events or activities typically take place in the classrooms of the program's writing courses?

2. What textbooks are used in each writing course? Why is the program using these textbooks? What instructional materials other than textbooks does the program use? How do these textbooks and other materials fit the goals and structure of the course(s)? Who chooses the textbooks and other instructional materials used in the courses?

3. How much time do teachers devote to individual conferences?

D. Responses to and Evaluation of Student Writing

1. At what point(s) in their composing do students receive responses to their writing? What kinds of responses do they receive? At what points during the course(s) do students receive evaluation of their progress?

2. What procedures do faculty use in evaluating students' writing (e.g., letter grades on each paper, letter grades on some papers only, no grades until the end of the course)? On what bases (standards) do faculty evaluate papers?

3. What processes are used to assure consistency across sections in evaluation of students' writing? How does the program assure that the bases for evaluation cohere with the goals of the program?

4. How does the evaluation of students' work reflect their achievement of the stated goals of the course?

E. Assessment

1. What tests and testing procedures are used in the writing program for such purposes as placement, exemption, determination of readiness to exit from a course or from the program, determination of eligibility to enter a more advanced program? What procedures are used to correct errors in placement? How do these procedures relate to the goals of the program?

2. Under what conditions are the assessment procedures conducted? Who conducts them? Who interprets and uses the results? What training do those who conduct the assessment have? If tests are scored by humans (i.e., not machines), what training do the scorers have?

3. What methods are used for continued monitoring of the assessment instruments to assure their current reliability and validity for the students and the purposes they are to serve? How frequently is the monitoring conducted?

III. Faculty

A. Status and Working Conditions

1. What percentage of full-time faculty at each rank, adjunct faculty, and graduate students teach writing? How many writing courses do faculty at each rank or status teach? What percentage of the writing courses are taught by faculty at each rank or status?

2. What are the qualifications for writing faculty, and how are they established? What training and experience in teaching writing do the writing faculty have? What professional organizations do they belong to? What is their record of research, publication, conference participation, and professional activity in composition and rhetoric?

3. What are the salary ranges by rank and category? How do these salary ranges compare to comparable departments? To neighboring, comparable institutions?

4. How are teaching, administration, and research in composition rewarded in terms of salary, promotion, and tenure?

5. How are adjunct faculty appointed? By whom? When in relation to the opening of a term? How are they evaluated? What is the length of their appointment? How are they reappointed? What percentage have multiple-year contracts? How are the adjunct faculty compensated in terms of salary and benefits? Are there step raises or cost of living increases for adjunct faculty? Are adjunct faculty compensated for preparation if a course does not fill or is covered by a full-time faculty member? Is there a departmental policy on percentage of part-time faculty? Do adjunct faculty attend department meetings and writing program meetings? Serve on departmental or writing program committees? What opportunities exist for adjunct faculty to develop curriculum, choose textbooks, formulate policy and procedures? What arrangements are made for office space, telephones, mailboxes, and clerical support for adjunct faculty?

B. Faculty Development

1. How is faculty development defined as a goal of the institution, the department or administrative unit, and the writing program? What are ongoing plans for faculty development in teaching writing?

2. What courses, speaker programs, workshops, teaching awards, etc. does the writing program offer or support to encourage excellence in teaching writing?

3. What opportunities for faculty development in teaching writing already exist? Who uses them? How do faculty find out about them? In what ways are faculty encouraged to avail themselves of these opportunities?

4. Are these opportunities available to adjunct faculty and teaching assistants?

5. Are issues of race and gender addressed in faculty development?

6. What financial resources are available for travel to workshops, conferences, and institutes related to teaching writing?

7. What avenues exist for writing faculty at each rank and status to design, implement, and evaluate faculty development programs best

suited to their needs and interests? How are faculty encouraged to develop their skills in composition research and teaching writing? What opportunities exist for learning about faculty development programs in writing at other institutions?

8. Does the department or institution support faculty development by offering paid leaves or sabbaticals for further education in composition studies and rhetoric, by publishing journals, by developing software or other media for use in teaching writing?

9. What support does the department or institution give for development of institutional and individual grants to improve writing instruction and curricula and for released time, overhead, and other support to carry out the grant?

IV. Program Administration

   A. Institutional and Program Structure

   1. What writing programs are there on campus (e.g., first-year composition, writing across the curriculum, technical writing)?

   2. What is the size and make-up of each of the departments or administrative units in which these programs are housed? What is the governing structure of each? How are these related administratively?

   3. What are the internal governing structures of the writing programs? Are there writing program administrators (e.g., director of first-year composition, composition committee chair, director of the writing center)? If so, what are the WPAs' administrative relations to other levels of administration? To whom are the WPAs responsible?

   4. If there are night school, continuing education, or non-degree programs, who determines how writing is taught in those programs? How is control exercised? Who is responsible for the teaching of writing in other departments or colleges within the institution?

   5. How are the teaching and tutoring of writing funded? Who controls these funds? On what are these funds spent? How does the funding of the writing programs compare to the funding of other programs on campus?

   6. Are institutional grant funds available for program development (e.g., curriculum development and assessment)? If so, have WPAs applied for and been awarded any of these grants?

   7. Who hires, promotes, and tenures the writing faculty throughout the institution? Who determines their salaries and assigns courses to them?

   8. How are new teaching positions determined and by whom?

   9. Who determines such things as class size, curriculum, and teaching load in the various programs?

   10. How are internal problems solved? Who decides on syllabi, testing procedures, textbooks, etc.? What procedures are in place for full-time faculty, adjunct faculty, teaching assistants, and students to shape policies?

11. What permanent or ad hoc committees related to writing programs exist? How are these committees appointed? Who serves on them (e.g., full-time faculty, adjuncts, students)? What do these committees do?

12. What are the procedures for negotiating student and faculty complaints about grading, teaching, harassment, learning atmosphere, and administrative processes and policies?

13. What administrative, clerical, and technical support is there?

14. How are the writing programs' histories documented (e.g., annual reports, status reports on progress toward multi-year development plans)? Who writes these histories and who reads them? How are they used?

B. Writing Program Administrators

1. How are the WPAs chosen and what are the lengths of their appointments?

2. What are the terms and conditions of appointments of the WPAs? Are these terms in writing?

3. What are the academic and professional qualifications of the WPAs? What are the WPAs' ranks and tenure statuses? Who decides the WPAs' tenures, promotions, and salaries?

4. What are the WPAs' teaching loads and how do they compare with other faculties' loads?

5. How much and what type of research are WPAs expected to do? To what extent are the WPAs' efforts in program development and institutional research considered scholarship?

6. How and by whom are WPAs evaluated? How are WPAs rewarded?

V. Related Writing Programs and Instructional Units

In many institutions the English Department's composition program is not the only place where writing instruction takes place. Others sites charged with teaching writing may include many of the following: writing centers, reading centers, learning centers, testing centers, disabled student centers, Writing-Across-the-Curriculum Programs, ESL and bilingual programs, tutoring services, correspondence and extension courses, telecommunications and long-distance learning courses and programs, high school bridge programs, writing proficiency programs and exams, and discipline-based writing programs in colleges of education, business, nursing, law, and engineering. Please address the relationships with the programs that are most pertinent to this visit. (Also include relationships that may become significant in the immediate or long term.) Briefly tell how you perceive the relationships between your program and the other academic units charged with writing instruction.

A. Administration

  1. To what extent do services offered by the writing program and other units overlap?

      a. Do their common goals and procedures reinforce each other or conflict?

      b. In what formal and informal ways (through scheduling, a coordinating committee, etc.) is each unit related to the writing program?

  2. How is each unit funded?

  3. How does each unit follow up on students who have used its services?

  4. How is credit determined for work in these units?

  5. What arrangements exist for the evaluation of each unit?

B. Curriculum

  1. How many students and faculty are associated with each unit?

  2. What is the profile of the students?

  3. How are students placed in or referred to each unit?

  4. What kinds of materials (books, computers, television) and techniques (tutoring, workshops) does the unit use?

  5. How do students learn about the unit?

C. Personnel

  1. What are the job descriptions for the director and teaching staff of each unit? How are the director and staff selected?

  2. What is the institutional status (faculty, full-time, part-time, graduate student, etc.) of unit personnel?

      a. How are they compensated for their work?

      b. How is their work evaluated?

  3. What provisions exist for training and professional development of unit staff?

You may not want to overwhelm consultants with background materials, but you may want to include the following in an appendix to the narrative report:

- Statistical information for the previous and current academic year: enrollments, class sizes, composition of the teaching staff, final grade distribution.

- A description of each course within the program(s) to be evaluated (objectives, syllabuses, texts, placement and exemption procedures, grading criteria).

- Copies of evaluative instruments.

- Materials pertaining to teacher training (both faculty and graduate students or adjuncts), including orientation meeting agendas, workshop descriptions, and syllabuses for training courses.

- School catalogues, department handbooks, and departmental student materials.

INDEX

A

AAHE. *See* American Association of Higher Education

Abbott, Robert, 118, 119

accountability, 72

"ADE Guidelines for Class Size and Workload for College and University Teachers of English", Appendix G

administration
  as teaching 34–36
  of university 12–14, 38–40, 44

Administrative Culture, 69–

Advanced Placement Exams, 252–63
  and writing, 254
  credit for, 252–63
  essay portion of, 254
  objections to, 254
  role in writing program, 252–63

Aisenberg, Nadya, 83

Altieri, Charles, 338–39

American Association of Community Colleges, 312

American Association of Higher Education (AAHE), 285, 300, 308, 312
  Assessment Forum, 304
  professional development, 303–04
  service learning, 304
  Summer Academy, 303–04

American Council on Education, 301–02, 307, 312

Ash, Roberta, 277

assessment, 71–72, 207–25
  contextual, 214
  direct measures of, 216–17
  directed self-placement in, 213, 215, 218–19, 223
  exit, 211–13, 219–20, 223
  holistic scoring in, 209, 211, 212, 217–19
  indirect measures of, 216
  knowledge construction in, 211
  local context for, 210–11, 15, 17, 220
  methods of, 210–22
  online submissions for, 218
  overview of, 208–09
  placement, 211–13, 215–219, 223
  program, 213-15, 220–22, 224, 122–23
  readers and, 211
  reflective practitioners and, 210, 212–15, 224
  reliability in, 208–09
  student portfolios in, 212, 218, 221–22
  teaching assistant training and, 122–23
  teaching portfolios in, 221
  testing companies and, 216
  validity in, 208–09, 222–224
  validity inquiries in, 209–10, 223
  Writing Across the Curriculum and, 282, 290

Association for Institutional Research (AIR), 312

Association of American Colleges and Universities (AACU), 300, 304–05, 308, 312
  Knowledge Network, 305
  "Preparing Future Faculty," 305
  publications of, 308

Association of Departments of English (ADE), 112, 307, 312

Association of Governing Boards of
    Universities and Colleges, 302–03,
    308, 313
Authority, WPA and, 80–84, 95–97, 98–99

B
Bakhtin, Mikhail, 194–95
Barr-Ebest, Sally, 166
Bartholomae, David, 101, 119, 192, 254–55
Bazerman, Charles, 244, 249, 265
Bear, John, 265
Beason, Larry, 207, 220
Bell, David V.J., 94–95, 96, 99
Benford, Robert, 275, 276, 277
Bergquist, William H., 287, 288
Berlin, James, 194–95, 257, 258, 335
Berthoff, Ann, 192
Bishop, Wendy, 88–89
Bizzell, Patricia, 193
Bloom, Lynn, 62–63
Bly, Brian, 119–120
Boyer, Earnest, 300
Brannon, Lil, 257
Britton, James, 187, 188, 189, 264, 265, 278, 284
Broad, Robert, 211
Bruffee, Kenneth, 265
Buckley Amendment, the, Appendix H
burnout
    antecedents of, 52–58
    avoiding, 58–62
    definition, 50–52
    WPA and, 49–65

C
Cambridge, Barbara L., 96, 303
campus environment, and WPA, 92
Carnegie Foundation for the Advancement
    of Teaching, 306, 313
case study, 75–76
CCCC. *See* Conference on College
    Composition and Communication
centers for teaching / learning, 268, 286
Chronicle of Higher Education, 307
Coles, William, 191
College Composition and Communication, 91, 93
Comley, Nancy, 335
community colleges, funding at, 19
composition requirement, 243–44
    role in institution, 243–51
computer-assisted instruction, 228–42
    classroom design for, 231–33
computers. *See also* computer-assisted
    instruction

in classroom design, 231–33
instruction with, 119
use in writing programs, 228–42
Conference on College Communication and
    Composition, 59, 112, 123, 185, 267, 300,
    306–07, 322, 336, 337
Connolly, Paul, 124, 140
Connors, Robert J., 243
Corbett, Edward P.J., 139–140
Cordes, Cynthia L., 50–55, 57–58
Cornell University, 23–32
Council of Writing Program Administrators,
    270, 271, 300, 306, 313, 316, 317–18,
    321, 322
    consultant-evaluator service, 321–22
    Journal of, 316
Cronbach, Lee, 223–24
Crossley, Gay Lynn, 88–89
Culler, Jonathan, 337
curriculum, 27–28
    conferences and 192–93
    critical pedagogy and, 194–96
    cultural studies in, 195–96
    Current-Traditional rhetoric in, 186–88
    design of, 200–03
    ethnography frameworks in, 197–98
    for teacher training, 141–52
    history of writing, 186–200
    of first year writing courses, 185–206
    of independent writing programs. *See*
        independent writing programs:
        curriculum of
    service learning and, 198–99
    workshops and 192–93
Dartmouth Conference, 188
David, Denise, 185–86
distance learning, 229
Dougherty, Thomas W., 50–55, 57–58
Dowst, Kenneth, 191

E
Eble, Kenneth, 35
EDUCAUSE, 305–06, 313
Elbow, Peter, 186, 192, 211
Emerson, Caryl, 340
Emig, Janet, 189, 265, 335
engagement, definition of, 51–52
English Coalition Conference, 197–98
"Evaluating the Intellectual Work of Writing
    Administration," 10–11, 94, 304, 306, 318,
    Appendix F
evaluation. *See* assessment: and teaching
    assistant training; and program

exit assessment. *See* Assessment: and exit

F
faculty development, 268, 279, 26, 28
   definition of, 157
   difference from professional
     development, 157
faculty full-time equivalents, 69
Faigley, Lester, 241, 243
Feminism / Feminist Theory, 97
   and WPA, 78–90
First-year requirement. *See* composition
   requirement
Fish, Stanley, 257
Freire, Paulo, 194, 278
FTE student. *See* full-time equivalent student
FTSE. *See* full-time equivalent student
full-time equivalent student, 18–19
Fulton, Carol, 160-61
Fulwiler, Toby, 265, 278, 279, 280

G
Gallop, Jane, 334–335
Garrison, Roger, 193
Garrow, John, 216–17
genre theory, 194–95
George, Diana, 69, 228
Gerber, John, 337
Gordon, Barbara, 185–86
Gottschalk, Katherine, 186
graduate teaching assistants. *See* teaching
   assistants; *See also* professional
   development: graduate teaching
   assistants
graduate student training, 337–38
"Guidelines for Self-study to Precede WPA
   Visit," Appendix I
"Guidelines for the Workload of the College
   English Teacher," Appendix D
Gunner, Jeanne, 81, 97

H
Harrington, Mona, 83
Harris, Jeanette, 228, 229
Hartzog, Carol P., 92, 130, 246
Heath, Shirley Brice, 194, 197
Herrington, Anne, 265
Hesse, Doug, 16
higher education, discourses in, 299–314
Hjortshoj, Keith, 30–31
holistic scoring. *See* assessment: holistic
   scoring in
Howard, Rebecca Moore, 86, 88, 96

Hult, Christine, 94, 97, 228
Huot, Brian, 208–09, 210, 211, 213, 271

I
independent writing programs, 25–26, 38–46
   and writing across the curriculum, 43
   curriculum of 45–46
   non-tenure track staff and, 41–43
   professional staff vs. faculty and, 41
   staffing of, 26, 41–44
   status of, 25, 39–41
   tenure track staff and, 41–43
influence, WPA and, 95–96, 99–101
instructors, part time, 118
Iowa, University of, 190–91

J
Jakobson, Roman, 264
Job description, 317–18

K
Killingsworth, M. Jimmie, 228
Kinneavy, James, 187–88, 265
Knoblauch, C.H., 257
Knowledge Network, 305
Krupa, Gene, 190

L
language across the curriculum, 284
   See also writing across the curriculum
leadership, 62–65
Licklider, Barbara L., 160–61
Louisville, University of, 220–21, 224

M
Mahala, Daniel, 284
Maimon, Elaine, 265, 266, 278
Management, 62–65
Maslach, Christina, 50–52, 55–58, 62
McAdam, Doug, 276, 277
McCarthy, John D., 276, 277
McClelland, Ben W., 96
McLeod, Susan, 25, 119, 265
McMillin, Gary, 166–81
McNaron, Toni, 82
McQuade, Finlay, 256, 257, 258, 259
mentoring, 320
Messick, Samuel, 223
Miller, Carolyn, 194
Miller, Hildy, 78–90, 97
Miller, Richard, 301
mission statement, 70–71
MLA. *See* Modern Language Association

Modern Language Association (MLA), 304, 307, 313, 336
Moffett, James, 187–89, 264
Morson, Gary, 340
Moss, Pamela, 214
Moxley, Joseph M., 80–81, 96, 97, 99, 108, 110

N
National Council of Teachers of English (NCTE), 326, 306–07, 313
NCTE. *See* National Council of Teachers of English
Neel, Jasper, 336, 337
North, Stephen, 338
Nyquist, Jody, 118, 119, 121

O
Ohmann, Richard, 240–41
Olson, Gary A., 80–81, 96, 97, 99, 108, 110
O'Neill, Peggy, 209

P
Parker, Palmer J., 276, 286, 291
Pemberton, Michael, 35
Perry, William, 190
Petraglia, Joseph, 197
Petrosky, Anthony, 192, 254–55
POD. *See* Professional and Organizational Development Network in Higher Education
Polin, Linda G., 92
Pollard, Rita, 185–86
portfolios, student, 212, 218, 221–22
    in assessment, 212, 218, 221–22
"Portland Resolution, The," 10, 94, 317–18, Appendix B
"Position Statement on the Preparation and Professional Development of Teachers of Writing," Appendix E
power, WPA and, 63–64, 80–84, 93, 94–97, 98, 106–113
Pratt, Mary Louise, 288
private institutions, 18
process theory of writing, 187–89, 193, 201
Professional and Organizational Development Network in Higher Education (POD), 157
professional associations, educational, 301–07
professional development, 270. *See also* faculty development: difference from professional development

American Association of Higher Education and, 303–04
and teacher training, 156–65
Association of American Colleges and Universities and, 305
benefits of, 159–160
definition of, 158–59
documenting of, 161–62
in terms of professional involvement, 163
in terms of scholarship, 162–63
in terms of self-promotion, 163–64
of teaching assistants, 117, 177
position statement on (*see* "Position Statement on the Preparation and Professional Development of Teachers of Writing.")
program staffs, 156–65
relation to adult education, 160
suggestions for, 162–64
tenure and promotion of WPA, 315–330
promotion
    in writing instruction, 331–41
    post-tenure, 326
    professional development and. *See* professional development: tenure and promotion of WPA
    WPA and, 315–330, 331–341
proposals, writing of, 73–74
public institutions, 18
Pula, Judith, 211, 217

R
Recchio, Thomas, 119
Russell, David, 27–28, 195–97, 265, 271, 277, 278, 284, 287
Ryder, Phyllis Mentzell, 186

S
SCH. *See* student credit hours
Schendel, Ellen, 209
Schnelker, Diane L., 160–61
Scholes, Robert, 255, 335
Schwarzbach, Fred S., 119
SCUP. *See* Society for College and University Planning
Selfe, Cynthia, 208, 212, 214, 229, 234, 235, 238, 239, 241
service learning, and American Association of Higher Education, 304
Shor, Ira, 194–95
Simpson, Jeanne, 68–77
Sledd, James, 318

small college, 91–105
Smith, William L., 212, 218
social context for writing, 193–95
social movement organizations, 275–77
  and macro-level concerns, 276, 279
  and micro-level concerns, 276–77, 279
Society for College and University Planning
  (SCUP), 306, 313
"Statement of Principles and Standards for
  the Postsecondary Teaching of Writing,"
  94, Appendix A
student credit hours (SCH), 19, 69

T
teacher education. *See* teacher training
teacher training, 84–85. *See also* faculty
  development; professional development
  and teaching portfolio, 128–29
    in assessment. *See* assessment:
      teaching portfolios in
  and Wyoming Resolution, 123–26
  curriculum, 141–52
  of teaching assistants. *See* teaching
    assistants: training of
teaching assistants
  curricula for, 141–52
    apprenticeships, 142–44
    methods courses, 146–48
    practica, 144–46
    requirements of 149–52
    theory seminars, 148–49
  duties of, 167, 180–81
  employment issues and, 178[–180
  evaluation of, 167, 168–76, 121
  hiring of, 43, 118
  mentoring of, 130–31
  professional development. *See*
    professional development: of teaching
    assistants
  training of, 28–29, 34–36, 139–155,
    117–138, 124–26, 139–155, 140–41, 167,
    168–76, 180
    trends in, 167–68
    program descriptions for, 124–26,
      176–78
    evaluation of, 122–23
teaching file. *See* teaching portfolio
teaching portfolio, 128–29, 164, 320–21
tenure. *See also* promotion
  and professional development, 315–30
  for writing instructors, 331–41
  planning for, 317–23

WPA and, 315–330, 331–41
Textbooks, 203

V
Vilardi, Teresa, 124, 140
Vopat, James, 253
Vygotsky, Lev, 194–95

W
Walvoord, Barbara, 265
White, Edward M., 25, 81–82, 92, 100, 120,
  122, 199, 212, 243, 267, 271, 283, 285, 308
Williams, Raymond, 288
Witte, Stephen P., 92, 243
Wolfe, Edward, 212
"WPA Outcomes Statement for First-Year
  Composition", Appendix C
Writing Across the Curriculum, 71, 101,
  106–107, 196, 264–74, 275–95
  administration and, 287–88
  administrative structures, 266
  assessment, 270–71, 282, 290
  centers for teaching/learning and, 268,
    286
  courses, 266–67
  faculty development and, 268, 279
  funding, 269, 281
  goals of, 284
  history of, 264–65
  influences on, 264–65, 278–79
  National Network of WAC Programs,
    267
  pedagodies, 265–66
  professional development and, 270
  program characteristics, 265–67
  research in, 270–71
  technology and, 268, 289
  theory, 264–65
  trends, 267–69
  workshops, 280–82, 289–90
  writing to learn, 266, 280
writing-intensive courses, 268, 282–83, 285,
  286, 288
writing in the disciplines, 27–32, 284. *See
  also* writing across the curriculum
writing programs
  budget for, 16–22, 25–26, 44
  capital funds, 20
  cost accounting in, 17, 22
  expenditure categories of funds, 20–22
  financial aspects of, 16–22
  fund accounting in, 17–22

independent status. *See* independent
   writing programs
placement within institution, 11–14, 23-32
responsibilities of WPA, 10–12
rotating directorship, 26
structure, 11
writing to learn, 266, 280
Wulff, Donald, 118, 119, 121
"Wyoming Resolution, The", 94
   Teacher Assistant Training and, 123–126

Y
Yancey, Kathleen Blake, 210, 213, 271
Young, Art, 265, 279

Z
Zald, Mayer N., 276, 277